Publishing Law

Publishing Law is a comprehensive guide to the law as it affects the publishing process. Written by the Copyright Counsel of The Publishers Association and a practising solicitor with many years experience of the publishing trade, this work will serve as a comprehensive handbook for all those who need a practical under stai ̃ ̃ ̃ ̃ ̃ ̃hors and age es in the pul

- copyright, m ̃ ̃ghts, commissionin ̃ ̃ ̃ ̃ ̃s, including online access and e-books
- libel and other legal risks such as negligence, privacy and obscenity
- infringement and defences such as fair dealing, trade marks and passing off
- consumer law, data protection, advertising and promotion, distribution and export

This fully updated third edition features:

- a new introduction on UK and EU law
- full coverage of electronic rights and e-commerce issues
- up-to-date coverage of changes in UK and EU legislation

Legal points are explained with reference to important statutes, cases and relevant trade practices. A revised glossary and lists of useful addresses and further reading are also provided.

Hugh Jones is Copyright Counsel to The Publishers Association and to the International Association of Scientific, Technical and Medical Publishers (STM). He also advises the Publishers Licensing Society on copyright issues. A qualified solicitor, he worked in publishing for fifteen years for law publishers Sweet & Maxwell and reference publishers Macmillan Press, before practising for eight years as a publishing and copyright lawyer at city law firm Taylor Joynson Garrett (now Taylor Wessing). He writes and lectures regularly, and is Treasurer of the British Copyright Council.

Christopher Benson is a solicitor at city law firm Taylor Wessing. He has been practising for over ten years as an intellectual property lawyer. He has considerable experience in the fields of publishing and copyright and also advises on all aspects of intellectual property law, both contentious and non-contentious, including copyright protection, trade mark protection and passing off, brand management, licensing, merchandising, sponsorship, franchising and advertising. He is a regular writer and lecturer on intellectual property matters.

Publishing Law

Third edition

Hugh Jones
and
Christopher Benson

Routledge
Taylor & Francis Group

LONDON AND NEW YORK

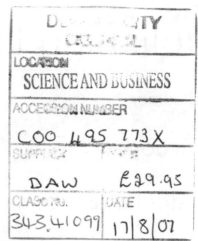
First published 1996
Second edition first published 2002
Third edition published 2006
by Routledge
2 Park Square, Milton Park, Abingdon, Oxon OX14 4RN

Simultaneously published in the USA and Canada
by Routledge
270 Madison Ave, New York, NY 10016

Routledge is an imprint of the Taylor & Francis Group

Typeset in Goudy by
HWA Text and Data Management, Tunbridge Wells
Printed and bound in Great Britain by
Antony Rowe Ltd, Chippenham, Wiltshire

British Library Cataloguing in Publication Data
A catalogue record for this book is available from the British Library

Library of Congress Cataloging in Publication Data
Jones, Hugh, solicitor.
  Publishing law / Hugh Jones and Christopher Benson.— 3rd ed.
    p. cm.
  Includes bibliographical references and index.
  1. Authors and publishers—Great Britain. 2. Press law—Great Britain.
  3. Copyright—Great Britain. I. Benson, Christopher, Solicitor. II. Title.
KD1340.J66 2006
343.4109'98—dc22   2005029924

ISBN10: 0–415–38425–7 (hbk)
ISBN10: 0–415–38427–3 (pbk)
ISBN10: 0–203–96987–1 (ebk)

ISBN13: 978–0–415–38425–5 (hbk)
ISBN13: 978–0–415–38427–8 (pbk)
ISBN13: 978–0–203–96987–8 (ebk)

To Marian
Who nurtured this project from the start

Contents

Preface to the third edition

It is nearly ten years since a fateful conversation at Frankfurt produced the idea of a readable, user-friendly book about law for busy publishing people. Commentators have been very kind about this modest book, on the whole, and it is gratifying to find ourselves looking at a third edition now. Our only reservation is that we are beginning to suspect we have a job for life, since the law – and publishing – show no signs of standing still, but perhaps this is the penalty for meeting a need.

We have altered the shape of the book somewhat in response to new legal developments and helpful suggestions from users. The slightly complex material on confidentiality, which was right at the beginning, has been moved to a new chapter 8, inserted to do justice to the fast-developing new law on Privacy. In its place we have provided a much shorter introductory chapter 1 on The Law and Publishing – giving readers a quick birds-eye view of UK law in its EU and international context, which we hope will be a more helpful and accessible start. In chapter 5, on individual contracts, some sections have been pruned to make way for expanded coverage of contracts for electronic publication, and two new sections on Online Access Licences and E-Book Agreements. This part of the book may need to expand further in future editions, if users find it helpful. Finally, we have for the first time included a list of further reading and sources, including relevant websites, in Appendix C.

Once again, we have been fortunate in having such generous help from our friends and colleagues. We would particularly like to thank Paul Mitchell of Taylor Wessing, recently elected chairman of the British Copyright Council, for commenting in detail on chapters 2 and 3. We must also thank Niri Shan, Tom Carl and Tim Pinto, also of Taylor Wessing, for their expert comments on chapters 7 and 8, Nick Cody for reviewing chapters 10 and 11, Peter Willis for his invaluable help with chapter 12, and Lorna Caddy and Nada Jarnaz for helping update a number of chapters. The Registrar of Public Lending Right, Jim Parker, once again kindly supplied new statistics of the PLR scheme in chapter 3.

Kate Pool of the Society of Authors and Kevin Stewart of Hodder Headline shared their unrivalled combined expertise in publishing contracts in chapter 4. Lynette Owen of Pearson, and Cliff Morgan and Sue Joshua of Wiley, made many helpful comments and provided useful material on chapter 5, as did James Shirras of Film Finances Ltd, and Brian Green of Book Industry Communications. Finally, the task of updating the section on US copyright law in chapter 8 was greatly eased by detailed and helpful comments from Mark Seeley of Elsevier.

Any errors or inaccuracies which remain are, of course, entirely our own work. As with the first and second editions, it would be helpful to know of any inaccuracies which slipped through the net, or even of any points which are unclear or potentially misleading – one of the main aims of this book is still to make this branch of law understandable by those it most affects.

Once again, readers should be aware how rapidly the law changes – particularly in this field. We hope that we have foreseen at least the major likely developments, but it cannot be stressed too strongly that the law is stated as accurately as possible at the date given below, when the proofs were returned. After that, it may well be wise to check with a publishing lawyer.

Hugh Jones
Christopher Benson
London, December 2005

Part I
The law, and original works

Publishing and the law

1

Anyone can be a publisher in the UK. You don't need professional qualifications, or letters after your name, or a practising certificate. All of us 'publish' opinions or other information every time we send an e-mail, or circulate anything that anyone other than the intended recipient may see (although there may be an argument about personal text messaging). Most of this is normal Internet and mobile phone traffic, the lifeblood of twenty-first century communication, and most of it – most of the time – keeps well away from the law. But what if an e-mail you send to a list of friends or colleagues defames someone's reputation? Or what if text or pictures you use on your website infringe someone else's copyright? The law can quickly become involved, even in such apparently domestic transactions, so anyone who is part of the full-scale business of publishing – either as an author, a publisher, or in any other capacity – needs to keep the law in mind all the time. That is what this book is about, and what it is for – a roadmap of publishing, for those who wish to stay within the law.

The rest of this book will broadly follow the chronological sequence of most publishing, so we will start at the beginning, with the author's first idea, and follow the process through copyright and contract, to the legal risks of publication to the outside world (such as libel), and on through sales and marketing to distribution and export (in hard copy or digital form). At every point, we will find that the law has a habit of getting involved. Those of us who are familiar with the law will not find this terribly surprising (although there is a school of thought that some of us should get out more). Those for whom law (especially English law) is an arcane mystery, may need a few more signposts along the way. So even before our author has his (or her) first idea, here is a brief introductory map of the legal system which governs most UK publishing – UK and EU law, linked to foreign laws in many cases via international treaties such as the Berne Convention.

UK AND INTERNATIONAL LAW

One of the most important things to understand about law is that most laws operate on a territorial basis – in other words, they are promulgated by nation-states for their own citizens and to regulate activities within their own territorial boundaries.

They do not generally apply anywhere else. This has strengths and weaknesses – if in the UK you create or publish an original copyright work (like this book) you will have the full protection of UK copyright law, but if you find your copyright is being infringed in, say, Turkey or China, there is nothing UK law itself can do to help you and any legal remedies you may have will largely be dependent on local Turkish or Chinese law and on local courts. As you can imagine, some countries have better laws (and offer better protection) than others. In an Internet age, this worldwide patchwork of very different legal regimes is already proving a challenge. If material which infringes copyright, or libels someone, is created in New Jersey, uploaded to a server there, hosted on a UK website and downloaded in France and Saudi Arabia, whose law should govern the resulting dispute, and whose courts should have jurisdiction to try the case? This is no tiresome technicality – for publishing today, this can matter a great deal, since some laws are relatively liberal while others can be positively restrictive.

Increasingly, of course, the countries of the world have tried to regularise all this by means of **international treaties**, so there is an **International Court of Justice** at The Hague (mainly referred to for war crimes), and a **European Court of Human Rights** in Strasbourg. However, these only operate in certain areas, and (as in the case of the European Court of Human Rights) their judgments may be regional rather than global, and normally enforced against individual member states. There is no truly global International Court, applying global laws. Many think the Internet will eventually require something similar, but it seems we are still a long way away from persuading all governments in the world to agree on what the global laws would be, and who should enforce them. Copyright, however, is comparatively well off, thanks to one of the world's most successful and longest-running treaties, the **Berne Copyright Convention** of 1886, now acceded to by well over 150 countries, which obliges members to apply reciprocal 'national treatment' in their own courts to works of other member states. National treatment means that the UK, for example, is required to give copyright works of other convention countries – such as the USA – the same protection in UK courts as it gives to UK works – and vice versa. The World Trade Organisation's **TRIPS Treaty** also requires member states to enforce copyright effectively (for more on this, see chapter 8).

EU LAW

The UK is of course a member of the **European Union**, comprising 25 countries at the time of writing, and like every other member state participates in its government, with nominated Commissioners holding portfolios at the **Commission** in Brussels, and elects MEPs to the **European Parliament** in Brussels and Strasbourg. Equally, apart from its own domestic laws, it is also subject to EU laws. The purpose of much EU law is to harmonise legal regimes across Europe, in pursuit of the famous 'level playing field'. These EU laws can be on a wide variety of topics – from fish farming to intellectual property – and commonly take the form of:

- **Regulations**, which have direct effect in the member states of the EU, or
- **Directives**, which as the name implies are directions to member states to amend their own laws in accordance with given rules.

Both these forms of law take precedence over domestic UK laws. The E-Commerce Directive of 2000 and the Copyright Directive of 2001 are examples of laws which particularly affect publishing in the EU. They are enforced by the **European Court of Justice**, which sits in Luxembourg, with 25 judges drawn from a variety of member states, and an Advocate General. A **Court of First Instance** was also established in 1988 to help with the case-load problem. In addition, there are **Decisions**, binding on those to whom they are addressed, and **Recommendations** and **Opinions** which have no binding force but which result from references by national courts to the European Court of Justice for interpretation.

Human Rights Law

The UK has been a signatory to the European Convention for the Protection of Human Rights and Fundamental Freedoms since 1950. However, in October 2000 the Human Rights Act 1998 came into force, thus bringing convention rights such as freedom of expression and privacy more centrally into UK law. When courts now interpret the law, they must do so in a way which is compatible with the Convention. In doing so, they must take account of the decisions of the European Court of Human Rights.

This, then, is the international and European context in which UK law now operates.

UK LAW

'COMMON LAW'

After the Romans departed (taking Roman law with them) the islands now making up the UK were a pretty lawless place. But over the centuries a body of Anglo-Saxon, and then Norman, law developed, based on cases decided by judges, and increasingly following set rules.

This became known as the common law of England (a key part of '**English law**'), and was administered by common-law courts. Separate laws developed in Scotland (**Scots law**) and Northern Ireland. Actions for breach of contract or negligence were (and still are) common-law actions. Separate ecclesiastical courts regulated matrimonial law, and Courts of **Equity**, such as the Chancery courts, could be appealed to for remedies (such as injunctions) based less on rules than on basic fairness and justice (hence 'equitable' solutions). The judges, however, played a crucial role. Meanwhile, on the Continent, the codified rules of Roman law continued to be influential, so a separate **Civil law** tradition grew up (and still operates, e.g. in France and Germany, based on civil Codes containing general principles, rather than a body of fact-based case law).

STATUTES

Although much of publishing law is still based on common law and equity, nowadays an increasing amount comes from **Acts of Parliament**, passed by Parliament in Westminster (also called **Statutes**), and subsidiary orders or **Regulations** made under those Acts, called **Statutory Instruments** (or S.I.s). Examples of Statutes relevant to publishing law are the Copyright, Designs and Patents Act 1988 (still the primary source of copyright law in the UK), the Trade Marks Act 1994, and the Human Rights Act 1998. Most of this legislation is introduced into Parliament in the form of government **Bills**, usually in the House of Commons, but Bills are sometimes introduced in the Lords, or often appear as Private Members' Bills: the Copyright (Visually Impaired Persons) Act 2002 began life as a backbench MP's Bill.

Often, the legal principles contained in Acts of Parliament need fleshing out in more detail, so may be followed by Regulations, which amplify – and perhaps amend – the original Act. A good example was the wonderfully-named Copyright (Librarians and Archivists) (Copying of Copyright Material) Regulations 1989, which followed immediately after the 1988 Copyright Act in order to clarify the permitted extent of library copying.

Here is an example of how the EU and UK legal system works:

- The UK term of copyright under the 1988 Copyright Designs and Patents Act was 'Life plus 50' (more precisely, 50 years after the end of the year in which the author died).
- In October 1993, the EU Parliament passed EU Directive 93/98/EEC (the Term Directive, sometimes called the Duration Directive), harmonising the term of copyright throughout the EU at 'Life plus 70'. Member states had until July 1995 to make the necessary changes.
- This required an amendment to the UK's 1988 Act, so the required changes were introduced by the UK Government in part by a Statutory Instrument called the Duration of Copyright and Rights in Performances Regulations 1995, which came into force (late) on 1 January 1996. From that moment, the UK term of copyright was increased by 20 years, to Life plus 70.

It will be seen from this how Acts of Parliament passed in Westminster come to be amended by laws created in Brussels, and also how important it is to keep track of any amending Regulations, many of which change the law quite dramatically.

CONTRACTS

All this important-sounding government activity should not blind us to the fact that we can make laws too. Or at least, that we can enter into agreements that the law will enforce, called **contracts**. Publishing is crowded with contracts, of course, from **licences**, which permit or authorise us to do things, to more complex agreements such as author contracts, which grant rights in return for a promise to publish and (usually) remuneration, to agreements not to do things at all, such as restrictive covenants. Some contracts need to comply with certain formalities (an exclusive licence needs to be in writing, and signed by the person granting it, for example), but as a general rule contracts do not necessarily need to be written at all. All this is set out in detail in chapters 4 and 5.

The law will enforce most reasonable contracts, so if one of the parties to a contract fails to comply with significant terms of that contract, the other party may bring a legal action against him (or her) for **breach of contract**. Usually, if the value of a case is £5,000 (£2,000 in Northern Ireland) and less than £15,000, it will generally be allocated to the **Small claims** track, which is within the **County Court**. Claims for over £15,000, or complicated claims, are allocated to a 'multi track' and can be heard in the **High Court**, depending on the claimant's choice of court and the nature of the claim. There is an appeal from there to the **Court of Appeal**, and from there in some cases to the **House of Lords**. Where cases involve questions of interpretation of EU law, the UK courts can appeal to the **European Court of Justice**. Decisions of these court cases are reported and published, and judgments – particularly of the higher courts – are followed by judges in later cases, thus establishing a system of judge-made law, known as **precedent**. So although an increasing amount of our law derives from politicians passing Acts of Parliament, judges still have a very important role in interpreting the law in order to reach decisions in individual cases.

If a breach of contract is proved, claimants are entitled to a remedy sufficient to restore them to the position they would have been in had the breach not occurred.

TORTS

Tort is the French word for wrong, so since Norman times a **tort** has meant a civil wrong (as opposed to a criminal wrong, which is a crime). Examples of torts are libel, negligence, nuisance, copyright and trade mark infringement, breach of confidence, malicious falsehood or passing off – wrongful or harmful acts which we may do to each other, and for which we may take legal action against each other in the civil courts (as with breach of contract, above).

Successful claimants in a tort action are entitled to a remedy sufficient to restore them to the position they would have been in had the tort not occurred.

CRIMES

Criminal offences, on the other hand, like murder or assault, are regarded as so serious by the State that prevention and punishment are taken out of our hands altogether in order for those concerned to be **prosecuted**, usually by the **Crown Prosecution Service**, or **H.M. Revenue and Customs** (formerly the Inland Revenue and H.M. Customs and Excise). Obscenity and indecency are criminal offences, as are blasphemy and incitement to racial hatred, all of which may affect publishers (see chapter 7). Certain activities infringing copyright, such as importing or possessing infringing equipment, are also criminal offences under the 1988 Copyright Act, for which there are set penalties, including **fines**, seizure or destruction of stock, or even **imprisonment**. Offences involving illegal importation are usually the responsibility of H.M. Revenue and Customs. Offences such as selling illegal or bootleg copies, e.g. of books, CDs or videos, are usually prosecuted by **Trading Standards Officers**, as are offences under the Trade Descriptions Act. So reputable publishers, as well as more recognisable criminals, may commit criminal offences.

On which happy note, we should perhaps complete our tour of the legal system which governs publishing in the UK, and turn our attention, in the next chapter, to an author starting to write a book.

Copyright

2

ORIGINAL IDEAS

All published works start with an original idea, and all ideas have an author. *The Oxford English Dictionary* equates author with '*originator*': in the classic publishing hierarchy, the inspiration of authors is the beginning, the process starts here. This is the classic blank sheet of paper (or the blank screen) which all authors encounter, in the back bedroom, on the kitchen table, or (in J.K. Rowling's case) in the Edinburgh coffee bar. When – finally – the original idea appears, is it protected at all by the law?

Possibly, but in different ways. A good publishing idea may have immense commercial value – it may generate not only profitable individual works but also entire series of profit-making publications as well as substantial other revenue, for example, from merchandising or film, TV or electronic exploitation. Even if the final finished works were written by others, none of what follows would have happened without the original idea. Despite this, it is not at all easy to protect original ideas as such; as a general rule, there is no copyright in an idea, and the less developed it is, the harder it will be to protect in any other way.

Some possible ways include:

- Trade mark protection – for a new children's character, for example (for more on this, see chapter 10).
- Confidential information – concepts, plots and other ideas imparted in confidence may be protected by the law of confidence in appropriate circumstances (see chapter 8).
- Copyright – particularly for material set down and developed beyond the idea stage, perhaps to substantial drafts, sketches or work in progress (see below).

INTRODUCTION TO COPYRIGHT

We saw above that there is no copyright in an idea. However, there might be copyright protection for some kinds of more developed material, once something is put into concrete form or given tangible expression. Copyright law will not protect you just for having a good idea, but it may protect you for doing something positive to express it – in effect, for putting it into a form where it can be shared with the rest of the world. The law recognises that doing this requires an investment of time and effort, and also some skill (quite apart from any financial costs, which may also be involved). It also carries with it a serious risk: once expressed in tangible, physical form, an idea can be copied by others. This has always been true – even before Gutenberg – but it is particularly true in an Internet age. So the law provides protection against copying for those who make that investment and take that risk, and thus an incentive for them to invest their efforts in more ideas in the future. This is one of the most important truths to grasp about copyright, and UK copyright in particular. Although it protects authors and their works – quite rightly – it is not only a reward for authorship, but a protection for investment. This explains why UK copyright law has developed in the way it has over the centuries, and it is unlikely that the UK's worldwide publishing business in its present form could exist without it.

What is copyright then, and why is it so important to publishing?

COPYRIGHT AND INTELLECTUAL PROPERTY

Copyright should, literally, be the right to copy; in fact in legal terms it is better to think of it as the right to *control* copying by others. Put a little more precisely, copyright in the UK is the exclusive statutory right, given (usually) to those who create original works, to exercise control for a specified period of time over the copying and other exploitation of those works. It therefore gives creators two different, but matching rights:

- an exclusive, positive right to copy and exploit their own works, or license other people (such as publishers) to do it for them; and
- a negative right to prevent anyone else from doing so without their consent, coupled with powerful legal remedies for copyright infringement if they do.

Under UK law, the emphasis has been very much on the second, negative, right: UK copyright was primarily a right to prevent other people from doing things. It is important to remember, though, that it is far from being an absolute monopoly, and was never intended to be; as well as a limited duration, after which works revert to the public domain, there are clear exceptions for purposes beneficial to society, such as 'fair dealing' for research and private study, or library and educational exceptions. (We will look at copyright infringement, and the various permitted exceptions under UK law, in chapter 9.)

Copyright may thus be grouped with the protection given to the owners of patents and the proprietors of trade marks, which (together with registered and unregistered designs, database rights, rights in performances, publication rights, moral rights and confidential information) traditionally make up the area of law known as 'intellectual property'. This term is not very precise, or very accurate (not every right is strictly speaking a right of property, for example), but it is a useful label for the increasingly important legal protection given to products of the mind: intellectual creations which, when applied commercially or industrially, are of some value to society, and worth protecting legally. In today's Internet society, intellectual property (the more scientific rights such as patents are sometimes called 'industrial property') is an increasingly important form of national and international legal protection for trade in all kinds of goods and services; not only for books, e-books, websites and databases, but also for films, DVDs, videos, computer software, distinctive trade brands, new drugs and other inventions. It is a key issue for all trading countries, and for trading blocs such as the EU and the World Trade Organisation, and intellectual property is normally fairly near the top of the agenda in international trade negotiations. Some developing countries, whose lack of infrastructure puts them on the wrong side of a growing 'digital divide', have suggested that intellectual property should be diluted to allow easier access, primarily to generic drugs, but this would harm local authors and publishers, who need copyright protection (for example, against piracy) even more than their colleagues in the West.

Before looking at modern copyright law in detail, it might be helpful to explain how we have got to this point, and how copyright law has developed over the centuries to meet the challenges of a fast-moving technological society.

FROM SCROLLS TO SCREENS: A BRIEF HISTORY OF COPYRIGHT

Although authors had a limited form of copyright and moral rights in the ancient world (plagiarism being punishable in Ancient Greece, for example), and Chinese block-printed books dating from the eleventh century Song Dynasty have been found with copyright claims, copyright only really started to develop as an organised system of legal protection in Europe when commercial copying first became possible in the fifteenth century with the invention of the printing press. In England the new printing process – introduced here by William Caxton – quickly came under the control of the Stationers Guild as part of a royal licensing system which, by the time of the Catholic Queen Mary, had as much to do with the suppression of heresy as the propagation of literature or learning. Parliament finally refused to renew any further Licensing Acts in 1694 after the Glorious Revolution, and the Stationers therefore lobbied Parliament for a proper statutory form of copyright protection.

The result was the first Copyright Act, the Statute of Anne of 1709. Under that Act, authors were given 'the sole right and liberty' of printing books for a fixed (renewable) term of 14 years, or 21 years for works already in print. Works had to be registered (of course) with the Stationers Company. This provided initially only a brief statutory monopoly, and continuing arguments about common law copyright were only finally resolved in favour of a fixed statutory term for published works in the historic case of *Donaldson* v. *Becket* in 1774. Unpublished works continued to enjoy an indefinite term of protection (now limited to 2039). The term was progressively increased through the eighteenth and nineteenth centuries, and extended to other works, such as paintings and photographs, but it remained, as today, a fixed statutory term, although increasingly this varied depending on how long the author lived.

To this developing national protection, the Berne Convention in 1886 added for the first time an international treaty system of reciprocal copyright protection, now (after a hundred years) accepted by over 150 nations. Key elements are:

- fully reciprocal 'national treatment'
- no requirement for formalities, e.g. registration, but works must be 'original'
- minimum protection for life of author plus 50 years.

A watered-down version of these requirements was included in the 1952 Universal Copyright Convention (UCC), established largely to accommodate the two superpowers, the USA and Russia, neither of which had yet joined Berne (they both since have). The UK joined the UCC in 1957.

The twentieth century was otherwise a century of rapid technological change, during which new advances such as films, broadcasts and computer programs were successively given statutory protection. The current UK Act, the Copyright, Designs and Patents Act, was passed in 1988 and came into force on 1 August the following year (referred to throughout the rest of this book as the '1988 Act'). It has already been heavily amended to take account of various EU directives, providing among other things for Rental and Lending Rights, legal protection of databases, and for extension of the term of copyright protection from life plus 50 years to life plus 70 for most works, including all works of EEA origin. Some of the most significant changes came when the UK implemented the EU Copyright Directive, designed to harmonise copyright protection across the expanding EU and enable full accession to the 1996 WIPO Copyright Treaty, bringing the Berne Convention more fully up to date with the digital society.

In addition, the World Trade Organisation has now replaced the old system of GATT trade negotiations, not only adopting Berne as the minimum copyright standard for member states, but also (via the 1994 TRIPS Agreement) requiring member states to provide sufficient and effective copyright enforcement. In an Internet world, this is already proving a challenge.

THE EU COPYRIGHT DIRECTIVE

Directive 2001/29/EC on the harmonisation of certain aspects of copyright and related rights in the information society (generally referred to as the EU Copyright Directive) was finally passed by the EU Council of Ministers on 9 April 2001 after two years of unprecedented lobbying, and implemented in the UK (late) via the Copyright and Related Rights Regulations 2003 (referred to in this book as the 2003 Regulations), which came into force on 31 October the same year. The following summary sets out the basic structure of this key Directive (still being implemented in other EU member states), together with references to the UK Regulations where appropriate. Further details of copyright enforcement provisions, and new 'non-commercial' wording for many copyright exceptions, are included in chapter 9.

CORE RIGHTS

Adopting wording drawn directly from the WIPO Copyright Treaty 1996, the Directive required member states to provide the following key rights for authors:

- *Reproduction Right* (Article 2) The exclusive right to authorise or prohibit direct or indirect, temporary or permanent reproduction by any means and in any form, in whole or in part. This was largely already covered in the 1988 Act.
- *Right of Communication/making available to the public* (Article 3) The exclusive right to authorise or prohibit any communication to the public of their works, by wire or wireless means, including the making available to the public of their works in such a way that members of the public may access them from a place and at a time individually chosen by them. This was new, and has resulted in changes to sections 16 and 20 of the 1988 Act (set out fully in chapter 9). Opinion is divided about whether the changes increase the scope of copyright protection already given under UK law.
- *Distribution Right* (Article 4) The exclusive right to authorise or prohibit any form of distribution to the public by sale or otherwise (already dealt with under the 1988 Act).

EXCEPTIONS

In addition to new core rights, there are 21 possible exceptions, set out in Article 5. The first (5.1) dealing with temporary copying, is mandatory; the other 20 are optional, forming an à la carte menu from which the 15 member states required to implement the Directive are inevitably making different selections – thus seriously limiting the chances of any real harmonisation. It is at least an exhaustive list, so that no further exceptions within the EU are possible.

- *Temporary Reproduction* (Article 5.1) This exempts from the Reproduction Right temporary acts of reproduction 'which are transient or incidental and an integral and essential part of a technological process and whose sole purpose is to enable [network transmissions or lawful uses] ... which have no independent economic significance'. Since it is the only mandatory exception, and every word was the result of such vigorous argument by all sides, it was included almost verbatim in the UK Regulations (regulation 8), giving a new Permitted Act of 'Making Temporary Copies' under a new section 28A of the 1988 Act (see chapter 9 for more on this). It is generally felt to be a workable compromise between the interests of rightsholders to protect their works against economically significant misuse, and the legitimate need for intermediaries, users and telecommunications companies to have a workable exception that will enable the Internet to function. There are more general provisions dealing with liability of intermediaries in the E-Commerce Directive.
- *Optional Exceptions* There is not space here to set out all 20 optional exceptions, particularly since the UK selected very few, sticking broadly to current 'fair dealing'

exceptions, such as criticism or review, or research or private study plus existing educational and library exceptions, many now subject to express 'non-commercial' criteria. However, there was also provision in the Directive for an exception for disabled people, which the UK utilised in passing the Copyright (Visually Impaired Persons) Act 2002, and which now permits making 'accessible' copies by visually impaired people (or on their behalf if no licensing scheme is available). The Act came into force on 31 October 2003, and licensing schemes are now established, including one operated by the Copyright Licensing Agency.

• *The 'Three-Step Test'* One very important proviso applying to all 21 exceptions is contained in Article 5.5. Using wording drawn directly from Article 9(2) of the Berne Convention, it provides that each exception should only be applied 'in certain special cases which do not conflict with a normal exploitation of the work or other subject-matter and do not unreasonably prejudice the legitimate interests of the rightsholder'. Although this wording was not reproduced in the UK Regulations, it still forms part of EU copyright law, and is likely to be an increasingly important yardstick for future interpretation.

TECHNOLOGY AND REMEDIES

Articles 6 and 7 required member states to provide protection against circumvention of technological measures, such as encryption, and rights-management information. Both these provisions were implemented in the 2003 Regulations. Article 8 (also implemented) further provided for sanctions and remedies, which must be 'effective, proportionate and dissuasive', including remedies against service-providers which it is hoped will lead to effective Notice and Takedown provisions suitable for the Internet age.

COPYRIGHT WORKS

INTRODUCTION: TYPES OF WORKS

Initially, as we have seen (above, p. 11), copyright only extended to books and other printed matter. However, definitions based on traditional packages such as 'books' are no longer specific or flexible enough for modern content industries like publishing, where individual creations – such as text, graphics, or sound recordings – may now need to be re-used and adapted in different combinations and in different forms (such as online services or websites). Each original element may also be created and owned by quite different people, who may wish to exploit them in different ways; it is important therefore to identify who owns the rights in each constituent part and deal with those rights separately. For this reason, it is better to think of books, journals, CD-ROMs or websites not as 'works' at all but as packages or bundles of works, each of which may need different treatment.

What copyright works, then, does UK law protect? Not every creation counts as a work. The works which may currently be protected are set out in section 1(1) of the Copyright, Designs and Patents Act 1988. These categories were only slightly altered by the 2003 Regulations, which removed the separate category of cable programmes, now included under broadcasts. Three general categories of works may now be protected:

(1) original literary, dramatic, musical or artistic works;
(2) sound recordings, films, broadcasts or cable programmes; and
(3) the typographical arrangement of published editions.

There is now a separate Publication Right in previously unpublished works, and a separate statutory Database Right, both dealt with in chapter 3. Copyright may still cover some original databases, dealt with below (p. 16).

If you want to secure copyright protection for a work in the UK, therefore, the first thing you will need to do is make sure that it falls into one of the above categories. There are other qualifying criteria which each individual work will also need to fulfil (see below, p. 33), but these three categories are the essential starting point. Many of the categories have been defined quite widely over the years – so that literary works, for example, now include computer programs and compilations – and we will examine each of the categories most relevant to publishing in turn. As will become obvious, a modern publication may contain several different copyright works.

LITERARY WORKS

Of all copyright works, literary works are still the most important for authors and publishers, although others (such as artistic works) are important too as we shall see. Under section 3 of the 1988 Act, a 'literary work':

- means any work (other than a dramatic or musical work) which is written, spoken or sung;
- includes a table or compilation (other than a database) and a computer program;
- includes a database which by reason of the selection or arrangement of its contents, constitutes the author's own intellectual creation;
- must be recorded, 'in writing or otherwise'.

'Written, spoken or sung'

A work does not need to be 'literary' in the colloquial sense in order to be a literary work, as long as it is written, spoken or sung. Some very un-'literary' written matter indeed has been given copyright protection in the past, such as business letters, football coupons, trade advertisements and examination papers: indeed, it is possibly more useful to think of 'literary' in the broadest context of sales 'literature' or business 'literature' than as having any necessary connection with Dickens or Proust. It merely needs to be written (or spoken or sung) and recorded, in writing or otherwise (see below). There is no requirement for written matter to be written in any particular language or notation, or even to use words at all: mathematical symbols and equations, scientific formulae or even circuit diagrams will be equally protected. However, a single invented word will not be sufficient to constitute a literary 'work'. Under section 178 of the 1988 Act 'writing' and 'written' include any form of notation or code, whether by hand or otherwise, and regardless of the method or the medium used.

Tables and compilations

Tables and compilations have been given copyright protection as literary works since the 1911 Copyright Act, and may be of considerable commercial value in published works today – in many cases forming the whole or virtually the whole of the work. Examples are TV listings, sports fixture lists, professional or trade directories, street directories, trade catalogues, websites, bulletin boards, or even – given sufficient originality in the selection (see p. 18 below) – schemes of chapters or sequences of topics or headings. However, compilations stored electronically are equally protected whether or not printed out or published in written form. UK copyright law recognises that an original compilation is more than the sum total of individual entries (which may or may not be literary or other works in their own right) and protects the selection and arrangement of those items as a separate copyright work. This new compilation may have value as much for what is omitted, as for what is included: however, there does need to be some evidence that some skill and judgement has gone into the selection and arrangement – we will consider this below, and under originality (p. 18). Compilations which are databases now have to satisfy a more rigorous test of originality to qualify for copyright protection (see below). This means that some compilations which enjoyed copyright protection in the past might not do so now. However, there are transitional provisions protecting databases created on or before 27 March 1996.

Databases

Although databases (however mundane) have traditionally been protected under UK copyright law as compilations, since the Copyright and Rights in Databases Regulations 1997 (implementing the EU Database Directive) came into force on 1 January 1998, databases have only been eligible for full copyright protection in the UK if they bear the hallmark of the author's 'intellectual creation'. With this proviso, they are still protected as literary works, and are now defined widely to include any collection of independent works, data or other materials which:

(a) are arranged in a systematic or methodical way, and
(b) are individually accessible by electronic or other means.

This broad definition would include not only commercial databases and most websites, but also newspapers and journals (and even this book) but probably not films, because of the requirements of individual accessibility at (b). However, none of these will be given copyright protection unless original, and revised section 3A(2) of the 1988 Act (inserted by the 1997 Regulations) now provides that:

a literary work consisting of a database is original if, and only if, by reason of the selection or arrangement of the contents of the database, the database constitutes the author's own intellectual creation.

This new intellectual standard was a dramatic change for UK copyright, which had previously protected quite mundane databases, whose authors – unlike their Continental counterparts – had to display not so much 'intellect' as 'sweat of the brow' (see below, p. 18). As a result, many basic, but commercially valuable, databases, such as alphabetical listings or directories, may not now be eligible for full copyright protection, now lasting in most cases for the life of the author plus 70 years. They may not, however, be unprotected if there has been 'substantial investment' in 'obtaining, verifying or presenting' their contents – in which case they may be protected now by a separate statutory Database Right, preventing unauthorised extraction or re-use, and lasting for a much shorter 15-year term, but renewable regularly in appropriate circumstances. There are transitional provisions protecting databases created on or before 27 March 1996 and which were protected by copyright on 31 December 1997. Database Right has recently been significantly narrowed by the Court of Appeal, applying the European Court of Justice's judgment in the *William Hill* case – this is dealt with fully in chapter 3.

Computer programs

Computer programs are specifically protected as literary works, having been given statutory protection for the first time by the Copyright (Computer Software) Amendment Act 1985. They are not defined in the 1988 Act, but would probably include any sequence or set of instructions in machine-readable form which are capable of causing a computer to perform a particular task or function. This would extend to programs held in most current forms, as long as they could be said to be held in notation or code and therefore 'written': this would clearly include print-outs, but equally computer chips, magnetic tapes, disks and recordings. Design material created in preparation for computer programs is now also protected as a literary work under the Copyright (Computer Programs) Regulations 1992.

'Computer-generated works' are also protected under the 1988 Act, and are defined as works generated by a computer 'in circumstances such that there is no known author of the work'. This difficult philosophical concept is probably best left to the experts: we will consider who owns such creations at p. 29.

Recorded in writing, or otherwise

A literary work will not be protected unless it is put into some permanent, or material, form or, in the case of electronic information, a retrievable form. The means of recording used is very widely defined: 'in writing, or otherwise' could include almost any form of record, and specifically extends to non-written media. This means that a speech or lecture will be protected as a literary work even if delivered without a text or notes, provided that someone (not necessarily the speaker) makes a record of it at the time; for example, makes a tape recording, or keys it into the memory of a lap-top computer. The same might be true of an interview, provided what was said had enough originality to qualify as a copyright work at all (see below).

It does not matter who makes the recording, and in fact there is no requirement that it should even be made with the speaker's consent. In many cases two quite separate copyrights will be created at the same time – copyright in the spoken (and recorded) words as a literary work, and a separate copyright in the recording, or a transcription of it, either as a new literary work or as a sound recording. Even a verbatim written report of a speech has been given separate copyright protection – in the famous case of *Walter* v. *Lane* in 1900 – where special skill is needed to write it down. As we shall see later, although such parallel copyrights may be dependent on each other, they may be owned by different people. For example, a photograph taken of a painting may be entitled to copyright protection if sufficient skill is used by the photographer (for example, in choice of angle, cropping or lighting). If the painting is still in copyright, there will then be two separate copyrights, which may well be owned by separate people, the artist and the photographer.

Originality

Copyright protection under the 1988 Act is not given to all literary works, but only to 'original' literary works: dramatic, musical and artistic works must also be original. The requirement does not extend to any other works, but since literary (and artistic) works in particular play such a central role in publishing, establishing originality in appropriate cases is clearly of great importance. So: what is 'original'?

For the purposes of copyright law, all that original means is that the work concerned should originate from the author: in other words, that he or she should not have copied it from anywhere else. Any evidence that you have saved yourself time and effort by copying directly from someone else, without sufficient original input from you, will rob your work of its originality and thus of its copyright protection. However, it does not need to display what we may think of colloquially as original thought, in the sense of unique perception or insight which no one else has contributed to the subject before. It is quite permissible to base your work entirely on common sources and existing material (provided you do not copy them) – the originality which is required is not so much original thought as original effort: an independent work which (however mundane or derivative) you have used your own time and effort, and your own faculties and skills, to create. (In America they used to refer to this as 'sweat of the brow' – however, following the 1991 US case of *Feist Publications Inc.* v. *Rural Telephone Service*, mere sweat is not now enough under US law. It will also not now be sufficient to protect databases in the EU – see above.)

On this basis, it is easy to see how English law has granted copyright protection to railway timetables and sports fixture lists, as well as to great works of literature. It also means that two or more very similar – or even identical – works could be created independently by different people, provided that each of them has expended their own skill and effort. Thus two photographers might take virtually identical photographs of the same scene, and two novelists may write strikingly similar stories: provided no copying had taken place, each one may constitute a separate copyright work.

Some copyright works are, by their very nature, bound to be similar, if not identical. Published mathematical tables are the classic example, since any two authors working them out properly are bound (one hopes) to arrive at the same result. A compilation such as a directory of professional names and addresses is bound to be very similar to another directory covering the same profession, but both will be protected if both are the result of independent skill and effort. Copying does occur, of course, and we will consider 'originality' again later on, under infringement of copyright (chapter 9). Many directory publishers include deliberate minor errors in their databases in order to expose copying: it is stretching coincidence a bit far to claim that, while expending your own skill and effort, you still nevertheless happened to reproduce exactly the same errors as someone else.

New editions, and even possibly revised reprints, will often contain enough originality to be protected as separate copyright works, provided that there is sufficient that is new. However, to create a copyright by alterations in the text, these must be extensive and substantial, rather than minor or merely cosmetic.

Abridgements may also be protected, including abstracts of articles (but abstracts may often be copied under section 60 of the 1988 Act).

Adaptations of a book by turning it into a play or a film will create new copyrights, if sufficient skill and judgement is used, even though the original work is reproduced in the new works.

Translations have always been given separate copyright protection in view of the obvious skill involved, even though – by definition – derived entirely from an existing work.

It is very unlikely that the title of a book would have enough originality to be protected as a literary work in its own right – unless it was unusually long. Indeed, it may not be a 'work' at all, and it may also not be a substantial part of another work (see chapter 9, p. 216). However, titles may in appropriate cases be protected as registered trade marks, given their necessary distinctiveness, or in some cases by the law of passing off (see chapter 10).

SUMMARY CHECKLIST: LITERARY WORKS

To summarise briefly so far: in order to be protected under UK copyright law as a literary work, a work must display the following features, among others:

- It must be written, spoken or sung (this includes tables, compilations and computer programs).
- It must be recorded, in writing or otherwise.
- It must be 'original'.

There are other qualifying requirements which apply to all copyright works, as we shall see (below, p. 33) but a work must fulfil at least the above three criteria if it is to be protected as a literary work at all.

ARTISTIC WORKS

Artistic works are defined in section 4(1) of the 1988 Act to mean:

(1) a graphic work, photograph, sculpture or collage, irrespective of artistic quality;
(2) a work of architecture being a building or a model for a building; or
(3) a work of artistic craftsmanship.

'Artistic' is not defined but, like 'literary', it is more a generic grouping than any particular cultural yardstick. As the definition shows, artistic quality is not required at all for graphic works, photographs etc., which are protected 'irrespective of artistic quality', but a specific artistic element does seem to be required for works of artistic craftsmanship: we will look at this further when we consider those works (below, p. 21).

Remember also that artistic works, like literary works, must be 'original' in order to be protected under the 1988 Act: a direct copy would be unlikely to be given copyright protection. It is arguable, however, that a professional (or at least a skilful) copy of a painting might constitute a new copyright work, even though it was an exact replica, and re-origination of old illustrations by a new computer process might also create new copyrights if sufficient skill and judgement were involved.

The artistic works most relevant to publishing are graphic works, photographs and works of artistic craftsmanship.

Graphic works

Graphic works are defined in section 4(2) of the Act as including:

- paintings, drawings, diagrams, maps, charts or plans;
- engravings, etchings, lithographs, woodcuts or similar works.

All such works are protected irrespective of artistic quality, so judges (fortunately, one may think) are not required to make value judgments about 'art'.

Together with photographs, this wide definition of graphic works must cover most if not all illustrations which may currently be contained in published or accessible works, or which are relevant to publishing; for example, the design of a new typeface. Note also that diagrams and charts are included, so that small and relatively mundane technical illustrations within the text or website, such as graphs, may be given copyright protection as artistic works just as much as more obvious pictures, provided they display sufficient originality.

Strangely, unlike many other works, there is no requirement under the 1988 Act that graphic works should be fixed in any permanent (or retrievable) physical form, although this is probably implied. In the case of a painting, however, there is some authority for saying that it must be put on to some permanent (or at least fairly fixed) surface.

As from 1 January 2006, if the UK passes the necessary legislation in time, artists who have created original works of graphic (or plastic) art will be entitled to an Artist's Resale Right (or *droit de suite*) to a percentage share of the sale price every time their work is resold (e.g. by a gallery). For more on this, see chapter 3.

Photographs

Section 4(2) of the 1988 Act defines a photograph as:

> a recording of light or other radiation on any medium on which an image is produced or from which an image may by any means be produced, and which is not part of a film.

Films are separately protected, and a single frame of a film would therefore now be protected as part of a film and not as a photograph, although the position was different before the 1956 Copyright Act came into force: the date the photograph was taken may therefore be highly relevant, to ownership, to whether or not any 'originality' is required, and also to how long copyright protection lasts (see p. 39).

The 1988 Act makes no distinction between negatives and positive prints: negatives, as the master copy, would certainly be protected, and prints may well be protected separately if they displayed sufficient originality. However, a straightforward photocopy would not qualify as an original copyright work.

Works of artistic craftsmanship

Original works of craftsmanship, such as furniture or ceramics, may be protected as registered designs under the Registered Designs Act 1949, or (since the 1988 Act) as unregistered designs: however, they may also in some circumstances be entitled to copyright protection as works of artistic craftsmanship if they are more than merely functional and display some 'artistic' element. It is not clear how significant this artistic element needs to be, or what relationship it needs to bear (if any) to the function of the item in question. A prototype for a suite of mass-produced furniture, and the arrangement of objects and the members of the pop group Oasis from an album cover, have both been denied copyright protection on this basis, but works with a more obvious artistic element, such as hand-painted ceramics, inlaid cabinets, stained glass, specialised printing and hand-tooled bookbinding would almost certainly be protected.

SUMMARY CHECKLIST: ARTISTIC WORKS

To be protected under UK copyright law:

- All artistic works must be 'original'.
- Graphic works (paintings, drawings etc.) and photographs must be original, but need not display any particular artistic quality.
- Paintings must be fixed on to a surface.
- Works of artistic craftsmanship must have an 'artistic' element.

DRAMATIC AND MUSICAL WORKS

Dramatic works

When dramatic works were first given separate statutory protection under UK law, in the Dramatic Copyright Act 1833, they were defined as including 'any tragedy, comedy, play, opera, farce or other dramatic piece of entertainment'. Now, under the 1988 Act, they are not defined at all, other than to specify (in section 3(1)) that they include a work of dance or mime. A dramatic work probably, however, needs to be capable not only of being performed in some way, but also of being acted, and hence needs to have an essential and coherent dramatic structure of its own: TV personality Hughie Green (as we will see in chapter 8) failed to prevent the New Zealand Broadcasting Corporation in 1989 from producing their own game show using elements very similar to *Opportunity Knocks*, since no actual scripts seemed to exist and what was taken had no dramatic structure or coherence of its own. The later cases of *Fraser* v. *Thames TV* (1983) and *De Maudsley* v. *Palumbo* (1995) confirmed that, to be protected, a dramatic work must be 'clearly identifiable and potentially realisable', and 'capable of being realised as a finished product'. Similarly, a singer giving a recital in the Wigmore Hall, although clearly performing, would be unlikely to be performing a dramatic work, unless a significant amount of action was involved.

The more recent case of *Norowzian* v. *Arks Ltd (No 2)* (2001) decided that a film could be a dramatic work for the purposes of the 1988 Act. The Court of Appeal held that the ordinary and natural meaning of a 'dramatic work' was a 'work of action, with or without words or music, which was capable of being performed before an audience'. A film would often, though not always, be a work of action and it would be capable of being performed before an audience. In making this finding the Court of Appeal recognised that cartoons could now be classed as dramatic works and as such receive protection under UK copyright law. They would still be protected as films, and the underlying drawings would also be protected as artistic works. Perhaps the most puzzling example of a dramatic work given by the courts is a film made using particular editing techniques (which was later used in a Guinness advertising campaign) because film works are already entitled to their own copyright protection under section 5B of the 1988 Act (see later).

Like literary and musical works, dramatic works must be recorded 'in writing, or otherwise'. They must also be 'original'.

Musical works

The 1988 Act, at section 3(1), helpfully defines a musical work as 'a work consisting of music'; it does however go on to tell us that such a work is distinct from any words or action intended to be sung, spoken or performed with it. Thus, lyrics of a song or the libretto of an opera would not be part of the musical work itself, but would normally be separate literary works, and choreography or other action would be a dramatic work: quite often these works would have been created and thus will be owned by different people.

Musical works, to be protected by copyright, must be recorded, in writing or otherwise – this may be by means of written scores or by being recorded onto tapes or CDs, or by being fixed by any other means. The recording itself will be a separate copyright work (probably either a literary work or a sound recording).

The Court of Appeal recently observed that the essence of musical work is combining sounds to listen to, in a way intended to produce effects on the listener's emotions and intellect – it is more than mere noise. The resulting sounds are protected by copyright, provided they are recorded in material form.

Finally, as with other copyright works in this group, all musical works must be 'original'. As has been seen with literary and artistic works, this implies no more than some significant creative effort and skill, and an absence of copying: it is not necessary to be Mozart. However, an original musical work must be more than a mere interpretation.

SOUND RECORDINGS, FILMS, BROADCASTS OR INTERNET TRANSMISSIONS

Sound recordings

Sound recordings were given separate copyright protection under UK law by the 1911 Copyright Act, as a response to the growing sale of phonographs and perforated rolls. The recording industry is now a major international industry and the opportunities for digital as well as mechanical copying are considerably more sophisticated, as the *Napster* and *Grokster* litigation in the USA has shown – involving not only unauthorised copying but also systematic uploading and 'peer-to-peer' file-swapping. In a decision which came as something of a relief to the music industry, the US Supreme Court recently found that the filesharing activities of Grokster were illegal and infringed copyright.

Sound recordings continue to be protected in the UK as separate copyright works under the 1988 Act, and are now defined (in section 5A(1)) as meaning:

(a) a recording of sounds, from which the sounds may be reproduced, or

(b) a recording of the whole or any part of a literary, dramatic or musical work, from which sounds reproducing the work or part may be produced, regardless of the medium on which the recording is made or the method by which the sounds are reproduced or produced. Thus, two separate kinds of sound recording are protected – those which are recordings of pure sounds (such as birdsong), and those which are recordings of other copyright works, such as recordings of famous actors reading books (literary works), or reciting plays (dramatic works), as well as – of course – recordings of music.

Modern film soundtracks are now protected not only as part of the films which they accompany (under section 5B(2)) but also as sound recordings separately from the films themselves (although the position may be different for soundtracks created before 1989).

In addition to copyright, the 1988 Act also introduced a limited rental right for sound recordings (and for films and computer programs) – we will deal with this later, when we look at the restricted acts which only a copyright owner may do (below, p. 220). There is, as yet, no blank tape levy in the UK.

There is no requirement that a sound recording should be original (unlike literary, dramatic, musical or artistic works). However, copyright will not protect a sound recording which is merely a copy of a previous sound recording (section 5A(2)).

Films

A film is a separate copyright work, defined in section 5B(1) of the 1988 Act as meaning 'a recording on any medium from which a moving image may by any means be produced'. This definition is wide enough to cover videos and DVDs, film downloads, and some aspects of computer games. Film soundtracks are now protected both as part of the films concerned, and independently as sound recordings (see above). In addition, a typical film will include many other copyright works, and the relevant rights will need to be acquired (or licensed) from the respective owners in order to make the film: these rights are collectively referred to in the film business as the 'underlying rights'. These might include, for example, the screenplay and the book or script (dramatic and literary works), the score (a musical work), graphics, cartoons or set designs (artistic works), as well as the soundtrack (sound recording). Individual frames or stills from a film are protected as part of the film, and not as photographs (see above, p. 21). This may be significant, since (for example) a photograph (as an artistic work) must be original, whereas the film need not be. Films, like sound recordings, do not need to be original; however, section 5B(4) of the 1988 Act provides that a film which is merely a copy of a previous film will not be protected by copyright.

Broadcasts

Broadcasts include not only traditional radio and TV broadcasts and cable transmissions, but also (since the Cable and Broadcasting Act 1984) direct broadcasting by satellite. The wide definition of broadcasts (in section 6 of the 1988 Act, as amended by the 2003 Regulations) effectively includes all transmissions including those sent via fixed, land-based routes (such as cable): broadcast means 'an electronic transmission of visual images, sounds or other information' which can lawfully be received by the public or which is sent for public presentation. Note: (1) that broadcasts may consist not only of pictures and sound but also of 'other information' – such as teletext; and (2) that an encrypted transmission is only regarded as being lawfully received by the public if they have access to authorised decoding equipment.

Broadcasts do not include Internet transmissions unless they fall into one of three categories:

(a) transmissions taking place simultaneously on the Internet and by other means;
(b) concurrent transmissions of a true event; or
(c) transmissions of recorded moving images or sounds forming part of a [scheduled] programme service offered by the person responsible for making the transmission.

These categories of transmission on the Internet will be treated as broadcasts. Other Internet transmissions will fall within the new section 20 of the 1988 Act. This deals with communication to the public, which includes both broadcasting and making a work available to the public. It is this latter right which will cover most Internet activities.

Internet transmissions

It is interesting that there is now no specific category of copyright work which relates to transmissions on the Internet which are not included in the category of 'broadcast'. Under the previous law, such a transmission would have been protected as a cable programme. That separate category of work has been abolished by the 2003 changes in the law. Cable programmes are now protected as a type of broadcast. Under the new law, works transmitted on the Internet are protected by the communication to the public and making available rights, but the transmission itself is not protected as such, unless it falls within the new definition of a broadcast, which excludes many types of Internet transmission.

TYPOGRAPHICAL ARRANGEMENTS

There is a separate copyright in the UK in typographical arrangements of published editions. It lasts only for 25 years from the end of the year of publication, and is owned by the publisher: the purpose is to protect the publisher's skill and investment in the composition and typesetting, so a separate copyright is given to the visual appearance of the printed page itself as well as to its contents. This means that, on a typical printed page there are likely to be several copyrights: a literary copyright in the text, and possibly in any compilation, artistic copyright in any photographs, charts or illustrations, and a separate typographical copyright, owned by the publishers, in the arrangement of the page itself. This protects a publisher of a public domain edition, say of Shakespeare or Milton: although the text is long since out of copyright, there may still be an enforceable copyright in the publisher's edition.

It is not clear whether this protection would be available to the creator of a website or an e-book. However, it seems likely that a conventional book, or similar text, might be reproduced via those media, and typographical copyright in the original edition might be infringed depending on the way it was reproduced.

A substantial part of the *whole* 'published edition' does, however, need to be copied. This is clear from the decision of the House of Lords in *Newspaper Licensing Agency Ltd* v. *Marks & Spencer PLC* (2001), where the NLA failed in a claim that Marks & Spencer had infringed typographical copyright in newspapers by operating an unlicensed cuttings service which circulated cuttings of individual articles to members of its staff, usually mounted as single items on plain sheets of paper. Was a single article, taken out of context, a substantial part of the whole published edition? The Lords thought not, and Lord Hoffmann spoke for the majority view when he said 'I find it difficult to think of the skill and labour which has gone into the typographical arrangement of a newspaper being expressed, in anything less than a full page'. For more on the need to copy a substantial part, see chapter 9.

Typographical arrangements do not need to be 'original' as such (unlike the artistic copyright which may exist in a new typeface) but they will not be protected if they merely reproduce the typographical arrangement of a previous edition. A publisher cannot therefore perpetually extend typographical copyright beyond 25 years simply by re-issuing the last edition. Typographical copyright was not affected by UK implementation of the EU Copyright Directive, other than by the introduction of a new wide-ranging exception for temporary copies, under new section 28A (see p. 13 above).

SUMMARY CHECKLIST: COPYRIGHT WORKS

It should be clear by now that a modern publication such as a book or a CD is unlikely to be a single copyright work, but a bundle of several different works. Before we go on to consider who *owns* each copyright, it may be useful to remind ourselves which works may most often be relevant.

Books and e-books

May contain:

- original text (literary work). The plot – if any – may be a dramatic work;
- quoted text from other sources (separate literary works);
- index, prelims, tables or compilations (literary works);
- illustrations/photographs (artistic works);
- overall compilation (particularly in the case of collective works such as encyclopaedias (literary works);
- databases (literary works and/or database right works);
- typographical arrangement (typographical copyright);
- jacket text and illustrations (literary and artistic works);
- computer programs/software (literary works), in the case of e-books.

CD-ROMs

May contain:

- original and quoted text (literary and possibly dramatic works);
- tables or compilations (literary works);
- illustrations/photographs (artistic works);
- overall compilation (literary work);
- databases (literary works and/or database right works);
- computer programs/software (literary work);
- accompanying manual/booklet (literary and artistic work and typographical copyright).

Multimedia CD or website

May contain:

- some or all works in a CD-ROM (see above);
- animations/graphics/cartoons (artistic works);
- video and film (films);
- music (musical work);
- lyrics (literary works);
- drama/plays (dramatic works);
- recordings of music, speech or other sounds (sound recordings);
- performances of works (rights in performances);
- broadcasts (insofar as a website is broadcasting).

Moral rights of authors may also now be relevant in relation to many of the above works – on moral rights generally, see chapter 3.

OWNERSHIP OF COPYRIGHT

Who owns all these different copyrights, and connected rights? Given the variety of copyright works which UK law protects, it might be thought that working out who owns which rights would be a complete nightmare – but in fact, in most cases, the underlying principle of copyright ownership is very simple. There are (of course) some exceptions (such as employee works) which we will come to, but, subject to those, the general rule is stated in section 11(1) of the 1988 Act:

The author of a work is the first owner of any copyright in it.

The search for a copyright owner is therefore in most cases the search for the author. And who, then, is the 'author'? Section 9(1) tells us: the author is the person who creates the work. As a general rule, therefore, the creator of a work usually owns the copyright in it.

It should not be forgotten that the rules governing who is the author of a work and who owns copyright in it vary according to when the work was made. In the notes which follow, we will focus on the current law, but for pre-August 1989 works it will often be necessary to refer back to the 1956 or 1911 Copyright Acts, or even earlier.

Ownership of copyright is unaffected by the EU Copyright Directive, or by the 2003 Regulations.

'AUTHORS'

As we saw in chapter 1, there is no copyright in ideas, so the author or creator of a novel or a play is not necessarily the person who had the original idea, but the person who first put that idea into concrete form. These may be one and the same person, of course, or they may have worked on the project together (in which case they may be joint authors), but they may also be completely different people. The law tries to find the real creator – the person who actually executed the work, the person who made it. This may vary according to the type of work. For example, the creators of a film will be more than one type of person, such as the producer and the principal director.

Someone who was merely putting a literary (or artistic) work onto paper at the instruction of someone else – a secretary writing a letter, or an amanuensis helping to take down a book, for example – would not be regarded as the author of that work. But where the work is not merely dictated, but is ghost written, then the ghost writer will own the copyright, because it is the ghost writer who has created the work which appears on the page. Appropriately enough (for ghosts) this was held in a 1927 case to protect the writings of a spiritualist medium, despite claims that the real 'author' resided in another world. And, in the same way, a reporter writing up a report of a speech (even, in one famous case, a verbatim report) would probably be regarded as the 'author' of that report and would own the copyright in it (although copyright in the speech itself would still be owned by the speaker).

Joint authors

In some cases, it may simply not be possible to identify separate copyright works, and say that X wrote this bit and Y wrote that. Where it is possible (for example where contributors write distinct chapters of a book or entries in an encyclopaedia) each one will own a separate copyright. Where it is *not* possible, but more than one person clearly contributed (as, for example, where a scientific research team publishes their findings) they are treated as joint authors.

In many cases, it will be a question of degree, whether what is created is a collection of separate works, or whether it is truly a joint work. Under the 1988 Act (section 10(1)) a work of joint authorship is:

> a work produced by the collaboration of two or more authors in which the contribution of each author is not distinct from that of the other author or authors.

Each of them must be authors, however: someone who contributed ideas and suggestions, but took no part in the actual writing, would be unlikely to be considered a joint author (although this is not completely impossible). This would be the case even if they made minor revisions, unless their revisions were unusually original. For example, members of the pop group Spandau Ballet failed in one case to prove that they made a significant and original contribution to the group's songs and, therefore, were not entitled to joint authorship in the songs with Gary Kemp, the main songwriter and lyricist. Contributions such as a saxophone improvisation in the song 'True' were held to be only examples of a performance (that any accomplished musician would make) rather than of the joint creator of a work.

Joint authors usually own the copyright as 'tenants in common' – under section 173(2) of the 1988 Act, no single joint copyright owner can publish or license the work without the consent of the others, and when a joint copyright owner dies the same rights and duties will pass to his or her heirs.

Collective works

In a collective work such as an encyclopaedia or dictionary, there is likely to be a copyright not only in the individual entries – normally owned by the respective authors – but also in the overall compilation of the collective work as a whole. The 'author' of that compilation is usually taken to be the person who was responsible for assembling it, and whose selection and arrangement it is. This might be one person, such as a General Editor, or one or more of the contributors (who might then be joint authors of the compilation) or even possibly the publisher.

Photographs

Under the 1988 Act, the author of a photograph is the person who creates it – usually the photographer. This means that copyright in all photographs taken after 1 August 1989 will be owned by the photographer, unless there is an agreement to the contrary or one of the exceptions applies (see below). For photographs taken between 1 June 1957 and 1 August 1989, however, the 1956 Copyright Act defined the author as the person who, at the relevant time, owned the material on which the photograph was taken – it may therefore be important to find out when the photographs were taken, in order to find out who owns the copyright. There may also be special provision for commissioned photographs under the 1956 Act (see below, p. 30–1).

Software and computer-generated works

Copyright in a computer program which is created by an identifiable human being will normally be owned by that person, as with any other literary work. In a case of a computer-generated work, however – generated in circumstances such that there is no human author – section 9(3) of the 1988 Act provides that the 'author' is the person who undertook the arrangements necessary for the creation of the work.

Typographical arrangements

Copyright in typographical arrangements of published editions is owned by the publisher.

Sound recordings and films

Under the 1988 Act, the author of a sound recording or a film is the person by whom the necessary arrangements for making it were made. In many cases this might be several people, but is most likely to be a record or film production company. In the case of a film, the principal director is an author. Also, in the case of a film, the Duration Directive, and 1995 Regulations made under it (see p. 36–9), have specified that copyright protection shall be calculated from the death of one of four possible categories of persons, but this does not change the position that the authors of a film are the producer and the principal director.

The soundtrack of a film is now not only treated as part of the film concerned but is also protected as a separate copyright work (as a sound recording) and copyright may thus be separately owned.

As pointed out at the beginning of this section, pre-1989 ownership may be different, and the complex provisions are beyond the scope of this book. In cases of doubt, specialist legal advice should be sought.

Broadcasts

The author of a broadcast under the 1988 Act is the person who makes the broadcast (provided he or she has at least some responsibility for its contents, and is not – like BT – simply a common carrier). Where more than one person is involved in making the broadcast, the broadcast may be a work of joint authorship.

Where a broadcast is relayed, the original broadcaster is the author, rather than the person making the relay.

Commissioned works

Unlike US provisions regarding Works for Hire (where the commissioner may own copyright in certain commissioned work), there are no special provisions in the 1988 Act relating to copyright in commissioned works in the UK, so for works created after 1 August 1989 the general rule of copyright ownership applies, and the author will normally own the copyright, not the commissioner (unless there is a contract providing otherwise, or a contract term which may be implied in appropriate circumstances). In fact (despite popular beliefs to the contrary) even before 1989 there has never been any general rule of law that if you commissioned a work you would automatically own the copyright in it. There were three very limited exceptions under the 1956 Copyright Act, covering certain kinds of commissioned artistic works, but these never extended to literary or other works. The exceptions were:

- commissioned photographs;
- commissioned portraits (painted or drawn);
- commissioned engravings.

A person commissioning such works after 1 June 1957 but before 1 August 1989 might own the copyright, if the work was made in response to the commission, and if he or she paid for it (or at least agreed to). There were somewhat similar provisions under the 1911 Copyright Act. Otherwise, subject to the rules set out above, the artist or photographer, like authors of literary works, would probably own the copyright in the normal way. For most commissioned works, therefore, unless one of the limited exceptions above applies, or unless there is an agreement to the contrary, it is likely that the author or artist, not the commissioner, will own the copyright.

WORKS BY EMPLOYEES

There is one major exception to the general rule that authors own copyright in their works, and that concerns works created by employees. Under section 11(2) of the 1988 Act:

> where a literary, dramatic, musical or artistic work or a film is made by an employee in the course of his employment, his employer is the first owner of any copyright in the work subject to any agreement to the contrary.

The position was broadly the same (save in relation to films) under the 1956 and 1911 Acts. There are two particular points to note.

'Employees'

The terms 'employee' and 'employment' refer to employment under what the law calls a contract of service or apprenticeship – in other words, someone employed under a contract of employment, rather than a self-employed person such as a freelancer. The contract of employment does not need to be full-time, or permanent, so part-time and temporary employees would be covered, but as Lord Denning said in one case, the person concerned does need to be 'employed as part of the business'. One traditional test, in cases of doubt, used to be the degree of control exercised by the employer – if the people concerned have little or no discretion over the way the work is done they are probably employees (although there are exceptions: directors, for example, may have considerable discretion but might still be regarded as employees for copyright purposes). It is usually reasonably easy to tell: in the 1916 case of *University of London Press Limited* v. *University Tutorial Press Limited* two external examiners were held *not* to be employees of London University, since they were not exclusively employed by London University, and prepared the papers in their own time, for a one-off fee: they therefore owned the copyright, not the university. In the more recent case of *Beloff* v. *Pressdram Ltd* (1993), Nora Beloff, the lobby correspondent of *The Observer* was held to be an employee on the basis, amongst other things, that she worked full time at the *Observer* and did not use her own capital for the job, and would be paid her salary whether or not the paper made a profit.

'In the course of his employment'

For the employer to own the copyright, the employee must have created it *in the course of* that employment, not merely while employed. A night security guard who wrote a novel while on duty would probably therefore own the copyright in it, since writing novels would be unlikely to feature anywhere in his (or her) job description. In other cases, such as lecturers preparing teaching manuals, or academic or scientific researchers publishing research papers, the position may be less clear-cut, and there is considerable pressure from some academic institutions for copyright in works created by their staff to be owned by the institutions, if the institution's facilities were used, even without any agreement or assignment. This is highly debatable under English law, but even where the work is done outside official working hours, it may still be in the course of employment. Ideally, such issues should be covered clearly in employment contracts.

Before 1989, under the 1956 Copyright Act (and earlier law) employers might also have owned the copyright (or part of it) in works of their employees which were created for publication in a newspaper, magazine or similar periodical. This only applies, however, to pre-1989 works.

MANUSCRIPTS AND ARTWORK

Before we leave the subject of ownership, it is important to remember that ownership of copyright in something is not the same as physical ownership of the documents or artwork, or other materials such as disks or tapes, on which it is recorded. Although ownership of physical materials might still be relevant to establish copyright in some older works – such as photographs created before 1989 – for most purposes now the two things are completely separate. An author delivering a manuscript, print-out or disks, or an artist delivering original artwork or photographs, will therefore continue to own those physical materials, and be entitled to their (reasonably) safe return, even if he or she does not own the copyright or subsequently assigns it to someone else. In the case of artwork, the artist will, by 1 January 2006 (if the necessary legislation is passed in time) be entitled to an Artists Resale Right of up to 4 per cent of *any* subsequent sales (see chapter 3). Since busy publishing offices are not always the best places to store valuable materials, many publishers in the delivery clauses of their contracts expressly disclaim any liability for loss or damage to manuscripts and other materials submitted to them; however, publishers are probably under a general duty at least to take reasonable care of an author's or artist's materials.

SUMMARY CHECKLIST: COPYRIGHT OWNERSHIP

- As a general rule, for modern works, the author of a work owns the copyright in it.
- Is the person concerned really the 'author'?
- Are there joint authors? If so, do all the copyright owners agree?
- Is there a separate copyright in any compilation, or a database right in any database?
- Have any computer-generated works, sound recordings or films been created? If so, who made the necessary arrangements, and who is the principal director of the film?
- Were any photographs taken before or after August 1989?
- Were any commissioned photographs, portraits or engravings created before August 1989?
- Was the author an employee?
- Did the author create the work in the course of that employment?

QUALIFICATION FOR COPYRIGHT PROTECTION

Although it is no longer necessary to register copyrights at Stationers Hall (or anywhere else), the work will not qualify for copyright protection under UK law unless it meets certain qualifying criteria. Works may qualify by virtue of:

- the author, or
- the country in which the work was first published.

These two 'points of attachment' for copyright protection are common to most Berne member countries: it does not matter whether it is the author or the place of first publication which qualifies for copyright protection, but one or other of them must. Often, of course, a work will qualify on both counts.

QUALIFICATION BY REFERENCE TO THE AUTHOR

A work qualifies for copyright protection in the UK if the author was at the material time a 'qualifying person'. A qualifying person is defined in section 154 of the 1988 Act and includes:

- a British citizen or a citizen of a British Dependent Territory;
- a British National (Overseas) or a British Overseas Citizen;
- a British subject or a British protected person;
- a person domiciled or resident in the UK (or another country to which the 1988 Act extends or has been applied);
- a body incorporated under UK law (or the law of another country to which the Act extends or has been applied);
- a citizen or subject of a foreign country to which the 1988 Act has been applied or extended by Order in Council (or who is domiciled or resident there).

Most of these terms are defined further in the British Nationality Act 1981. For most practical purposes, an author will qualify, at least as 'resident', if at the material time he or she lived at a home address in the UK, or the relevant foreign country. Foreign countries are periodically added by Order in Council, in accordance with the UK's Berne, UCC and other treaty obligations (see chapter 9, p. 246).

The 'material time' is:

- for unpublished works, when the work was made;
- for published works, the date of first publication.

(If the author dies before publication, the material time is immediately before his or her death.)

COUNTRY OF FIRST PUBLICATION

If for some reason copyright protection does not attach to a work by virtue of the author's nationality or other qualifying status, it may still do so if it was first published in the UK, or another qualifying country to which the 1988 Act extends or is applied.

What is 'first publication'? Indeed, what is 'publication'?

Publication

Publication, under the 1988 Act, takes place when copies of the work are issued to the public with the licence of the copyright owner. This would cover most publishing, but not for example the delivery of a speech or lecture, or the exhibition of a painting (unless copies were subsequently issued). Note that copies, in the plural, must be issued, although making the work available to the public via the Internet will count as publication in the case of literary, dramatic, musical and artistic works. A local intranet might be sufficient if access to it was sufficiently wide. It is not necessary that works should be issued for commercial sale: private or free circulation would probably count as publication. The work will not be 'published', however, if publication is a purely token gesture and 'not intended to satisfy the reasonable requirements of the public' – what the 1988 Act describes as 'merely colourable'.

First and simultaneous publication

First publication, although not defined, simply means what it says: the first time authorised copies are issued to the public. So if a copyright owner, or his or her licensee, first issues copies of a work to the public in the UK, that work will qualify for copyright protection under UK law, irrespective of the nationality of the author. Works of (say) US authors would therefore have qualified for copyright protection under UK law if they were first published here, even before the USA joined the UCC or Berne Conventions.

Publication also counts as first publication, even if simultaneous publication takes place somewhere else: 'simultaneous publication' for these purposes means publication within 30 days. So a US work simultaneously published in New York and London with a gap of no more than 30 days between publication dates would count as first published in the UK. (Under the 1911 Copyright Act, the simultaneous publication period was only 14 days – this shorter period continues to apply to works first published before 1 June 1957.)

SUMMARY CHECKLIST: QUALIFYING WORKS

- Was the author a qualifying person at the material time?
- If the author does not have a relevant British qualification (such as nationality or residence) is the author a citizen or subject of a qualifying foreign country?
- For a published work, did the author qualify at the date of first publication?
- For unpublished works, did the author qualify when the work was made?
- If the author is not a qualifying person, was the work first published in the UK (or another country to which the 1988 Act applies)?
- If not first publication, was there 'simultaneous' publication within 30 days?
- Did publication satisfy the reasonable expectations of the public?

DURATION OF COPYRIGHT

AUTHORS' LIVES

As we have seen, copyright in the UK is primarily a statutory right, and ever since the first Copyright Act of 1709 it has had a fixed term, or duration. After that, it expires and the protection ends. Although the first statutory copyrights only lasted for 14 years, they could be renewed for a second term if the author was still alive at the end of the first one, so from the outset the length of copyright protection has been linked to how long the author managed to stay alive. After various increases, the Berne Convention countries agreed each to adopt the same minimum term of copyright protection for literary and artistic works, starting from the moment of creation of the work and lasting until 50 years after the death of the author (sometimes referred to as 50 years 'post mortem auctoris', or '50 years pma'). At the time of the 1911 Act this was thought sufficient to protect two generations of the author's heirs (on the assumption – presumably – that each generation produces an heir at the average age of 25) and seemed a suitable compromise between those who argued that free access to literature required a shorter fixed term and those who felt that copyright should benefit the author's estate in perpetuity. It is not a perfect formula, but during the course of the twentieth century the Berne period gained widespread international acceptance. Countries belonging to the Universal Copyright Convention (see p. 248), adopted a shorter minimum period of 25 years pma, but the Berne period of 50 years is now the minimum period adopted by most countries.

For convenience and certainty, since the exact date of authors' deaths is often hard to prove, the 50-year period of copyright is deemed to run, not exactly from the 50th anniversary of the author's death but 50 years from the end of the calendar year in which the author died. So if an author died on 1 July 1945, copyright in the author's works would expire on 31 December 1995. It is important to remember this: for authors who die in January this can mean virtually a whole year's extra copyright protection.

EU HARMONISATION: LIFE PLUS 70

This widespread international standard did not, however, provide a level enough playing field for the European Commission, since it only provided a minimum, and some EU member states (such as Germany and Spain) provided longer terms. In addition, some countries like France gave longer protection to certain works, and, in certain cases, to account for the war years of both world wars.

The EU attempted to deal with this lack of harmony in 1993 by Directive 93/98/ EEC – variously called the Duration Directive, or the Term Directive – which provided for the copyright term for literary, artistic and other works to be harmonised upwards to 70 years pma throughout the EU and EEA. Member states were required to implement the necessary changes to their domestic laws by 1 July 1995, and the increased term now applies to all EEA-origin works which were protected in at least one member state on that date. The UK implemented the Directive (late) by means of the Duration of Copyright and Rights in Performances Regulations (1995). The USA has also now increased its own term of protection to life plus 70 years under the Sonny Bono Term Extension Act of 1998 (see p. 251).

THE 1995 REGULATIONS

Because the Duration Directive extended protection for works protected at 1 July 1995 'in at least one member state', each member state's implementing measures had to provide not only for *extensions* of copyright periods which were still running, but also for *revivals* of copyright in works which had gone into the public domain in their own country during the previous 20 years, but which might still be protected in, for example, Germany or Spain. Following the *Phil Collins* decision of the European Court of Justice in 1993, this was especially true if the author was (or would have been) an EU national. In the UK, this means that works by authors such as Thomas Hardy, John Buchan or Rudyard Kipling will have come back into copyright, having previously been in the public domain. The needless confusion and uncertainty caused by this retrospective law is likely to continue for several years to come. In addition, the much-vaunted harmonisation is unlikely to result for some time, since it was left to each member state to decide several crucial questions, each in their own way:

• Who should *own* the revived or extended copyright?
• What – if any – royalties would the new owners be entitled to?

* What protection or compensation would be available for those publishers (and others) who had exploited previously public domain works in good faith?

The UK's 1995 Regulations came into force on 1 January 1996. As well as longer protection for newly created works, they provided for:

(1) *extensions of copyright* for relevant works in which copyright still subsisted in the UK at 31 December 1995; and
(2) *revivals of copyright* for works whose terms of copyright expired before 31 December 1995 in the UK but which were still protected by copyright in another EEA member state on 1 July 1995.

The 1995 provisions did not apply to Crown or Parliamentary copyright, or to computer-generated works.

Extensions

The owner of an extended copyright is generally the person who owned the copyright immediately before commencement (1 January 1996).

In addition, any copyright licence, any term or condition of a copyright agreement, or any waiver or assertion of moral rights which existed immediately before commencement, and which was for the (then) full period of copyright, will continue to apply during the period of extended copyright (subject to any agreement to the contrary).

Revivals

Following the *Phil Collins* decision of the European Court of Justice (see above), this is now likely to cover the works of all EU and EEA authors who died between 1925 and 1945, provided they were protected in another EEA state (most probably Germany) at 1 July 1995. Depending on the year of the author's death, the revived copyright may last for anything from a year or so to an extra 20 years.

The new owner of any revived copyright is generally the person who owned copyright immediately before it expired. This is at least even-handed between publishers and authors: the last owner may have been a publisher, or equally a literary estate. If the former owner has died (or, in the event of a company, ceased to exist) the author or his or her estate will acquire the right; however, there may be some problems in tracing rights ownership.

Any waiver or assertion of moral rights in force immediately before copyright expired will continue to apply during the period of revived copyright: there are now detailed provisions for exercise of moral rights after an author's death.

Acquired rights

The Directive required member states to protect acquired rights of third parties: although it was not entirely clear exactly what this meant, it was the only express provision protecting those, like publishers, who had invested in good faith in editions of public domain works, only to find themselves potentially infringing a new, revived copyright. The 1995 Regulations protect such publishers in relation to revived copyrights in two ways:

(1) *Non-infringing acts* After commencement (1 January 1996), it is not an infringement of any revived copyright to do anything in pursuance of 'arrangements made' before 1 January 1995, or to issue to the public copies of the work made before 1 July 1995 (in both cases, at a time when the work was in the public domain). There are similar provisions relating to anthologies or adaptations, although these are slightly unclear.

(2) *Licences of right* There is considerable comfort for publishers of previously public domain works: 'any acts' (including copying, or issuing copies to the public) will be treated as licensed by the new owner of the revived copyright, subject only to payment of 'such reasonable royalty or other remuneration as may be agreed' (or, in the absence of agreement, arbitrated by the Copyright Tribunal). The acts will be treated as licensed from the outset (even though any royalty is not agreed or arbitrated until later), but the publisher must give reasonable notice to the new copyright owner of an intention to do the acts concerned (before the publisher does any of them).

Previous exclusive licensees will find that they may be in competition with any number of non-exclusive licensees of right under the above provisions, but on the other hand there does seem to be a reasonable basis for protection for those who seek to exploit (or continue to exploit) previously public domain works in good faith. The requirement to give notice may, however, cause publishers some difficulty, particularly where the identity of the new copyright owner is not immediately obvious. And whether and how far the Copyright Tribunal – not thus far very much involved in publishing arbitrations – will be asked to arrive at a definition of 'reasonable royalties' remains to be seen. At the time of writing it seems that most publishers, authors and agents are setting reasonable rates between themselves (bearing in mind that all Licences of Right are by definition non-exclusive).

Works not of EEA origin

Section 12(6) of the 1988 Act (inserted by the 1995 Regulations) provides that when the country of origin of a work is not an EEA state and the author is not an EEA national, the duration of copyright is that to which the work is entitled in its country of origin, subject to two provisos:

- the work cannot have a longer term of protection in the UK than it would have had if it had been of EEA origin;
- (for works in existence on 1 January 1996 and protected by copyright in the UK on 31 December 1995) this provision would not reduce the period of copyright protection which the work enjoyed under the old law.

The overall effect of this is that works not of EEA origin may also enjoy the extension (or part of it) and in appropriate cases revival of copyright where the term of protection in their country of origin exceeds that granted in the UK prior to 1 January 1996.

DURATION OF COPYRIGHT IN INDIVIDUAL WORKS

In addition to harmonising – or attempting to – the period of copyright protection for literary and artistic works, the Duration Directive also continued important provisions for duration of copyright in other works such as films, and for certain neighbouring rights. We shall deal with these and the relevant UK provisions in turn below, when we look briefly at each kind of work.

Literary, artistic, musical and dramatic works

The term of copyright was previously 50 years pma: it was increased in the UK from 1 January 1996 to 70 years pma (that is 70 years from the end of the calendar year in which the author died (see above, p. 36)). Photographs benefit from the 20-year extension, like other artistic works: this is a double extension for pre-1989 and pre-1957 photographs which were calculated for a fixed period from the year of first publication, and from the year the photograph was taken, respectively: for all photographs the term is now 70 years from the end of the year of the photographer's death.

Works of joint authorship

The Duration Directive and the 1995 Regulations re-inforced the existing UK position, under which the term of copyright (now increased to 70 years pma) is calculated from the year in which the last surviving (known) author dies.

Anonymous and pseudonymous works

Under the 1995 Regulations the term is increased to 70 years from the year it was made, or (if it was published during that period) 70 years from the end of the year in which the work is made available to the public. However, this only applies when the author is truly unknown – when the pseudonym adopted leaves no doubt as to the author's identity (or the author's identity is revealed) the term of copyright will be 70 years pma, as in literary, artistic, musical and dramatic works above.

Computer-generated works

The 1995 Regulations exclude computer-generated works from the provisions of the Duration Directive: the term of copyright in the UK is still the term provided in the 1988 Act; that is, 50 years from the end of the calendar year in which the work was made.

Posthumously published works, and publication right

Under the 1956 Copyright Act, copyright in posthumous literary and artistic works ran for 50 years from the year of first publication. With effect from 1 August 1989, the 1988 Act provided a fixed period of 50 years from 1 January 1990 for unpublished works in existence at 31 July 1989. These periods are unchanged by the 1995 Regulations. However, if the new provisions would give a longer period of protection (e.g. life plus 70) to a work unpublished at 31 July 1989, the longer period of protection will apply. Works created on or after 1 August 1989 enjoy the normal copyright period (e.g. life plus 70), calculated in relation to the author's life, whether they are published or not.

Where posthumous first publication in the UK or elsewhere in the EEA took place after the then period of copyright protection had expired, Article 4 of the Duration Directive provided for a new publication right. This right is to be owned by the first publisher of the work, and lasts for 25 years from the end of the year in which the work is first made available to the public. The UK has implemented these provisions in the Copyright and Related Rights Regulations 1996 (see chapter 3).

Unpublished works

Unpublished works were at one time protected in the UK by a perpetual common law copyright, but this was abolished by the 1911 Copyright Act. The transitional provisions of the 1988 Act provided that works which were still unpublished when the 1988 Act came into force (1 August 1989) should be protected for 50 years from the end of that year – that is, until 31 December 2039. They still are, unless the period of protection given by the new provisions would give a longer period of protection, in which case the longer period will apply.

Typographical arrangements

Copyright in the typographical arrangement of published editions is unaffected by the 1995 Regulations, and continues to last for 25 years from the end of the year in which the edition was first published.

Sound recordings and films

Under the 1988 Act, copyright in both sound recordings and films expired 50 years from the end of the year in which they were made (or, if they were released before then, 50 years from the year of release). Following the Duration and Copyright Directives and the 1995 and 2003 Regulations, there are two significant changes:

(1) for sound recordings, the 50-year period remains the same, but the definition of 'release' is now replaced by 'publication', which now includes any (authorised) making available to the public (by being played in public or communicated to the public);

(2) for films, the period of copyright is increased dramatically to 70 years from the end of the year in which the last known of four persons connected with the films dies:

    (a) the principal director;

    (b) the author of the screenplay;

    (c) the author of the dialogue;

    (d) the composer of the music (if it was created specifically for the film, and actually used).

If the identity of *none* of these people is known, copyright expires 70 years from the year the film was made, or (if it was made available to the public before then) 70 years from the year it was made available.

In the (unlikely) event that no one falls into the categories (a)–(d) above, then the Regulations (and section 13B(9) of the 1988 Act) provide that the extension will not apply and copyright will expire 50 years from the year the film was made.

Broadcasts and cable programmes

Copyright – owned by the relevant broadcasting organisations – continues to last 50 years from the end of the year in which the first transmission was made, whether by wire or over the air, by cable or satellite.

Copyright in a repeat broadcast or cable programme expires at the same time as copyright in the original broadcast or cable programme.

Crown and Parliamentary copyright

The Crown claims copyright in every Act of Parliament, and in all works created either by the Queen personally, or by an officer or servant of the Crown in the course of his or her duties: this is called 'Crown Copyright'. Crown Copyright is largely controlled and administered by HMSO. Under the 1988 Act (unchanged by the 1995 Regulations) Crown Copyright lasts for 125 years from the year the work was made, if the work remains unpublished commercially. Official papers are often never published commercially, but simply made available for inspection after 30 or more years. If the work is published commercially within 75 years of its making, copyright lasts 50 years from the year of first publication.

Parliamentary copyright exists in Bills and other works made under the direction or control of either House: it lasts for 50 years from the end of the year in which the work was made. A similar copyright is owned by certain international organisations. These also are unaffected by the 1995 Regulations.

Universities' copyright

The universities of Oxford and Cambridge, Edinburgh, Glasgow, St Andrews and Aberdeen, and the Colleges of Eton, Westminster and Winchester secured perpetual copyright in 1775 in works printed by them, in which they had been given or bequeathed the copyright. This perpetual copyright was limited by the 1988 Act, and any such copyrights will now expire at the end of 2039. The works concerned may of course qualify for copyright protection on other grounds, in which case longer terms of protection may apply.

Peter Pan

J. M. Barrie's famous play went out of copyright at the end of 1987, but the 1988 Act contained special provisions to enable the trustees of the Great Ormond Street Hospital to continue to collect royalties in perpetuity in respect of certain uses of the play. Following the 1995 Regulations, it is likely that all Barrie's works, including *Peter Pan*, came back into copyright in the UK as from 1 January 1996, and will continue in copyright until the end of 2007: presumably the hospital will continue to receive royalties during this period (unless some other arrangement is agreed) and after 2007 the provisions of the 1988 Act will continue.

SUMMARY CHECKLIST: DURATION OF COPYRIGHT

- UK copyright is a statutory right, and now always has a fixed term of years.
- That term may vary, depending on the work, and it may be calculated in relation to the date of the author's death, or in relation to creation or first publication of the work, or to the year it was 'released' or first made available to the public.
- The Berne Convention international minimum for literary and artistic works is 50 years from the end of the year in which the author died.
- Within the EU, the term of copyright in literary, artistic, musical and dramatic works has been harmonised upwards by the Duration Directive to 70 years pma.
- The 70-year term applies to all EEA-origin works which were protected in at least one member state on 1 July 1995.
- The 70-year term (or part of it) also applies to certain works not of EEA origin, depending on the term of protection for those works in their country of origin.
- Within the UK, this meant that some existing copyrights were extended, but also that some works will have come back into copyright, having previously been in the public domain.
- For the current UK position, it is necessary to check the relevant provisions of the 1995, 1996 and 2003 Regulations (and the 1988 Act, as now amended).

Other rights of authors and publishers

3

MORAL RIGHTS

INTRODUCTION

In addition to copyright, authors now have in the UK personal statutory rights relating to their works and their reputations, called moral rights. They are quite separate from the copyright itself, and remain attached to the author personally, or the author's estate, even if the copyright is later assigned to someone else, such as a publisher. They cannot be sold or assigned to anyone else (although they can be inherited) but they can be waived: we will consider waiver further, below.

The idea of authors having personal moral rights is (relatively) new to UK law, although *droit moral* has been well-established in France, and elsewhere in Europe, for some time: indeed, the Continental view of copyright itself is primarily as an author's right (*droit d'auteur*) – quite different from the pragmatic economic right which has developed in the UK. With our different mercantile traditions, some in the UK initially regarded moral rights as dangerously romantic and suspiciously foreign, but they have been a (Berne) Treaty obligation of the UK for some time, and are now included in our 1988 Copyright, Designs and Patents Act.

Moral rights are unaffected by the EU Copyright Directive, and are specifically stated (Recital 19) to be outside its scope. There have been suggestions of an EU Moral Rights Directive, but at the time of writing this seems unlikely.

Article 6 *bis* of Berne

Moral rights as a species come in all shapes and sizes: consider, for example, the thought-provoking *droit de repentir*, which in countries where it applies (not the UK) allows an author to have second thoughts entirely and insist on withdrawing a work, even after publication (there is usually provision for compensation). Only two moral rights, however, are specifically written into the Berne Convention (at Article 6 *bis*): the right to claim authorship of the work (the right of paternity), and the right to object to distortions, mutilations or other derogatory treatments of the work which would prejudice the author's honour or reputation (the right of integrity). All member countries are obliged to provide for protection of these two key rights.

The 1988 Act

The 1988 Copyright, Designs and Patents Act now provides for four statutory moral rights in the UK:

* The Right of Paternity.
* The Right of Integrity.
* The Right to Prevent False Attribution.
* The Right to Privacy of Certain Photographs or Films.

They are, however, severely hedged about with restrictions, as we shall see.

THE RIGHT OF PATERNITY

Section 77 of the 1988 Act gives the author of a copyright literary, dramatic, musical or artistic work, and the director of a copyright film, the right to be identified as the author or director of the work whenever the work is published commercially, performed in public, or communicated to the public, or issued to the public as part of a film or sound recording (or, in the case of an artistic work, exhibited in public, or a visual image of it communicated to the public). Given that communication to the public includes making available to the public on the Internet, the paternity right may have considerable relevance to Internet exploitation. In the case of commercial publication, this means that the author has the right to be identified in (or on) each copy or, if that is not appropriate, in some other way 'likely to bring his identity to the notice of a person acquiring a copy'. This might require careful consideration if the information is only available online, or as part of a website. The identification must be 'clear and reasonably prominent'. The author may specify a pseudonym, or some other form of preferred identification (for example, initials). The right lasts for as long as the work remains in copyright.

In a recent case, the claimant claimed that his moral rights had been contravened by a number of articles not attributed to him which he claimed 'exploited' a number of articles written by him. While he accepted he was not the author of the other work, he argued that he was entitled to be identified as the author under section 77 of the 1988 Act, as he was the originator of the ideas. The court found that the moral right contained in section 77 is, in relation to a literary work, concerned with the authorship of a written paper and not with crediting the originator of the ideas embodied in the paper. The claim was accordingly struck out.

Although this new statutory right now complies with the UK's Berne obligations, it is accompanied by a number of restrictions, some of them quite significant.

THE WORK MUST BE IN COPYRIGHT

The paternity right only applies to 'copyright' works: the works must meet the various criteria for copyright protection in the UK (see chapter 2), and the period of copyright must still be running. It also only applies to copyright literary, musical, dramatic or artistic works, or films – sound recordings, broadcasts (including cable programmes), and typographical arrangements are not covered.

PUBLICATION MUST BE COMMERCIAL

In the case of a book or similar publication containing literary and/or artistic works, the author's right of paternity operates to give the author the right to be identified when certain acts take place. These include 'commercial' publication, performance in public or communication to the public or inclusion in copies of a film or sound recording issued to the public. This therefore rules out token or nominal publication, or anything that is not intended to satisfy the reasonable requirements of the public. By implication, the book must be reasonably widely advertised to its intended market, and be available in quantities capable of fulfilling a likely minimum of orders. In the case of communication to the public, including transmissions on the Internet, the requirement that the act is done commercially does not apply. Care needs to be taken, therefore, with Internet uses.

THE RIGHT MUST BE ASSERTED

The right of paternity is the only moral right that needs to be expressly 'asserted' by the author before it can be enforced. Joint authors must each assert independently. Many commentators have argued that this formal requirement seriously weakens the right's effectiveness and may even be contrary to the Berne Convention (which normally bans any requirements for formalities). In steering the 1988 Act through Parliament, however, the UK government relied on the actual wording of Article 6 *bis*, which does not require any absolute right of paternity but only a right to 'claim authorship'. Section 78 of the 1988 Act therefore requires assertion.

The assertion may be included:

- in an assignment of copyright (which must be in writing); or
- via some other written document signed by the author.

The former method binds not only the person to whom copyright is assigned but also all those whose claims stem from theirs – whether they personally knew about the assertion or not. The latter method binds only those 'to whose notice the assertion is brought', which is why many author contracts now provide not only that the publishers themselves will credit the author but also that a similar contractual obligation will be written into any sub-licences.

The author must therefore assert his or her right positively and in writing. What most often now happens is that a form of assertion is printed on each printed edition of the work, this being seen as the most practical method for an author to put the world generally on notice of a new right. For publications only available online, an equivalent method of public notice may need to be found. Note that it is *only* the paternity right which needs to be asserted: all-embracing phrases such as 'the author's moral rights are hereby asserted' go further than is strictly necessary.

Assertion is not retrospective so if an author allows a work to be published without asserting his or her right of paternity, and later decides to assert, the publisher cannot be sued in respect of sales already made. Once the publisher is on notice of the author's assertion, however, all copies subsequently sold must identify the author in accordance with the Act.

THE RIGHT DOES NOT APPLY TO EVERY WORK

No right of paternity attaches to authors of certain works. The following are the most important:

- computer programs, computer-generated works, or typeface designs;
- works created in the course of employment (where the copyright is originally owned by the employer and the employer has authorised the publication complained of);
- works made for the purpose of reporting current events;
- works written for publication and published in a newspaper, magazine or similar periodical;
- works written for publication and published in a 'collective work' such as an encyclopaedia, dictionary or year book.

The last exception seems at first sight to cover all major (even multi-volume) works of reference, but it must surely be a question of degree. Where individual articles or entries are significant contributions to the literature in their own right, it will probably still be advisable to identify the author in accordance with the Act – unless one of the restrictions applies (for example, that the right has not been asserted, or has been waived).

THE AUTHOR MAY CONSENT, OR WAIVE THE RIGHT ALTOGETHER

Under section 87 of the 1988 Act, none of the author's moral rights will be infringed if he or she consented to the acts concerned. This is perhaps only reasonable; however, section 87 also goes much further and provides that all the author's moral rights, including the right of paternity, may also be *waived*, partially or completely. This is in sharp contrast to the Continental position – in France, for example, the author's *droit moral* is 'perpetual, inalienable and imprescriptible' – and has been strongly criticised as a further serious weakening of the author's rights in the UK.

Under the 1988 Act a waiver may be general and unconditional, or it may be limited in some way: it may apply only to certain works, or kinds of works, or it may apply only in certain circumstances, for example, as in some contracts, only in so far as necessary to exploit subsidiary rights, such as film or book club rights. It may also be conditional, and it may be made subject to revocation.

Waivers do not have to be in writing, and section 87(4) specifically allows for informal waivers (implied by the author's conduct, for example) under general common law principles. However, such implied or informal waivers may be difficult to prove, and if a reliable waiver is needed it is probably advisable to take the hint in section 87(2) that moral rights 'may be' waived by a written document signed by the author.

SUMMARY CHECKLIST: THE RIGHT OF PATERNITY

- Is the work a relevant copyright work? Is it one of the excluded categories of works?
- Has it been published commercially, or otherwise exploited?
- Has the right been asserted?
- Has the author consented, or waived the right?

THE RIGHT OF INTEGRITY

If the right of paternity is the Berne Convention's primary moral right of authors, the second key right enshrined in Article 6 *bis* is almost as important: the right of authors to object to 'derogatory treatment' of their work. This is usually referred to informally as the Right of Integrity. The right is now set out in section 80 of the 1988 Act, which provides that authors of copyright literary, dramatic, musical or artistic works, and directors of copyright films, have the right, in specified circumstances, not to have their work subjected to derogatory treatment. Like the Paternity Right, the Right of Integrity lasts for as long as the work remains in copyright.

DEROGATORY TREATMENT

What, one may ask, is 'derogatory treatment'? Does it cover what publishing contracts often refer to as reasonable editorial changes?

There are in fact now two separate questions:

- Do the particular acts complained of amount to a 'treatment' at all?
- If so, is that treatment 'derogatory'?

'Treatment'

The 1988 Act defines treatment to include any of the following things done to a work:

- adding to it
- deleting from it
- altering it
- adapting it.

Specifically excluded from this list, however, are translations, or musical arrangements or transcriptions which amount to no more than a change of key or register. The exclusion of translations might seem hard to justify, given their frequency, and the ease with which a bad translation can ruin an author's reputation, but ministerial statements prior to the 1988 Act suggest that those may, ironically, have been the very reasons for exclusion – coupled perhaps with the fact that contractual remedies are usually available in such circumstances, under the translation rights contract (see chapter 5).

What if the work is entirely untouched and unchanged, but is placed in an unflattering or unfortunate context (perhaps included in a website next to racist or indecent material)? Under the 1988 Act if none of the four positive acts listed above had occurred, the placing of the work in that context would not amount to a 'treatment' at all, and could not therefore infringe the integrity right. So a composer whose music was faithfully played and recorded could not complain of a breach of the integrity right if that recording then featured in the sound track of a documentary film condemning the political regime under which the composer lived and worked (as Shostakovich and a number of other Soviet composers found in a celebrated US case after the Second World War).

'Derogatory'

The 1988 Act (section 80) provides that:

> The treatment of a work is derogatory if it amounts to distortion or mutilation of the work or is otherwise prejudicial to the honour or reputation of the author or director.

'Distortion' and 'mutilation' are strong words. 'Prejudicial to ... honour or reputation' also implies an objective standard, similar in strength to the various definitions of defamation (see chapter 7). It seems likely, therefore, that it will not be the author's opinion (or injured feelings) alone which will provide the yardstick for what is or is not prejudicial to their honour or reputation: authors will have to produce objective evidence that their honour or reputations have actually suffered, or are likely to.

Derogatory treatment will clearly include complete mutilation or emasculation of a work, or a complete misrepresentation of the author's real views or philosophy. Indeed, if the treatment is that serious there would probably also have been an action for defamation anyway.

Editorial 'improvements' in general are therefore now highly unsafe, particularly where the risk of breaching the author's right of integrity is accompanied by the risk of defamation, or breach of contract. In the case of breach of contract this will particularly be so where the contract is an informal one, with no express provisions allowing the publishers to make 'reasonable' (or any other) changes.

In a more standard publishing agreement, it is likely that there will be some provision for reasonable alterations, and if the alterations made broadly comply with the terms of the contract it is unlikely that a claim of derogatory treatment will succeed, since the author will have consented – via the contract – to the changes made (see below).

Where alterations go *beyond* any contract, however, an action for breach of contract may well succeed and there may also now be derogatory treatment. There might also be an issue of false attribution.

'Bad Boys Megamix'

Although a music case, the injunction granted to George Michael in 1991 is still instructive as one of the few reported occasions so far, since the 1988 Act, on which an issue of derogatory treatment was considered by the UK courts. Michael complained that five of his early tracks, recorded in the days when he was a performer with Wham!, had been used without his consent in a 'Megamix' medley: the tracks (he alleged) had been edited, some words had been changed, and fill-in music from elsewhere had been added. Clearly, a 'treatment' of the works had taken place, since there were both deletions and alterations (and possibly additions also – although 'filler' music linking separate tracks might not strictly speaking 'add' to the tracks themselves) – but was the treatment 'derogatory'? Michael argued that the megamix 'completely alters the character of the original compositions'. The judge, adopting a somewhat cautious approach, first pointed out that:

> It is not, in my judgment, self-evident that taking parts of five different works and putting them together necessarily involves a change of character or modification.

However, on the arguments before him he took the view that it was at least arguable that such treatment amounts to distortion or mutilation within section 80(2)(b) of the 1988 Act, and therefore granted Michael's application for an injunction.

That particular case went no further, and there have been few cases since: in one of the most recent, it was decided that the addition of a rap line to a sound recording did not in itself amount to derogatory treatment of the musical work recorded. There was no evidence that rapping of the kind added was prejudicial to the honour or reputation of the author.

LIMITATIONS ON THE RIGHT OF INTEGRITY

As with the right of paternity, the author's Right of Integrity will only apply if:

- the work is a copyright work;
- the work is published commercially (other uses may also suffice: see p. 45 above).

The Integrity Right does *not*, however, need to be 'asserted'. The right does not apply to the following works, among others:

- computer programs or computer-generated works;
- works made for the purpose of reporting current events;
- works written or made available with the consent of the author for publication and published in a newspaper, magazine or similar periodical;
- works written or made available with the consent of the author for publication and published in a 'collective work' such as an encyclopaedia, dictionary or year book;
- works created in the course of employment (where the employer owns the copyright, authorises the treatment concerned and – where the author is identified – provides a 'sufficient disclaimer').

Most of the above exceptions are similar to the list of exceptions to the right of paternity (see above, p. 46), apart from the provision for a disclaimer in employee works, and the omission of typeface designs from the list – the Paternity Right does not apply to such designs, but the Right of integrity *does*.

The Right of Integrity also does not apply to anything done to avoid the commission of an offence, or complying with a statutory duty, or (as with the BBC or possibly organisations such as the Internet Watch Foundation) to avoid anything which offends against 'good taste or decency or which is likely to encourage or incite to crime or lead to disorder or to be offensive to public feeling'. This last exception now provides a let-out for the BBC even where alterations are significant structural changes – although it was decided in a 1967 case that deletion even of a few (crucial) words from a play could be 'structural', it would not now amount to derogatory treatment if (as in that case) the BBC's cuts were motivated by a desire not to offend public feeling. As with employee works, however, there must be a 'sufficient disclaimer' (if the author is identified).

Finally the Right of Integrity will not apply:

- to anything done with the author's consent; or
- if the author has waived the right.

SUMMARY CHECKLIST: THE RIGHT OF INTEGRITY

- Is the work a relevant copyright work? Is it one of the excluded categories of works?
- Has it been published commercially, or otherwise exploited?
- Has any 'treatment' of the work taken place?
- Has the work been added to, deleted from, altered or adapted (except by translation)?
- If so, was the treatment 'derogatory'?
- Did it distort or mutilate the work?
- Was it otherwise prejudicial to the author's honour or reputation?
- Did the author consent, or waive the right?

FALSE ATTRIBUTION

Authors not only have a moral right of paternity – to be credited as the author – but also have its converse: the right *not* to be credited with things they did *not* write. This is known as the right to prevent false attribution, and is now contained in section 84 of the 1988 Act. Of the four moral rights contained in the 1988 Act, it is the only one to have existed before in statutory form: there was a very similar right in section 43 of the 1956 Copyright Act.

The right applies to literary, dramatic, musical and artistic works, and to films and (unlike the paternity and integrity rights) can be exercised by any 'person' – they do not have to be authors.

The attribution complained of may be express or implied, and the right will be infringed wherever a false attribution:

- is included in copies of a work issued to the public; or
- is in (or on) an artistic work exhibited to the public.

In the case of *Alan Clark v. Associated Newspapers*, the late MP, Alan Clark, brought an action for false attribution against the publishers of the *Evening Standard* newspaper. One of the Standard's journalists wrote a regular column entitled 'Alan Clark's Secret Election Diary' (together with a picture of Mr Clark) which was intended to be a parody of Mr Clark's well-known diaries. The court used a similar test under section 84 as in the law of defamation, namely that it was necessary to determine what single meaning was conveyed to the reasonable reader. Since the articles contained clear and unequivocal false statements attributing authorship to Mr Clark, he therefore proved his false attribution claim.

The right may also be infringed by false attributions contained in public performances or showings, or communications to the public, but only where the person concerned knew or had reason to believe that the attribution was false. There are also secondary offences of possession, or dealing with, copies of works containing such attributions, but again where the presence of the attribution was known, and was known to be false.

The right is an entirely personal right, allied to a person's reputation rather than to any copyright works he or she may have created – it does not therefore last for the full term of copyright, like other moral rights, but only for 20 years after the person's death.

As with other moral rights, it often overlaps with other legal remedies – in this case with the existing laws of defamation and passing off. (Alan Clark also succeeded in proving passing off against the *Evening Standard* because he had a substantial reputation as a diarist which would have been important to the readers in deciding whether to read the articles, because the readers were misled and he suffered loss.) Indeed, where other, more traditional, remedies exist it may well be that judges will prefer to use those and will pay less attention to specific statutory moral rights. The damages awarded to the singer Dorothy Squires in *Moore* v. *News of the World* (1972) may be instructive: for a report of a newspaper interview falsely attributed to her as her own writing ('How My Love for the Saint Went Sour by DS talking to WT'), the jury awarded £4,300 for libel but only a nominal £100 for false attribution under the 1956 Act. This may have had something to do with the judge's guidance:

> Nobody suggests that if she is entitled, it should be a shilling or something contemptuous; but it should be a very much more modest amount than you would give for libel if you find the damages for libel have to be assessed ... I cannot suggest a figure, but something small ... some gentle, gentle amount for a rather technical cause of action.

THE RIGHT TO PRIVACY OF CERTAIN PHOTOGRAPHS OR FILMS

Some countries – the USA for example – have significant and substantial laws protecting personal privacy, but a general privacy law is still in the process of developing in the UK under the Human Rights Act 1998, particularly following the *Naomi Campbell* and *Michael Douglas* cases (see chapter 8). This limited moral right to privacy, contained in section 85 of the 1988 Act, is not really a moral right at all, and applies only to certain photographs and films which are commissioned for private and domestic purposes (such as wedding photos).

Under the 1956 Act, the person who commissioned such photos (usually the happy couple) owned the copyright in them, and could thus control the use made of them. Under the 1988 Act, however, this rule was changed (see p. 30) and the author (that is, the photographer) now owns the copyright. This would have meant that professional photographers could make unlimited copies of wedding photos they had taken and could, for example, sell them to national newspapers if the bride or groom subsequently became newsworthy. It was to prevent this limited, but very real, danger that section 85 was passed. Those commissioning such photos or films can now prevent:

* copies being issued to the public;
* the works being exhibited or shown in public or;
* the works being communicated to the public.

The right lasts for as long as the work concerned remains in copyright.

REMEDIES FOR INFRINGEMENT OF MORAL RIGHTS

Section 103 of the 1988 Act provides that an infringement of a moral right:

> Is actionable as a breach of statutory duty owed to the person entitled to the right.

Damages may be awarded, and an injunction may be granted in appropriate cases. There is also express provision for a disclaimer, to be approved by the court, 'dissociating the author or director from the treatment of the work'.

DATABASE RIGHT

As explained in chapter 2 (p. 16), copyright in the EU no longer protects databases unless they bear the hallmark of 'the author's own intellectual creation'. This intellectual standard may prove a difficult test for straightforward listings or alphabetical directories, so a new (freestanding) right to prevent unauthorised extraction or reuse was provided for by the EU Database Directive. The right was called Database Right in the UK, and implemented here by the Copyright and Rights in Databases Regulations 1997. The Regulations came into force on 1 January 1998.

Under the Regulations, there may be a Database Right 'if there has been a substantial investment in obtaining, verifying or presenting the contents of the database'. Following the *William Hill* case (below), and the European Court of Justice's ruling in that case, the question of where the investment has been made is key (particularly whether it was truly in 'obtaining' the data).

'Substantial' is a test of quality as well as quantity (provided, again, that the investment is in obtaining (etc.), rather than creating, the data). 'Investment' includes any investment, whether of financial, human or technical resources, and 'database' is widely defined to mean any 'collection of independent works, data or other materials arranged in a systematic or methodical way and individually accessible by electronic or other means'. Whether there has been 'substantial investment' involves an assessment of the resources used to locate the constituent materials, to collate them, verify them and present them. Any investment relating to the *creation* of the materials (as opposed to obtaining them) is irrelevant to the question of whether there will be database right for the database in which they are contained.

The right is owned by the 'maker' of the database, who is defined as the person whose initiative is responsible for the relevant obtaining, verifying or presenting, and who assumes the risk of the necessary investment. As with ownership of copyright itself, however, this general rule of ownership does not apply to databases made by employees in the course of their employment: these will be owned by the employer. There will be no database right unless the maker was at the material time (usually when the database was made) an EEA national or resident, or a body incorporated or based in the EEA (including partnerships or other unincorporated bodies).

The Database Right lasts for 15 years from the end of the year in which the database is completed. This term can be effectively renewed if substantial new investment can be demonstrated as a result of 'substantial change', including the accumulation of successive additions, deletions or alterations – in other words, a significant new edition or re-origination but not a mere reprint.

Under Regulation 16 'a person infringes database right if, without the consent of the owner of the right, he extracts or re-utilises all or a substantial part of the contents of the database'. Repeated and systematic use of insubstantial parts may amount to use of 'a substantial part', provided (following the *William Hill* case) that the sum total of what was taken would enable the defendant to reconstitute and re-publish a substantial part of the whole database, in a way which would conflict with normal exploitation of the database. Extracts can be permanent or temporary, and by any means or in any form. 'Re-utilisation', however, must involve making the contents available to the public, albeit by any means.

There are two exceptions for certain limited purposes. Fair dealing by a lawful user 'for the purpose of illustration for teaching or research' will not infringe a database right as long as the source is indicated. Use may also be permitted where it is not possible 'by reasonable inquiry' to identify the maker and it is reasonable to assume that the 15-year term has expired.

It is clear from all of the above that UK Database Right is a distinct and individual statutory right whose operation depends on close consideration of a number of key definitions, some of which are now narrowly defined. Was there a 'substantial investment' initially, was it in *obtaining* , as opposed to creating, the data, and was 'a substantial part' extracted or re-utilised? In *British Horseracing Board* v. *William Hill Organisation Ltd* (2005), the Court of Appeal reversed an earlier decision of the High Court that William Hill had 'extracted' a substantial part of the BHB horseracing database by taking information from its daily data supply and loading it onto computers for the purpose of making it available on its own website, and the later transmission and loading of that data onto its website for access to the public was a 're-utilisation'. Interestingly, this was despite the fact that the BHB database was a single database in a constant (daily) state of updating and refinement. In the judge's view, this meant that 'as new data are added, so the database's term of protection is constantly being renewed'. The Court of Appeal referred several questions to the European Court of Justice, which delivered its ruling in November 2004 (along with rulings in a group of similar sports fixture cases). The Court of Appeal followed this ruling, with William Hill succeeding in its appeal. The decision and rulings make it clear that the Database Right is concerned with obtaining (verifying and presenting) data and not the creation of the data itself. 'Obtaining' in this sense does not include the act of selecting and arranging fixtures. Instead, the right is concerned with the promotion and protection of investment in data storage and processing systems.

This is a narrow distinction in many cases. Many databases are comprised of relatively simple data with most of the resources being ploughed into sorting through that data. Where the obtaining of the content, the verification and the presentation do not involve much investment beyond creating the data, the right will not apply. In creating most databases, there is often a single process that involves creation of data, its obtaining, verification and presentation, and it may be difficult – if not impossible – to separate these processes one from another. There is some hope, however. Even though the database does not attract the database right, the database owner may still be entitled to copyright protection in respect of the content, i.e. the data itself, provided that the data passes the test for protection as a literary work and provided that the database owner is also the owner of the copyright in that data. Where the database shows signs of 'the author's own intellectual creation', the database may well attract copyright protection and he owner can take advantage of a longer term of protection. As explained above, though, this intellectual standard may prove a difficult test for straightforward listings or alphabetical directories.

PUBLICATION RIGHT

Publication Right is a new statutory right in the UK, introduced by the Copyright and Related Rights Regulations 1996. It protects people who publish for the first time in the EEA original literary, dramatic, musical and artistic works and films in which copyright has expired, but which were never previously published during their copyright terms anywhere in the world. To qualify for the new right, the publisher of the work must, at the time of first publication, be a national of an EEA member state.

The new right will benefit many editions of previously unpublished works in EU and EEA member states, which do not have typographical copyright, but in the UK it will overlap extensively with existing rights; both typographical copyright and the final stages of perpetual copyright in unpublished works (which is not due to expire finally until 2039). Many unpublished works in the UK continued to have perpetual copyright under the 1911 and 1956 Copyright Acts, until the 1988 Act ended that arrangement for good by providing that works remaining unpublished when it came into force (1989) would enjoy a maximum of a further 50 years' protection – i.e. until 2039. So some unpublished works may still be protected by copyright until 2039, and the key requirement of Publication Right (that copyright must have expired) may often not apply until then.

Publication Right may benefit any 'person' who satisfies the criteria set out in the Regulations, and 'publication' is given a very wide meaning (including any (authorised) communication to the public, such as making available via electronic retrieval systems, rental or lending, performance, exhibition or broadcast) so if ancient manuscripts, diaries or pictures which seem to have some publishing potential are found in the attic, it may be advisable to exercise some caution before they are given or lent to anyone else, or even displayed in a museum or library. However, the criteria are fairly exacting:

- the work must have been protected by copyright
- copyright must have expired without the work being published
- the work must still be unpublished
- the person publishing the work must be an EEA national and must first publish the work in the EEA.

For most unpublished works in the UK, at least the second of these criteria may not be satisfied until 2039. For works which do qualify, though, Publication Right may prove a valuable new right, effectively conferring all the rights of a copyright owner. The right lasts for 25 years from the end of the year of first publication.

HUMAN RIGHTS

Following the coming into force of the Human Rights Act 1998, it seems likely that a general right of privacy – and perhaps a number of other key rights – will develop as part of UK domestic law. For a fuller treatment of this, and some early decided cases, see chapter 8.

PUBLIC LENDING RIGHT

After vigorous lobbying by authors such as Maureen Duffy and Brigid Brophy, a Public Lending Right for authors (PLR) was established in the UK by the Public Lending Right Act 1979, and came into effect in 1982. The first payments were made in 1984, and payments have been made annually ever since: payment is entirely out of central government funds. The scheme is administered by a Registrar of Public Lending Right and a small staff, supported by an advisory committee representing interested bodies, including the responsible government department, the Department of Culture, Media and Sport.

The PLR scheme provides for authors (and others, such as illustrators) throughout the EEA to receive payments in proportion to the number of times their books are borrowed from public libraries in the UK: borrowings are recorded from a sample of 30 library authorities around the UK and the results grossed up annually to arrive at an estimate of the national loans of each book. Over £75 million has been distributed to authors since the scheme started.

No author may currently get more than £6,000 per annum (although this is under review) – 291 authors received the maximum amount in the financial year 2004/5, and most of the 33,000 authors currently registered for PLR (it is necessary to register in advance) will receive less than £100. The total government funding for the PLR scheme in 2004/5 was £7.4 million – working out at a rate per loan of exactly 5.2p.

In order to participate in the PLR scheme, and benefit from any modest annual payments which may be on offer, it is necessary to register with the PLR Registrar (his address is set out at appendix B). Those entitled to register include not only authors, but also other persons who have contributed to the text or illustration of a published book: this would include illustrators, photographers, editors and translators, who will receive a share of any PLR payment generated by loan of the book. Those registering must be resident in the EEA.

Payment continues for 70 years after the death of the author or contributor, in line with of the term of copyright.

PLR is more of an issue elsewhere in the EU now, following the 1992 Directive on Rental and Lending Right, which required all member states to make provision for a similar system. Very little happened for many years, with some member states believing an opt-out for public libraries was possible (not in fact true, without 'remuneration' to authors). The EU Commission launched infringement proceedings in 2004 against several countries for inadequate implementation, and at the time of writing a number of cases are still before the European Court of Justice.

ARTISTS' RESALE RIGHT (*DROIT DE SUITE*)

Although not strictly speaking an authors' right, the new Artists' Resale Right will be of considerable importance to many artists and merits a mention here. Artists' resale rights provide for artists or their heirs to receive a percentage of the sale price of their works of art when they are re-sold by auctioneers, dealers or galleries (often at vastly inflated prices). The idea is not new, since it is already written into the Berne Convention and the legislation of 11 EU member states (France has had *droit de suite* since 1920), but it took a long time for the Resale Right Directive 2001 to be passed, and then only after a protracted conciliation procedure between the EU Parliament and Council, during which the UK, among others, objected that such a right would seriously damage the London art market. In the end, a compromise solution was reached, under which the Directive was adopted (on 3 July 2001), but implementation by member states (normally 18 months) would be delayed until 1 January 2006 at the earliest, and – for states such as the UK which did not apply resale rights when the Directive comes came into force – a further four years to 1 January 2010. In fact, it appears the UK will now implement the Directive, under the draft Artists' Resale Right Regulations 2006. Key elements of the Regulations are likely to be:

- the Right will be limited to genuine re-sales, rather than first sales;
- the work must still be protected by copyright;
- private sales (as opposed to gallery, auction or other commercial sales) will be excluded;
- the Right may not be assigned or waived (although it may be bequeathed, but only to a human being or a charity);
- it is very likely that the Right may only be administered collectively, via a collecting society such as DACS.

Under the Directive, resale rights could apply to any sale of an original work of (graphic or plastic) art where the price exceeds €3,000 – a limit which may exclude smaller sketches, engravings and photographs but will include many paintings and sculptures. Member states have an option to apply the right below that level also, and it is likely that the UK will opt for a lower threshold of €1,000.

The Directive provides for a sliding scale of rates as follows:

- 4 per cent for the bottom band up to €50,000 (or 5 per cent at each state's discretion)
- 3 per cent from €50,000 to €200,000
- 1 per cent from €200,000 to €350,000
- 0.5 per cent from €350,000 to €500,000
- 0.25 per cent for any amount over €500,000.

It is likely that the UK will opt for 5 per cent for the bottom band.

In addition, the maximum an artist can receive in resale right on any single sale is €12,500. The EU Commission has agreed that once the Council has given the go-ahead it will open negotiations to extend artists' resale rights internationally.

Part II
Commissioning: publishing contracts

Author contracts 4

HOW A CONTRACT IS MADE

In this chapter we will look at contracts generally – what they are, legally, and how they are made – and then examine in some detail the contract which is in many ways the most important contract in publishing – the publisher's initial contract with the author. Whether publication is to be in print on paper or in digital form, or for a book or journal article, or for other web-based content, this will raise a number of important issues, such as ownership and control of rights, which we will need to come back to again and again, so we will spend some time on these. In chapter 5, we will go on to look at some other key publishing contracts, such as contracts with contributors, and co-publishing and subsidiary rights deals, including electronic rights.

WHAT IS A CONTRACT?

A contract is an agreement that the law will enforce. That sounds rather simple, and it is: contracts are in essence very simple things. You do not need to sign a 20-clause standard form document in order to have a binding contract with someone – indeed in most cases you do not need any writing at all. The 20-clause document may be important later on, in granting rights and confirming your agreement on a number of detailed points, and we will look at such important details in the second half of this chapter. But you may well find you have an agreement that the law will enforce long before you get to that stage. There are two separate elements to consider:

(1) '*An agreement*' There must actually be an agreement between the parties concerned; all that this means is that the parties:
  • must have reached a clear agreement on a specific matter, and
  • must have intended 'to enter into legal relations' – intended, in other words, to make a binding legal commitment to each other on the matter.
(2) '*That the law will enforce*' The agreement must be legally enforceable – so the parties must be capable of entering into binding contracts (which will not, for example, be declared void because one of them is under age, insane, or incapable through drink), the bargain must not itself be illegal or contrary to public policy, and must either be under seal or in writing (for certain types of contract) or –

more usually – must be supported by some 'consideration': something (almost anything) of value must be given or promised in return for the promises made.

We will look at these various criteria below, but assuming that most authors and publishers are over 18, not insane or (completely) drunk, and that their agreement is (on the whole) legal and decent, the most important requirements for an enforceable publishing contract are likely to be these:

- a clear agreement;
- an intention to be legally bound by it;
- some valuable consideration to seal the bargain.

We now know, following the 1991 decision of the Court of Appeal in *Malcolm* v. *OUP* (see below, p. 64) that these simple key requirements can be met long before a formal written contract is signed, or even discussed, and that a publisher may become bound contractually to publish a book, even during what have traditionally been thought of as mere 'pre-contract negotiations'.

CLEAR AGREEMENTS: OFFER AND ACCEPTANCE

For a contract to exist, a clear agreement must be reached, with no significant misunderstandings: the parties must not be at cross-purposes. One side must make an offer in clear terms, and the other side must accept that offer on basically the same terms, otherwise no contract can come about. Let us suppose that Routledge makes an offer to two authors (who shall be nameless) to publish at a (fairly) reasonable royalty a third edition of a 310-page book them on publishing law, to be delivered by 1 October 2005. That is a fairly clear 'offer'. If accepted, they clearly intend it to be legally binding, and the provision for a royalty means there will be valuable 'consideration'. Suppose then, however, that the authors reply: 'Thank you for your offer; we are happy to confirm that we will write a 1,288-page loose-leaf text, including precedents, on publishing law on the terms you have set out.' Is there a contract? No – because the offer, to publish a 310-page book, has not been accepted: what has happened is that the authors have made a counter-offer, to deliver something altogether different and more ambitious. Routledge may like this new offer, and decide to accept it, or the parties may continue negotiating, and reach agreement sooner or later, either on the original terms or on revised terms, but until the offer and acceptance match each other no contract exists.

Acceptance by conduct, and offers to treat

Silence does not imply acceptance (even if the offer attempts to provide that it will) but offers may be accepted by *conduct* as well as by written or spoken words. Suppose that an author and publisher are discussing a draft contract but for one reason or another never actually sign it. The basic terms of the offer contained in the proposed contract may still be accepted or confirmed by either or them if they start to act on the basis of those terms – for example, by delivering the book on time, or by commencing production. If publisher and author both continue to 'perform' the terms of the contract, even though it was never signed, it will increasingly bind them, on those terms. However, if it is left unsigned, and there is no separate agreement on these points, the publisher may well find that it has no more than an implied licence to publish (and perhaps deal with certain subsidiary rights) on a non-exclusive basis, and would not have been granted an assignment of copyright, or any exclusive publishing licence (both of which must be in writing, and signed).

Does a bookshop make an offer when it displays a book in the window at a certain price? Suppose the price label is out of date: can a customer 'accept' the offer and claim there is a binding contract at the old price? No – because shops in those circumstances are not making binding offers, but merely offers to come in and enter into negotiations – what the law calls 'offers to treat'. So if our canny customer takes the book to the till and offers the old price, it is then open to the bookseller to reject that offer and instead make a counter-offer to sell it at the correct price.

INTENTION TO BE LEGALLY BOUND

Both parties must intend to enter into legal relations, and intend that their agreement will bind them legally. An agreement to meet in the Festival Hall Bar at 7 p.m. is *not* usually intended to be legally binding, and if one party is late and as a result they both miss the first half of the concert (because the late one has the tickets) there may be a serious row but there will be no breach of any contract. An agreement by an office syndicate to share in National Lottery winnings, however, or an agreement by an author to deliver a manuscript on disk to a publisher by a specified date *are* both normally intended to be contractually binding. It will be a question of fact in each case.

If one or other party wishes to negotiate, but avoid any binding legal commitment for the time being, it is possible to achieve this by marking all correspondence 'Subject to Contract', so that it is clear that the necessary intention to conclude a contract is not yet present.

CONSIDERATION

So that there is no doubt that the parties mean what they say, an agreement is not generally binding under English law unless:

- it is signed and witnessed as a Deed, or made under seal (for some formal assignments, or certain transactions involving land); or
- it is supported by some valuable 'consideration'.

For most publishing contracts therefore – even informal, verbal ones – this means that there must be consideration – either consideration now, or a promise of future consideration to come. An upfront fee or an advance would be present consideration – an undertaking to pay future royalties would count as future consideration. Sometimes of course both exist, but both are equally valid in the eyes of the law.

Although money normally features somewhere, 'consideration' does not actually need to be in the form of convertible currency, provided it is of some economic value. It also does not have to represent an adequate commercial price – it can be purely nominal, for example £1. A promise by a magazine publisher to publish in book form articles by the athletes Harold Abrahams and Eric Liddell (later made famous in the film, *Chariots of Fire*) for a payment of '4d per copy' was held by the Court of Appeal in 1922 to be sufficient consideration to form the basis of a binding publishing contract, even though virtually no other details had been settled. Despite the reservations of the court ('I cannot but wonder that publishers and authors enter into agreements as indefinite as this'), '4d per copy' is perfectly clear, and sufficient, consideration.

Mutual promises can be good consideration for each other, provided that both of them have an economic value to the party to whom they are made: arguably, a publishing agreement which is not signed as a Deed and which makes no mention of fees or royalties or anything else of economic value – even free author's copies or offprints – might well lack the necessary consideration to be binding, even if it contains a firm commitment to publish, since although the act of publishing will cost the publisher money it may not in itself convey anything of economic value to the author (except perhaps for academics whose promotion or even tenure may depend on it). Most publishing agreements, however, are quite clearly of economic value to the author.

VERBAL CONTRACTS

A publishing agreement does not need to be in writing (although it helps) and a publisher can be bound by even a purely verbal agreement, provided it has the necessary ingredients listed above. This has been clear since the case of *Malcolm v. OUP* in 1991, when a number of verbal assurances, made over the telephone to an author, Mr Malcolm, by OUP's then editor, Mr Hardy, were held by the Court of Appeal to constitute a binding contract.

Mr Malcolm submitted a manuscript to Oxford University Press. Their in-house editor, a Mr Hardy, and an outside reader, both liked it, but thought it too long, and Mr Hardy suggested substantial cuts. Now, Mr Malcolm had had a number of unsatisfactory experiences with other publishers at this 'pre-contract discussion' stage, and made it clear to Mr Hardy he was looking for a firm publishing commitment before embarking on any more revisions, which he estimated could well take up to six months' work. There followed two telephone conversations, both of which Mr Malcolm – with unusual foresight – tape recorded. In the second telephone conversation Mr Hardy made some crucial remarks, which should be required reading in every editorial department:

> … we would like to do it. That is to say, I mean I know you want a commitment sufficient to take you through the last stage of revision and that's what I am offering.

It seems to me that because it's such a risky venture I am not going to be terribly generous financially, erm … I mean what I think we should agree is that you have a fair royalty.

The Court of Appeal – reversing an earlier decision by the High Court – found that in these circumstances all the necessary elements were present to create a binding contract, and therefore found that OUP's refusal to publish after all was indeed a breach of contract.

The court made a number of important findings:

- No special formalities are required for publishing contracts, and it does not matter if contract details such as exact royalty terms, print number or format are all left to be agreed later; an agreement is not incomplete in law simply because it calls for further agreement on some key points later on, as long as the parties have settled the essential elements of the bargain.
- In this case, there was a clear agreement – that Mr Malcolm would deliver, and OUP would publish, a specific book (indeed the author was busily revising it to OUP's own specifications).
- There was a sufficiently clear intention on both sides to enter into legal relations: Mr Malcolm had made clear his determination to have a firm commitment before doing any more work and Mr Hardy had offered that commitment. As Lord Justice Leggatt put it:

It is difficult to know what was meant by 'a firm commitment' other than an intention to create legal relations … to suggest that Mr Hardy intended to induce Mr Malcolm to revise the book by giving him a valueless assurance would be tantamount to an imputation of fraud.

- There was also sufficient 'consideration' for the contract, in the shape of Mr Hardy's promise to pay a 'fair royalty'. This vague phrase is not a recommended method of settling consideration for a publishing contract, but it is (just) sufficient in law. '4d per copy' was sufficient consideration in 1922 (see above p. 64) and 'a fair royalty' appears to be equally sufficient today.

On this basis Lord Justice Leggatt and a majority of the court concluded that OUP did enter into a binding contract to publish Mr Malcolm's book, for a fair royalty ('it follows that in my judgment when Mr Hardy used the expressions 'commitment' and 'a fair royalty' he did in fact mean what he said and I venture to think it would take a lawyer to arrive at any other conclusion').

A final – equally important – finding by the court was that specific performance of a publishing contract might be ordered in appropriate cases – in other words, that the publisher should be ordered to publish the book – and it is important to bear this in mind. In most cases, however, courts will avoid making such orders, since they will be difficult, if not impossible, for the court to enforce. If (as here) an award of damages for breach of contract is a viable alternative, courts will normally prefer to award damages (on damages generally, see chapter 9).

In the more recent case of *Sadler* v. *Reynolds* (2005), involving a verbal agreement with a ghostwriter for an autobiography, the High Court similarly found that a prominent football chairman who told a well-known sports reporter that he wanted him to write his autobiography, for a 50:50 split of a £70,000 advance which the reporter had negotiated, was in breach of contract when he subsequently gave the ghostwriting contract to someone else. The Court awarded the reporter his £35,000 half of the deal by way of damages, plus a further £1,000 for loss of opportunity.

PARTICULAR CONTRACTS AND LEGAL CAPACITY

CONTRACTS WHICH NEED WRITING

Although verbal contracts are binding in most publishing situations, there are some kinds of contracts which must be in writing. Others do not need to be in writing themselves, but some written evidence must exist to support them. In addition, some specific assignments or grants or licences must be written.

Contracts which must be in writing

- Bills of exchange, promissory notes, and bills of sale;
- Regulated consumer credit agreements;
- Hire purchase and consumer hire agreements.

Contracts for which written evidence must exist

- Marine insurance contracts;
- Contracts of guarantee;
- Contracts for the sale (or other disposition) of an interest in land.

Assignments or grants which must be written

- Assignments of copyright (under section 90(3) of the 1988 Act);
- Grants of Exclusive Licences (under section 92 of the 1988 Act).

In both of these last two cases, the assignment or grant must not only be in writing, but also *signed* by, or on behalf of, the copyright owner. If it is not, it will be unenforceable as a legal right (although an equitable interest might in some cases exist). Note that under the Electronic Communications Act 2000 electronic signatures will be recognised as valid evidence of authenticity.

ILLEGALITY

The law will not enforce a contract to do something which is legally wrong, such as the commission of a crime, or a tort (such as a libel), or which is otherwise contrary to public policy. Thus contracts which promote sexual immorality or which pervert the course of justice are void and unenforceable, as are certain kinds of gaming and wagering contracts. Contracts to finance other people's litigation in return for a share in the proceeds (formerly an offence known as 'champerty') are unenforceable (although contingency fee arrangements are now permitted in the UK for libel cases). Also illegal are contracts in restraint of trade, and contracts the purpose of which is to procure the breach of an existing contract: so that publisher B, wishing to entice an author away from publisher A, cannot sign the author up to a more attractive deal knowing it to involve the breach of the author's existing contract – the new contract will be unenforceable, and publisher B will probably be liable to an action in tort from publisher A for procuring a breach of contract.

INCAPACITY OF THE PARTIES

Not everyone is legally capable of entering into binding contracts. Those who might *not* have the necessary legal capacity at the relevant times, and whose contracts would therefore be liable to be declared voidable (i.e. where the parties have the power to avoid the legal relationship by invalidating the contract or to avoid the contract and continue), include the following.

Minors

The age of legal capacity was reduced from 21 to 18 by the Family Law Reform Act 1969 (so those of us who were 19 or 20 when the Act came into force all missed out on coming of age parties). Until people have reached their eighteenth birthday, they are not fully capable of entering into binding legal contracts – they are known as minors (previously 'infants'). This is designed to protect the young from unwise contracts – particularly from contracts which (as in the case of many young pop singers or sports stars) might involve very large sums of money and which would significantly restrict their future freedom. On the other hand, those who do business with minors in good faith may also need protection – if for example they supply valuable goods to them on credit, or pay them advances. In order to balance these two objectives, the law will as a general rule uphold minors' contracts if they are for 'necessaries', or are otherwise – on the whole – for the minors' benefit. In a well-known publishing case in 1966 (*Chaplin* v. *Leslie Frewin (Publishers) Limited*) Charlie Chaplin's son – who was then a minor – was held to be bound by a book publishing contract under which he had already been paid significant advances, since the contract was itself for his benefit and also enabled him to make a start as an author; equally, it would have been unfair to deprive the publisher of the opportunity to recoup his advances.

Mental patients

If you are insane, you are considered by the law to be 'incapable of intelligent consent'. However, insanity is not always a permanent state and those suffering from insanity often have lucid intervals during which they are quite capable of entering into rational agreements. A contract made by a mental patient is therefore not void from the outset, but may be declared void by the patient later if it is not for his or her benefit, particularly if the other party knew of the insanity and took advantage of it. Equally, a beneficial contract made while insane can be *affirmed* later on.

Drunkards and drug abusers

Rather like the insane, those who enter into contracts while their faculties are completely incapacitated through drink (or, by analogy, drugs) may plead their extreme drunkenness or incapacity as a defence in any subsequent actions under those contracts. But they may do this only if:

- their condition completely prevented them from understanding the transaction; and
- the other party knew this.

Most publishing lunches nowadays would be unlikely to have the necessary effect. In any event, if the drunkard ratifies the contract later on, when sober, he or she will become liable in the normal way.

Those acting beyond their authority

Companies which enter into contracts for activities which are not within the company's objects as set out in its Memorandum and Articles of Association may well be acting *ultra vires*, or beyond their authority, and such contracts may be open to challenge, for example by the shareholders. For this reason, most Memoranda and Articles are drafted as widely as possible, but something clearly *ultra vires* may still be declared void. One way of avoiding this risk is to provide that the object of the company is to carry on business as 'a general commercial company' – since 1991 this authorises a company 'to carry on any trade or business whatsoever'.

Similarly, partners may not always have authority to bind a partnership in contracts unconnected with the partnership – such contracts may need to be ratified later on.

Employees who are allowed regularly to negotiate contracts such as publishing directors, or commissioning editors may, however, often be considered to have apparent authority to do so, and a contract made in good faith with such employees may well bind the company. Publishers should therefore bear in mind that if they give employees business cards describing them as 'Publisher' or 'Commissioning Editor' and send them off to Frankfurt and Bologna and on commissioning tours around universities, they may well be bound by any apparently reasonable contract they may make (however strenuously the board or publishing committee may object later on).

Similarly, agents – such as commercial or literary agents – may in some circumstances also go beyond the scope of their authority, but (depending on their particular terms of appointment) most agents will have considerable implied authority to enter into reasonable contracts on behalf of their principals.

Finally, contracts entered into by bankrupts may not always be enforceable, unless affirmed by their trustee in bankruptcy. However, a contract – such as a royalty agreement – which produced *income* for a bankrupt (or his or her creditors) would almost certainly be affirmed.

THIRD PARTIES

Until November 1999, there was an established legal doctrine (known as privity of contract) that contracts could not be enforced against or enforced by third parties (those not party to the contract). Therefore, pre-1999, if a publisher contractually agreed with an author to pay all royalties to a friend of the author, the friend could not compel the publisher to pay the royalties to him, because he was not a party to the contract. These rules were the subject of much criticism.

Dissatisfaction about the situation led to the introduction of the Contracts (Rights of Third Parties) Act 1999, which created a wide-ranging exception to the doctrine of privity of contract. It provided (subject to exemptions such as employment contracts) that a third party could acquire rights under a contract, if, and to the extent that, the parties to the contract so intend.

The Act states that a third party will be able to enforce a term of the contract if:

* the contract expressly provides that he or she can do so; or
* it clearly identifies him or her (by name, description or class of persons) and the benefit conferred.

The effect of this legislation is that the 'friend' in the example above could use the Act to enforce his contractual right to payment against the publisher, as could any other third party promised a contractual benefit.

SUMMARY CHECKLIST: BINDING CONTRACTS

* Are both parties legally capable of entering into contracts?
* Has a clear agreement been reached between them?
* Has a specific offer been accepted (in substantially the same terms)?
* Did both parties intend the agreement to bind them legally?
* Is there valuable 'consideration' (however nominal)?
* Is the contract one which needs to be in writing (for example, if it is to include an assignment of copyright)?
* Might it be illegal, or against public policy?
* Might it be voidable, for example if entered into by a minor or someone acting beyond their authority?
* Is a specified third party entitled to a benefit under the contract, and, if so, is this what the contractual parties intended?

AUTHOR–PUBLISHER AGREEMENTS

STANDARD FORM AGREEMENTS

After all the discussions and pre-contract negotiations (and, possibly, the lunch) there will come a point of decision, yes or no: either the author or the publisher (or both) will decide they do not wish to take the idea any further after all, or both of them will decide that they are ready and willing to go ahead, and to commit themselves to do so by signing a formal publishing contract. They may already have agreed the basis of a deal (indeed, as we have seen above, they may already have a binding contract) but now they will want to confirm in legally binding terms what they have already agreed, and settle a number of other detailed matters at the same time. They will want an agreement that enables them to do two key things:

- to make mutual undertakings to each other (I will write the book or supply the content if you publish it);
- to acquire rights (in the publisher's case, all the rights it needs to publish and exploit the work, and in the author's case the right – amongst other things – to a reasonable share in the proceeds).

Most publishers with any experience will have some kind of standard author agreement; in the case of a large publishing company it is likely to be a detailed printed or word-processed document of 20 or more clauses. It will, however, reflect that publisher's own experience: every clause will be there for a good reason, but it will – of course – be drafted from the publisher's point of view. This does not necessarily mean that it is unfair or unreasonable, but authors need to bear its origins in mind. Equally, most major literary agencies have their own standard author–publisher contracts, which not surprisingly are drafted much more with the author's interest in mind: for example, fewer rights are normally granted to the publisher, and the financial terms to the author are usually better. Whose version is used depends entirely on the relative negotiating strengths of the parties. A literary agent representing a successful author is likely to be in a strong position to deal on its own standard terms, whereas a publisher taking the risk of publishing an unknown author will prefer to use its own standard contract initially.

In recent years, Minimum Terms Agreements have been agreed between several publishing houses and the Society of Authors and the Writer's Guild on behalf of their members: these are more author-centred and either involve the grant of a more limited publishing licence, or (more often) a review after perhaps 10 years, so that more control is kept in the author's hands.

Even so, dealing on the other side's standard terms can still represent a serious negotiating disadvantage, especially if detailed terms are not properly explained or understood. If in doubt, ask. If no satisfactory explanation is forthcoming, get a second opinion from your professional body, or from an independent lawyer with experience of publishing contracts. And, when dealing with any standard form contract, bear the following points always in mind:

- The law will enforce most reasonable agreements which reflect what both parties want (for the few exceptions, see above, p. 66–9).
- From a legal point of view, most clauses of most contracts are therefore fully negotiable.

THE STANDARD AUTHOR–PUBLISHER AGREEMENT

Most good publishing contracts deal with the same basic points, although sometimes in a different order and sometimes (as we have seen) from very different points of view. In the rest of this chapter we will follow the sequence of topics in the standard author–publisher agreement which is probably in most widespread use, the first precedent in Charles Clark's admirable source book, *Publishing Agreements* (sixth edition, 2002). Comparisons with other versions, such as agent's contracts or Minimum Terms Agreements, will be made as we go along. You may find it useful to refer to your own version at the same time.

THE PREAMBLE: THE PARTIES AND THE WORK

It may sound rather obvious, but it is a good idea to say clearly right at the beginning of any publishing contract who you are and which precise publication you are talking about. Both sides are taking on significant legal obligations, so it is necessary to know who it is exactly who will be bound by those obligations. It is also essential to know how far those responsibilities extend, so 'the Work' needs to be clearly defined; whether it is a traditional book or journal, e-book or online service, it is often sensible to set out a precise specification (content, format, number of illustrations etc.) in a separate appendix at the end. Finally, although strictly speaking it is not legally necessary, if the contract is not already pre-dated it is highly desirable if the last person to sign the contract also *dates* it clearly so that everyone knows when the rights and obligations start to run (and, in some cases, when they finish). There might be difficult problems of evidence later on, otherwise.

The parties

The parties need to be carefully defined. In the case of 'the Author' (sometimes the 'Proprietor'; for example, where there is a literary estate) it is normal for the term to be defined to include the Author's executors and (sometimes) administrators, where the Author dies or becomes incapacitated, and also his or her 'assigns': we will deal with assignments below.

In the case of 'the Publisher' it is customary to include the Publisher's successors in business, should the company be taken over (as has been known) and often also other related publishing imprints, so that a publisher will retain the option to publish the work under another imprint if that seems more appropriate at the time, but limited (usually) to subsidiaries, or imprints elsewhere in the same group.

'Assigns' and assignment

The parties are often defined to include their respective 'assigns'. As a general rule of law, either party to a contract may freely assign their rights under that contract (unless there is a specific provision in it to the contrary) but not their *duties*. The person to whom the rights are assigned (called 'the assignee') may take over the entire benefit of the contract from the person doing the assigning ('the assignor'): it is also possible, of course, to assign specific rights separately, such as the copyright.

The author may wish to assign the benefit of the contract to a spouse or relative, or to a separate company (perhaps for tax reasons). Equally, the publisher may wish to assign copyrights or publishing licences under individual contracts, or whole lists of contracts, as part of a sale to another publisher in due course. If this is envisaged – or might be – it is important to make sure that the wording of the contract allows for this: the definition of both parties should include their respective 'assigns', and there should be no ban, or undue restriction, on assignments later on in the contract, unless this is what both parties want. A separate clause permitting (or prohibiting) assignment may often be the clearest solution.

Any continuing *duties* and obligations of either party may *not* generally be assigned without at least the implied consent of the other – particularly in a contract involving continuing skill and judgement on both sides, as with many publishing contracts. Either party may quite justifiably have reservations about the possibility of future assignment of continuing obligations by the other. The publisher may be unhappy about the author assigning any remaining personal obligations – for example, to take part in publicity or serial interviews, or to keep a reference work up to date – to a third party, or a company, less able to meet these obligations, and may require a letter of inducement from the author beforehand by way of reassurance. The author may have equal fears that any continuing obligations of the publisher – to promote and exploit the Work effectively, for example, and pay royalties – may be assigned to a different company altogether, with less feel for the market or the Work concerned and about which the author quite possibly has strong views. Where such personal obligations remain, it is always advisable (and may be essential) to obtain the express consent of the other party before any assignment, if this is possible. In many cases – such as the sale of a list – it is usually advisable to arrange for relevant contracts to be 'novated' (newly executed, and signed by the new parties), so that:

- the relevant rights are re-affirmed;
- the new publisher clearly takes over both the benefit and the burden of the contract.

Some agents' contracts include non-assignment clauses, usually towards the end of the contract, banning assignment by the Publisher without the prior written consent of the Author, sometimes with a proviso that such consent shall not unreasonably be withheld. And a typical Minimum Terms Agreement might provide that the Author shall be consulted in advance on all in-company assignments from one imprint to another, and outlaw assignments to outside third parties altogether (unless they are acquiring a substantial part of the company's business or at least an entire imprint). This can make sense, but both parties should think carefully whether such restrictions on their future activities are in their long-term interests, particularly if the proposed restriction is not mutual, but affects only one side.

Acquisition of an entire company – usually by a purchase of shares – will not normally involve any individual assignments, and will therefore probably not be prevented by non-assignment clauses in individual author contracts.

RIGHTS GRANTED

From a publisher's point of view, one of the main objectives of an author contract is to acquire rights. By far the greatest part of a typical publisher's business consists in exploiting other people's copyright works, and that exploitation may cover many languages, forms and media and involve publishing activities in all corners of the globe: it is essential therefore that it should all be clearly licensed by the copyright owner. Every author contract should therefore make it clear who owns the copyright, (is it the author, or the author's employer?) and what publishing rights that owner grants to the publisher. Ownership of electronic publishing rights , including Internet rights, is very important today, even if at first sight the work may not appear to have much immediate scope for digital exploitation, even as part of a larger database. It is prudent to consider at the outset who will be best placed to exploit such rights in due course, together with other key rights. Whether they are granted to the publisher, or reserved by the author or agent, the contract should make the position as clear as possible. This will ensure:

- that author and publisher (and the rest of the world) clearly know who controls which rights;
- that the publisher can safely sub-license individual rights to others;
- that rights can effectively be assigned or transferred;
- that all licensed activities can be protected legally against copyright infringers (around the world if necessary).

There are two ways for a publisher to acquire the publishing rights it needs:

(1) by obtaining an assignment of the entire copyright from the copyright owner; or
(2) by being granted a publishing licence – in terms wide enough to cover all the publishing 'activities' envisaged.

Full copyright or a licence?

It is more common for authors to retain their copyrights and for publishers to be their exclusive licensees, but there may be areas of publishing where an assignment of the full copyright makes sense if both sides agree – such as major works of reference or multimedia works, often with hundreds of different contributors, where the publisher will want to retain overall long-term control. It may also be an issue for multi-contributor works and in some territories in protecting the work against international piracy. In most other cases, however, a sole and exclusive publishing licence, drafted in wide terms if necessary (including a very robust clause allowing the publisher to take legal action if necessary), will probably meet most publishers' needs. It has been likened by a number of commentators to taking a lease of a house rather than buying the freehold – a long lease for all practical purposes will probably be just as valuable. Although the image is helpful, the analogy is not entirely accurate, since a freehold should last forever whereas copyright in most cases expires 70 years after the author's death. While the copyright lasts, however, a full assignment of it is the closest to a freehold a purchaser can get. And an assignment is generally irrevocable, while a licence can usually be revoked (for example for breach of its terms).

If a full assignment of copyright is needed, remember that in order to be effective under the 1988 Act it must be *in writing*, and *signed* by or on behalf of the copyright owner. Do not assume that just because an assignment letter has been sent off to the author a valid assignment has somehow magically taken place – it hasn't. Copyright will not be assigned until the author or their representative actually signs.

Sole and exclusive licences

If you grant someone the 'sole' right and licence to do something you are undertaking not to grant a similar licence to anyone else, but you are not necessarily ruling out the possibility that you may continue to do it yourself (although this has usually been implied). An 'exclusive' licence, on the other hand, is now defined under the 1988 Act and clearly excludes not only other potential licensees but also the person granting the licence. An author granting both a sole and an exclusive licence to a publisher is therefore granting complete control of all the publishing activities listed. It is by far the most powerful right to have, short of a complete assignment, and under the 1988 Act gives such licensees in the UK the same rights and remedies against copyright infringers as if they were full assignees (we will look at remedies further in chapter 9). Like assignments, however, exclusive licences must be in writing and signed by or on behalf of the licensor.

Scope of the licence

The activities licensed

In the process of publishing, the publisher will need to do a number of things which UK law treats as 'restricted acts', and which may only be done with the copyright owner's licence or permission. We will look at restricted acts more fully in chapter 9, but – in due course – bearing in mind the 2001 EU Copyright Directive, a publishing licence now probably needs to include:

- the right to reproduce (which would cover copying);
- the right to communicate and make available to the public (which would include online access);

- the right to distribute (in hard copy form); and
- the right to sub-license others to do the same.

Arguably, the traditional grant of rights to 'produce and publish' would cover at least the first and third of these, but in the light of recent case-law there may be some doubt about whether the second was fully included. If the parties wish, it may avoid uncertainty in due course to adopt up-dated wording similar to that above, which reflects not only the new EU copyright regime, but also the latest international standards adopted by the WIPO Copyright Treaty 1996. It may be advisable to adopt a belt and braces approach and grant 'the right to reproduce, publish and distribute, communicate and make available to the public'. (Alternatively, if appropriate, the right to communicate and make available to the public could be left to a separate grant of subsidiary rights later on, and subject to different terms – see below.)

The right to make an 'adaptation' may also be needed if, for example, translation rights are included. It is important that the licence should cover not only the Work as a whole, but also any 'substantial part' of the Work since otherwise this may also be a copyright infringement. Again, we will discuss this more fully in chapter 9.

There are other restricted acts, such as public performance of the work which are normally covered – if appropriate – under subsidiary rights (see below, p. 88).

Formats

The licence may cover 'all forms and media', which although not very specific at least makes the intention clear, or it may be restricted to 'volume' form only. 'Volume' rights normally include all the publisher's own hardback and paperback editions, including promotional, mail order and premium sales and book club sales, together with royalty inclusive export sales of bound copies or sheets. Although there is no unanimously agreed definition of volume rights, the term quite probably also includes anthology, digest book condensation, and picturisation book rights, and may include other rights too which relate to exploitation of the verbatim text of the work as a whole (but see next paragraph). One-shot periodical rights were expressly held to be included under a grant of volume rights in *Jonathan Cape Ltd* v. *Consolidated Press Ltd* (1954), where a substantially complete work was published in a single issue of *The Australian Women's Weekly* without the consent of the publisher, Jonathan Cape, who owned the volume rights. If the entire work is published, the fact that it appears in non-book format does not of itself prevent publication from being in 'volume' form.

However, this must now be considered in the light of alternative methods of digital delivery, such as downloadable text or hand-held devices such as e-books. If the complete verbatim text is published or made available in this form, such exploitation might arguably be considered as part of the main volume rights, but publishers, authors and agents generally agree nowadays that it is necessary in such cases to have an express grant of rights, and even then perhaps only for a limited term, such as three years. This is very likely to be an issue if the publisher wishes to license audio downloads, or to make the work available for online searching via Amazon's Search Inside or Google – this may be highly beneficial for both author and publisher, but it is very unlikely that such use (often involving digital access to the entire text) would fall under 'volume rights'.

At the time of writing, there have been no UK cases on this point, although two recent US cases might be instructive. In *Tasini* v. *The New York Times* (2001) the US Supreme Court held that publishers of 'collective works', such as newspapers and magazines who were publishing articles by freelance writers – usually without any signed contract or grant of rights – did not automatically have the right to go on to exploit those articles in electronic databases. And in *Random House* v. *Rosetta Books* (2001), even where the publisher did have exclusive rights to publish a number of long-established authors 'in book form' it was held that this did not necessarily give exclusive rights over e-book exploitation of the same text (although since the e-publisher secured consents directly from the authors there might in some circumstances be a separate non-competition issue under the contract – see below, p. 78).

Volume rights do not include other subsidiary rights such as serial rights or film rights, but these, like electronic rights, are often the subject of additional specific grants of rights under the royalties and subsidiary rights sections (see below, pp. 87 and 91). It is absolutely crucial to make sure that all the forms and media in which publication is envisaged are included somewhere and that the parties agree who has the right to exploit the work in which formats; translation rights may be vital to travel books, for example, and merchandising rights to children's books – neither of these are included in volume rights. Publishers with experienced rights managers are normally quite capable of exploiting such rights, but many agents prefer to retain them; it will be for the parties to decide who is best placed to control these rights. If in doubt, seek advice, or refer to Lynette Owen's indispensable guide: *Selling Rights*.

Languages

Licences often cover the English language only, but sometimes include all languages. The restriction to English only would deprive the publisher of the right to publish (or more likely to license) translations, unless translation rights are granted later on (see below, p. 90). As in the section on Formats above, this should be clearly agreed.

Territories

Licences may be granted to publish worldwide (or preferably 'throughout the Universe', not in order to secure the Venusian and Martian rights – although doubtless that will come – but in order to remove any doubts about satellite broadcasting). Alternatively, they are often limited to specific territories of the world (often listed in a Schedule), but in some cases, of course, Internet publication may transcend such market divisions and worldwide licences may be more appropriate or even unavoidable. It is entirely for the parties to agree who is best placed to exploit the Work in each part of the world – many publishers will have the capacity to exploit internationally, either online via the net or in hard copy, or the author or agent may prefer to retain some rights (for example North American or US rights) for themselves. Note, now, that exclusive UK rights are no longer exclusive if the rest of Europe (specifically, the EU and EEA) are open territories shared with other publishers: under the Free Movement of Goods Provisions in Article 28 of the Treaty of Amsterdam (see chapter 13, p. 323) a US edition lawfully on sale in (say) Belgium cannot be prevented from entering the UK. There may be other territories whose local copyright laws might make exclusivity difficult to enforce, such as Australia or New Zealand: if these territories are likely to be important to you, it may be worth taking further advice.

Duration

Finally, it is very important to specify clearly for how long the licence granted lasts. Many publishers will seek a licence for the full term of copyright (now, in the EU and USA, increased to 70 years after the author's death), and in the case of some works, especially textbooks or major reference works, the publishers may well need the life of several editions before the Work will truly come into profit. If the full term of copyright is agreed, it is advisable to include not only the current term, but also any extensions, renewals and revivals (on Duration generally, see chapter 2, p. 35–42).

Some Minimum Terms Agreements provide for a shorter licence period of, say, 20 or 30 years: 10-yearly reviews are fairly common. Again, it will be for the parties to agree what suits them (and that particular work) best, but a publisher accepting a licence for a limited period should be aware of the risks of investing heavily in establishing a work (and perhaps an author) only to find that the licence, or part of it such as the paperback rights, terminates after 10 or 20 years.

DELIVERY, APPROVAL AND ACCEPTANCE

Delivery of the Work is the author's primary responsibility under the contract, so the publisher will want to make sure:

- that it is actually delivered, in the required format and more or less on time;
- that, when it arrives, it accords with the contract;
- that any necessary revisions and improvements can be made, or – failing that – the contract can be terminated on a reasonable basis.

Equally, the author will want to see a fairly clear commitment to publish the Work (and possibly within a given timetable) if it is delivered substantially as per contract, and that if things do go wrong there is a reasonable agreement about any advances and, particularly, that the rights can be reclaimed.

There are a number of other important considerations to bear in mind: not least, what amendments might be 'reasonable' in the light of what was agreed, and the author's moral rights, and how both Author and Publisher can disentangle themselves from the contract if the Work as originally agreed clearly isn't going to happen. We will explore all these tricky issues – and some possible solutions – in more detail in chapter 6, but when considering the contract wording itself, these are the points to bear in mind:

- In the event of a dispute, it is the wording of the contract which will prevail – so make it as clear and unambiguous as possible.
- Agree clearly the time and method of delivery (for example on disk) and what happens if it is late.
- If time is of the essence, say so: otherwise it is unlikely the Publisher will be able to terminate the contract simply because the Work is not in bang on time.
- Agree in advance any acceptance criteria. Refer if possible to known yardsticks: a requirement that the work 'shall conform to a reasonable extent to the specifications set out in the Appendix' (or possibly the synopsis) is fairly easy to pin down in any subsequent dispute, but beware generalised phrases like 'of a standard which might reasonably be expected' (by whom?), or other question-begging adjectives such as 'acceptable' or 'satisfactory'.
- Agree a specific procedure and a timetable for any revisions, and do not forget that the author will usually have a moral right of integrity (see chapter 3, p. 47).
- Consider the effects of terminating the contract: will the Publisher retain an option, and what happens to any advance? The circumstances may be different, depending on whether the work was commissioned or not, and how much work in progress exists. It is also advisable to make it clear if (and how) the rights are to revert to the Author; reversion is implied when a contract containing a licence is terminated, but the rights will not necessarily revert where there was an assignment, unless there is clear provision for this (probably by means of a formal re-assignment).

COMPETING WORKS

Many publishers' contracts contain non-competition clauses under which the Author promises as long as the contract lasts not to undertake any other works which might reasonably be considered either to compete directly with the contract Work or to 'affect prejudicially' its sales or other exploitation. These are often expressed to cover not only directly competing works, but also abridgements or expansions of the same material, if done without the Publisher's consent. Such restrictions may be an understandable way of protecting the publisher's investment, particularly in the case of STM or professional textbooks or services, but they must be drafted tightly and not so widely that they would amount to a total ban on any further writing in the area: that would almost certainly be an unreasonable restraint of trade (see p. 312), which the courts might refuse to enforce (particularly if the publisher already had the option of suing for breach of an exclusive licence). This will particularly be the case where the author is an acknowledged expert in the area concerned: such a ban might prevent the author not only from developing his or her reputation and career, but quite possibly from earning a living. Many contracts get round this problem by specifically allowing authors to use their material for professional purposes, e.g. for training or seminars, or similarly for academics in their own teaching.

WARRANTIES AND INDEMNITIES

In publishing a work, a publisher takes a number of significant legal risks. If the Work contains statements defamatory of other people, the publisher will be liable legally for publishing them just as much as the author; equally, if any material is obscene, it is the publisher who will be prosecuted, for publishing an obscene article. The wider the publication, the greater the risk, so a website or bulletin board accessible worldwide may require special vigilance. There are a number of other legal risks, which we will discuss fully in chapters 7 and 9, and for this reason the publisher will normally require certain warranties and indemnities from the Author to protect against them. This does not mean that the publisher should become complacent about the need for in-house vigilance and, if necessary, outside legal advice (such as libel reading), or the need for adequate insurance cover, but it is generally thought to be reasonable that the author (who after all knows the work better than anyone else) should either disclose any known risks or else warrant that the Work is safe to publish.

Which warranties are sought, and which are given, is of course a matter for the parties to agree. Many publishers' standard contracts contain full lists of warranties – an agent's contract may contain only one or two. However few or however many there are, they should all be taken seriously. Breach of a warranty will probably not entitle the Publisher to terminate the contract altogether (see p. 95), but it will provide an action for damages, so together with the indemnities which are usually required each warranty should give the author pause for thought.

The warranties most commonly given are these

That the Author has full power to make the agreement

Not everyone has full legal capacity to enter into binding contracts – for example the mentally ill, children under 18, or those acting beyond their authority (for a full treatment see above, p. 68). The Author's warranty on this point will give the Publisher some protection against the risk of the contract subsequently being declared void.

That the Author is a qualifying person

Following the 1988 Act it is now common to seek a warranty that the Author is at the material time a 'qualifying person' under section 154 of the Act. As we saw in chapter 2 (p. 33) the Work may qualify for copyright protection in the UK either on the basis of first publication here or in another qualifying country, or alternatively on the basis of the Author's nationality or other status. Clearly, the place of publication is outside the Author's control, but the Author may be able to warrant that he or she is (for example) a British citizen or British subject, or domiciled or resident here, or a citizen of another EU member state: the full list of nationality and status qualifications is set out on pp. 33–4. It is often helpful to put the warranty in context by phrasing it thus: 'The Author warrants that he/she is a British citizen, or is otherwise a qualifying person under section 154 of the 1988 Copyright Designs and Patents Act.'

That the Author is the sole author of the Work and owns the rights granted

It is important for a publisher that the Author owns all the relevant rights, and that there are no rival claimants such as employers or joint authors. As a general rule, you cannot grant rights you do not own (see p. 270–1).

That the Work is original to the author

A literary or artistic work will not be protected as a copyright work unless it is 'original'. Under UK law the standard of originality required is not very high (see chapter 2, pp. 18–19), but there must be some evidence of skill and judgement, and individual effort. The Author will not own the copyright unless that effort is his or her own effort – if anyone else's effort is involved there may be joint authors, or possibly a claim for copyright infringement (see below).

That the Work has not previously been published, or any of the rights previously assigned or licensed

As we saw in chapter 2, first publication can be one basis for copyright protection and also, as we saw in chapter 3, a claim for Publication Right, so it is important to know that there will be no rival claims from any previous publications. The warranty against previous publication is usually limited to the territories covered by the agreement, and often to the specific formats covered (such as volume form) although sometimes it covers any forms. It may be particularly important for the publisher to be reassured that the Work has not already appeared on the Internet, or perhaps under Open Access conditions required by a research funding agency, or even within a local intranet, or is not about to: for many STM or academic works, such prior publication might significantly reduce any commercial market, particularly if free of charge.

It will also be important to the publisher to know that an assignment or exclusive licence has not previously been diluted by the grant of some particular rights elsewhere: for example US rights or French language rights. Such previous grants or licences will normally survive any new agreement, and the new publisher's licence will be subject to them. So if it turns out that US rights have already been granted elsewhere, the new publisher will not have worldwide rights after all, but only worldwide rights minus the US rights previously granted. Authors (and agents) are usually therefore asked to warrant that no such previous grants have taken place.

That the Work does not infringe any existing copyright or other right

Since printing and issuing copies of a work to the public may be just as much a copyright infringement as copying, the publisher will be just as much at risk of any legal action as the author: this is therefore a fairly crucial warranty to seek. Ideally it should cover not only copyright infringement as such but also infringements of any other rights of third parties, which would include for example any breaches of the terms of any previous licence, or contract, or any breaches of confidentiality, or moral rights, or database right or any trade mark infringement. For some specialised works, such as medical textbooks, there may be a need for specific warranties relating to the moral right of privacy in certain private photographs or films, or in some cases (particularly where US photographs are involved) that necessary consents or clearances or patient releases have been obtained. Don't forget that there is now a developing law of privacy in the UK, and that there may be obligations of confidentiality, not just for revelations in celebrity books (ghostwritten or otherwise) but also applicable more widely, e.g. to educational or academic authors. For more on this see chapter 8.

That it contains nothing defamatory (or libellous)

This is a key warranty, and possibly now the most important of all, if only because of substantial damages awarded for libel by some juries (see chapter 7, p. 162). As with copyright infringement, the publisher will be equally at risk with the author for publishing any defamatory statement, and so might anyone else involved in the publication, such as editors, printers and distributors, as well as Internet service providers (although there may be defences of innocent dissemination, or temporary and transient copying). Defamation (which includes libel) is therefore a very serious risk indeed and should be actively borne in mind at all stages by author and publisher alike. A sober reading of chapter 7 might be a useful starting point. Above all, if either of them has any reason to suspect that a particular passage may be defamatory – the author when writing, or the editor when editing – it cannot be stressed too strongly that the safest policy is to *tell someone*. If there is any doubt, it may make sense to have some passages (or the whole Work) read for libel by a lawyer who knows about such things, and share the cost if appropriate. It is *infinitely* better to do this at an early stage than to run the risk of going ahead regardless and hoping no one will notice. They (or their lawyers) always do. Defamatory statements, like viruses, can be dealt with if caught early enough, but once they are published, that is that: the damage is done.

Is it reasonable that the author should bear the risk? The author knows better than anyone else whether (and where) there might be defamatory passages and is in the best possible position to do something about them. If they are not disclosed at the outset then it seems fair for the author to bear the resulting legal risk. Some agents' agreements and Minimum Terms Agreements seek to limit the Author's liability to passages 'unknown to the publishers' – this very significantly dilutes the value of the author's warranty, and rather begs the question: 'When?'. There might well be an argument for sharing the risk if a libel is disclosed during the course of writing, or at least between delivery and proofs – when it still might be said the publisher has a realistic opportunity to do something about it – but if a libel only comes to light after the Work has gone for press it may be thought that the Author, not the Publisher, should bear the risk.

It is, of course, possible to insure against the risk of libel (and other associated risks such as malicious falsehood), and many publishers now have comprehensive libel policies. It is also possible in some cases to add specific authors to the policy as coinsured. However, insurance premiums are increasingly expensive, and the level of cover is usually subject to a substantial excess and may not cover the largest awards. It seems likely that an author's warranty will be required for some time to come.

That it contains no obscene, blasphemous or otherwise unlawful material

Obscenity, like defamation, is a real risk in publishing and is not solely restricted to illustrated sex manuals: text can be obscene if it encourages drugs, or violence, for example, and the criminal penalties, including fines and imprisonment, can be severe (see chapter 7). Consider also the risk of publishing 'indecent' material, particularly photographs of children. Blasphemy is still an offence – so be careful what you say about Jesus Christ – and there are other possible offences such as seditious libels, incitement to racial hatred, or offences under the Official Secrets Acts which may well pose a serious legal threat to a published work. All these topics are dealt with fully in chapter 7.

That all statements are true and that no formula, recipe or instruction will harm the user

This is a fairly wide-ranging warranty, but is particularly common in contracts relating to STM and consumer books. The warranty is normally restricted to all statements 'purporting to be facts' but is still quite a wide guarantee; authors often insert a proviso 'to the best of their knowledge and belief'. This is a less all-embracing warranty, but may be more acceptable in some circumstances: it still gives the publisher some reassurance that the author will at least have checked. Similarly, there is usually a proviso that the warranty will only apply to recipes, formulae or instructions 'if followed accurately'.

Indemnities

The warranties given are normally accompanied by an indemnity, under which the Author undertakes to indemnify the Publisher against any legal actions or claims, including associated costs and expenses, caused by breach of any of the warranties given (indeed, there is often a separate warranty that the book has not been and is not the subject of any claim, complaint or proceeding). Many contracts also provide for costs associated with claimed (as opposed to actual, or proved) breaches, which may equally involve significant costs and possibly out-of-court settlements. This may require some discussion between authors and publishers, since there may be cases where credible *prima facie* claims are made – but not proved – which the author may wish strenuously to resist but which the publisher (who has a publication to get out) will want to settle as quickly and cheaply as possible. It may also be a condition of some insurance policies – such as libel insurance – that the underwriter's views on whether to settle should prevail. Authors may feel that their publishers should defend them – and their honour – to the hilt in such circumstances, but sooner or later more commercial considerations may well prevail. It is usually wise to make express provision for alterations to be made on the advice of the Publisher's legal advisers.

Finally, it is important that any warranties and indemnities should last for as long as the legal risks may continue to exist – which may be long after the book has gone out of print or the agreement itself has terminated. A sentence or a clause to the effect that 'the warranties and indemnities shall survive the termination of this agreement' will achieve this.

THE PUBLISHER'S RESPONSIBILITY TO PUBLISH

If the Author's main responsibility under the contract is to deliver the Work, the Publisher's is to publish it (at the Publisher's expense). A legal commitment to publish may arise even out of an informal, verbal contract (see *Malcolm* v. *OUP* above, p. 64) but it is better to have it in writing if possible. Most authors, for obvious reasons, will look for such a written commitment before signing a publishing contract, although there may be circumstances in which author and publisher agree that the work will be delivered but not considered for publication until some later date – such agreements are probably not publishing agreements at all, but merely options.

Where a firm undertaking to publish is given, it is normal to include a proviso that this shall be unless prevented by circumstances beyond the Publisher's control (to allow for events such as war, fire, flood or terrorist attack). A contract for a tie-in publication linked to a specific event, such as a TV series or a royal wedding, might also have a proviso giving the Publisher the option not to publish if the event is called off – the payment clause, including the terms of any advances, will need to provide for this. It is also advisable to specify whether publication depends on timely delivery and what happens if the author fails to deliver on time.

A crucial issue may be whether the publisher undertakes to publish within a particular time-scale, and if so when. Topicality may be a key issue not only for current affairs publications but also for many professional or scientific texts, where the area covered is constantly changing (the law is a good example). On the other hand, the publisher will want some reasonable flexibility to launch new works at optimum times, and also to allow for necessary changes to the publishing programme. Twelve or 18 months from delivery (and perhaps 'acceptance' – see above, p. 77) are both common undertakings, sometimes with a maximum period running from the date of the contract. Phrases not linked to any specific timetable, such as 'with reasonable promptitude' or (worse) 'within a reasonable period of acceptance' are not generally of very much effect, and it may be advisable to include a provision for the Author to put the Publisher on notice to publish after the author considers a 'reasonable period' has elapsed and terminate the contract and reclaim the rights if publication does not then take place within, say, six to nine months.

PERMISSIONS, ILLUSTRATIONS AND INDEX

Most publishing contracts contain provisions covering the inclusion of necessary extra materials, such as quoted extracts or illustrations, which the author may have taken from elsewhere and copyright in which is likely to be owned by other people. It is absolutely essential to make sure that copyright permission to reproduce such material is obtained before publication, and preferably before the work is delivered (if a realistic amount of time for the necessary – and frequently delayed – correspondence has been allowed), otherwise there may be a serious risk of copyright infringement. Note, however, that defences such as fair dealing may sometimes be available for quoted extracts (see chapter 9).

It is equally important to ensure that the permission given actually covers all the formats, territories and languages in which the Publisher is proposing (or at least realistically intends) to exploit the Work – the wording of any permission obtained should therefore follow as closely as possible the wording of the Author's own grant of rights to the Publisher (see above, p. 73). With some copyright owners, this may require some negotiation, so allow plenty of time. If the permission offered falls short of what is required – a picture agency may only be prepared to grant rights to reproduce their image of a painting or a photograph (as opposed to the original) in certain territories or in English-language editions, for example – then both author and publisher may need to reconsider whether that material can be used at all. It is not enough to write off to the copyright owners and then simply assume that permission will be given in due course: copyright owners are not obliged to license their material for use by others if they do not wish to. Bear in mind also that many permissions may extend only to one edition of the work – if a second edition, or e-book version, is planned, it may be necessary to renew the permissions. Note, finally, that adapting a copyright work, e.g. re-drawing 'after X's picture', is also likely to require permission.

Responsibility for arranging, and sometimes paying for, permissions is almost always the author's, although this is entirely a matter for agreement, and in appropriate cases (such as major works, anthologies or highly illustrated works) the publisher will often share the cost or sometimes take over the responsibility altogether. This may be particularly necessary if the publisher wants to acquire permission for electronic use, where the negotiations may be harder (and more expensive).

As to indexes, many authors prefer to do their own, but good indexing is a professional skill in itself, and a tired author is not always the best indexer. Where the index is particularly important to the success of the work (as for example with a major work of reference) the contract should provide expressly for the kind of index required, when it should be supplied and who should do the work (and – if an outside indexer is required – who should pay their fee).

PRODUCTION, PROMOTION AND PROOFS

All matters relating to physical production, promotion, and sale of the work are normally reserved for the Publisher's sole discretion and control, although in many cases a publisher will be willing to consult authors on matters of taste or style such as illustrations or jacket design. The key commercial issue of the price is usually for the publisher alone to decide, although the author may wish to be consulted on this as well as on the publication date itself, perhaps with a provision that the publisher's decision shall be final or that consent will not unreasonably be withheld.

Editorial changes to the work itself (beyond 'house-style' amendments already agreed, or specified in the contract) may not normally be made without the author's consent, particularly if they might amount to derogatory treatment and thus infringe the author's moral right of integrity (see chapter 3, p. 47–50). Where individual authors do not have the final say over editing (e.g. as part of a multi-author team) it will be advisable for the publisher (or, more likely, the work's Editor) to make sure each author is credited appropriately (for more on these moral rights issues, see chapter 3). Publishers will usually provide proofs, but will want an undertaking from the author that they will be returned within a reasonable time (14 or 21 days are typical) and, if not (if the author is away, or ill, for example), that the publishers may pass them for press themselves.

Alterations to proofs made by the author above an agreed level (usually 10 to 15 per cent of the cost of composition) are usually charged to the author or deducted from royalties.

ROYALTIES AND ADVANCES

As we have seen, unless a contract is made under seal, or executed as a Deed, it must be supported by valuable 'consideration' (see above, p. 63). Although the Publisher's undertaking to publish may in some circumstances count as adequate consideration, the consideration most authors want to see is money. This may be in the form of a one-off fee but is more often expressed as a royalty on sales. This has the advantage for the publisher of minimising the upfront risk (if no sales are made, no royalties will be paid) and it has the potential advantage for the author of a direct financial link with any success the work might have: the better it sells, the greater the rewards the author will get (particularly if the royalty rate itself increases, via a sliding scale). There is often provision for a payment on account, in the form of an advance.

Needless to say, money can be a fertile source of author–publisher disputes (particularly where the contract is not as clear as it should be) but it is beyond the scope of a book like this to suggest financial terms; such commercial issues are matters for the parties to negotiate, in circumstances which may vary widely. From a purely legal point of view, there are perhaps only two golden rules:

- Be sure both sides fully understand all the terms being proposed (including the likely effect of discounts, and the meaning of phrases like 'net receipts').
- Be absolutely clear about what is finally agreed.

For good specialist commentaries see Clark's *Publishing Agreements* or Lynette Owen's *Selling Rights*. Issues which tend to crop up most frequently include the following.

Advances

Publishers are not legally obliged to give advances (unless they have contracted to do so, of course) but many do. Advances are normally regarded as payments on account of all future royalty earnings (royalty and subsidiary rights), and are recoupable from the author's royalty account in due course; a large advance may therefore take some time to be earned back, before positive royalties start being paid – 50 per cent of the author's anticipated royalty earnings from the publisher's first printing is not untypical, although of course advances vary widely depending on the type of publication, the status of the author and the presence or absence of a literary agent.

It is advisable to make it clear in the agreement whether outstanding advances already paid are to be repaid by the Author if, for example, the work is never delivered (or is delivered but rejected) or, in some cases, as a prerequisite to reversion of rights. There will be greater pressure for outstanding sums to be repaid where termination is perceived to be the Author's fault (or results from the author's 'material breach'), and less if termination is the fault of the Publisher; for example, by allowing the work to go out of print or following some other breach of contract.

The editions covered

Make sure *all* likely editions are covered somewhere. The most common categories for volume sales are:

- *'Home' full-price hardback*: the publisher's own hardback. 'Home' may mean the UK and Ireland, or possibly now the EU and EEA (see p. 324). This is the 'base royalty' and is often calculated on a sliding scale.
- *Home cheap hardback*: a publisher's hardback at two-thirds or less of the full price: usually with a lower royalty.
- *Home trade paperback*: the publisher's own paperback: royalties are normally lower, but print-runs can be much higher. Again, sliding scales might apply.

- *Home mass-market paperback:* either issued by the publishers or licensed to a paperback house – smaller format, lower price, and even lower royalties – but even bigger print-runs. The author's consent may be required for this kind of sale, perhaps not unreasonably to be withheld.
- *Export editions:* export versions of all four home categories above – usually based on net receipts, often sold at discounts of 50 per cent or more, and with correspondingly lower royalty rates.
- *Small reprints:* usually 1,000 to 1,500 or less (or 5,000 to 7,500 for paperbacks). Since small reprints are often uneconomic, the publisher often reserves the right to offer a lower royalty – often the lowest of the above rates. In order to prevent regular small reprinting, some contracts provide that the publisher may only do this once in any 12-month period, and not less than two years after publication. However, modern print-on-demand technology is making small reprints less necessary, although issues are already arising between authors and publishers about appropriate royalties for print-on-demand sales, and what relation the price should bear to the main editions.
- *Promotional and premium sales:* special editions, often under a different imprint, as part of someone else's promotion or special offer: this could mean cornflake packets, so the quantities may be high but royalties will be at low rates. The author may have strong views about this kind of sale: prior consent is advisable.
- *Book club sales:* normally regarded as 'volume' sales, although not usually in the publisher's imprint. Discounts given to book clubs can be very high indeed, but they are generally felt to be a positive extension to the publisher's own market. Authors may well have views about book club editions, and consent (or at least prior consultation) is often written into the contract.

The author's moral right of integrity (see p. 47) should also be taken into account, since book clubs may wish not only to provide editions of the complete work, but also digest or condense it with a relatively free hand. It is therefore not uncommon for book club clauses to contain either an express consent to such treatment, or a partial waiver of the author's right of integrity (or at least an agreement to waive the right in the future) insofar as it becomes necessary in order for the publisher to exploit the book club rights effectively.

- *E-book sales:* sales in e-book format are now dealt with under volume rights, involving delivery of the complete verbatim text via a website to an individual purchaser in electronic form, downloadable onto a PC or a handheld device. Royalties are under continuing discussion in the industry. For other electronic exploitation, see subsidiary rights, below.

The basis of royalty calculation

It is essential to be clear in the contract how each given royalty percentage is calculated: are home hardback sales at 10 per cent (say) based on the UK published price, or are they 10 per cent of the net receipts (which normally means income actually received, or recommended retail price less any discount)? This can make a large difference to the sums the author will get if a significant proportion of the publisher's sales are likely to be at high discounts. Export sales are often at 60 per cent to 70 per cent discounts: bear this in mind if, say, the US market is going to be important. Equally important: is Europe home or export? Home sales may often also be at comparatively high discounts, if via major chains of bookshops: 50 per cent to 60 per cent is not unusual (although the average trade discount in the UK is probably closer to 35 per cent or 40 per cent). Mail-order sales are sometimes at no discount at all (so a net receipts calculation might make little difference).

Both publisher and author need to be clear about the likely markets and the probable basis of sales to each; it is infinitely better to sit down and talk about it, and eliminate any misunderstanding, at the outset, rather than wait for unpleasant surprises in the first royalty statement.

Free copies

Royalties are not usually paid on copies given away in the interests of promoting the work (such as review copies), or lost or damaged copies.

SUBSIDIARY RIGHTS

What are they?

Non-volume rights, such as TV or merchandising rights, are usually grouped together in a publishing contract under the generic heading of 'Subsidiary Rights'. A typical full list is given below. The division is not very precise, and many of the rights (such as electronic and book club rights) may appear confusingly under both volume and subsidiary rights: perhaps the most useful distinction to keep in mind is that, generally speaking:

- Volume rights license the publisher's own publishing.
- Subsidiary rights give the publisher the right to sub-license exploitation by others.

So in the case of electronic rights, the publisher might want both: the right to sell its own e-book or online versions, and also the right to license digital use by others, for example as part of a database, or to be accessed as part of search engines such as Amazon and Google. In all such cases, express author consent is very likely to be needed.

The grant of rights

As with the main grant of rights clause (see above, p. 73), the first and most important thing to check in a subsidiary rights clause is: does it actually grant the rights required? This may be crucial, because the main *grant* of rights clause may cover volume rights only, and may make no mention of subsidiary rights – so unless the particular rights the publisher wants are separately granted here, the publisher may not get them. The actual words 'the Author hereby grants' (the rights concerned) should ideally appear, preferably shortly followed by 'to the Publisher'. Simply listing some subsidiary rights, with some agreed percentages, may not be enough (although a limited grant of rights may be implied).

Ensure that the rights are granted in the correct terms – so that they cover the required formats, territories, languages (where appropriate) and period of time, and (crucially) that they are expressly stated to be 'exclusive' if that is what author and publisher want. A grant of rights will be regarded as non-exclusive unless it is expressly stated to be exclusive (and signed by the author).

Authors' consent

Some grants of subsidiary rights may be conditional upon the Publisher first securing the Author's consent before exploitation can take place, or at least consulting him or her; this may apply to the whole list of rights, or be a specific requirement of certain rights only – electronic rights, book club, digest and condensation rights are frequent examples. To get round the publisher's need to do some deals quickly in the author's absence, some contracts require consent only 'wherever practicable'; in other cases, where the author is available but they can't agree, there may be a provision that the author's consent 'shall not unreasonably be withheld'. Ultimately, it is a question of bargaining position, and who wants to retain effective control – and who is best qualified to use it. Author consent is not normally required for low-income exploitation, such as anthology and quotation use, or use by print-handicapped people (see later).

Waivers of moral rights

Contracts now often include a conditional waiver of the author's moral right of integrity (or an agreement to waive it in the future), insofar as it may be required in order to exploit the subsidiary rights. Book club sales often require this flexibility: so also do film and TV deals. See pp. 132 and 137, and on moral rights generally, see chapter 3.

The list of rights

Subsidiary rights most frequently dealt with include the following:

- *First serial rights:* the right to publish an extract or series of extracts in a newspaper or magazine on or before (or commencing on or before) publication – these can be extremely valuable, both to sales of the work and to the circulations of the periodicals concerned, and are often optioned. If a newspaper wishes to offer access to the work via its website the terms – and timing – for this should be specifically agreed.

- *Second and subsequent serial rights:* serial rights *after* publication has taken place – these are normally less valuable (whenever the licence was signed).
- *Anthology and quotation rights:* some quotations may count as fair dealing for the purposes of criticism and review, if accompanied by sufficient acknowledgement, and copyright permission need not therefore be sought (see chapter 9) – these rights cover all other substantial quotations and extracts.
- *Digest rights/digest book condensation rights:* these are, respectively, the right to publish an abridgement of the work in a single issue of a newspaper or periodical, and the right to publish an abridgement in separate volume form. They are sometimes grouped together under 'condensation rights', for both magazines and books.
- *One-shot periodical rights:* the right to publish the complete work in a single issue of a newspaper or periodical. These are also now regarded as part of volume rights, following *Jonathan Cape Ltd* v. *Consolidated Press Ltd* (1954) (see above, p. 75).
- *Licensed paperback rights:* for paperback editions sub-licensed to another publisher.
- *Hardcover and educational reprint rights:* the rights to publish straight hardback reprints (in someone else's library series, for example) and educational reprints, usually annotated.
- *Book club rights:* see p. 117, and for dealings with book clubs, see p. 118.
- *US rights:* the USA may be a major market: these rights may be sold directly or via an agent. They will usually take the form of a straightforward licence to publish, for a royalty on the US price plus – usually – an advance, or will accompany a sale of bound stock or sheets (or a co-edition) and be dealt with under volume rights (see p. 75). Permissions may need to be re-cleared for US editions (see p. 84).
- *Strip cartoon rights (also known as picturisation rights):* the right to make such visual adaptations may be highly valuable, particularly for children's books.
- *Translation rights:* these may be licensed separately, or accompany a co-edition deal for bound copies in the foreign language concerned: in either case, the foreign publisher will be responsible for arranging a translation of a satisfactory standard, and will normally pay an advance and a royalty (see chapter 5, p. 113). Note that the territories covered should be made clear: a Portuguese translation may sell more copies in Brazil than in Portugal.
- *Dramatisation and documentary rights:* usually cover theatrical, radio and TV rights to the work in dramatised form.
- *Single-voice readings:* the right to read extracts directly from the work, either on radio or TV or as part of other public performances. *A Book at Bedtime* is a good example.
- *Film rights:* if Hollywood is likely to be interested, it is important to ensure that these rights are effectively exploited. If the publisher is not best placed to do this, the author or agent may wish to reserve these rights themselves (for exploitation of film rights, see chapter 5, p. 131).
- *Audio and video rights:* audio cassettes, often spoken by famous actors, are a growing market. Video rights are often dealt with separately from the film rights. These

rights used to be combined under the heading 'mechanical reproduction rights' and included CDs, analogue and digital tapes and those strange black vinyl things we used to buy called gramophone records. Given the speed with which formats are replaced nowadays, such clauses now usually extend the right not only to formats known at the time but also to 'those hereafter invented'.

- *Merchandising rights:* the right to exploit titles or characters from a successful work can be as profitable, if not more profitable, than the work itself. It is therefore worth making sure that these rights are included, particularly for children's books. They are often associated with film rights; indeed, merchandising rights achieved some kind of apotheosis in the film of *Jurassic Park* when the T-shirts and other merchandise actually featured in the film itself. On the exploitation of merchandising rights, see chapter 5. Titles, logos and characters with merchandising potential should also normally be registered as registered trade marks (see chapter 10).
- *Electronic publishing rights:* it is important to distinguish between the publisher's own electronic exploitation of the work (for example, as an e-book) and other, sub-licensed, exploitation. Older contracts may not make this distinction, and may group 'electronic rights' together (although that phrase has little meaning today). Until recently, the publisher's own e-book exploitation of the verbatim text of the complete work might have been dealt with under volume rights (on this, see the section on Formats, above p. 75), while digital exploitation, use or access sublicensed to others such as via an online database, aggregator or research engine, or access via a site licence might fall under subsidiary rights. It is likely now that in both cases author consent will be highly desirable, and possibly essential. At the time of writing, there have been few (if any) UK cases on this issue, although two interesting US cases are noted in the section on Formats, p. 76 above.

Exploitation and uses which may need to be considered separately are set out in chapter 5. Whatever form of digital use or access is required, or envisaged, it cannot be stressed too strongly that there is no substitute for a clear grant of specific rights each time. The author's, or agent's, consent is likely to be required (or at least be strongly advisable) for some forms of exploitation, and care should be taken to ensure that the author's moral rights are not infringed. Some electronic rights may only be available for limited terms, or may require renegotiation after, say, three years. Financial terms currently vary widely.

- *Reprographic reproduction rights:* photocopying is still a fertile source of copyright infringement in the UK, but collective licensing schemes run by bodies such as the Copyright Licensing Agency are now more widely available.
- *Non-commercial rights for the print-handicapped:* Braille, or tape (or computer) recorded copies for the Royal National Institute for the Blind and other registered blind users have usually been licensed free of charge by the publisher. A licensing scheme for organisations representing visually impaired people (such as the RNIB) to make 'accessible copies' on their behalf was established by the Copyright

Licensing Agency in 2003 following the Copyright (Visually Impaired Persons) Act 2002. At the time of writing, a joint pilot scheme is under discussion between RNIB and rightsholders to find a secure and viable method of using publishers' own digital files to provide quicker accessible copies of the titles visually impaired people most often need.

All other rights are reserved

Any rights not expressly set out in the agreement are normally taken to be retained by the author: there is often an express provision making this clear. This will include Public Lending Right, which under the Public Lending Right Act 1979 is given solely to the author (on PLR generally, see p. 56).

SALES STATEMENTS, ACCOUNTING AND VAT

Publishers' royalty statements have been the subject of grim humour for as long as anyone can remember, but most publishers now have computerised royalty systems to keep track of royalties and other rights revenue, and most now pay their authors twice a year rather than the traditional annual payment. Educational and academic publishers still tend to pay annually, however, as do some professional imprints. Payment – when it comes – should normally be no longer than three months after the relevant accounting date (usually 30 June and/or 31 December).

Small credits, say £50 or less, are often carried over to the next accounting period. It is also common for the publisher to keep a reserve against returns – stock apparently sold to bookshops, but then returned under normal sale or return terms later on. Ten per cent to 20 per cent for hardbacks is not unusual, and some reserves (usually for paperbacks) can be as high as 30 per cent. However, there is often provision, particularly in agents' contracts and Minimum Terms Agreements, that any significant subsidiary rights revenue should be paid out as agreed to the Author within 30 days of receipt, provided any advance has been earned back.

Royalty statements themselves should be as clear and informative (and accurate) as possible: if the contract does not specify the standard of information to be supplied, there is a Publishers' Association/Society of Authors Model Royalty Statement for guidance.

With the best will in the world, however, computer errors can still occur (as anyone who has a bank account will know) so most contracts provide that the Author – or his or her appointed representative – may examine the Publisher's accounts in person during normal business hours. Who bears the costs of this normally depends on whether, and to what extent, errors are actually found.

Authors who are registered for VAT will be required to notify the Publishers and supply them with their VAT number: by agreement with Customs and Excise (which collects VAT), royalty statements can be treated as the author's tax invoices and VAT is added in the normal way.

COPYRIGHT

Where the Author assigns the full copyright to the Publisher, this should be set out in clear wording under the main grant of rights clause (see above, pp. 73–4). But even where the Author retains the copyright, this should still be made clear here, and some special words are still advisable. As we have seen (above, p. 12) the Berne Convention forbids formal registration requirements of any kind, but it is still advisable for copyright protection under the Universal Copyright Convention (UCC) that a copyright claim should be printed on all copies of the work, containing the following information:

- The letter C in a circle (©) now a worldwide copyright symbol.
- The name of the copyright owner.
- The year of first publication.

There is no stipulation in the UCC that the information should be printed in any particular order but it is customary to print it thus:

© Hugh Jones and Christopher Benson 2006

The word 'copyright' is sometimes also printed before the ©, although this is not strictly necessary.

UK works have carried the UCC symbol for many years, because prior to its joining the Berne Convention in 1989 the USA belonged to the UCC but not Berne: the printed notice above was therefore essential to secure copyright protection in the USA. Since 1989 this has no longer been necessary for US protection, but there are still some countries which belong only to the UCC, and UK works should therefore keep the notice. It is also convenient to combine it with any assertion of the author's moral right of paternity (see p. 45), and a contractual undertaking to print such an assertion is now common. For the fullest protection of the right of paternity it is also advisable to include a term to the effect that such assertions will also be a condition of any sub-licences.

COPYRIGHT INFRINGEMENT

We will deal with this more fully in chapter 9: suffice it to say here that the publisher will necessarily bear the burden of protecting the work, once published, against pirates and other copyright infringers around the world, and where the author retains the copyright the publisher will therefore need clear authority from the author, as copyright owner, to do so. Exclusive licensees under the 1988 Act have the right to take legal action and join the copyright owner as a party to any action in the UK (on giving an indemnity against costs), but it is still advisable to confirm this in the contract. It also gives the author and publisher the opportunity to agree on the practical control of any such legal action (including the terms of any compromise or settlement), whether the Author is required in any way to contribute to the costs and, if so, whether the Author will receive a corresponding share of any net damages.

AUTHOR'S COPIES

Most publishers will give authors at least six personal copies of their works, plus one or two copies of each sub-licensed edition (such as translations or US editions). Some are more generous than others. The latest Minimum Terms Agreements give 12 hardbacks and 20 paperbacks, but publishing economics may not always make that possible. Additional copies, not for resale, are usually available at a discount (but like any trade customer, the author may need to haggle over these).

REVISION OF THE WORK

With some kinds of works, such as educational, professional and reference texts, keeping the work up to date once published is almost as important as publishing it in the first place. In such cases author contracts will usually contain a clause requiring the Author to prepare new editions when they become necessary. It may be appropriate to provide for a fresh advance to be agreed at that time. It is prudent also to give the Publisher the option of commissioning some other (competent) person to do the work of updating, should the Author be unwilling or unable to do so (for example, through illness or death). The fees payable to such persons will then be deducted from the royalties payable to the author, or the author's estate – quite reasonably.

Who decides when new editions are required? This may be an important issue, and it is worth checking the wording of the contract to see what it says. Often the decision is for the publisher alone to make, or sometimes dependent upon mutual agreement – the author is unlikely to be in a position to insist. This perhaps is fair enough (it would be unreasonable to force a publisher to publish against its will and arguably unenforceable anyway), but if more regular new editions (or a more flexible system) are likely to be needed this should be agreed at the outset.

REMAINDERS

Remaindering is a sensitive issue, but most publishers know when a book has ceased to have any further sales potential and may want the power to remainder their remaining stock. Some agents' contracts forbid this within a specified period without the author's prior written consent: where this is not practicable it may be equally effective to ensure that, while the publisher retains the option to remainder, the author will at least have (say) 30 days' notice, and the right to purchase part or all of the remaining stock at the expected remainder price (which will probably be fairly low, as will any royalty). Publishers should bear in mind that such a clause is fully enforceable, like any other clause of the contract, so if they fail to notify the author and remainder the book regardless they may face an action for damages for breach of contract. This was confirmed in one case, where a lecturer won damages against Cassell for breach of such a clause, on the grounds that she had been deprived of the (very real) chance to sell the books cheaply herself to her own students.

TERMINATION OF THE CONTRACT, AND REVERSION OF RIGHTS

Just as it is essential that rights granted should be granted for a specific period of time, so it is equally important that any grounds for early termination should be clearly set out. In the early clauses governing delivery and acceptance (see p. 77) the Publisher is normally given grounds for termination of the contract if the Work does not come in at all, or is unacceptable when it does – it is therefore in the author's interests to have similar grounds for termination if the *publisher* breaches any terms of the contract later on – for example, by not paying royalties on time, or allowing the work to go out of print.

All rights granted should revert to the Author (in the case of an assignment of copyright, there may need to be specific provisions for formal re-assignment). Reversion is usually without prejudice to any sub-licences or other contracts properly entered into while the agreement was in force, or any outstanding claims or monies owing.

The most common grounds for termination and reversion are:

- Material breach by the publishers of any terms of the contract (such as failure to publish), and failure to remedy the breach within a specified period (one to three months is normal).
- Insolvency of the publisher's business (or a substantial part of it) – including administration, receivership, winding-up and (in some cases) arrangements with creditors.
- Failure by the publishers to keep the work from going out of print (and failure to reprint after a given period of notice). It is important to agree what 'out of print' means – does this refer only to the publisher's hard copy edition? With print-on-demand technology, works may effectively be available and 'in print' for ever. For some specialist, slow-moving works this may suit both parties well; in other cases it may be advisable to consider termination and reversion of rights when sales fall below a certain level (for, say, two successive years).

OPTIONS

There is a school of thought that no option clause is enforceable. This is not strictly true – but a future option for no fixed consideration ('on terms to be agreed', for example) may be difficult to enforce. Generally speaking, the more specific the option, the easier it will be to enforce legally. A sweeping option over the author's next six works may be extremely difficult to enforce, and may well be in restraint of trade if it unduly restricts the author's future writing (see above, p. 312), but an option on the next one or two defined works (of fiction, say, or for children) and on specified terms (such as 'the same terms', or 'terms no less favourable') may well be enforceable and bind the author.

It makes sense to provide a clear timetable for the publishers to exercise the option, and provide for the author's freedom to go elsewhere if they do not (or if they cannot agree terms).

MORAL RIGHTS

This may be a suitable place to include an assertion of the author's moral right of paternity, as required under section 78 of the 1988 Act. The paternity right – the right to be credited as the author – is the only moral right which needs to be asserted (in writing) under UK law before it can be enforced: on this generally, see chapter 3, p. 45.

AGENCY

Where an author is represented by a literary agent, the agent's standard contract will usually contain a clause authorising the agent to receive all monies payable under the contract on behalf of the author. Since authors and agents do occasionally fall out, it should also specifically provide that payment to the agent would be a good and valid discharge of the debt – so that the publisher, having paid royalties to the agent in good faith, will not then get embroiled in arguments about payment of the agent's commission later on. It is not generally necessary or advisable to sign an irrevocable appointment or authorisation: if an author wishes to revoke that particular payment arrangement, and be paid direct, he or she should be perfectly entitled to do so. There may then be a separate contractual dispute between author and agent about the agent's commission, but there is no reason why the publisher should become involved in that. There is a long-standing trade practice among literary agents that an agent will expect commission on *all* monies payable to the author under contracts which that agent negotiated – even long after the agent's appointment has been terminated. Such matters are entirely dependent on the author's contract with the agent: see chapter 5, p. 142.

RESERVATION OF TITLE

Although this is implied, it is advisable to make it clear that no rights or licences or other interests are granted to the Publisher other than those specifically set out and granted in the contract. A provision to this effect is often usefully included at the end of subsidiary rights clauses.

ASSIGNMENT OR NON-ASSIGNMENT

Many agents' contracts contain non-assignment clauses, which forbid any assignment of the benefit and burden of the contract to any third party without the Author's consent: sometimes (and in some Minimum Terms Agreements) the objection is waived in the case of third parties who are at the same time acquiring the whole or a substantial part of the Publisher's business. Non-assignment clauses may seriously restrict the future value of the rights granted and the publisher's capacity to deal with them commercially, and should be carefully considered. The (significant) implications are discussed above, pp. 72–3.

ARBITRATION

Many publishing contracts contain provisions for arbitration in the event of any disputes. It is important to recognise that because such provisions are deemed to be distinct and separate from the main contract (even if they are contained in a clause embedded in the contract), generally such clauses will survive the termination of the contract. Therefore, both Author and Publisher will continue to be bound by an arbitration clause, even after the contract itself has come to an end. If one party unilaterally terminates the contract, the other party may (equally unilaterally) invoke the arbitration clause. Both parties should therefore consider how they would actually want any disputes to be resolved before agreeing to such a clause.

The Arbitration Act 1996 has consolidated the previous legislation (Acts of 1950 and 1979) and applies to all arbitration proceedings commenced after 31 January 1997. References to arbitration are of two kinds, conventional (where the parties agree to refer any dispute to a mutually agreeable tribunal and not to a court) and statutory (where the Act lays down default provisions where the parties have not decided on the mechanics of the arbitration procedure). The Act encourages the former approach and generally will not interfere where the parties make their own arrangements by written agreement.

There are a number of arbitration methods. In some cases each party will appoint their own arbitrator, and agree to be bound by the decision of those two people, or (if they cannot agree either) a third arbitrator who they appoint (called their 'referee' or 'umpire'). Where the dispute can be reduced to written submissions, without any (or much) need for oral hearings, such arbitrations can be relatively quick and inexpensive. A full-scale arbitration including hearings with lawyers on both sides, can however be just as expensive as a High Court action – indeed, more so, since the parties will have to pay for the arbitrators whereas judges are free. Following the civil justice reforms under Lord Woolf, even High Court actions are now expedited so that there is more pressure on the parties to settle, and small claims in the County Court can be relatively straightforward

The Publishers Association offers a confidential Informal Arbitration Procedure, which can be quick and inexpensive, except in very complex cases, but there is as yet no industry-wide arbitration scheme for publishing as a whole.

GOVERNING LAW AND JURISDICTION

It is essential to make it clear which country's laws will govern the interpretation and enforcement of the contract. For most UK publishing contracts it will be advisable for this to be English law: note that Scots law is a separate legal system and may require separate advice.

Bear in mind that a contract offered by a foreign publisher is likely to specify their law as the applicable law – in the case of a US co-edition, for example, this may mean that the relevant state law (such as Delaware, or New York) will govern the contract, and any disputes arising under it.

If no applicable law is specified in the contract itself, there are statutory rules which UK courts will apply. As a general rule, they will apply the law with which the contract is most closely connected: in the context of publishing contracts this will usually mean the law of the party who is primarily to perform the contract. In the case of contracts entered into since 1991, if the contract is entered into in the course of a trade or profession, it is presumed that it is most closely connected with the country where the party who is to effect the performance which is characteristic of the contract has, at the time of conclusion of the contract, [its] ... principal place of business (or, if the contract is to be effected through a secondary place of business, *that* place of business). If the contract is for a UK-based publisher to (say) supply sheet stock to New York, UK law will prevail. If it is for the New York based publisher to perform, New York State law will apply.

It is important to note that whose law applies is a different issue from whose courts have jurisdiction to hear the case. UK courts regularly hear cases involving issues of New York or other foreign laws. A good contract should always therefore provide for whose courts will have jurisdiction; in most cases, preferably UK (or English) courts.

In the absence of any express provision, there are complex rules governing the right of UK courts to assume jurisdiction over a dispute. These vary, depending among other things on whether the defendant is based inside or outside the EU.

The Brussels Convention on Jurisdiction (which was not binding Community law) was replaced in December 2000 with a binding EU Regulation on Jurisdiction, Recognition and Enforcement to ensure that rules of jurisdiction and enforcement of judgments are dealt with consistently in the EU. The Regulation broadly confirmed the 'country of origin' principle embodied in the E-Commerce Directive that persons (including companies) domiciled in member states must be sued in their own courts. However, this was subject to certain exceptions. For example, in contracts for the sale of goods or delivery of services (including website services), consumers (or others) could sue in the courts of the place of performance of the contract. This would usually be in their home courts in a sale of goods case (place of performance is deemed to be where the goods were or should have been delivered). The same will probably apply in a provision of services case (place of performance is deemed to be where the services were or should have been provided). At the time of writing, the issue of Applicable Law is under discussion by the European Parliament, and various amendments to the relevant Conventions have been debated. It seems likely that discussions will continue for some time. For more on this highly complex question, see chapter 11.

STAMP DUTY

Until the Chancellor's Budget of March 2000, intellectual property rights were considered to be types of 'property' for stamp duty purposes and therefore transfers attracted stamp duty. From 28 March 2000, transactions in intellectual property are exempted from stamp duty, in order to foster an environment in which innovation and invention are encouraged. The exemption applies to transfers and licences of patents, trade marks, registered designs and copyrights.

Note that where property sold under a transfer instrument for more than (currently) £60,000 consists partly of intellectual property (IP) and partly of other property chargeable to duty, an apportionment of the sale price will be made to determine the amount chargeable to duty. If the value of the transaction (involving both IP and non-IP transfers) is below £60,000, it is necessary to include at the end of the contract a clause in approved form saying so.

Other contracts

5

ACADEMIC/PROFESSIONAL/STM AUTHORS

CONTRACTS FOR SPECIALISTS

Some authors (lucky things) write for a living: many authors earn their living primarily doing other things, but can sometimes be encouraged (or provoked) into writing on topics connected with their work or their research. Increasingly now their writing will be published in electronic form as well as (or instead of) the traditional hard copy formats. They are often experts in their fields, with established (often international) reputations, and their names as authors, or as members of an editorial team, will sell all kinds of publications and services to what are often highly profitable specialist markets. Even if they are not all yet acknowledged experts, they are all specialists. The works they create tend to have distinctive features, and these need to be reflected in the publishing contracts which they sign. We will highlight these features in this section: bear in mind, however, that most of the general legal principles set out in chapter 4 will still apply as well.

For convenience, we will use the abbreviation 'specialist works' throughout this section to refer to all academic, professional or STM works, and we will call their authors 'specialist authors'.

COPYRIGHT: TEAMS AND INSTITUTIONS

Specialist works are often highly detailed and complex, and may require contributions from several different authors: indeed, a major work may need hundreds of contributors all over the world and an international editorial board. More straightforwardly, two colleagues may co-author a text, or co-host a website, or jointly write up some research. At both ends of the scale, it is equally important:

- to ensure that *all* those involved in the project are under contract;
- to be clear who is doing what;
- to agree who owns the copyright (and other rights) in all the work(s) which result;

- to make sure that the publishing activities envisaged are fully licensed by all those owners.

To make absolutely sure, a publisher investing in a major project may wish to seek a full assignment of copyright from all the contributors involved (including editors): such assignments will give the publisher complete control of the material, but they must be in writing and signed by or on behalf of each contributor (see above, p. 74). The contributors may in most cases be allowed to re-use their material elsewhere, such as within a university intranet, or on their own websites or for professional lecturing purposes, but it is advisable to confirm the details of this. In other cases a sole and exclusive publishing licence may be sufficient (provided it is wide enough to cover all forms of exploitation envisaged), including digital use and online access, but it is still essential to make sure that all the relevant copyrights and other rights are covered by the licence(s) given, so that no rights will be infringed.

Copyright

Depending on the publication, a number of different copyright works might be created, including a range of literary, artistic and other works: for the full list, see chapter 2, p. 14. As well as the obvious ones, such as text and illustrations, do not forget copyright in any overall compilation or database, and also – if it is available electronically – copyright in any computer software. All these copyrights will probably be owned by the people who created the works, but with specialist writing or research teams there may be joint authors to consider (p. 28) – in which case, if there is a risk they might fall out, it may be advisable to legislate for this in the contract since, as joint authors, neither will have the right to publish (or license) the work without the consent of the other. Also, it may well be that some of the employee authors will have created the works in the course of their employment, in which case their employer (which may be their university or company) might own copyright in the works they create, not them (p. 31). They might also, of course, have been persuaded to assign their copyright to the institution or company concerned, and some institutions such as universities are increasingly requiring this.

Other rights

Many collective works nowadays might amount to a database (for the conditions, see chapter 3). Assuming – as is likely – that the publisher, or other 'maker', of the database has made a 'substantial investment in obtaining, verifying or presenting the contents of the database', that person will be entitled to a statutory Database Right to prevent unauthorised extraction or re-utilisation. It is highly advisable to make it clear in each case whether the right is to be owned by the publisher, or any other 'maker' of the database concerned. The right lasts for 15 years, but is renewable thereafter. For more on this see chapter 3.

With collaborative works, there may also be issues of confidentiality to consider – if draft research findings (say) are circulated confidentially, it may be a breach of a duty of confidence to publish them without consent (see p. 199). Such a duty might be owed to a fellow researcher, or to an institute or other employer.

Also, for material created after 1 August 1989, do not overlook authors' moral rights, which are likely to be more than usually significant for specialist writing, where academic or professional reputations are at stake. Moral rights may not apply to certain 'collective works' such as dictionaries and encyclopaedias (see pp. 46 and 49), but if they do there will be at least three moral rights to consider:

- the right for each author to be identified (this right must be specifically asserted);
- their right to object to derogatory treatment of their work (especially if editorial changes are planned);
- the right to prevent false attribution.

(For moral rights generally, see p. 43.) These rights may not apply to any acts done with the author's (or in some cases, the copyright owner's) consent, and will also not apply where the rights have been waived. For smaller contributions or for major works, complete waivers may be appropriate; for others, it may be necessary to rely on partial waivers or contractual consents.

WARRANTIES

For specialist works, warranties may need to be revised to take account of joint authorship, or limiting to the author's particular contributions to the work, rather than applying to the work as a whole – clearly, a specialist author cannot be expected to make warranties about other people's work. However, the personal warranty against plagiarism which amounts to copyright infringement may be particularly important in an academic work, and the warranty against libel may prove useful to protect the publisher against academic vendettas carried on in the footnotes. This is particularly true if the work is going to be published worldwide on the net.

The warranties should ideally also include negligent mis-statement (although negligence will be hard to prove – see p. 185) and should cover statements of fact, and the reliability and safety of formulae or instructions. It may also be advisable to require the author to provide for safety warnings, to put users on notice of any hazards arising out of dangerous experiments or procedures, and refer to any appropriate safety precautions or standards or codes of practice.

Some specialist authors may only feel able to warrant that statements of fact are true 'to the best of their knowledge' – the publisher may be willing to accept this risk, particularly if adequate insurance is in place. On warranties generally, see pp. 79–82.

QUOTATIONS, ILLUSTRATIONS AND PERMISSIONS

These are likely to be important in all specialist works, particularly source books or anthologies. Some textual quotations may freely be used, for example if they count as fair dealing for the purposes of criticism or review (see chapter 9, p. 227), but otherwise permission to reproduce all quoted extracts and illustrations must be obtained from the copyright owners. Most publishers will place responsibility for this – including, where appropriate, paying any permissions fees – on the author, but for a major project where permissions are likely to be a significant item, the publishers may be willing (in fact, may prefer) to arrange this themselves.

Where the author is responsible for permissions, it may be advisable to specify an agreed financial limit. It is also advisable for the publisher to have copies of any permissions correspondence, for future reference.

CORRECTIONS

In specialist works, last-minute corrections may be essential to take account of recent research or knowledge, or legal or technical changes. The work may be unsaleable without them, if it becomes dangerously unreliable or out of date. It is advisable for the publisher to be alerted well in advance if there is a risk of significant corrections. It is also important to agree who will pay for them; otherwise, the authors may find themselves paying substantial sums for dealing with changes which the book needs, but which were totally outside their control.

ROYALTIES AND FEES

One-off fees may be more appropriate for a multi-author work, or where the copyright is assigned: many specialist authors are happy to write for money upfront (or at least on delivery and acceptance), especially where there is some academic or professional kudos involved as well. The timing of the fee payment may be crucial – most contributors will prefer to be paid when they have delivered their own work, and not wait until the last (and slowest) contribution comes in, still less until publication. Advance payments may get round this problem. There should also be provision for fee payments if for some reason the project collapses and the work is never published.

Consider, also, any reprints or further exploitation of the work, including electronic exploitation and whether further fees or royalties may be appropriate then, if the contribution is a significant proportion of the whole work (or the part of it to be exploited). If the material later proves suitable for electronic exploitation, such as inclusion in an online database, or for website or search engine access or local site licensing, the contract will need to allow room for a suitable new payment structure for such use in due course, including aggregator or subscription services. Ideally, this should allow for exploitation by the publishers themselves, as well as any exploitation or access sub-licensed to others (see further, on this, pp. 85–92).

Another factor to consider in contracts for specialist works is the need to phase out royalty payments in a realistic manner where an original author or editor retires or dies. In order to keep the work up to date, and maintain its reputation against rivals, it will be necessary for co-authors to take over, or for new editors to be brought in, and to be paid at realistic rates. As they prune old text and contribute new original material of their own, each edition or update for which they are responsible will contain a smaller and smaller proportion of the original author's copyright material, so it is reasonable that the royalty rates payable to the author or author's estate should decline also. Many specialist contracts now provide for the original author's royalties to continue for one, or perhaps two, further editions but then to cease; an alternative method is to agree a gradually declining percentage, over perhaps three or four editions.

REVISIONS

A publisher who has taken full assignments of copyright will normally have complete freedom to revise and update a work, although in many cases the publisher will still prefer to give the author first option to make any revisions. The fact that the publisher owns the copyright will normally mean that the author's moral right of integrity will also not apply to any changes the publisher authorises unless the author is identified, and even then not if there is a sufficient disclaimer. In the case of a publishing licence, however, this will probably not be the case, and provision should be made in the contract for revised editions. In any event, many specialist authors will want to retain at least a first option to make any required revisions themselves.

COMPETING WORKS

Non-competition clauses may have particular significance for specialist authors whose reputations often depend on their writing. They must not be drafted so widely as to amount to an unreasonable restraint of trade (see p. 312) and specialist authors must not be so prevented from writing in their own field that they cannot develop their work properly or earn a living. If such clauses are to be enforceable, it is advisable to be as clear as possible about the level of competition restricted: a blanket ban on a whole subject is unlikely to be upheld, but directly competing works at the same level in the same market may well be prevented. To avoid any doubt, it may help to list some or all of the activities which *may* be undertaken, such as limited website access, journal articles, conference papers or anthologies.

REMAINDERS

As we saw in chapter 4, p. 94, the courts are willing to enforce an author's contractual right to be consulted before any remaindering. Where the contract contains such a right, damages may be payable to an academic author (for example) who could have sold the remaining copies to students had he or she known the remaindering was about to take place.

GENERAL EDITORS

DON'T FORGET THE EDITOR

As we saw in the last section, major projects often require whole teams of contributors, and the General Editor – there usually is one – will probably be a contributor too. He or she will probably need a quite different type of contract from that of the typical contributor, however, because there are two quite different legal matters to sort out:

- the Editor's practical duties and responsibilities in relation to the team and the project as a whole;
- the Editor's rights (including copyright) in the material produced, and any associated warranties or liabilities.

COMMISSIONING AND DELIVERY

It is essential that the Publisher and the Editor should agree on the scope of the Editor's role, and set this out as clearly as possible in their contract. Does the Editor commission the work – and the contributors – from scratch, or is the publisher doing this? If the Editor does it, it will be advisable for the agreement to settle:

- the overall scope of the work, including length and schedule;
- the management of contributors, and responsibility for ensuring each of them is put under contract with the Publisher;
- any responsibility the Editor has for negotiating fees or other payments and budgets for these;
- who is responsible for clearing and paying for permissions;
- the Editor's duty to review and edit each contribution, and powers of acceptance, amendment or rejection;
- who decides on any extra text (is this entirely at the editor's discretion, or only as necessary in the Publisher's opinion?).

The schedule itself is (of course) usually crucial – note that time will not normally be regarded as being of the essence unless the Editor's contract (and those of contributors) expressly makes it so.

COPYRIGHT AND MORAL RIGHTS

The Editor is likely to own copyright in:

- his or her own contributions as a contributor;
- any other original material he or she creates (such as introductions, forewords and so forth);
- the overall scheme and plan of the work as a whole, as a compilation.

If the Editor does the work, and creates the works, in the scope of employment (by a university or research institute, for example) it may well be that the employer will own the copyright – in which case any publishing contract should be with them (but preferably including the editor in his or her personal capacity too). The Publisher may wish to secure a full assignment of all the relevant copyrights – in which case this should be in writing and signed by or on behalf of the assignor – or may seek a sole and exclusive licence in terms wide enough to cover all forms and media envisaged.

If the work amounts to a database (see above, p. 16) it is likely that the Publisher or 'maker' will have a Database Right to prevent unauthorised extraction or re-use, for 15 years.

The Editor is likely to have the same statutory moral rights as individual contributors over his or her work. Unless one or other of the exceptions applies (see chapter 3, pp. 46 and 49), these are likely to include the right to be credited as the editor (this right must be specifically asserted), the right to object to derogatory treatment, and the right to prevent false attribution. These rights may not be assigned but they may be waived. On waiver, and moral rights generally, see chapter 3.

If the Editor is responsible for procuring assignments of copyright and waivers of moral rights from contributors, the contract should make this clear, although it will probably be more appropriate for the Publisher to negotiate for these.

WARRANTIES

The Publisher will want the usual warranties (see pp. 79–82), covering at least the Editor's own contributions, and (crucially) any amendments, alterations or additions which are made to the contributor's text or other material. It is important that there should be no gaps in libel cover (for example) – libels can be introduced just as much by editorial additions (or deletions) as by original text.

CORRECTIONS

Does the Editor get an extra correction allowance, or is there one overall percentage? Ideally, the Editor will share with the Publisher the responsibility for keeping corrections under control.

BUDGET, FEES AND EXPENSES

All fees and other expenses payable to the Editor, or on his or her behalf, should be settled at the outset. These may include royalty payments (and any advances) or fees, and also any honorarium. In particular, a budget for expenses such as travel and any overheads such as secretarial support should be agreed.

It may be advisable to clarify in the agreement whether the Editor has any responsibility at all for negotiating fees with contributors (or even paying them) and, if not, to confirm that the Publisher will do this and hold the editor harmless against any liability for such payments.

REVISIONS AND NEW EDITIONS

It is desirable to agree who initiates these, and what happens if Publisher and Editor cannot agree. If the Editor is unwilling or unable to edit a revision or new edition, the Publisher will need the right to bring in someone else and pay them for the work they do out of any royalties or fees which might otherwise have been paid to the Editor, or the Editor's estate.

Remember that any moral right of integrity (to object to derogatory treatment) the Editor might have, and which has not been waived, will last for as long as the work remains in copyright, as will the Editor's right of paternity (to be credited as the editor). In the event of a dispute, the converse right – to prevent false attribution – might also be important, and may stop the Publisher putting out a new edition under the Editor's name if it contains substantial amounts of material which the Editor did not write or of which the Editor disapproves. This right lasts for 20 years after the Editor's death.

Finally, remember that any substantial investment of time, skill or money in a database will trigger a renewed 15-year term of Database Right (owned by the publisher or other 'maker').

CONTRIBUTORS (TEXT AND ILLUSTRATIONS)

COMMISSIONED WORKS

Commissioned work (literary or artistic) has distinctive features which any contract will need to reflect, but it is otherwise substantially the same as any other original work. Contrary to what many people think, the copyright position in the UK is also now fundamentally the same, so that the author, artist or photographer usually owns the copyright (but see below on the US position). Much of what was said in chapter 4 about author–publisher agreements will thus apply here too, as will the comments about specialist authors at the beginning of this chapter.

The illustrations in some works can be more valuable than the words – indeed some publications (children's books, for example) might consist almost entirely of pictures. In such cases the illustrator will for contractual purposes become the primary author. In others, the publisher will probably need two separate contracts, with author and illustrator, reflecting the contribution the illustrator has made and granting the publisher the necessary rights in what the illustrator has produced. For the important issue of ownership of the artwork (and possible Resale Right) see below.

DELIVERY AND ACCEPTANCE

Where a project depends on many contributions, the schedule and delivery requirements for each one are likely to be much less flexible. Time may well be of the essence – if so, this must be expressly stated, so that if the work doesn't come in the publisher will have the option of cancelling the contributor's contract and re-commissioning the work from someone else.

There should be provision for what happens if the contribution is delivered but is unacceptable. For text, most General Editors will want considerable freedom to require alterations, or reject the contribution altogether – this should be agreed in advance, and set out in the contract. It is common in contributors' contracts for hard-copy works for the contribution – if it comes in at all – to be accepted for one edition only. For digital or online works, a more realistic future timetable may be necessary. If a contributor is dropped, there should of course be appropriate arrangements for reversion or reassignment of his or her rights.

Since so many decisions about illustrations are matters of suitability and taste, most delivery schedules allow for submission and approval of roughs, as well as finished artwork.

It also makes sense to provide for the possibility that illustrations will not be felt to be suitable after all. A termination fee (known as a 'kill fee') is usually agreed in advance to cover such an eventuality. If rights are to revert to the illustrator, this should be made clear as well.

EDITORIAL CHANGES AND MORAL RIGHTS

For text, it is important to agree in the contract whether and how far the publisher, and any editor, can make the editorial changes which they may consider necessary, since these may well involve quite heavy revisions in the interests of uniformity or overall style. Although for some projects it may be appropriate to have a proviso that no substantial alterations may be made without the contributor's prior written approval, it is probably more usual for the editor to be given a free hand.

In these circumstances it is essential either to secure a full waiver of the contributor's moral right of integrity, or at least to include a clear consent to such alterations in the contract (since moral rights will not apply to any acts which are done with the author's consent).

Otherwise, there will be a danger that significant editorial changes to the contribution may amount to derogatory treatment, and thus infringe the contributor's moral rights (unless one of the 'collective work' exceptions applies – on all this generally, see chapter 3, pp. 46 and 49).

The moral right of paternity to be credited as the author (or artist or photographer) will not apply unless the contributor specifically asserts it.

COPYRIGHT

Generally speaking, in the UK the fact that work is commissioned makes no difference to copyright ownership (which is normally vested in the author). However, the position is different for 'Works for Hire' in the USA, where the commissioner may own copyright provided there is a signed document making clear that this is the intention of the parties. There were some limited provisions in the UK relating to commissioned photographs, portraits or engravings prior to 1989 but these have never extended to literary works. So a UK contributor of commissioned literary or artistic work will almost certainly own the copyright, unless:

- there are joint authors; or
- the contributor is an employee, and wrote the work in the course of that employment.

These exceptions, and copyright generally, are dealt with fully in chapter 2, pp. 28 and 31. Whoever owns the copyright, the publisher will want to secure a sufficient grant of exclusive publishing rights to cover all likely exploitation of the work, including digital and online access, and possibly – in the case of commissioned text – a full assignment of the copyright. Full copyright assignments must be in writing and signed by or on behalf of the copyright owner in order to be effective.

Not all contributors will be willing to assign copyright in their work, so a publisher embarking on a major project would be well advised to raise the question with each contributor at an early stage and not, for example, leave exchange of formal commissioning letters until right at the end, when it may be too late to re-commission someone else. Without a signed written assignment, the publisher will not acquire the copyright, and indeed if there is no agreement at all the best that the publisher will get is an implied non-exclusive publishing licence, probably for one edition only.

If a contributor is unwilling to assign his or her copyright, the publisher will need to decide whether that particular contributor is crucial to the project, and if so whether a sole and exclusive licence will suffice. In that case, it will be highly desirable for the publisher to obtain an undertaking that the contributor will not assign the copyright elsewhere without giving the assignee written notice of the publisher's exclusive licence.

With illustrations (particularly of characters), bear in mind any merchandising potential including sale of photographs as posters, animated cartoon, film and TV rights, and any possible electronic exploitation.

Bear in mind also the desirability of registering characters and logos with merchandising potential as registered trade marks – and consider who should be the proprietor of the marks. For more on trade marks, see chapter 10.

OWNERSHIP OF ARTWORK

Do not forget that ownership of copyright in something is quite different from ownership of the physical material on which it is recorded. An illustrator may assign copyright in illustrations but still own the original artwork – which may of course have a substantial value of its own, for resale or exhibition purposes (particularly in view now of the forthcoming Artist's Resale Right in the EU – see below). When completed artwork or photographs are delivered, therefore, the publisher should remember that they are probably someone else's (valuable) property (unless of course the publisher already owned them, or has purchased them separately) and take reasonable care of them. It is also probably useful for publishers and illustrators to agree on a reasonable level of mutual access, so that the publisher can have access to the material for publicity or promotion purposes, even after it has been returned, and the artist can include the work if required in exhibitions. Particularly valuable artwork, or negatives, may need to be specially insured while under the publisher's control: if so, it will be necessary to agree a valuation, and decide who is paying the premium or whether this is to be shared.

ARTISTS RESALE RIGHT (DROIT DE SUITE)

From 1 January 2006, if implementing legislation is passed in time, there will be an Artists Resale Right in the UK and in most countries throughout the EU, giving artists a percentage royalty of between 4 or 5 per cent and 0.25 per cent on all subsequent commercial sales of their works above a value of €3,000. For more on this, see chapter 3.

WARRANTIES

The usual warranties will be needed (see above, pp. 79–82) but relating of course only to that contributor's particular contribution(s). The warranties that the work is original, and contains nothing defamatory, are particularly important for text. In the case of scientific or technical material, the warranties may also need to cover safety warnings and refer to appropriate codes and standards. Where recognisable likenesses of identifiable human beings are included, it may be advisable (as in many medical texts) to block out faces, or to ask an artist or photographer for an undertaking that they will secure a form of release, or written consent, from any such identifiable people. In some cases the subjects may be entitled to a Human Right of Privacy.

ILLUSTRATIONS AND PERMISSIONS

In the case of contributors writing text to order, so to speak, it is important to be clear about any other, non-text, material which may also be required and which the contributor might wrongly assume is being commissioned by the publisher from somewhere else. This would include not only quoted text, illustrations and photographs, but also charts, graphs, diagrams and maps. If these are not created by the contributor, and they are still in copyright, then permission to reproduce them will be needed from the copyright owners, and the contract will need to specify who is responsible for getting those permissions and who pays for them.

PROOFS

It is not uncommon for the contract to give the editor the right to correct and pass text proofs on the contributor's behalf if the schedule requires this.

FEES AND EXPENSES

It is customary for a one-off fee payment to cover all uses of the work, and all future exploitation, but it is advisable to check this. If an older contract refers to 'existing' (i.e. pre-digital) formats and media only, or is not clear on the point, it will probably be necessary to agree additional fees for any electronic exploitation, including site licence or website access licensed by the publisher, as well as online search, aggregator or subscription services.

For artistic works, if the agreed fee does not clearly cover exploitation in all forms and media, it may be necessary to agree additional fees for some kinds of exploitation, such as merchandising or electronic exploitation. It is also desirable to agree in advance how any extra payments are to be split between the author and illustrator if (as is likely) the words and illustrations are exploited together.

Expenses should also be clarified – for a major commissioned work the publisher may be willing to meet (allowed) expenses, but in general artists and illustrators are expected to meet the costs of materials and roughs, and photographers are expected to pay for their own developing, printing and enlarging, and also for the hire of any studios, props or other equipment, as well as assistants and staff. If separate budgets need to be fixed for these items, this should be clearly agreed.

TRANSLATORS

TRANSLATORS AND TRANSLATIONS

A significant proportion of the works we want – or need – to read have to be translated from other languages, and this supports a substantial international trade in translation rights – for physics and computing textbooks as much as great literature. We shall look at translation rights contracts later, pp. 123–6: in this section we will look first at the equally important contract with the translator (whose skill – or lack of it – can make or break a work).

COPYRIGHT AND TRANSLATIONS

Under UK law, if you translate someone's work into another language you are making an adaptation of that work. Since adaptation is one of the restricted acts which only copyright owners can do or authorise (see chapter 9) you will need the copyright owner's permission; otherwise, you will be in danger of infringing their copyright (for this reason, a translator might need some assurance that the publisher actually has the relevant translation rights, and may seek a warranty to cover this risk – see below).

At the same time, creating a translation (even an unauthorised one) creates a new original copyright work, and as with most copyright works – apart from employee works – the copyright in that is owned by the person who created it: in this case, the translator. A publisher commissioning a translation will not own the copyright simply by virtue of having commissioned the work – if the publisher wants to own the copyright, it will have to be assigned by the translator in a written, signed document. Publishers often do seek a full assignment of copyright, particularly for reference or STM works; alternatively, they will need an exclusive licence in terms at least as wide as the translation rights deal, including any digital or online exploitation.

Whether or not the translator retains the copyright, there will need to be two separate copyright claims on the title pages: one relating to the original work, the other covering the translation.

MORAL RIGHTS

Even if copyright has been assigned, it is important to remember that the translator may still have statutory moral rights – and so, indeed, may the original author. We will look at the two key rights below: see generally, on all this, chapter 3.

The right of paternity

This right – to be credited as the author – needs to be asserted before it can be enforced under UK law, and this limitation applies to the original (foreign) author's right as much as to the English translator's (even though the foreign author may not have needed to make any assertion in his or her own country). However, it is probably advisable to err on the safe side and credit both author and translator fully: most publishers will want to do this anyway.

The right does not apply to translations created in the course of employment, where the employer owns the copyright and has authorised the acts (or, presumably, omissions) complained of.

The right of integrity

Although a bad translation can do serious harm to an author's reputation, section 80 of the 1988 Act expressly excludes translations from the definition of a 'treatment' – so, by definition, even the most appalling translation cannot be a derogatory treatment of the original work under UK law (because it is not a treatment at all).

It *is* possible, however, to subject the translation itself to derogatory treatment, by making additions, deletions, alterations or adaptations which are bad enough to amount to 'distortion or mutilation', or are otherwise prejudicial to the honour or reputation of the translator. There are as yet few decided UK cases on this, and it may be that it will prove difficult in practice to satisfy a court that a publisher's alterations in this context are sufficiently bad to amount to derogatory treatment. Translators who have assigned their copyright will also have the difficulty that anything done with the consent of the copyright owner will not infringe the right of integrity unless the translator is identified, and then not if there is a sufficient disclaimer – there are also exceptions for works written for publication in newspapers, magazines or other periodicals, or in collective works such as encyclopaedias, dictionaries or year books (for a full list of exceptions, see chapter 3).

DELIVERY AND ACCEPTANCE

One of the key undertakings a translator will be asked to make is to render a 'faithful and accurate' translation, not only in reasonably good and accurate English but also true to the style, spirit and character of the original work. This is usually accompanied by a specific undertaking to translate the whole work, and not to make any alterations, additions or omissions without the publisher's (and probably the original author's) consent.

Since the publisher is often required under the translation rights contract to submit the translation, or specimen sections of it, to the original foreign publisher for approval, there is usually a requirement to this effect in the translator's contract too. Given the difficulties of checking work in another language, the material may only be given a fairly cursory structural check, but the original author may be entitled under the contract (or under a more informal agreement resulting from the licensing correspondence) to examine the work, and it is therefore advisable to allow a reasonable period of time for approval. Needless to say, it is also advisable to provide for what happens if amendments are required, and who pays for them, and also what happens if the translation for some reason is rejected altogether – specifically, do the rights in that particular translation revert to the translator (see below), and is he or she paid a proportion of the agreed fee, or merely allowed to keep any advances? All this should be spelt out as clearly as possible.

WARRANTIES

The publisher will want a warranty that the translator will not introduce any objectionable new material, particularly nothing that is defamatory, obscene or indecent or otherwise illegal, and nothing that infringes the copyright or other rights of anyone else. In return, the translator may often seek a counter-warranty and indemnity from the publisher that the original work being translated does not itself carry any such legal risks, since these would put the translator at risk too.

Since the work is not the publisher's own, any such warranties are unlikely to go beyond those given by the original publisher of the work, and the best warranty the publisher of the translation may feel able to give is 'to the best of the publisher's knowledge and belief'.

FEES

Fees – normally at a rate per thousand words – are more common than royalties, but translators are increasingly being regarded as secondary authors and in some cases a royalty may be more appropriate. Payment of fees is usually preferred on delivery – for obvious reasons – although the publisher may wish to hold some instalments of the payment back until final approval or even publication. Some payments might be made to the translator on signature of the contract, some on delivery and acceptance, and some on publication.

TERMINATION

Normal termination provisions will usually apply – on rejection, breach, or insolvency, for example (see p. 95) – but it is important to make clear what rights, if any, will revert to the translator in these circumstances. Since the publisher is likely to have exclusive translation rights for that work in a relevant language, then as long as those rights are still in force the publisher is not going to want the translator to publish or exploit the original translation or any part of it without its consent (particularly if it was rejected and the publisher has had to go to the trouble and expense of commissioning a new one).

SUBSIDIARY RIGHTS CONTRACTS

RIGHTS DEALS

As we saw in the last chapter, it may be important for a publisher to have the right not only to produce and publish the work itself, but also to sub-license others in different areas to do so too. There may be a market for electronic or online exploitation or a Russian translation, or a film or TV version, in which case the relevant subsidiary rights will need to be licensed (see pp. 88–92). Indeed, the revenue from rights deals may well mean the difference between overall profit and loss for a publisher, and may even exceed that derived from the publisher's own publishing. Some authors and agents will prefer to retain and exploit subsidiary rights – or some of them – themselves; in other cases a publisher with an experienced rights manager will probably prefer to control such exploitation itself (in which case the publisher must make sure it *has* the rights in the first place – see p. 88). Whoever ends up doing it would be well advised first to consult Lynette Owen's indispensable guide to *Selling Rights* (fifth edition due in 2006).

In the rest of this section we will concentrate on the legal issues arising out of agreements for some of the key subsidiary rights.

PAPERBACK RIGHTS

In these days of 'vertical publishing', it is increasingly common for one publisher to undertake both hardback and paperback editions (although mass-market paperback rights may still be licensed to a separate paperback house). Not all publishers are in a position to undertake both, however, and sub-licensing paperback rights is still therefore a major business, at Frankfurt and elsewhere. In the case of authors with proven sales records, there may be a full-scale auction of the paperback rights, with considerable sums changing hands by way of advance.

Grant of rights

As with the original publisher's main grant of rights from the author (which must be checked, see p. 88), it is essential that the rights then granted by the original publisher to others – and their limitations – are clearly spelt out. The roles are of course reversed for such sub-licensing: the original publisher, having up until now been the author's (and others') licensee of the head rights, now becomes a licensor of individual subsidiary rights to others. The original publisher will usually now become 'the Grantor', and 'the Publisher' will now be the paperback publisher acquiring the rights.

The Publisher will almost certainly want exclusive rights to produce and publish the work in all paperback formats: if this is not possible, the Publisher will at least want to know which other paperback editions already exist, or are planned. Has the Grantor already published its own trade or educational paperback, or e-book, or is the work available online? Is any book club edition (paperback or otherwise) licensed, or being planned? If any competing paperbacks exist (or might), a licence for 'all paperback editions' will not be possible and it will be advisable to specify as clearly as possible exactly which paperback rights are being granted. It may be necessary to refer to markets (such as mass-market) or to specific formats (such as A or B format). In the case of book club paperbacks, the Publisher may wish to avoid possible conflict by seeking an undertaking from the Grantor that it will not license any such book club editions without the publisher's prior consent. Similar considerations may apply to low-cost editions or reprints for major export markets such as India or (increasingly) China.

Although it is unlikely that a paperback publisher would acquire translation rights, the grant of rights should also specify the language(s) covered (English-language only, or in other, or all languages) and the territories included – specific territories (such as the USA), lists of territories (such as the EU or EEA, which should be clearly set out, preferably in a Schedule) or the whole world. Any 'open' territories should also be carefully considered, bearing in mind the EU's free movement of goods within Europe (see p. 323).

Duration and timing

Paperback licences are normally granted for a limited term rather than for the full term of copyright; it is therefore essential to specify what the term is going to be. Eight years from the date of the contract is the most common period: in some cases, such as an encyclopaedia or dictionary or other non-fiction title which is likely to be revised regularly, paperback rights are granted edition by edition. There is usually provision for renewal of the licence thereafter, on terms to be agreed.

It is also advisable to agree well in advance – and as clearly as possible – what the timing of the licensed paperback edition is going to be. Since the appearance of a cheaper paperback is bound to affect sales of the hardback and other existing editions, it is normal to provide a breathing space of at least six months or a year before the paperback may be published: earliest and latest dates are often specified. There may also be external events to consider, such as film or TV tie-ins which may be a reason to allow for early release of the paperback with a tie-in cover.

Timing may be particularly crucial in the case of US paperback editions, whose larger home markets and print-runs may lead to highly competitive prices in a number of open markets around the world. Beware, in particular, of leaving Europe (specifically the EU and EEA) as an 'open' territory if you wish to retain UK exclusivity (see p. 323) and, equally, the problems of parallel importation into territories such as Australia: it may be worth the original publisher considering a simultaneous (or earlier) export edition of its own in order not to lose some open markets completely.

Finally, the timing of an English language paperback may be highly relevant to markets which are already (or may be) served by a foreign-language translation. A Dutch or Swedish translation (for example) could be killed stone dead by the untimely appearance of an English paperback in either territory, since in both places English is widely spoken and read.

Warranties

Any warranties given by the Grantor should ideally match those it has itself received from the author, although the new Publisher will usually require a warranty that the work has not previously been published in a particular format in the territory concerned. If any new or additional warranties are required the Grantor should carefully consider whether it is willing (or able) to bear the risk.

Alterations and permissions

Given that the author (probably) has a moral right of integrity, it is now even more important to keep amendments to the work itself under control; to be on the safe side, no abridgements, expansions or alterations to the work should be allowed without at least the Grantor's consent, and the author's consent (or waiver) may also be necessary in order to avoid any claim of derogatory treatment (see p. 47). Exceptions are sometimes allowed for alterations made on the advice of the paperback publisher's lawyers, on giving due notice to the Grantor (the Grantor – and its own lawyers – will then need to consider whether its own editions are at risk).

The Grantor may supply originals of artwork or prints, or other supplementary material, but it is vital to check that any original copyright permissions granted for this do actually extend to paperback publication in the territories covered: it may well be necessary to renew many (or even all) of the permissions if they do not include the re-use of the material in sub-licensed editions (for example, under different imprints).

Copyright and credits

The Grantor will want to ensure that its original copyright claim, including its name and the date of first publication, are included in all subsequent paperback editions (for UCC copyright notices, see p. 93). This is also an opportunity to ensure that the author's name appears in its customary form with due prominence, and (if appropriate) to include an assertion of the author's moral right of paternity, to be identified as the author (for the wording of assertions, see p. 45). The Grantor usually supplies duplicate production material to cover this.

Royalties and accounts

The normal considerations will apply (see chapter 4, p. 85), although royalties under paperback licences are usually paid twice a year. A percentage of this (normally 50 per cent or more), although different percentages may apply to home and export sales, will of course go to the author. It is common for a paperback publisher to wish to make some reserve against returns, and there may be a small reprint clause.

Termination and reversion

Apart from the normal termination provisions – for breach or insolvency, for example – the Grantor will want the right to terminate the licence if the Publisher allows the paperback edition to go out of print or fails to put it back on the market within, say, 9 or 12 months of formal notice to do so. Conversely, when the licence expires, or comes to an end for other reasons, the Publisher will probably want a reasonable sell-off period to clear remaining stocks.

BOOK CLUB RIGHTS

Britain, like the USA, has a vigorous, healthy book club market, the larger clubs, such as Book Club Associates (BCA), claiming well over a million members. BCA and Readers Union each contain a large number of individual clubs, and there are also many other independent clubs: some of them are general book clubs such as BCA's Literary Guild, and others specialise in particular areas, such as the Mystery and Thriller Guild (BCA) and the Gardener's Book Society (Readers Union). All of them operate primarily by mail order. Members are regularly recruited via national press advertising, often being induced to join with loss-leading 'premium' offers of the 'four books for £1' variety, with in most cases a modest annual purchasing obligation thereafter.

Although the larger clubs will demand substantial discounts, there can be significant economies of scale on both sides: not only to the club's members, in reduced prices, but also to the licensing publisher, in increased print-runs and lower unit costs.

Such a large, distinct market, dominated by one or two major players, has obvious competition law implications (see chapter 13) and indeed BCA and Leisure Circle were the subject of a Monopolies and Mergers Commission report in January 1988. The clubs have, however, by and large managed so far to remain within UK competition law by agreeing a measure of self-regulation. Prior to the demise of the Net Book Agreement, this was under the Book Club Regulations and a Concordat supervised under the auspices of the Publishers Association. When the Net Book Agreement died in 1997, the Book Club Regulations died with it, since they applied only to net books. However, the Concordat applied to all books, and still survives.

Concordat between book clubs

A Concordat signed between the leading book clubs in 1983 and updated in 1988 encourages competition 'on an equitable basis'. It was not dependent in any way on the Net Book Agreement and at the time of writing remains fully in force. It facilitates reasonable access to titles by competing clubs (particularly smaller clubs), and provides for example that:

- No club will seek exclusive rights for more than three years or for an edition of less than 3,500 copies.
- No general club will attempt to deny titles of specialist interest to smaller clubs.
- No single club will attempt to obtain exclusive rights over complete categories of titles (such as atlases, dictionaries or year books).

Licensing book club rights

Selling bound copies

Despite the considerable degree of self-regulation which surrounds book clubs in the UK, and the occasional attentions of the Office of Fair Trading, the larger clubs still undoubtedly occupy a pre-eminent position and can command discounts from licensing publishers of well over 60 per cent – often as high as 75 per cent or even over 80 per cent. However, publishers are not always negotiating at a disadvantage. The following licensing points should be borne in mind:

(1) It is advisable for publishers to deal only with recognised clubs, or those subscribing to the Concordat.
(2) If the club is to have an exclusive licence, it must order at least 3,500 copies.
(3) No exclusive licence may last for longer than three years (although an initial exclusive licence may be extendable by a further non-exclusive licence).
(4) Timing may very well be crucial: in which case time should be clearly stated to be of the essence. Publishers will normally be required to specify their own publication date. Any penalties for late delivery should be spelt out, and it should also be made clear at what point – if at all – the club has the right to cancel the order altogether.

(5) The normal warranties and indemnities will apply (no copyright infringement, or defamation, for example) and the publisher must therefore make sure it has the necessary book club rights itself and has re-cleared any permissions which do not already cover book club editions.
(6) The licence should normally provide for termination if the club exhausts its stock within the licence period and does not re-order.

BCA now operate on the basis of one master contract with each supplying publisher, supplemented with individual purchase orders. The other clubs operate on purchase orders only.

SAME LANGUAGE RIGHTS: CO-EDITIONS AND JOINT VENTURES

As we have seen, even in the English language, there may be forms and media of exploitation which publishers, authors or agents cannot develop alone; there may also be key English-language markets (such as the USA) where the market may require local promotion and distribution and may best be serviced by a local publisher with daily hands-on contact and goodwill. In many such cases, a straightforward licensing deal may be sufficient, but in others a more collaborative co-edition agreement may be preferred. For newer or more complex products, a formal division of functions, responsibilities and profits (or losses) may be necessary, usually best set out in a co-publication or joint venture agreement.

Co-editions

Unlike a standard licence, where the proprietor simply grants a publisher a licence to print its own local edition in return (usually) for a royalty on sales, a co-edition normally features a combined printing operation in which the local publisher will buy copies (or sheets) in its own imprint at an agreed price per copy. This requires more of an upfront payment from the local publisher, but can give a realistic price and provides economies of scale to the proprietor, who can print more copies and thereby reduce the unit cost. It also gives the proprietor more control over the production process which is often an important factor, for example for illustrated or children's books using four-colour printing.

Whoever's standard terms are used – a US co-publisher will often propose its own version – the following points should be covered.

Rights granted and territories

Local publishers will normally want exclusive rights in their home territory, but that territory will usually need careful definition, as will any 'open markets' in which either publisher's edition may sell, particularly Europe. The European Union's rules on free movement of goods (see p. 323) mean that an open market edition lawfully on sale in any EU or EEA member state cannot be prevented from entering the UK, despite licensing terms to the contrary – so that making the UK an 'exclusive' territory may in effect be unenforceable if, say, Belgium or Germany are open. Of particular importance today is whether the proprietor or local publisher is to make the work available via the Internet, and if so how – either downloadable as an e-book, or accessible in some other form – and when. The parties should be very clear about this, since any such exploitation may have a dramatic effect on sales expectations.

The other forms and media in which territorial rights may be exploited also need careful definition: are only volume rights granted, or may the local publisher sell electronic versions in that territory, or exploit subsidiary rights such as film, TV, paperback, serial and book club rights? Can the rights be sub-licensed or assigned? (Not normally without consent, but if so this must be stated.) It is advisable for the proprietor to reserve all rights not expressly granted.

Term of licence

A US co-publisher may expect to be granted a licence for the full duration of copyright. However, this may sometimes be resisted if inappropriate (or impossible, if the UK publisher only has a limited term of rights from the author), in which case a five- or seven-year licence is more usual, or perhaps a restriction to the number of copies supplied, with termination to take place when copies are exhausted. For major educational and academic works, it is often preferable to limit licences to the life of a single edition. It is customary to provide for the term to be extended, if required, by mutual agreement, together with an option to take further copies of a reprint or new edition.

Delivery and timing

If time is of the essence, say so – equally, specify any mutually agreed publication dates. The proprietor will be expected to undertake shipment of the publisher's copies by a certain date – often in agreed stages – but this may need to be conditional upon the publisher's timely supply of film or electronic files for any permitted local amendments: both sets of dates should be clearly set out. Final delivery details will also need to be specified: which shipping agent, who will supply documentation, whether advance copies by air are required, and time limits for any complaints.

The price

Payment should be in an agreed currency, if necessary at an agreed exchange rate, (perhaps providing for a five per cent or other fluctuation either way, any excess to be borne equally). The price is often held for a limited period only. Payment is often staged, for example with one-third payable on signature, one-third on delivery, and one-third 30 or 60 days later. Is there an advance? Is the price royalty-inclusive or royalty-exclusive? Does it include freight and insurance, and are the terms ex works, CIF or FOB, or delivered to the licensee's warehouse? (See Glossary in appendix A.)

Even though the price may be a royalty-inclusive price per copy, it may still make sense to specify annual sales statements and accounting and the usual provisions for audit, if only to monitor any subsidiary rights exploitation and be forewarned of any need to re-order or reprint.

Local alterations

Where the proprietor is producing copies, the publisher will usually be required to provide film or electronic files of any permitted amendments or alterations (in good time within the schedule). Consider carefully any substantial amendments proposed, and bear in mind the author's moral right of integrity (see p. 47), and the similar rights of illustrators and other contributors: ideally, no amendments should be permitted without consent.

Permissions

It is crucial to check that any copyright permissions apply to *all* the territories and media to be exploited: some may need to be re-cleared if the original clearance was restricted to publication in the original language, for a limited market, and/or under the original publisher's imprint. For a major reference or illustrated work permissions can be very expensive indeed, so it is best to agree as early as possible who will undertake the task of securing necessary permissions, and also who will pay, or how costs will be shared.

Copyright notice and credits

The proprietor will need to ensure that its own copyright credit appears (see p. 93), and any assertion of the author's right of paternity. It is also advisable to require the publisher to take all necessary and reasonable steps to protect the copyrights (and any trade marks) locally, including local registration where required.

Warranties and indemnities

Make sure that any warranties match those already given by the author, or (if not) that it is safe or reasonable for the proprietor to give them. Often this may be a matter for the insurers on either side – it may not be possible for a UK publisher, for example, to warrant with any certainty that nothing in a book will infringe US law (although a warranty about UK law may be perfectly reasonable). It is normal to limit warranties to the licensor's own national law.

Termination

As with all licences, any co-edition agreement should provide clearly for termination under specified conditions: normally breach, insolvency or change of control, or allowing the work to go out of print (with no reprint order in hand with the proprietor). It may be advisable to provide for arbitration in the event of any dispute – particularly if the applicable law is not English law.

Joint ventures

For more ambitious or elaborate projects (such as a large series of illustrated books or a major multimedia product), one publisher may not have all the skills – or finance – necessary. It may make sense in such circumstances to enter into a formal joint venture agreement with another publisher or with a film or TV company or software house – there may often be several parties involved. Joint venture agreements may be entered into at the outset, with all participants sitting down well in advance to plan the contributions – and profit shares – each will make, or sometimes relatively late in a project's development, for example to bring in extra finance, or distribution skills. As a general rule however, the earlier such agreements can be reached the better.

There are a number of key points to watch.

Define the product

It may be a single book such as an encyclopaedia or CD-ROM, or a series or online database or a multimedia product involving several partners: however many partners are involved, agree as soon as possible on your mutual aims, on the form and the scope of the enterprise, and define any product(s) as clearly as you can, including delivery media. A detailed specification for the product attached as a schedule might be advisable. Include any agreed details such as a General Editor or particular contributors, or intended price or format.

Decide who does what

Agree what each of you brings to the party – be it text, illustrations, other copyright material, software, or simply finance, and how the various publishing functions will be split up – how any research will be tackled, who will undertake design and production, who will be responsible for clearing permissions and underlying rights, who will do the promotion, marketing and distribution, and who will account for the proceeds, and distribute any profits (or losses).

Timing

If there are specific launch targets, write them in. Agree in particular when the joint venture agreement starts to run, and if it has a fixed term, when it will terminate.

Budget

Budget – and re-budget – carefully, bearing in mind that for a new project in an unfamiliar medium cashflow may be crucial. Agree on allowable costs – what each party may claim back from the project before any profits are shared out. Include any administrative overheads if necessary (such as subsidiary rights management), and distribution costs such as freight and insurance. Needless to say, agree clearly how any profits will be shared out and what will happen in the event of losses.

Ownership of rights

Assuming all necessary permissions have been granted and underlying rights secured, it is important to specify clearly who owns which copyrights and also how any new copyrights which are created – for example in a new compilation or database – are owned: it may be necessary for a joint venture company to acquire the rights. Do not forget other key rights, such as trade marks in any names or logos: will these be registered, and who will be the proprietor and licensed users?

Termination

Don't forget to provide a get-out route if it all goes horribly wrong, and allow for individual opt outs if necessary. Agree initial terms, grounds for early termination and suitable notice periods, with arbitration provisions if necessary. Most importantly, agree who will own which rights post-termination in the joint venture product itself, including work in progress, roughs and artwork. Agree the applicable law which will govern any disputes which cannot be settled by arbitration and which country's courts will have jurisdiction (see p. 97).

TRANSLATION RIGHTS

Not all works have the potential to sell in translation, but many UK works do – non-fiction as well as fiction. For most UK publishers and agents, selling translation rights can therefore be a major source of revenue, and a significant way of extending the market for an author's work. It can also be an effective way of combating unauthorised translations (including those given compulsory licences under some local copyright laws) and piracy of the English edition, in the territory concerned.

Not surprisingly, most publishers and agents who regularly sell translation rights will have one or more standard-form contracts, either for a straightforward sale of rights, or for a co-edition deal. We will deal here with sales of translation rights: co-edition deals are dealt with later on pp. 119–23.

Rights granted

Before translation rights are granted to others, it is highly advisable to check that the person who wants to grant them – usually the publisher, or the agent on the author's behalf – owns or controls them in the first place. You cannot legally give what you do not have. Publishers in particular often assume that they control foreign language translation rights when in fact their publishing licence from the author covers English-language volume rights only. If this happens, any accidental omissions can usually be remedied by a quick phone call to the author or agent and a simple exchange of letters, but this is not always possible. The author or agent may well have plans of their own, and indeed may already have sold the relevant rights to someone else. If in doubt, check.

Once the rights are secured, they will normally be sub-licensed to individual foreign publishers for separate languages and territories. Most local publishers will want exclusive rights in their territory; this is usually acceptable, provided that (within Europe) it does not fall foul of EU competition law (see chapter 13), and provided that the territory, formats covered and the length of time the licence lasts are clearly defined. Does a Portuguese translation licence cover the whole world (so that it may therefore sell in Brazil, and former colonies like Macau), or just Portugal itself? Does it cover hardbacks only, or paperback and book club editions, and even perhaps other forms of exploitation in that language such as digital access or online use. Most importantly, how long does the licence last? Five to eight years from signature is fairly common, depending on the work and the local publisher's plans; licences are normally renewable thereafter. In the case of major reference works and non-fiction works which are likely to be revised, a grant of rights may extend to one edition only, rather than a fixed term of years. All rights not expressly granted should be reserved to the Proprietor.

Publisher's responsibility to publish

Once the rights are granted, the Proprietor will want to ensure that an accurate translation appears reasonably promptly. The local publisher is normally required to undertake that it will commission a faithful and accurate translation by a competent translator (from the original language, based on the latest edition, and with no unauthorised alterations, omissions or additions – see above, p. 113) and will publish it at its own risk and expense within a specified number of months. If publication does not take place within the given time-scale, the licence will normally terminate and the rights revert, so it is advisable to allow reasonable time for the translation itself (especially if approval is required) as well as local production. The Proprietor will normally wish to be informed of the actual publication date. To assist with production (and accuracy) the Proprietor may supply duplicate film or electronic files, or otherwise may wish to see samples of any illustrations to be reproduced directly from the original edition in order to assess their quality.

Warranties

The local publisher will normally seek the standard English law warranties from the Proprietor: that the work is not, for example, an infringement of someone else's copyright and has not previously been published in that territory before – any warranties outside the Proprietor's own control should ideally match, and not exceed, those originally given by the author (see chapter 4, p. 79). The publisher may want the right (on notifying the Proprietor) to remove passages which on local legal advice may be actionable in the territory concerned.

Permissions and illustrations

Copyright permissions for extracts and illustrations may need to be re-sought for foreign language editions; it is important to agree who is going to undertake this (and who will pay any new fees). For a major work, it may be a complex and time-consuming task, and the Proprietor may prefer to arrange it and charge the publisher the cost plus an administration fee. If the local publisher is going to do it, it may be advisable for the Proprietor to ask for written proof that it has been done.

Illustrations may present unique problems for foreign translations of children's books: pictures that are perfect for one country may not be acceptable in another (for example, on grounds of racial mix, or on moral, social or religious grounds). Some pictures may need to be omitted or replaced; in some cases, a complete set of fresh illustrations better adapted to the local market may need to be commissioned by the local publisher, in which case they will need to be costed in.

Copyright notice

As the making of a translation creates a new copyright work (see above, p. 111) there will normally be two separate copyright lines – one for the original author, or whoever now owns copyright in the original work, and one for the translator, or whoever owns copyright in the translation. The Proprietor will also probably require details to be included of the Proprietor's original edition, so that it is clear the translation is an authorised arrangement.

In some territories, there may be local registration or other legal formalities before copyrights can be protected; the local publisher should be obliged to make the necessary arrangements, and also undertake to comply with any local copyright regulations.

Advance and royalties

Sometimes a lump sum fee is agreed for a limited print-run, but royalties are probably more common. It is important to be clear what price is to be used as the basis for calculation – local selling price, retail or recommended retail price (minus any VAT) or average wholesale price (used in most central and East European countries). An advance is normally required, with part at least of the payment due immediately on signature of the agreement; there is often a provision that if the agreement is not signed, and the first tranche of the advance paid, within a given period (such as 60 days of the contract date), the licence will terminate and the rights revert to the Proprietor.

The usual detailed accounting information should be required (see above, p. 92), and it is also wise to agree the currency in which royalties are to be paid; not all local currencies are fully convertible, and payments in blocked currencies which cannot be sent outside the country concerned are of limited use to foreign rights owners (although they may be better than nothing).

Publishers in most countries without fully convertible currencies now find it easier to hold hard currency accounts or to purchase hard currency in order to make licence payments.

Updates/new editions

The publisher will normally want an option on any new or revised editions, on the understanding that all changes notified will be incorporated. The licensor would normally require a new contract to cover any new edition.

Termination and reversion of rights

The normal provisions for termination of the licence will apply, for example for insolvency or breach (see above, p. 95), but special attention may need to be paid to the terms on which rights may revert if a translation goes out of print. Does 'out of print' mean only in the local publisher's home territory, or in all territories (so that a Spanish edition, say, might still be 'in print' if it is available in South America)? Consider also what the position will be if the bound stock is exhausted but the publisher wishes to keep the translation available via print-on-demand. There may also be a need for a provision that the licence will terminate and rights will revert if sales of the translation fall below a certain minimum level in any single accounting period (or perhaps any two periods in succession).

MERCHANDISING RIGHTS

Some publications – particularly children's books – may contain names, characters, designs or illustrations which are popular enough in their own right to be exploited not only via the medium of books but also on T-shirts, stationery, mugs and other merchandise (hence the label 'merchandising rights'). Film and TV exposure usually helps. The characters of Beatrix Potter were early examples of successful merchandising, widely licensed now for a range of merchandise such as children's crockery and other nursery goods; other examples are A.A. Milne's Winnie the Pooh, Harry Potter and Batman. If handled properly, such exploitation, across a wide range of goods, can add very considerably to the earning potential of the original work (and in some cases exceed it).

Where a work has merchandising potential, the author or agent may grant the merchandising rights to the publisher, together with other publishing rights, or they may retain them for separate exploitation. They may be a key element, for example, of film or TV deals. Exploitation may be bit by bit, product by product, in which case the publisher or agent may end up dealing with multiple licences for a whole range of goods; alternatively (and increasingly nowadays), the rights might be licensed in one go to a specialist merchandising company which, in return for a commission on revenue, will then take on the task of seeking out, and sub-licensing, suitable manufacturers and products. Whoever handles the rights, there are a number of key points to bear in mind, two of the most important of which are:

- protection of rights;
- quality control.

Grant of rights

You can't grant merchandising rights if you don't own them or control them yourself. So the first and most essential thing to do is check the contract. If you are a publisher, check your author contract to see that it contains a specific grant of rights, or a clearly inclusive grant of rights such as 'all subsidiary rights' or 'any other rights'. If an author or agent, make sure that merchandising rights have not already been granted elsewhere. And if you want to use original illustrations as well as names of characters, make sure that the illustrator, or other rights owner, has granted you merchandising rights in them too (otherwise – if agreement cannot be reached – you may need to recommission new illustrations).

Assuming – subject to all the above – that you do have the relevant rights, you will need to consider the terms on which you are going to sub-license them (or some of them) to others.

In particular:

- Will the rights granted be exclusive or non-exclusive? (This may depend on your view of the market, and the status of the particular licensee.)
- Will the licence cover the world, or a specific territory or territories? (Merchandising rights are often licensed country by country.) Will it cover Internet or other electronic exploitation?
- How long will the licence last? (Three- or five-year terms are common, usually renewable, and often with a sell-off period at the end.)

Product specifications and approval

Unless an overall licence is being granted, the products on which the names or images may be exploited by that licensee must be clearly specified and described in as much detail as possible (for example, T-shirts or different sizes of greetings card or items of breakfast crockery). They are usually set out in an appendix. Any products that the licensor wishes to exploit itself (such as videos, or electronic publishing and games) should be expressly reserved.

The licensee should have a clear obligation to seek out (actively) potential sub-licensees and, in some cases, distributors and propose the most suitable ones for particular products to the licensor; once selected, the licensee should be responsible for their regular supervision and control. All sub-licences should be in a form approved by the licensor, and should not exceed the term of the original licence. If there is not already an agreed plan, it is advisable in the interests of quality control to set out a regular procedure for submission and approval of product proposals, within set timetables. It should be clear that the products selected should in no way reflect adversely on the image, reputation or goodwill of the licensor, and the licensor should at all times retain a right of rejection or veto. This quality control should not only apply to initial prototypes or mock-ups and packaging, but also continue after the products have been launched, with regular samples submitted for approval, either at random or on demand. The licensor needs to be satisfied at all times that the products are suitable in themselves, and manufactured to a high enough standard. They must also be safe; the licensee must take legal responsibility for any product liability, for example for defective goods, or for breach of any safety standards (and insure where necessary). Needless to say, once approved, there should be no changes without consent.

Promotion and marketing

The licence will normally specify merchandise to be on the market within a given timetable. There is often a launch deadline, within a given number of months or by a particular deadline (for example to tie in with a film or TV series). Thereafter, the licensee should undertake to continue advertising, marketing and distributing the licensed products within the agreed territory. All packaging and promotional material should conform to samples – the licensor may also wish to specify the choice of media used. It is customary for the licensee to undertake to sell only to reputable wholesalers or retail outlets, and the licensor may exclude certain kinds of sales (for example premium sales, or door to door) and retain the right to order the suspension of sales to any particular outlet of which it disapproves.

There will usually be agreed sales targets: quarterly targets are common. If targets are not met (sometimes two or more in succession) the licence will normally terminate, and the rights revert to the licensor.

Copyright and trade marks

The names, characters or illustrations being merchandised will probably be copyright works and quite possibly registered trade marks too (for more on trade marks, see chapter 10). It is essential in any merchandising licence that all these copyrights and trade marks should be expressly acknowledged and recognised by the licensee and on the products themselves. A copyright claim in agreed form, with the name of the copyright owner (see p. 93) should normally appear on all relevant products and packaging, and a trade mark notice, in the UK usually ® or ™, next to all words, phrases or logos which are registered trade marks. If the merchandising licence is for an overseas territory, it may be necessary to make the licensee responsible for registering any copyrights or trade marks locally – this should be done in the licensor's name, not the licensee's. The licensee may, however, need to be recorded as a licensee at the Trade Marks Registry and the parties may need to supply details of the licensing agreement.

In addition, of course, it is very likely that the product itself will constitute a new copyright work, in which case it will be desirable in order to avoid any conflict for the new copyright to be acquired from the manufacturer or designer and assigned back to the licensor; it will normally be the licensee's responsibility to see that this is done.

Infringements and insurance

It is customary to require the licensee to exercise vigilance on the licensor's or proprietor's behalf against any unauthorised copying or use, and notify them of any infringements at once so that any necessary legal action may be taken. The licensor will normally indemnify the licensee against any legal risks and costs arising from permitted use, provided any claims are notified at once, and the licensee will normally give a corresponding indemnity to the licensor for any activities outside the terms of the agreement. The licensee is normally well advised to arrange general liability insurance of its own, although mutual insurance, to spread the risk, is sometimes agreed.

Moral rights

Bear in mind that an illustrator might not only own copyright in original illustrations but also now have personal moral rights in them, particularly a right of paternity – to be credited as the illustrator and a right of integrity – to object to derogatory treatment (see chapter 3). If the illustrator agrees, these rights may be waived, either unconditionally or insofar as necessary to exploit the particular merchandising rights concerned.

Royalties and commissions

There may be an initial one-off fee for permission to test the market over, say, a one-year trial. Thereafter fees or royalties entirely depend on the popularity and marketability of the character, design or name being licensed: the range is normally between 5 per cent and 15 per cent of the invoice price, but higher commissions – up to 45 per cent – are not unknown for major licensees with a proven track record. Any percentage commission should cease with the end of the licence agreement.

Quarterly sales figures and accounts are usual – the normal requirements to keep accurate accounts, and to allow inspection for errors, should apply. Payments should be made for all sales in the period, irrespective of whether the licensee has yet been paid.

Non-assignment and Key Men

A merchandising licence is normally non-transferable and non-assignable without the licensor's prior consent in writing. There is also often a stipulation (called a 'Key

Man' clause) that the licence will end, and the rights revert, if any key individual within the licensee's organisation departs, or at least giving the licensor the option to terminate if this happens.

Termination

Termination is usually on the normal terms, for example, for breach or insolvency; merchandising licences may also terminate if a Key Man leaves the licensee, or there is any other unacceptable change in the control or management of the licensee.

On termination, the licensee should arrange the termination of any sub-licences, with due notice, and arrange for any samples, artwork or other materials to be returned and any unsold stock to be delivered up (usually at cost) or certified as destroyed. Manufacturing equipment, such as moulds, may need to be destroyed. Needless to say, any outstanding payments should be paid forthwith.

FILM AND TV RIGHTS

Making a feature film or TV series is an immensely complex – and expensive – business, and negotiating rights with film and TV companies is not a recommended pastime for the faint hearted. For the right literary 'property', however, it can be a highly lucrative form of exploitation, not only in fees and royalties from the film itself but also in increased exposure and sales of the book. Sometimes film rights are optioned before the property is published, as happened in the case of the first Harry Potter book and the film adaptation of John le Carre's *The Constant Gardener*. In other cases the film might appear many years after publication of the book, the most obvious recent example being *The Lord of the Rings* trilogy directed by Peter Jackson, which appeared more than 40 years after the publications of J.R.R. Tolkien's novels, although the author had sold the film rights before his death in 1973 and an animated film had appeared in 1978. Film and TV rights often therefore need long-term management and, since the media involved are so different, control of them is often retained by the author's agent rather than granted to the publisher of the book.

Underlying rights

A film or TV producer or production company wishing to make a film based on a book which is still in copyright will need to clear the 'underlying' literary rights at the outset (and, equally, any artistic, musical, dramatic and other rights which may be involved). Initially, as a rule, clearing the rights does not involve actually acquiring them outright; at this stage the film is still an idea only and may never be made, so they may never be needed. What happens first almost invariably is that the producer will seek to secure an option.

Options

The advantage of an option, rather than an outright purchase of rights, is that it enables the film producer to reserve the underlying rights for a (comparatively) modest upfront fee whilst spending anything up to two years preparing a script, finding investors, putting together the necessary film finance, and finding a director, leading actors and suitable locations. It also limits the copyright owner's risk, by avoiding a full grant of rights until it is certain that the film will actually be made and that the producer is able to pay for the rights.

Unless the subject is very topical, options are normally granted initially for a year or 18 months, for a non-returnable fee which is usually not more than 10 per cent of the total intended purchase price (for low-budget films, it may be lower). The option is usually extendable for one or two further 6- or 12-month periods, in case developing a satisfactory script and putting together the finance proves harder than expected (it often does). During the option period, the producer will need the right to make certain uses of the literary work concerned; specifically, to copy extracts and make an adaptation in the form of a screenplay to show potential investors, or even to make a pilot if TV rights are being acquired.

The exact rights (and media) over which the option is granted should be set out clearly: the usual way of doing this is to cross-refer to the intended final Acquisition document (see below) and attach it as an appendix to the option.

If the project falls through, and the option is not exercised within the option period, the rights owner should ideally have the right to buy back any new copyrights created in (for example) the screenplay or any other adaptations of the work – although a producer who does not own the underlying rights, and whose option has expired, will not be able to do much with scripts or other material without infringing existing rights.

Acquisition and assignment

If and when the option is exercised, the Acquisition agreement may then be signed, under which the balance of the purchase price is paid, and in which the necessary film rights are finally granted. This may be via an assignment of the copyright, but now often takes the form of a sole and exclusive licence of (specified) film rights, usually for the full term of copyright, although the period of exclusivity may be limited to 10 or 15 years, for example for made-for-TV films. 'Quitclaims' are often required at the same time, under which the relevant (usually English-language) publishers confirm that they have no conflicting interest in the film rights.

It is essential to set out clearly what rights are included (and which are not), and particularly whether TV rights are included. The definition of 'film' in the 1988 Act would normally include TV programmes, so it is important to be clear about this: if it is not the intention to grant TV rights, a narrower definition of films should be used, such as 'theatrical feature films'. Most producers will want both the film and TV rights, for obvious reasons – a TV channel will, not surprisingly, usually seek to acquire unlimited film and TV rights, but even if the film is being made primarily for theatrical (that is, cinema) exploitation, the producer will still usually wish to show it on television. If, despite this, TV rights are not available the producer may require a 'hold back' clause, restricting the proprietor's own exploitation of TV rights for an agreed number of years.

The rights granted will normally include most or all of the following:

- the right to make one or more films (including TV) plus re-makes, prequels, and sequels;
- the right to show the work in public;
- the right to broadcast the work (including excerpts or trailers, and including TV satellite and cable);
- the right to make adaptations of the work (such as dramatisations and screenplays);
- the right to issue copies to the public (including video rental);
- the right to distribute the work online;
- 'publicity rights': to create written synopses (usually of up to 5,000 or 10,000 words), and broadcast and publish extracts;
- the right to compose music to accompany the work, and the right to make sound recordings;
- the right to use the author's name, likeness and biographical details for promotional purposes;
- the right to publish a 'book of the film' (often withheld by the rights owner);
- associated merchandising rights.

If the film is not made within a specified number of years (for example, five) the Acquisition agreement should provide that the rights revert to the owner, perhaps upon payment of an agreed sum. This is often calculated by reference to the sum originally paid by the producer and also possibly the further amounts the producer has spent in developing the project. During that period it is advisable for the rights owner to specify that the film rights should not be assigned without its consent, at least not without a full novation (see p. 72).

There will normally be warranties and indemnities on both sides: the producer will want the usual warranties covering the original work (see p. 79), and the owner will often seek a specific indemnity covering any liability arising out of changes made in the film.

Producers and production companies will normally insist on a full waiver of the author's moral rights – at least insofar as they relate to film exploitation form. The right of paternity is not likely to be infringed, since specific on-screen credits are usually agreed in the Acquisition agreement, but the author's right of integrity (to object to derogatory treatment) may become an issue unless the author is willing to consent generally to 'treatments', as defined in the 1988 Act, being made: 'any addition to, deletion from or alteration to or adaptation of the work' would include most changes a film director would need to make.

Payment of fees or royalties depends on the status of the author, and the nature of the adaptation. Usually, the purchase price will be a fixed sum, possibly with a further sum on top calculated by reference to a percentage of the film's budget, up to a cap. Most rights owners will also be entitled to a share of the 'net profits'. It is, however, essential to define 'profits' clearly – after deducting the cost of production, financing, distribution and deferments, there may not be very much 'profit' left at all. On top of this, there should be repeat fees, and additional revenue from any re-makes, prequels and sequels. Payments in respect of TV exploitation are normally triggered by the first broadcast or transmission.

DVD distribution may generate significant revenue in due course, which may entitle the rights owner to additional specific payments or simply contribute to 'profits'. Bear in mind that under the Copyright and Related Rights Regulations 1996, implementing the EU Directive on rental and lending rights, authors and screenwriters who have transferred their rental rights in films to the relevant producers have an unwaivable right to 'equitable remuneration' from any such rental exploitation.

ELECTRONIC RIGHTS

In 1996, when the first edition of this book appeared, the Internet was a relatively specialised, academic network, only just beginning to open up for business and general social use. Some thought that its primary relevance to publishing then lay in the extent to which researchers and e-enthusiasts might buy books about computers. Today, publishing is part of an Internet world in which information published in electronic form can be accessed worldwide more or less instantaneously by anyone with a PC and a server. This opens up new opportunities for exploitation and licensing of data (and sound and visual images), but as we now begin to see it also poses threats. Subscriber-based online databases such as the legal database LEXIS can monitor and control the copyright data which licensed subscribers receive, and the use they make of it, but the Internet has few such controls (yet). Between these two extremes, Internet service providers offer more or less 'closed' systems or networks such as AOL and CompuServe – these may offer subscribers Internet access as part of the package, but they also offer a variety of other services, some free and some chargeable. By far the most frequently visited websites offer hardcore pornography. Not surprisingly, there have been a number of high-profile cases of copyright infringement on the net, notably the 'peer-to-peer' swapping and downloading of unauthorised music files uncovered in the *Napster* and *Grokster* litigation, together with libel and (depressingly) incitement to racial hatred. Some method of international control for the net is still required, but national courts have increasingly intervened to prevent infringing or illegal acts affecting their citizens or territory. Digital Rights Management (DRM) systems are also increasingly providing rightsowners with a means of monitoring and controlling use of their words even on the net. DRM is of course much more than just encryption – it enables rightsowners to identify their intellectual property via metadata identifiers such as DOI, the Digital Object Identifier, increasingly being developed for the publishing world (a similar system is in operation for musical works) and giving the opportunity to describe the rights on offer, fees and access conditions for potential users in a reliable licensing environment. It can also track usage and collect appropriate revenues.

Publishers are increasingly licensing their works directly online, often to groups of authorised users via site licences (e.g. for academic institutions, or library consortia). This raises specific access and security issues (see the following section on Online access licences, p. 138). However, for e-book sales, where the complete verbatim text of a work can be downloaded by an individual purchaser via a website to a PC or handheld device, or for online journal access, the publisher may be in a position to exploit the rights directly, perhaps buying in conversion, storage and distribution services off the peg, or may prefer to sub-license the rights altogether.

Whatever the nature of the electronic use, or platform, it is important to separate the publisher's own exploitation of the work from exploitation which may be sub-licensed to others. The former is increasingly being regarded as an aspect of volume rights which the publisher will normally expect to control. The latter is normally dealt with under subsidiary rights, which may be granted to the publisher for sub-licensing, or may be retained by the author or agent, depending on who is best placed to exploit them. This means that no easy assumptions can be made about who owns electronic rights. In fact, as the *Tasini* litigation in the USA has reminded us (see chapter 4, p. 76) it is, arguably, safer for publishers to assume that they *don't* have electronic rights, unless they have a very clear, documented, grant of the exact rights they wish to exploit.

Acquiring electronic rights

As explained above, in order to license electronic rights (however that phrase may be defined) you first need to own them, or acquire them. From the publisher's point of view, this means acquiring a specific grant of the necessary rights from the copyright owner, usually the author. However, most publishing contracts more than 20 or so years old make no mention of electronic rights, and even more recent agreements may be somewhat vague on the two key issues of:

- what rights exactly are granted; and
- what will be paid for them.

(Often the second of these is left 'to be agreed', although arguably this reduces the 'grant' to a mere option.)

The golden rule is: *never assume*. A publishing contract decades old, which granted 'all rights', or 'publishing rights' (even 'including all subsidiary rights') at a time when the relevant type of digital exploitation could not possibly have been in the minds of the parties, cannot safely be assumed to grant those specific digital exploitation rights now. A more recent phrase such as 'electronic rights' might be sufficient to cover straightforward exploitation of the verbatim text in digital form, via CD-ROM or e-books, but it might not be specific enough to license more general Internet use or access. With the current rapid development of technology, it cannot be stressed strongly enough that a specific platform for electronic exploitation must be supported by an equally specific grant of rights – especially if (as is often the case) substantial investment is proposed. If it isn't clearly provided for in the contract already, it is highly advisable to secure an additional, specific, grant of rights from the rights owner(s). (There may be more than one – in the case of a children's book, for example, a fresh grant of rights may well be required from the illustrator as well as the author. A simple exchange of letters will normally suffice.)

The initial grant of rights: author–publisher licensing

In the early days of electronic licensing, publishers were often advised to 'acquire broadly, and license narrowly': this seemed to make sense from their point of view, but has increasingly been resisted by authors and agents. Some publishers (especially reference and periodical publishers) may be in a sufficiently strong bargaining position with their authors and contributors to be able to insist on a full buy-out of electronic rights, but in other cases the author will want some evidence that the publisher actually intends to *exploit* those rights, and has the skill and capacity to do so. If all the publisher is doing is acquiring rights pre-emptively, just in case they may be needed later on, authors – particularly those with agents – may feel it unwise to do more than grant a first option, reserving the rights generally until a firm proposal can be made which refers to a defined platform and product, and offers specific payment terms. A publisher who controls all other publishing rights in a work, however, will at least want some reassurance by way of undertaking that the author or agent is not going to exploit the work electronically elsewhere without prior consultation.

If electronic rights are granted, it is advisable to specify as far as possible what rights exactly this rather vague phrase includes. There will be particular types of exploitation which the publisher may wish to see expressly included, or which an author equally may wish to withhold. In this context it is important to distinguish and deal separately with the 'products' which can be based on, include or be derived from the text being licensed, and the 'distribution media' for those products. For example:

Product categories:

- original text in digital form including e-books and journals available online;
- online versions or editions of major works, e.g. OED and the Grove music dictionaries;
- information databases and multimedia products, which include the text;
- entertainment/leisure software (such as video games and DVD) derived from the text or its characters;
- recordings of performances/readings of the text; film based on text.

Distribution media:

- Internet and online access;
- CD-ROM for home or office use;
- broadcast (including digital broadcast)/public performance/cable transmission;

- open/closed network distribution rights including site licensing;
- pay-per-view and payment for use.

These distribution media options may vary in relation to each of the various product categories being licensed. Also, of course, the appropriate royalty structure and percentages may vary.

The key to maximising commercial potential is to divide rights by reference to actual market sectors. It is essential to avoid giving away rights to an operator in one sector which may limit the exploitation and marketing of the text in another sector. Otherwise, these rights may remain unexploited and commercial opportunities may be missed. Equally, when defining the scope of 'distribution media', many problems can be avoided by tying the licence and any exclusivity down to the 'distribution media' and particular product categories or even only the licensed product itself. Again, this means driving licensing practices by reference to market sectors and not the technology that delivers to them.

The following points should generally be borne in mind:

- Is the licence exclusive or non-exclusive?
- Are the rights limited to electronic use of the (unaltered) verbatim text (arguably, simple storage and retrieval should be part of volume rights anyway)? Does this include e-book and online delivery?
- May the work only be used complete, or may it be condensed or abridged, manipulated or altered?
- May it be used in a compilation with other works? Does this include an interactive/ multimedia version?
- Is the licence limited to delivery platforms currently in existence or is the intention to include 'any other devices hereafter invented'?
- Is the licence for all languages (human and machine) and all territories? (Bear in mind that territorial limits may be of limited effect with Internet use.)
- What payment methods are available (fees, payments per use, subscriptions, royalties based on net receipts, or dealer price?) and what proportion will the author/contributor get?
- Does the licence last for the full term of copyright, or only for a limited term of years?
- Do (or should) the rights revert to the author if they are not being exploited (or if a product is launched, but then allowed to go 'out of promotion')?

Major publishers planning (or investing in) ambitious online or multimedia works may prefer to commission authors, illustrators and other contributors specifically for those projects, and take full assignments of copyright from them in their work – or at least sole and exclusive licences for all such exploitation for the full term of copyright. In other cases, where a full buy-out does not seem appropriate, authors and agents may prefer to grant electronic rights for limited periods at a time (perhaps for as little as five years) with provision for the rights to revert if the publisher or other licensee concerned has not exploited them within a given period. Following the EU Rental and Lending Directive, it will also be important to deal with authors' rights to 'equitable remuneration' on the rental of films based on their work.

The author's moral rights – particularly of paternity and integrity (see pp. 44 and 47) should also not be forgotten, where they apply (for exceptions, see pp. 46 and 49). Unless moral rights are going to be completely waived, it will be necessary to make sure that authors who have asserted their paternity rights are credited adequately, and also that the works are not subjected to derogatory treatment, and – ideally – are not subjected to any significant 'treatment' at all, without the author's consent. As with film and book club rights it is possible with rights in electronic media for authors to waive moral rights conditionally – in other words only insofar as necessary in order to exploit the text in accordance with the licence.

Electronic licensing and joint ventures

Owners or licensees of electronic rights – such as publishers – may seek to exploit those rights in a number of different ways. Some will have the experience and resources to develop electronic products themselves in-house – but this may be difficult initially for a traditional publisher. Some will acquire electronic publishing expertise by bolt-ons or buy-ins of existing teams from outside, but again this can be expensive. Most will rely on straightforward licensing or sub-licensing to service providers already in the market, or – where more active collaboration is required – joint ventures. As electronic publishing develops, many will use a mixture of all these strategies. As with all such licensing, however, many legal constraints are imposed; at the end of the day it is largely a question of who has (or is perceived to have) the relevant expertise, and who you trust.

Key issues which should be covered in any such licence include the following:

- Is the licence exclusive or non-exclusive (for example where only part of the work is to be used) and can the rights be sub-licensed to others? Some licensees and producers may need exclusivity in order to enter the market effectively: bear in mind any possible conflict with existing film or TV rights.
- Define the languages (computer as well as human) and the territories (where appropriate) in which exploitation may take place.
- Define the permitted platforms (for example Internet, or CD-ROM, or use on a hand-held device) if necessary; in some cases it may be advisable to license only a specific format or product.
- Agree on (and cost in) any necessary backup facilities, helplines or other support overheads: who will provide for these, and how will any costs be shared, or deducted? Will the author(s) need to be involved in regular revisions or updates, and on what terms?
- If necessary, specify permitted kinds of use, any restrictions on authorised or permitted users and in appropriate cases consider a site licence, restricting use to particular geographical sites (such as offices or university campuses – for more on this, see online access licences, below).

- May the work be altered or adapted in any way, and may it – or parts of it – be 'bundled' with other works? Think seriously about the integrity of the work (including the author's moral rights): will you retain a right of consultation (or even veto) over any changes? With a new product in a new medium, quality control may be crucial – don't leave approval until it's too late. Agree, if necessary, a staged consultation/approval procedure as the product develops, and retain the right to withdraw approval and terminate the licence as and when necessary.
- How long will the licence last (three to five years is common)? Is there a launch deadline or specified release date? Consider the circumstances in which you might wish to terminate the licence early and regain the rights: breach of key terms (such as non-payment, or unauthorised use), unsatisfactory sales performance or failure to meet agreed targets, and the usual termination and reversion provisions, for example, on insolvency.
- Be clear about ownership of all relevant copyrights, and any other relevant intellectual property rights such as any trade marks. In the case of a joint venture, the joint venture company may need to acquire the rights. Do not forget to renew any necessary copyright permissions (and agree who will do this – and pay any fees).
- Provide adequately for any moral rights of all relevant authors, and any required waivers (see pp. 46 and 89). If possible ensure that any sub-licences are also made subject to the author's moral rights. Agree specific credits, not only to the authors but to the licensing publisher, and ensure that this covers advertising and packaging as well as the product itself. Be particularly careful about any permitted use of brand names, logos or trade marks.
- Agree clearly what is to happen about money – who gets what and when. For a compilation or multimedia work, this may involve agreeing on the comparative 'value' of each work included: bear in mind that text occupies far less space on a CD than pictures, yet may be far more valuable in selling the product. Allow for the value of any digital amendments which individual rights owners may need to make, but equally bear in mind the high upfront development costs a software house may incur. Agree a payment system appropriate for the product and medium concerned – this may be a familiar royalty structure, or payments-per-use, or a proportion of agreed profits (as in the film and TV industries). In each case be clear about the method of calculation to be used. In an unfamiliar environment, it may be wise to provide for a review of financial terms after three to five years, and perhaps minimum revenue in a given period.

ONLINE ACCESS LICENCES

Publishers are increasingly making the works they publish available online, as well as in hard copy form – in many cases, such as STM journals, there may soon be few examples which are not available simultaneously online. Given that 'digital is different', and that digital access enables unlimited perfect copying at the click of a mouse, online licences need considerable care. However, for many the rapidly growing demand for online access represents a major publishing market – not just a threat, but an opportunity.

Licences for online access raise a number of key issues. The notes which follow reflect a variety of current experience, including site licences for academic or library use.

THE LICENSEE

Be specific, not just in defining the licensee itself, but also in listing all addresses or sites which the licence is to cover. This may most easily be done in an appendix or schedule to the licence, which can then be updated if necessary without having to amend the main contract. It is useful to require contact details, e.g. of a licence administrator or technical contact.

AUTHORISED USERS

It is important to identify as precisely as possible which categories of users will be entitled to access. In the case of an academic institution, will this cover full-time faculty staff, researchers and librarians only, or include temporary, contract or visiting staff? All students, or only those registered full-time at that institution? Some flexibility is usually needed, e.g. to allow for joint degrees and linked research teams (and even walk-in users, if agreed), provided all those concerned are made subject to the relevant terms and conditions, and can gain access only via the licensee's secure network, either via designated and supervised terminals or from an authenticated IP address.

LICENSED MATERIAL

Set out clearly what is licensed and what isn't – if necessary title by title, but at least which online services and electronic products, and any other content available (and for which, obviously, the publisher owns or controls the necessary electronic rights). Detailed listings may be done more easily in appendices or schedules.

ACCESS LICENCE, AND TERM

Online licences are normally non-exclusive and non-transferable – it is highly advisable to spell this out – and it is clearer if they refer to specific licensed activities or permitted uses, and are made subject to any other terms and conditions (such as payment of the fee). Be clear about the dates on which the licence will commence and end, and what happens at the end of the term – will it automatically terminate (unless renewed) or will it continue from year to year?

INTELLECTUAL PROPERTY

It is advisable to confirm on both sides that the works licensed are copyright works, and confirm any other intellectual property or other rights, such as trade marks. Licensees are often required to use reasonable endeavours to protect relevant IP rights, or at least to notify any breaches. It is common to reserve to the publisher all rights not specifically granted in the licence, for the avoidance of doubt, and to prohibit removal of, or interference with, authors' names or the publisher's copyright notices or trade marks.

PERMITTED AND PROHIBITED USES

The more clearly these can be set out, the better – two separate lists is the clearest method. Consider what proportion of the licensed material may be stored, viewed, downloaded, copied and printed, and for what purposes. Can it be copied or linked to other authorised users, or even more widely? Commercial use or re-use is usually prohibited, as is uploading to any network other than the designated intranet or secure network – if so, it is wise to be very clear about this.

UNDERTAKINGS AND OBLIGATIONS

These are often stated to be mutual, so that the licensee clearly undertakes not only to pay any fees and charges but also, for example, to make access available only via the secure network, to promote the terms and conditions to all authorised users, to take reasonable steps to terminate any unauthorised access and deal with any copyright infringement reasonably under its control. On the publisher's side, the licensee may look for a continuing obligation for availability and uninterrupted online access, at least as far as reasonably possible and as far as can be predicted.

TERMINATION

It is usual for either side to have the right to give written notice to terminate, subject to an agreed period of notice, as well as the usual provisions for termination due to insolvency or material breach. It is sensible to specify how long access may continue after termination, and whether any licensed material (e.g. CD-ROMs) should be returned, or whether local files should be destroyed or deleted.

E-BOOK AGREEMENTS

While many publishers – particularly STM publishers – are making their own content available by licensing access directly to users themselves (see previous section on Online access licences), the hoped-for e-book market, aimed more at readers of trade books and consumer titles such as dictionaries, has been slower to develop. This may be because the technology for hand-held devices is still developing (although the Palm Pilot and Rocket eBook are well established, for personal organisers and e-books respectively); it may partly be because the trade paperback in printed form is still comparatively popular, user-friendly and cheap. However, hand-held devices are expected to get smaller, lighter and cheaper, with easier on-screen reading, and many publishers are entering into contracts with suppliers of conversion, storage and distribution services to make their titles available via this route.

The following notes deal with some of the key issues often raised by such licences.

TITLES AND E-VERSIONS

It is important to define carefully:

- The titles to be included (usually in an appendix, and often with a delivery timetable for key titles), and
- The e-versions to be created, in which formats, and usually for which titles (depending on the particular features of each one), and any approval requirements.

RIGHTS GRANTED

The publisher will need to grant the specific rights necessary for conversion into electronic versions, usually using the licensee's own conversion processes, and if necessary to store, sell, distribute and offer access on the publisher's behalf; such grants of rights are normally non-exclusive and non-transferable. The licensee may require confirmation from the publisher that the publisher does actually own or control (or have cleared) the relevant electronic rights, not only to each title but also to any third party material included (or, if not, that such material will have been removed).

TERM OF LICENCE

Given the speed at which technology is developing, licences are currently short: three to five years is fairly usual.

COPYRIGHT AND IP RIGHTS

It is advisable to confirm that copyright in the titles concerned (including the final e-versions) rests with the publisher, and there is usually a provision that the licensee should credit the copyright on every version. There may also be a need to make provision for protecting or crediting the authors' moral rights. However, although it is customary to specify that the licensee acquires no rights in any of the publisher's trade marks, the licensee will often need the right to make use of relevant trade marks, subject usually to a right of approval, and a proviso that no alterations will be made without consent.

CHARGES AND PAYMENTS

There may be conversion charges, or charges for any of the services bought in (which should be set out clearly), but there are normally royalty arrangements for e-versions sold. These seem to range currently from 35 to 65 per cent of the list price (or in some cases, net price received), depending on whether, for example, the titles are trade or professional titles. It is advisable to be clear about the timetable for any payments, e.g. quarterly or monthly, and audit arrangements – it is important to ensure that complete and accurate records of sales are kept, and regular sales reports are supplied.

WITHDRAWAL AND TERMINATION

It is sensible to provide for withdrawal of any individual title or titles, on reasonable notice, as well as for termination of the entire licence (on the usual terms, e.g. breach of a material provision, or insolvency), again on reasonable notice. It may be necessary to specify arrangements for return or deletion of any material or files held in electronic form.

OTHER ELECTRONIC AGREEMENTS

Given the developing nature of electronic exploitation and licensing in the publishing trade, and the rapid pace of change, it is impossible – and probably invidious – in a book like this to do more than try to highlight a few key principles, which we have tried to do in the preceding sections. It is very likely that this section of the book will expand considerably in future editions. Meanwhile, for other kinds of electronic licences in current use, see the growing list of precedents in *Clark's Publishing Agreements* (sixth edition, 2002; a seventh edition is in preparation).

AGREEMENTS BETWEEN AUTHORS AND AGENTS

We looked in some detail in chapter 4 at literary agents' own standard publishing contracts, in the context of the author–publisher agreement. In the final section of this chapter we will take a quick look at the legal relationship between agents and authors themselves.

Most established literary agencies now enter into some kind of written agreement with authors who they take on, usually in the form of an extended letter. It is possible in some circumstances for an agent to acquire actual or implied authority to represent someone else (called their 'principal') *without* entering into a written agreement, but this is not generally recommended as a long-term business practice, and it is always advisable to record such agreements in writing as soon as possible – if only to confirm the extent of the agent's authority, and (the source of most disputes) what payment or commission they will be entitled to receive.

Where there is an agreement, the terms of that agreement will govern the relationship; there is, however, probably also an overriding obligation on all agents to perform their duties in good faith and with reasonable care and skill. Contracts with all commercial agents within the EU are now regulated by the Commercial Agents Directive, implemented in the UK in the shape of the Commercial Agents (Council Directive) Regulations 1993. Some of the key criteria include the following:

- there should be no conflicts of interest;
- the agent's powers or duties should not be delegated without consent;
- agents should not make secret profits or undeclared commissions;
- agents have a right to be indemnified by their principals when acting within their authority;
- all agents have a right to reasonable remuneration.

The entitlement to reasonable remuneration normally comes to an end straightaway when the agency is terminated, unless the contract provides otherwise. However, although this makes sense for most commercial agencies, it does not allow for agents (such as literary agents) who – apart from a share of any advance – are paid substantially by means of a commission on long-term future earnings. Most literary agency agreements therefore expressly provide that the agent's agreed commission will be paid on *all* future earnings, from all sources, which derive from agreements which that agent actually negotiated (or, in some cases, agreements signed by the author while the agency was in force, even if the agent was not directly involved). If the author accepts this, it means that many agents will continue to be paid commission on their former author's titles long after the agency arrangement itself has been terminated. For this reason, most agents' standard publishing agreements include a clause irrevocably appointing them as the author's authorised recipient for all monies payable on that particular title. Some authors may not be willing to make an irrevocable appointment – there is no legal reason why agency appointments should not be revoked at any time if the author wishes later to be paid direct, or via some other agent, but there will then be a separate contractual issue between the author and the agent about outstanding commission. There is, however, no reason why the publisher should become involved in this: it is entirely a matter between author and agent.

For authors wishing to enter into an agreement with an agent, the Association of Authors' Agents maintains a professional code of conduct. Some general guidance, and comparison of commission rates, may be found in various annual publications such as the *Writers Handbook* and the *Writers and Artists Yearbook*. Carole Blake's book *From Pitch to Publication* has a sample letter.

Part III
Delivery, editing, and obligations on publication

Delivery, editing, and obligations on publication

6

DELIVERY: ACCEPTANCE OR REJECTION

DELIVERY

The emotional trauma and sheer physical effort of delivering a completed copyright work has often been likened to childbirth (usually by men). It is probably true that few authors – apart from the most experienced – realise quite what they are letting themselves in for when they sign their publishing contracts; first-time authors in particular may underestimate what is required (although a good agent or editor should spot this). In addition, even the best organised authors may be overtaken by unexpected events, especially if they have any kind of family or social life and a full-time job to hold down too. As a result:

- the work may be delivered late; or
- bits of it – or the whole thing – may not be of the standard expected.

A good publishing contract will foresee both these eventualities and make provision for them (see chapter 4, pp. 77–8).

Non-delivery or late delivery

Time will not be regarded as being of the essence unless the contract expressly says that it is (it often does, for example, if the work is a contribution to a major reference project on a tight schedule, or linked into some external event such as a royal wedding). Where time *is* of the essence, non-delivery by the specified date will normally be an automatic ground for termination of the contract, although in many cases – particularly where the author is not to blame – a publisher may retain the option to keep the contract alive a while longer if there seems a reasonable prospect that the work will come in soon and there is in fact a little leeway in the schedule.

Where time is *not* stated to be of the essence, late delivery may still constitute adequate performance of the author's contractual obligation to deliver (indeed, an author may deliver 20 years late and still perform the contract, if the publisher is prepared to wait that long). All other things being equal, two or three months either way would almost certainly be regarded as reasonably acceptable performance, and a publisher might find it difficult to terminate the contract on grounds of non-delivery alone if the author had a reasonable excuse for being late and was ready and willing to deliver in, say, three months time. Beyond that, however, it is probably advisable to confirm any revised schedule in a formal exchange of letters, varying the delivery terms of the original contract; otherwise, the author will be at increasing risk of termination for breach of contract, particularly where the publisher makes it clear (preferably in writing) that continued lateness will not be acceptable. It is important, however, to look at all the surrounding circumstances, and bear in mind any informal meetings or telephone conversations, or any previous dealings between the parties, as well as actual correspondence; a publisher may impliedly extend a delivery deadline by conduct as well as by a formal letter.

Acceptance

If and when the work does finally come in, the publisher will want to check as soon as possible whether it conforms to the publishing contract – whether it is, in fact, the thing contracted for. Any specified formats and delivery requirements – such as delivery on disk – should also be complied with. Under general contract law principles, there is probably only a limited window of opportunity here for the publisher either to reject the work on clear grounds as being unacceptable – not a sufficient performance of the contract by the author – or else expressly or impliedly accept it. Putting the work into production (or even editing, or marking up for house style) might well constitute implied acceptance, so that even if unacceptable defects were discovered later it might then be difficult for the publisher to reject the work as a whole. Accepting delivery of a work should therefore not merely be a process of passive collection, but should involve at some point a positive inspection and approval of what is delivered. For most works, the person to do this will be the commissioning publisher or in-house editor: for major works the approval of a general editor or section editor may be required. Whoever it is should be aware of the contractual significance of what they are doing – once a work is substantially accepted, then the publisher is to all intents and purposes probably stuck with it.

As to what is or is not 'acceptable', this will be entirely governed by the publishing contract, whether written or informal. Where no written contract exists, or where the contract does not refer to any specification or acceptance criteria (it is surprising how many do not) then any reasonably competent work of approximately the right length in the subject area concerned would probably be sufficient to perform the contract. Most good publishing contracts, however, contain at least some acceptance criteria, ranging from a full detailed specification set out in an appendix – probably the clearest method – to generalised phrases such as 'of a standard which might reasonably be expected' or sometimes just the single, and wonderfully simple, word 'acceptable' (which, unless further defined, probably does not mean very much, but can give the publisher very wide discretion, particularly if 'in the Publisher's sole opinion').

Rejection

What happens if the work – or a substantial part of it – is not acceptable to the publisher? The general rule in law is that the contract will prevail; if the publisher has a wide discretion under the contract, or if what the author delivers cannot reasonably be regarded as fulfilling his or her obligations under the contract, then the publisher may well have the right to reject it and terminate the contract in accordance with any relevant termination provisions. An author commissioned to write a 300 page textbook who delivers instead a 50-page pamphlet (this has been known) is clearly not delivering the work contracted for. Similarly, an article or research study commissioned for inclusion in a post-graduate STM journal which turns out to have no references or footnotes and to be written at a much lower level would also be a fairly obvious candidate for rejection, provided that the requirement to write at post-graduate level had been clearly agreed. But what if the publisher simply does not like the work, or is disappointed by it?

If it complies with the contract, but just isn't as good as hoped for, then the publisher will probably not have the right to reject the work for that reason alone, unless the contract gives the publisher virtually complete discretion. In most cases, the publisher's only remedy will be to persuade the author to improve it (see below), and if that still does not produce the desired result, make the most of what was clearly a commissioning mistake.

Rejection, if it happens, should be in accordance with any procedures set out in the contract: the publisher may have the option either to reject at once, or to put the author on notice to make specified alterations or improvements to bring the work up to contract standard within a given timetable, and then to reject if this is not done. Where improvements are feasible, some contracts give the publisher a further option of commissioning a competent editor to make the necessary improvements and deduct the cost from the author's royalties or other earnings in due course (this would now be subject to the author's moral rights, on which see further below).

Disputes

There are often disputes surrounding rejection of a work and termination of the contract may not always turn out to be as straightforward as the publisher might hope. Where the contract gives the publisher absolute discretion, and the work as delivered is obviously not in accordance with the contract terms, there should be little cause for dispute, but in other cases – particularly where alterations are involved – there may be considerable disagreement. If such disputes cannot be resolved amicably between the parties, many contracts provide arbitration clauses as a means of avoiding full-scale litigation. Arbitration clauses normally survive termination of the contract, and can usually be invoked unilaterally by either party, but formal arbitration is not always any quicker or cheaper than pursuing a claim in the High Court (see p. 97). It is still, therefore, comparatively rare in publishing disputes; most are settled one way or another between the parties.

In the event of rejection and termination it is important to confirm:

- what happens to the rights granted under the contract; and
- what happens to any advances, or other payments made.

In most cases the author will quite reasonably want his or her rights back, and most contracts provide for all rights granted to revert under such circumstances so that the author can still exploit the work, even if this will now have to be elsewhere. If the author assigned full copyright to the publisher (or someone else) under the contract, this may have to be formally re-assigned; to be effective, this should be in writing, and signed by or on behalf of the current copyright owner (see p. 74).

Advances, though always a fertile area for dispute, are either a matter for the contract or entirely at the publisher's discretion: where the publisher has paid an advance (or advances) the publisher will normally be entitled to ask for these to be repaid if the work is rejected unless they are clearly stated to be non-returnable.

SUMMARY CHECKLIST: DELIVERY

- Is time of the essence?
- Has the delivery schedule been revised (even impliedly)?
- Is the work delivered the work which was contracted for?
- Does it comply with any 'acceptance' criteria in the contract?
- Are there any grounds for rejection?
- Is there any rejection or disputes procedure?
- What happens to the rights and any advances?

EDITING AND ALTERATIONS

Once a work is accepted, it may be sent straight off for production as it is (particularly if it comes in on disk) but in the great majority of cases the publisher will want to edit it first. This mysterious process frequently leads to disputes, and horror stories abound of uncontrolled, demented editors mutilating what were previously perfectly publishable works. In reality, of course, editing varies widely from publisher to publisher, some doing little more than marking up to conform with agreed house style, and others adopting a more interventionist role. From a legal point of view, the position is fairly clear: subject to any agreement to the contrary, a publisher who contracts to publish an author's work is obliged to publish that work substantially as delivered by the author, and is not entitled to adapt (or 'improve') it without the author's consent. This is particularly so now that authors have a moral right of integrity and other moral rights in the UK under the 1988 Act. We will consider the implications of the right of integrity below.

AGREEMENT BY CONTRACT

As a general rule, authors will not be entitled in law to prevent editorial changes to which they have freely consented. Even their moral rights (see below) will not apply to anything done with their consent. Consent may be express (and set out, for example, in a contract) or implied – perhaps by conduct, or a previous course of dealing – but implied consent may be harder to prove. Most publishers will therefore seek the author's express consent in advance to the level of editorial changes they think they might need to make by including a specific clause to that effect in the publishing agreement. What changes may or may not be permitted will therefore become a question of interpreting the relevant wording of the contract.

Contracts, as we saw in chapter 4, vary widely but most publishing agreements try to give the publisher some leeway at least to make necessary and reasonable alterations in accordance with any agreed specifications, and the relevant house style. Where a detailed house style book is available this should ideally be made available to the author well before the time the contract is signed and expressly referred to in the contract itself: you cannot generally incorporate express terms into a contract which have not been disclosed and agreed by the time the contract is signed.

In addition, many contracts give the publisher the right to make alterations on the advice of its legal advisers, for example to remove passages which might be libellous or obscene, or which might otherwise be in breach of the author's warranties (see pp. 79–82). Libel is a particular risk (see p. 161), and it may be advisable to have any suspect passages read for libel by a lawyer who specialises in this kind of work and knows what to look for; many publishers retain lawyers to do regular libel reading for them, since a legal opinion may often be required at short notice.

Any alterations beyond the level clearly provided for in the contract, or otherwise agreed by the author, are highly dangerous, and where they cause damage to the author or his or her reputation may entitle the author to bring an action for breach of contract, infringement of moral rights, or – in severe cases – for defamation. Editors who feel an author's work could be 'improved' should therefore keep any urge to rewrite it firmly under control.

NECESSARY CHANGES

A publisher might be entitled in an emergency to make last-minute deletions, or minor consequential amendments, in order to avoid publishing infringing or illegal material (such as defamatory or obscene matter) and the moral right of integrity in particular does not apply to anything done to avoid the commission of an offence or comply with a statutory duty. However, in the absence of a clear contractual right to make the changes concerned, changes the publisher considers 'necessary' may not always be entirely safe: if time allows, it is always advisable to consult the author, and ideally get the author to make the changes personally. Obtaining the author's participation, or at least express agreement, will give the greatest possible protection against future claims by the author, for example, of breach of contract, or defamation. In addition, anything done with the author's consent cannot infringe his or her moral rights.

IMPLIED CONSENT

An author's consent to alterations may be implied in some circumstances – by the author's conduct (in accepting previous changes, for example), or in some cases by the nature of the publication or the list itself: where an author submits a contribution to a periodical or a major work known to be edited to a certain standard, or submits a work to a series or list of titles with a distinctive house style of its own, then it is quite likely that he or she will be deemed to have consented to a reasonable level of editorial changes consistent with those standards or styles. Where the changes made go a significant way beyond what might reasonably be expected, however, an author may well have a cause of action, for example for breach of contract or infringement of moral rights (see below).

MORAL RIGHTS

As we saw in chapter 3, authors now have statutory moral rights in the UK. In the context of editorial alterations, the two moral rights most likely to be in issue are:

- the right of integrity – the right to object to derogatory treatment of the work; and
- the right to prevent false attribution – the right not to be wrongly described as the author of something in fact written by someone else.

The right of integrity

We considered this key moral right fully at pp. 47–50; to recap briefly, section 80 of the 1988 Act gives the author of relevant copyright works (including both literary and artistic works) the right not to have those works subjected to 'derogatory treatment' – additions or deletions, alterations or adaptations which are so serious that they amount to distortion or mutilation of the work, or are otherwise prejudicial to the author's honour or reputation. The right lasts for as long as the work remains in copyright. Infringement of the right is actionable by the author as a breach of statutory duty, and the author may be entitled not only to appropriate damages but also to the grant of an injunction.

Potentially, therefore, this is a powerful right which editors embarking upon in-house alterations should bear constantly in mind. It is, however, hedged about with limitations and restrictions under the 1988 Act, and may not apply in every case. The limitations are set out in full in chapter 3.

The right to prevent false attribution

Under section 84 of the 1988 Act, authors (indeed any persons) have the right not to have material written by others falsely attributed to them (see pp. 51–2). Adding to the existing law of defamation, this is a new statutory right designed to protect authors' reputations from harmful association with work which they did not write, and over which they had no control, but which the publisher may try to pass off as theirs. Since it is a right protecting personal reputations, rather than the integrity of copyright works themselves, it lasts not for the full period of copyright but only for 20 years after the person's death. As with other moral rights, infringement of the right is actionable as a breach of statutory duty.

The right of paternity

Do not forget that the author is also likely to have a right of paternity – the right to be credited as the author in a clear and reasonably prominent way every time the work is published commercially. There are a number of exceptions to this right such as employee and collective works (for a full list, see p. 46), and the right also crucially depends on being asserted by the author. Where it applies, many contracts therefore provide for an assertion of the right to appear in a prominent position – usually together with the UCC copyright notice (see p. 93). Most publishers will have no difficulty about crediting their authors prominently on the works themselves, but it is important to remember that this is now a statutory right. It is also equally likely to apply to authors of copyright material other than text, such as artists, illustrators and photographers.

SUMMARY CHECKLIST: EDITING

- Are alterations really necessary?
- Has the author consented to alterations (for example, in the contract)?
- Do author's moral rights apply to this type of work?
- Has the author waived his or her moral rights?
- If not, can the author make any alterations personally, or at least be consulted?
- Is there any danger that the author's moral right of integrity may be infringed?
- Might there be a risk of false attribution?
- Has the right of paternity been complied with, and has it been asserted?

PERMISSIONS

Most published works contain extracts or quotations from other copyright works, and often reproductions of complete works such as illustrations, maps or photographs. If these works are still in copyright – older illustrations, for example, may by now be in the public domain – it will be an infringement of the owner's copyright to reproduce any substantial part of those works without permission. A court may award the copyright owner damages or an account of profits, delivery up or destruction of infringing stock, and in appropriate cases an injunction preventing publication (see chapter 9). It is therefore crucially important to check the copyright status of all such material as soon as possible and ensure that permission to reproduce it is obtained from the copyright owner well before the work goes into production – preferably before or soon after delivery. Most publishing contracts require the author to arrange (and sometimes pay) for all such permissions and indeed give a warranty and indemnity against any copyright infringement which may take place, but this of course does not help the author, and is not always sufficient to remove legal risk from the publisher, who is very likely to be joined as a co-defendant in any legal action. It will also not cover any copyright permissions necessary for material not included in the author's work itself, for example, an illustration or photograph selected by the publisher for advertising. Editors should therefore check as soon as possible:

- whether permissions have already been obtained by the author (preferably in writing);
- if not, which existing copyright works have been reproduced, at least in substantial part (if the author does not have a reliable list, the editor should compile one);
- whether they are still in copyright, or have fallen into the public domain (for duration of copyright, see p. 35). As a general rule, a literary or artistic work is still likely to be in copyright if the author died less than 70 years ago;
- whether they may be copied without permission under the fair dealing provisions of the 1988 Act: for example, limited extracts reproduced for the purpose of criticism or review, and accompanied by a sufficient acknowledgement (see p. 228).

This may remove the risk of copyright infringement from a number of extracts, but in all other cases permission should be sought from the copyright owner straightaway.

Who should arrange (and pay for) permissions is a matter for the author and publisher to agree, if they have not already agreed it in the contract. For large-scale works, such as dictionaries and encyclopaedias, or for multimedia works, clearing permissions might be a major undertaking, so whoever does it needs to allow plenty of time. It is worth remembering the following points:

- Owning copyright means being able to prevent others from copying your work, so the copyright owner may say 'no'. It is highly dangerous to write off a batch of letters and just assume that permission will be granted in due course – it may not be.
- The copyright owner may demand a permissions fee, particularly if a print or transparency is supplied as well. Museums and galleries are raising increasing amounts of revenue from this source, even for works which are themselves long since out of copyright (since the authorised reproduction which is supplied is of course a new copyright work). These fees can mount up very quickly: it may therefore be necessary to reconsider some of the more expensive ones if production budgets are tight. Give yourself time to consider all this, and if necessary select something else.
- If permission *is* given, check that the licence covers all formats, languages and territories in which the work is likely to be exploited (if permission is only granted for the UK, for example, including that extract or illustration in a French edition would not be licensed).

- Bear in mind that some permissions may only be given for one edition at a time – for example, of a dictionary. If subsequent editions are planned, these permissions will need to be renewed.

What happens if you cannot find out who – if anyone – owns the copyright? In the case of extracts from a book, the obvious place to start is the publisher of the most recent published edition: even though copyright in the literary work may vest in the author, the publisher will normally handle permissions requests. If, however, the publisher is no longer in business, and the author cannot be traced personally (for example, via the Society of Authors, Public Lending Rights Registrar, or simply via the telephone directory) then you will have to accept the risk that, if the work is still in copyright, publishing a substantial part of it without express permission may well be infringing someone's copyright. If the owner subsequently appears (possibly after publication) then he or she may have a legitimate claim of copyright infringement. There is no absolutely secure protection against such a possibility, but evidence that the copyright owner was difficult to trace, and that you had made serious efforts in that direction – not merely sent off a single letter – would probably be taken into account by any court. So also would the fact that you had credited the copyright owner, via a suitable acknowledgement. Any sums you had set aside by way of royalty or fee, against the possibility the copyright owner may one day turn up, would also be convincing evidence of good faith. The only entirely safe course of action, however, is not to copy the material at all.

There have recently been proposals by the US Copyright Office for permitted copying of such 'orphan works' in the USA, provided 'reasonably diligent' searches have been made (including relevant databases), and provided the copyright owner – if he or she ever turns up – is paid a reasonable licensing fee. There are currently no such proposals for the UK, although such schemes may often be felt to have practical advantages.

PRODUCTION AND PROOFS

Although it is a solidly established trade practice that publishers will supply the author with proofs of the work for correction before it is sent for press, there is no general legal obligation on them to do this, and in some cases there may simply not be time. However, most publishing contracts provide for proofs, which therefore gives the author a contractual entitlement to see and approve them, on the terms set out in the contract. These normally provide for proofs to be returned within a reasonably prompt schedule – 14 or 21 days is common. In many cases the publisher will retain the right to pass the proofs for press if the author does not return them on time, or cannot check them personally or arrange for someone else to (or simply cannot be contacted). Most contracts also make it clear that the supply of proofs is an opportunity to correct errors, not an open invitation to revise and rewrite sections over which the author may have had second thoughts (and which can be expensive). It is therefore common for an upper limit to be set on any author's corrections: 10 or

15 per cent of the cost of composition is fairly standard (although what the cost of 'composition' actually is where the author has supplied the work on disk might need to be separately agreed: 10 per cent of the cost of editorial revisions alone might not pay for very many corrections). Whatever the percentage, it is important to consider when signing the contract whether this is appropriate for the work concerned – in the case of a scientific, technical or professional text, for example, unforeseen new standards or legislation, or new research findings, may make corrections at proof stage essential if the work is not to be seriously inaccurate and misleading, and the contract should allow sufficient flexibility for this.

If an index is necessary, the contract should say so, and specify whether the author is to do this or whether it is the publisher's responsibility (and who pays).

Most other aspects of design, production, promotion and marketing are normally reserved to the publisher's sole discretion, and most publishing contracts reflect this. The price at which the work is sold, and the discounts and other terms of trade which would apply, are also normally entirely under the publisher's control. However, some Minimum Terms Agreements or agents' contracts provide for the author to be consulted on subjective matters of taste and style, such as design or the jacket.

OBLIGATIONS ON PUBLICATION

PRINTERS AND PUBLISHERS' DETAILS

Under what remains of the Newspapers, Printers and Reading Rooms Repeal Act 1869, it is a legal requirement in the UK for anyone who prints commercially 'any paper' (probably including a book):

- to 'carefully preserve and keep' at least one copy for at least six months, and
- to write or print on it 'in fair and legible characters' the name and address of the person commissioning the printing,

subject to a fine on summary conviction for failure to do so. In addition, subject to a similar penalty, printers of 'any paper or book whatsoever' intended to be 'published or dispersed' are required to print their own name and address on the first page (or on the front, if a single sheet only).

The requirement does not extend to Parliamentary papers, or to things published by public or local authorities, or to banknotes, and there are simplified requirements for the Oxford and Cambridge presses. The obligation was also further relaxed by the Printers' Imprint Act 1961, in order to exclude printed matter consisting only of:

- a greeting, invitation, 'or other message in a conventional form', or
- a picture representing only a geometrical, floral or other design or a registered trademark (or any combination of these).

LEGAL DEPOSIT

Most countries have a legal deposit requirement of some kind, requiring deposit with the national library (or libraries) of one or more copies of most significant publications published in that country. In the UK, the requirement goes back at least 400 years, and is generally regarded as a necessary contribution to the national heritage, for the use of scholars, researchers and other authorised library users. Under the 1911 Copyright Act, publishers and distributors are still today legally obliged to supply to the British Library one copy of each publication issued or distributed to the public in the UK within one month of publishing it. This covers all publications, except that some categories need only be deposited on specific request by the British Library – these include trade advertisements, local railway timetables, calendars and appointment diaries, educational posters and examination papers. All other publications (except newspapers) should be sent to the Legal Deposit Office at the British Library in Boston Spa, West Yorkshire (the full address is set out in appendix B).

In addition, five other legal deposit libraries are entitled to receive copies (but only on request). These are:

- the Bodleian Library, Oxford
- the University Library, Cambridge
- the National Library, Scotland
- the National Library of Wales, and
- the Library of Trinity College Dublin.

These copies, if requested, should be sent to the Agency for the Legal Deposit Libraries, 100 Euston Street, London NW1 2HQ (further contact details, again, are in appendix B).

Compliance with these requirements has been relatively straightforward for most publishers and deposit librarians, but following the Legal Deposit Libraries Act 2003 the Secretary of State for Culture, Media and Sport has been authorised to issue Regulations extending the deposit requirements to electronic publications as well. This raises a number of important issues of definition: how wide is the category of 'publisher' in the online, Internet age, and what kind of electronic 'publication' is – or should be – liable to UK legal deposit? How do you deposit a website or an online database? Is everything downloadable and accessible in the UK liable to legal deposit here?

Publishers and deposit librarians have been discussing these issues in a Joint Committee on Legal Deposit (JCLD) for some time, and agreed a Voluntary Code of Practice in 2000 dealing with offline electronic publications such as CD-ROMs. A statutory Legal Deposit Advisory Panel has now been set up under the 2003 Act to advise the Secretary of State on suitable Regulations for further categories of both offline and online publications, including for example e-journals, and it is likely that the Panel will build on the experience already gained by JCLD and its various working groups. The first Regulations are unlikely to appear before late 2006, or 2007.

Part IV
Publish and be damned

Defamation and other risks

7

DEFAMATION

LIES, DAMNED LIES AND DEFAMATION

Every publication which contains statements of fact or opinion runs the risk that some of them may be untrue, or unjustified. However hard authors and editors try, a certain number of inaccuracies will always slip through the net and get published. Some will not matter very much, or will simply look unfortunate. Some, more serious, mis-statements may raise allegations of negligence, and we will look at negligent misstatement below (p. 185). There is a particular category of untruth, however, which publishers would be well advised to avoid at all costs, and that is any untrue statement which might be taken to impugn a person's reputation. In essence, this is what defamation is.

It is not necessarily illegal to publish untruths about someone: English law has considerable sympathy for the concepts of free speech and freedom of the press. These are now enshrined in the Human Rights Act 1998 which gives everyone the right to freedom of expression. However, at the same time, the law also seeks to protect citizens from the publication of false allegations which may harm their reputation. It is not always easy to balance these opposing needs. There usually comes a point, however, where a critical or disparaging comment becomes a recognisably more serious allegation of fact, or of unsupported opinion: at that point, if it or the facts on which it is based is untrue, the law may intervene and decide that it becomes libellous.

It may also become expensive, because ever since the Libel Act of 1792 it has been settled law in the UK that damages for defamation are not a matter for judges to settle, but are primarily for a *jury* to decide. The Court of Appeal has stated that 'the question whether someone's reputation has or has not been falsely discredited ought to be tried by other ordinary men and women and ... it is the jury who are the people of England'. This remains a fundamental principle of English law. Juries (and judges), however, can be unpredictable. In the libel case concerning allegations by the *Sun* newspaper that Bruce Grobbelaar took bribes for fixing football matches, the Court of Appeal overturned the jury's verdict which had been in the footballer's favour. The House of Lords overturned the Court of Appeal's decision on liability (finding that the *Sun* was liable) but reduced the jury's award of damages from £85,000 to £1.

The purpose of an award of 'general damages' by the court is to cover the following:

- Vindication – to show to the world at large that the allegations were false;
- Compensation for damage to reputation; and
- Compensation for injury to feelings (e.g. pain, suffering, humiliation and embarrassment). However, damages under this head cannot be recovered by corporate claimants (as companies do not have feelings).

Whatever they think the actual damage to the claimant's reputation was, a jury may also decide to punish a defendant for behaviour of which it disapproves, particularly if the defendant has repeated the libel or failed to take opportunities to apologise. They might not care for your defence, or think much of your witnesses. At a time when reports of six-figure advances and cheque-book journalism appear regularly in the media, they may have great sympathy for a lone individual fighting to clear his or her name against what they see as a wealthy publisher or newspaper, and may award substantial damages. For a publisher seeking to defend a defamation action, therefore, it means that the financial risks of losing a case – including the costs – are impossible to calculate with any certainty in advance and can be considerable.

Awards of general damages by English juries at one point reached levels in excess of £1 million – the record is still held by an award of £1.5 million to Lord Aldington for allegations of war crimes contained in a book by Count Tolstoy. Following a Court of Appeal decision in December 1995, however, in which the court reduced an award of damages to Elton John against the publishers of the *Sunday Mirror* from £350,000 to £75,000, it is now open to judges to give much clearer guidelines to libel juries on what may or may not be appropriate damages, and most now do. These guidelines may take account, among other things, of the maximum sums normally available for personal injury awards. In the opinion of the court:

> It was rightly offensive to public opinion that a defamation claimant should recover damages for injury to reputation greater, perhaps by a significant factor, than if that same claimant had been rendered a helpless cripple or an insensate vegetable.

In 1996, a jury awarded £45,000 to Victor Kiam (the businessman appearing in the Remington electric razor advertisements) for allegations of insolvency published in the *Sunday Times*. In another case in the same year, the Court of Appeal substituted an award of £40,000 in place of a jury's award of £100,000 for allegations that the claimant was a pimp and exposed men whom he introduced to prostitutes to the risk of blackmail by the KGB. The Court stated that it was difficult to imagine any defamation action where even the most severe damage to reputation, accompanied by maximum aggravation, would be comparable to physical injuries such as quadriplegia, total blindness and deafness, where top of the range awards were £130,000 (now about £200,000). The highest award made, at the time of writing, was to two individuals in 2002 following the publication of untrue allegations that they had physically, sexually and emotionally abused a number of children. Each claimant was awarded general damages of £200,000, the maximum amount of damages said to be available in libel proceedings, as the court felt that they were entitled to be vindicated and recognised as innocent after such serious allegations.

It is unlikely now that there will be any further seven-figure general damages awards, but even at the new, more realistic, levels the financial risks can still be considerable. The losing party will frequently have to pay the winning party's legal costs if the matter proceeds to trial, which are often substantial (usually running into hundreds of thousands of pounds). We look at the important issue of legal costs below (p. 181).

If a successful claimant has suffered actual financial loss, which they are able to prove, then he or she may be able to recover 'special damages' in addition to an award of general damages. The claimant must, however, prove that the loss was suffered as a result of the defamatory publication and also that it was a reasonably foreseeable consequence of the publication. In 2004, the court struck out a special damages claim for £230 million pounds. Collins Stewart Limited, a stockbroker, sued for libel on an article published by the *Financial Times*. It claimed the meaning of the allegations was that they were guilty of gross impropriety in the way in which they carried on business, and had committed or acquiesced in serious criminal offences, in particular insider dealing. Collins Stewart sought special damages on the basis that the share price of the parent company had fallen relative to comparative companies but the court decided that this measure was too uncertain to be accepted as a legal basis on which to found a claim for special damages. At the time of writing, the remainder of the claim is ongoing.

WHAT IS DEFAMATION?

Any statement in a book or journal or newspaper, or any other published matter (an advertisement, e-mail or website, for example), runs the risk of being defamatory if it contains an untrue allegation or imputation which disparages the reputation of another. *All* those elements must be present, before a statement can be libelous:

- It must have been published (or in the case of slander, spoken) to a third party.
- It must be understood to refer to the person complaining about it.
- The allegation must bear a defamatory meaning.

We shall look at each of these categories in turn. But first, a distinguishing note about libel and slander.

LIBEL AND SLANDER

Broadly speaking, libel is defamation in written or permanent form (such as a book or newspaper): slander uses the more transitory medium of face-to-face words and gestures. Traditionally, printed libel was felt to have a more serious long-term effect on a person's reputation than words spoken during an argument or at a public meeting. Spoken words might be forgotten, but words you had printed would still be there the next morning.

As a result, there is a distinction between libel and slander: in an action for libel, damage is regarded as self-evident, and does not have to be proved; in order to succeed in an action for slander, however, claimants must normally provide evidence that they have incurred a specific quantifiable loss. The only exceptions are:

- accusations of a crime punishable by imprisonment;
- allegations of contagious disease;
- imputations on a person's ability to carry on an office, business or profession, or on the reputation or credit of a trader;
- imputations of adultery or unchastity in women.

Technology has rendered this distinction between libel and slander increasingly out of date. The printed word is no longer the only permanent medium capable of inflicting damage, and words spoken on radio and TV, and via cable services and satellite broadcasts, are all now specifically treated as libels (since the Broadcasting Act 1990). Accessible or retrievable messages delivered via a computer network – such as the Internet – are also now regarded as libels 'permanent' enough for damage to be assumed. This is also true of e-mail as well as bulletin boards.

DEFAMATORY MEANING

Before an action for defamation can proceed, the trial judge must decide whether the words complained of are capable of bearing a 'defamatory meaning'. Because it is possible to defame a person's reputation in a number of different ways, there is no single test for defamation, but several. Judges have sought to remedy each category in a succession of cases since the seventeenth century. Generally speaking, a statement will be defamatory of a person today if it tends to do any of the following:

LOWERS THEM IN THE ESTIMATION OF RIGHT-THINKING MEMBERS OF SOCIETY GENERALLY

A statement may still defame you, even if it does not fall under any of the other categories, if most normal, decent people would tend to think the worse of you as a result. It would almost certainly be defamatory, for example, to say that you have a criminal record, but it may also defame you to say that you regularly drink and drive.

DISPARAGES THEM IN THEIR OFFICE, PROFESSION, CALLING, TRADE OR BUSINESS

You may defame someone not only in their personal or social capacity, but also at work, for example by alleging immorality or hypocrisy of a politician or a clergyman, professional misconduct or incompetence of a lawyer or doctor, plagiarism of an author, or fraud, false accounting or general lack of creditworthiness of an agent or publisher.

EXPOSES THEM TO HATRED, CONTEMPT OR RIDICULE

It was defamatory of a man in 1680 to allege that his wife beat him, and possibly still is. Anything which exposes someone to ridicule is actionable, particularly if they have a professional or social position to protect (even repeating a story they originally told as a joke against themselves). It is certainly defamatory to publish a statement causing someone to be despised – for example by falsely accusing them of child abuse, or even perhaps cowardice. In 1996 the actor, director and writer Stephen Berkoff sued over a film review which stated that 'film directors from Hitchcock to Berkoff are notoriously hideous-looking people'. The Court of Appeal held that the words were capable of exposing him to ridicule.

In a contrasting case in 1998, the defendant published an article about the opera singer Jessye Norman who had allegedly become stuck in swing doors. The article stated that when advised to release herself by turning sideways, the singer replied 'Honey, I ain't got no sideways'. The singer sued stating that the words, which she had not spoken, exposed her to ridicule as they conformed to a degrading racist stereotype of an African-American. The Court of Appeal held that in the context of the publication – which was affectionate rather than critical – the words were not capable of bearing a defamatory meaning.

CAUSES THEM TO BE SHUNNED OR AVOIDED

Even if an allegation inspires only sympathy, rather than contempt, it may still be defamatory if it has the effect of causing people to avoid you, or excluding you from the society in which you normally move. Imputations of insanity or serious disease (such as leprosy) often had this effect in the past, even though they implied no blame or discredit. In the *Berkoff* case mentioned above, the words in question were held not to be capable of causing people to shun or avoid the claimant.

SOCIAL CONTEXT

In deciding whether a particular set of words is capable of being defamatory or not, a judge will have to bear in mind two things: current social standards and what the 'ordinary reader', applying those standards, would think. These standards may change, of course (and do), and what right-thinking members of society may have thought in our grandparents' day may not strike us as defamatory at all.

SOCIAL STANDARDS

It was defamatory to say of a man during the First World War that he was German, or to say someone was a Communist in the 1920s, and the word 'appeasement' was capable of being defamatory in the 1930s. However, it was not regarded as defamatory to say of someone in the 1920s that they had worked during a strike, even though they were active trade unionists, since ordinary, decent members of society then were clearly not expected to strike, or even belong to trade unions. The standard is of society *generally*, not of any particular group. So, to say of a person that they have given information to the police is not necessarily defamatory, since right-thinking members of society generally – even today – are expected to do their civic duty and assist the police, despite the fact that it may make you unpopular with your neighbours.

THE ORDINARY REASONABLE READER

The objective test for defamation is not what the writer intended or had in mind in writing the words complained of, but what an ordinary reader would have thought when he or she read them. This hypothetical ordinary reader is not merely a reasonable person of normal intelligence but also moves about in society, probably reads newspapers and watches TV, has a reasonable sense of humour and is fairly up to date with common linguistic usages, including current slang. As the House of Lords said in one case: 'The ordinary man does not live in an ivory tower. He can and does read between the lines in the light of his general knowledge and experience of worldly affairs.'

Thus, in the classic 1930 case of *Tolley* v. *Fry*, the depiction of a champion amateur golfer apparently advertising a Fry's chocolate bar was defamatory, since the ordinary reader would assume that he would have been paid for such sponsorship and had therefore prostituted his amateur status. The advertisement itself did not say that, but that is what the ordinary reader would have thought.

The ordinary reader is not, however, unduly suspicious or cynical. A 1964 case held that to say officers of the City of London Fraud Squad were inquiring into the affairs of a company did not mean the company was guilty of fraud: although some cynics might have thought so, the ordinary reader would not necessarily conclude that the company was guilty simply because an inquiry was under way. The article was capable of meaning that the company was suspected of fraud, which was a less serious, but still defamatory, meaning.

CONTEXT OF THE STATEMENT

The ordinary reader is taken not just to read headlines (which are often sensational in nature), but also to read the article accompanying the headline. In 1995, the House of Lords held that a prominent headline or a headline and photograph could not found a claim in libel in isolation from the related text of an accompanying article which was not defamatory when considered as a whole.

In that case, the actor and actress who played the characters Harold and Madge Bishop in the soap *Neighbours* sued when their faces were superimposed onto a photograph of a couple engaged in sexual intercourse. The headline read 'Strewth! What's Harold Up To With Our Madge?'. However, the body of the article discussed a computer game which superimposed the faces of celebrities onto the bodies of porn stars and stated that the celebrities had nothing to do with it. The single natural and ordinary meaning to be ascribed to the words of the allegedly defamatory publication was the meaning which the article taken as a whole conveyed to the mind of the ordinary, reasonable, fair-minded reader. Accordingly, the claimants could not rely on a defamatory meaning conveyed only to the limited category of readers who only read headlines.

HIDDEN MEANINGS AND INNUENDOES

Words are normally to be construed in their 'natural and ordinary meaning' – might reasonable people understand those words in a defamatory sense? To call someone a thief or a murderer is fairly plainly defamatory. Remember, however, that the ordinary reader is also capable of reading between the lines. Words not so plainly defamatory in themselves may still carry a defamatory *innuendo*, when read in context, or when used against certain people. The classic example of innuendo meaning is *Tolley* v. *Fry* mentioned above. The special fact known by certain persons which made the advertisement defamatory was that the claimant was an amateur golfer. Similarly, to describe a person as voting Liberal Democrat is not defamatory *per se*, but it could be if the person concerned is a well-known Labour supporter, because it would imply the person was a hypocrite, or even a liar.

Even if the specific facts which you are describing are true, it is still dangerously easy to go beyond those specific facts and draw a more general *inference* which might *not* be true, and would therefore be defamatory. To say of a publishing company that they were once found to have committed a trading standards offence in their advertising would not be defamatory, if it was true, but it might become defamatory if you then go on to imply from that that they are the sort of publisher that regularly defrauds the public with misleading advertising. A tour operator might on one occasion have sent tourists to a non-existent hotel, but if you publish an inference that they habitually do so they might well have an action against you for defamation.

THE REPETITION RULE

Every re-publication of a libel is a new libel. It is not a defence to say that you are simply a commentator or reporter repeating a statement made by someone else: defamatory statements do not somehow come into the 'public domain' once published or uttered, so that the subject thereafter becomes fair game. A libel is a libel, and the more often it is repeated – even as a 'rumour' or as an attributed quote – the more damage it can do and the more libel writs it may provoke. Different newspapers repeating the same story can *all* therefore be sued (and often are), and a remainder merchant or bookshop re-publishing an old title as a remainder might well find that they are repeating an old libel.

Where a publisher repeats a statement made by somebody else then the publisher is treated as having made the statement. So, the statement that 'the BBC reported that X is a terrorist' *means* that 'X is a terrorist', not that the BBC reported it. This is known as the 'repetition rule'. Furthermore, when it comes to proving the truth of the allegation, the rule states that it is not sufficient simply to point to the fact that the BBC was accurately quoted. The publisher must prove the substance of the allegation, namely that X is a terrorist (which, in this example, is an extremely difficult thing to do).

LEVELS OF MEANING

According to the courts, a defamatory allegation will usually have one of three levels of meaning. The highest level is 'guilt' (level 1), so for example, the statement that 'X is a thief' has a level 1 meaning. In order to succeed in a defence of justification at this level, which we deal with below (p. 171), a publisher would have to prove that the claimant is in fact guilty of theft (e.g. by pointing to a criminal conviction). The second level of meaning is 'reasonable grounds to suspect'. Statements will be attributed this level of meaning if the imputation is that the claimant is or was under suspicion. To say that someone has been 'accused of' or is 'alleged' to have committed theft would usually bring it under this level of meaning. To justify this level 2 meaning, one would generally need to prove that the reasonable grounds to suspect existed at the time the statement was published (justification of this level of meaning is explained further below on p. 172). The third (and lowest) level of defamatory meaning is 'grounds to investigate'. Stating that someone has been or is currently being investigated of a wrong doing but denies the allegations is likely to convey this level 3 meaning. Such a statement could be justified by proof of the grounds on which the investigating body brought the investigation. However, such information may not always be available to the publisher.

IDENTIFICATION

Once you have established that a statement is defamatory, a claimant must still prove that he or she, personally, is identifiable as the target before he or she can succeed in a defamation action. The words must not only be defamatory, and be published, but they must also be published 'of the claimant': that is, the finger must point at him or her. Put another way, the words complained of must be capable of being understood by reasonable people to refer to the claimant, so that those who know him or her would think that they were the person referred to.

It is not necessary that you should actually be named. If you are well known as the head of a particular publishing house, or the leader of a religious cult, or even the headteacher of a school, then you may be sufficiently identifiable to have an action for defamation – on the grounds that you were known to be responsible at the time, or must at least have known what was going on. 'A wealthy benefactor of the Liberal Party' secured damages on one occasion on the grounds that there were so few wealthy benefactors of the Liberal Party that everyone knew the words referred to him. Authors and publishers should therefore take great care over 'fictionalised' accounts of real-life situations or events. However much the names are changed, if it would be clear to any reasonable person which actual people or companies are being described, those concerned might well have an action for defamation.

It would not be defamatory, however, to make generalised statements about *all* members of a broad group or class, such as members of the Garrick Club or the Groucho Club: the statement must be taken to refer to the claimant personally, or to an identifiable group. To say that 'all lawyers are thieves' is not defamatory (however shocking), but it may be defamatory to criticise a particular group of lawyers, or a particular jury: each of them would then have an action.

Authors, and their publishers, should be particularly careful how they select names of fictitious characters, particularly if they are planning to put those characters in compromising positions. A humorous article in which a fictitious character called Artemus Jones appeared on the Continent 'with a woman who is not his wife' was held to be defamatory in 1910, when a real Artemus Jones turned up with several witnesses, all of whom claimed they thought the article referred to him. It would be similarly dangerous to publish unflattering references to any fictitious, but named, character, for example a fat actress: a real actress who happened to have the same name and who was a little plump may be able to prove that her friends (and potential theatrical employers) thought the references were to her. Selecting names of wicked aristocrats, dissolute women, or any other fictitious rogues or crooks, should therefore be undertaken with great care.

Nevertheless, in a 2001 case, the *Sunday Mirror* published, in five consecutive issues, a pornographic advertisement for an adult Internet service provider. The advertisement contained a photograph of a woman holding a telephone to her ear saying 'See me now at www.internet.com if you have access to the net, join on line now'. The claimant sued for defamation alleging that, as the photograph was the spitting image of her, people who knew her would believe she was appearing on a pornographic website as well as in the advertisement. In fact the photograph was of a glamour model who had consented to the publication.

The court held that the advertisement was objectively capable of referring to the claimant. Furthermore, it referred to the case involving Artemus Jones mentioned above and confirmed that innocence was no defence in such a case. Nevertheless, the court decided that Article 10 of the European Convention on Human Rights, which protects freedom of expression, prevented the law of defamation applying in the 'look alike' situation. The judge stated that it would impose an impossible burden on publishers if they were required to check if the true picture of someone resembled someone else who, because of the context of the picture, was defamed.

Nonetheless, the general rule is: if you think there is any risk you may be identifying a real person, do everything you reasonably can to check that no one of that name and description already exists, and if still in doubt, pick another name.

Finally, bear in mind the risk of juxtaposition of unconnected pieces of text or photographs. This can apply to any publication including advertisements. It is a risk particularly run by periodical and newspaper publishers. One extreme example of this was Jason Donovan's successful libel action in 1992 against *The Face* magazine, when his face was superimposed on to a photograph of someone else wearing a T-shirt which read 'Queer as Fuck'. It can be done quite innocently and accidentally, however: it is possible to defame someone simply by printing their photograph, or some other reference to them, next to quite unconnected text which is critical or unflattering of other people – a picture of a reputable literary agent next to an article on corruption or tax evasion, or of a happily married author next to a piece about prostitution or pornography. The fact that you did not intend any defamatory reference will not necessarily give you a defence, if the friends of those people would assume the piece referred to them. Those responsible for final page make-up should therefore be made well aware of the risks.

PUBLICATION

A statement in order to be libelous must be published to a third party. This means that any communication to someone other than the person being defamed counts as a publication. Most publications or information services put on to the market will, by definition, satisfy that requirement. Three points in particular should be noted.

LIABILITY FOR PUBLICATION

All those involved in a publication are *prima facie* liable for defamatory statements contained in it. This includes not only the original author of the words concerned, but everyone else who has taken part in publishing them. This could potentially include the author, editor, sub-editor, publishing director, publisher and proprietor. Responsibility can also extend to the printer, distributor, bookseller and even newspaper vendor. Nevertheless, anyone who is not the author, editor or publisher of the statement, may have a defence if they can show that they took reasonable care in relation to the publication and did not know, and had no reason to believe, that what they did contributed to the defamation (see below). One of the most important issues is the liability of Internet service providers for defamatory remarks on sites which they host (as to which see the section on innocent dissemination at p. 178 below).

ONLINE PUBLICATION

In a case in December 2001, the Court of Appeal held that every time someone reads an article in a newspaper's online archive, the newspaper is considered to have made a fresh publication. Thus, the limitation period (which is one year) begins again for each communication. In theory, this means that a publisher can potentially be open to a libel suit forever.

JURISDICTION

For the purposes of English defamation law, publication takes place in the jurisdiction where the matter is viewed. So if a foreign publisher sells some copies to people in

England or Wales (whether in hard copy or online form), it will be publishing in England.

Depending on where the claimant and the publisher are domiciled, the courts may need to consider whether the allegedly defamed person has a connection to the United Kingdom (e.g. by virtue of his reputation, family or business connections). The cases of *Don King* v. *Lennox Lewis* and *Richardson* v. *Schwarzenegger* make it clear that the English courts will not distinguish between those who deliberately publish in the UK and those who do so incidentally and without intending to target any particular jurisdiction. Generally, the greater the connection which the claimant has to England, the more likely it is that the English court will seize jurisdiction of the proceedings. Thus, if the claimant is an English citizen or has a significant reputation in England, it is likely that the court will refuse to stay the proceedings, even if the publisher is based in the US and most of the readers are in the US.

However, where the number of publications in England is so insignificant that there was no real or substantial tort, the English court is likely to strike out the claim as an abuse of process. In the case of *Dow Jones* v. *Jousef Jameel* (2005), the Court of Appeal struck out a claim against the *Wall Street Journal On-line* as there had only been five subscribers to the publication in the jurisdiction. In the circumstances of the case, the costs of the litigation would have been out of all proportion to any damage which could have been suffered by the claimant.

DEFENCES

Once a claimant has proved that the words complained of were defamatory, that they refer to him or her, and that they were published by the particular publisher concerned (note that claimants do *not* need to prove that the words were false), then the burden of proof shifts to the publisher: they must then prove (if they can) that there is a valid defence. English law provides a number of possible defences to an action for defamation. We will look at them in turn, but the main defences are:

- truth or justification
- fair comment
- absolute or qualified privilege
- innocent dissemination.

JUSTIFICATION

With one very limited statutory exception (below) it is an absolute defence to a charge of defamation to prove that the statement you published was true. It is not necessary to prove that every word of the statement is true, provided that it is substantially true. Minor errors of detail, which do not form the main substance, or essence, of the libel, will not prevent a defence of justification from succeeding.

What is the position, however, if the fact which turns out to be untrue is not some minor detail of time or place, but is also defamatory itself? It used to be the position that every defamatory statement of fact had to be separately justified, but under the Defamation Act 1952 this is no longer the case. Section 5 of the 1952 Act provides that a defence of justification will still succeed 'if the words not proved to be true do not materially injure the claimant's reputation, having regard to the truth of the remaining charges'.

Remember, however, that if you go beyond individual facts and make a much more serious general inference or innuendo which is *not* true, a defence of justification may not protect you. All material allegations must be substantially true.

It is no defence to claim afterwards that you were merely repeating rumours which genuinely existed, although the meaning may not be defamatory if you make it clear at the time of the statement that what you are saying is only a rumour. As a general rule, the truth you must prove is the truth of the sting of the article – not the fact that it was being rumoured. It is therefore important, if you are going to plead justification as a defence, to have reliable witnesses who will be prepared to testify in person as to the main fact on your behalf at a trial. If they are likely to become unreliable or disappear altogether, it may be in your interests to secure an witness statement from them, or at least ensure that they have kept a written note, or some other record such as a tape recording, but such evidence will not always be admissible.

The conduct rule

A publisher seeking to justify a statement which imputes a meaning of 'reasonable grounds to suspect' (a level 2 meaning) can generally only succeed by adducing convincing evidence relating to the conduct of the individual claimant. This is referred to as the 'conduct rule'. Evidence of existing credible allegations in the hands of a defendant publisher at the time of making the statement has been held by the courts not to be sufficient to justify such a meaning. For example, if the meaning of the publication is that there are reasonable grounds to suspect that X is a fraudster, it is not enough to prove that someone else (e.g. the police or the government) believes X is a fraudster. The publisher must prove that the conduct of X gave the publisher reasonable grounds for the suspicion (for example, that he used a false name when signing cheques). In summary, the conduct rule states that a defence will generally only succeed if the publisher is able to prove the level 2 meaning by concentrating on the conduct of the claimant which gave rise to the suspicion at the time of publication.

Spent convictions

The one exception to the general rule that truth is an absolute defence is the statutory provision relating to 'spent' convictions under the Rehabilitation of Offenders Act 1974. It is considered socially useful that relatively minor offences should be erased from the public memory after a certain period of time – the periods vary from three to ten years, depending on how serious the original offence was. After such convictions have become 'spent', evidence relating to them will not generally be admissible, but such evidence *will* be available in defamation actions to support a plea of justification, provided the original publication was not made with malice. We will deal more fully with 'malice' below, but for practical purposes here this is a very restricted exception.

FAIR COMMENT

English courts have long recognised a limited right of fair comment, by accepting it as a valid defence to a charge of defamation. This does not protect every form of comment, but it does provide a real defence for honest opinions, based on real facts and honestly expressed, on matters of public interest. To succeed in a fair comment defence, the defendant must prove four things:

(1) The statement must be an opinion.
(2) The opinion must be honestly held.
(3) The facts on which it is based must be true.
(4) The comment must be on a matter of public interest.

Even if the defendant can prove these things, the defence will not succeed if the claimant can show that the publication was made maliciously. Here, malice means an improper dominant motive such as making the statement knowing it was false, being reckless about its truth or falsity, or making the statement deliberately to injure the claimant.

Fair comment must be based on true fact

The statement must clearly be recognisable as personal opinion, but it must be opinion *on* something. It is not fair comment simply to express random opinions on other people. So to say of a well-known entrepreneur that they are not fit to be a director of a British company, without any supporting facts, would not normally be regarded as fair comment. If, however, you said that in your opinion the person was unfit to be a director because they had just been convicted of specific crimes (and that was true), then your comment is likely to be held to be fair comment.

It is very important to separate opinion from statements of fact. Fair comment must be based on true facts, but it is still recognisably comment. If it consists merely of fresh, unsupported allegations of (untrue) fact, or is mixed up with such statements, it may not be defensible as 'fair comment' at all. Something that is clearly intended to be healthy, vigorous comment may still be found to be defamatory if it contains strong inferences of (untrue) fact. A book reviewer might run such a risk, if he or she significantly misdescribes the book being reviewed, for example in basing criticism on its irresponsible approach to some topic such as adultery or child abuse when in fact the book does not adopt that approach, or even deal with those topics at all. If you impute to an author that they have written something which they have not in fact written, you are making an allegation of fact, not making a fair comment – and that allegation of fact might well be defamatory.

Reviewers and columnists are as much at risk from this as anyone else, even though they may think their copy is self-evidently fair comment. So too are biographers, and even those who write Letters to the Editor, if they make allegations of fact which are untrue. The House of Lords has held that the writer of a letter to a newspaper has a duty to take reasonable care to make clear that he is writing comment, and not making misrepresentations about the subject matter on which he is commenting.

If any passage of text which includes both fact and opinion is giving concern, therefore, it is a good idea to run the following tests:

• Are all the facts stated (and quotations) true and accurate – and can we prove it?
• Is any 'comment' honestly held and based on true facts?

If the answer to either of the above questions is 'no', a defence of fair comment may not succeed.

Fair comment and honest opinion

'Fair comment' may be profoundly biased and deeply unfair as long as it is an honest opinion. To succeed in a defence of fair comment, the defence need only establish that the statement was objectively capable of representing an honest opinion, or in other words that any person, however subjectively unreasonable, might honestly have held those views. The opinion need not be 'fair' in the colloquial sense of reasonable, fair-minded, balanced or even-handed. Commentators and critics are expected to express vigorous, often highly subjective, opinions. However, your defence may still fail if the claimant can show that you were not in that particular case being *subjectively* honest, and for example did not honestly hold those views yourself; or were motivated by some improper ulterior motive, such as malice.

'Malice', for these purposes, is any improper motive, including not only personal spite and ill-will but also any desire to cause injury, directly or indirectly – usually to the person who is defamed, but also including his or her family, or company, for example. Seeking a personal benefit without any desire to harm others can also be malice. Evidence that someone has gone ahead with publication of a statement, knowing it to be false, is *prima facie* proof of malice. A refusal to apologise, or offer any amends, once it has become clear that the statement is false or misleading, may also in some circumstances be regarded as malice. Similarly, a failure to give the other side a reasonable opportunity to state their own case, or comment on criticisms prior to publication, may be seen as malicious, especially if the allegations are likely to cause damage. Product reviews in trade journals which make imputations about a company may particularly be at risk from this. In the 1994 *Yachting World* case, a yacht was given a poor review and the manufacturers claimed the review implied that they had made dishonest representations about the yacht's performance. The review was held to be defamatory and malicious because the makers were not given an opportunity to comment on the review, which questioned the company's integrity in a way which was likely to cause serious damage.

Fair comment and public interest

Finally, fair comment must be comment on a matter of public interest. Nowadays, public interest is fairly widely defined to include any matters in which the public might have a legitimate interest, including (up to a point) the private lives of politicians or public officials. It covers, by definition, comment on all published works available to the public at large, such as books, plays, newspapers, theatrical or musical performances, exhibited paintings, or photographs. It would probably *not* include the private lives of authors, but it may well include their public activities and equally the public conduct of anyone else in a public role, such as doctors, teachers or company directors. The question is for the judge to decide, but few matters are now considered not to be of any public interest.

PRIVILEGE

English law regards some occasions as being self-evidently of public interest, and therefore protects statements made on those occasions from any actions for defamation. Such statements are said to be 'privileged'. The law will protect them, however untruthful they may turn out to be, in order to give the greatest possible freedom of speech to those who are regarded in the public interest as having a social or professional duty to speak freely.

Privilege comes in two kinds: absolute privilege, and a lesser form of conditional privilege known as qualified privilege.

Absolute privilege

As the name implies, statements carrying absolute privilege are completely protected from defamation actions, even though they may have been made maliciously or with reckless unconcern for the truth. Statements made by MPs or peers in Parliament are absolutely privileged, as are statements made in court, or during quasi-judicial proceedings, for example before tribunals, inquests or courts martial. Statements made by government ministers, senior civil servants or officers of the armed forces in the course of their official duty are absolutely privileged. So too are official Parliamentary or government reports such as Reports of Select Committees or White Papers.

In addition, the following reports are absolutely privileged:

(1) *Hansard*. This is the official daily report of proceedings in Parliament.
(2) *Contemporaneous court reports*. The Defamation Act 1996 provides that fair and accurate reports of proceedings in public before any court in the UK, the European Court of Justice, the European Court of Human Rights and any international criminal tribunal established by the United Nations are also protected by absolute privilege, provided they are published 'contemporaneously', that is in the next reasonably available issue or broadcast if in a newspaper or on the radio or TV.

Apart from the above two examples, second-hand reports of statements, for example in newspapers, are *not* generally protected by absolute privilege, although they may be given qualified privilege.

Qualified privilege

The essence of qualified privilege is the public interest for a particular recipient to receive frank and uninhibited communication of information from a particular source. Although only a conditional form of protection, qualified privilege still gives considerable protection to many statements even if they turn out to be untrue, made on matters of public interest, or in the context of a social or professional duty, provided that they are made without malice (as defined on p. 174 above in relation to the defence of fair comment). The publication must be in the public interest, not merely of interest to some of them.

The leading case on qualified privilege is *Reynolds* v. *Times Newspapers Limited*, where Albert Reynolds, the former Irish Taoiseach (prime minister) and leader of the Fianna Fàil party sued for defamation over an article, which he alleged meant that he had deliberately and dishonestly misled the Irish Dáil (Parliament). The article failed to give an account of Mr Reynolds's side of the story. The judge held that the newspaper could not rely on the defence of qualified privilege even though the reported matter was political in nature. This issue went all the way to the House of Lords, which rejected the argument by *The Times* that the law should recognise a generic qualified privilege for the publication by a newspaper of political information affecting the people of the United Kingdom.

The House of Lords held in 1999 that in order to succeed in the defence of qualified privilege for a statement published without malice, the publisher must be under a legal, social or moral duty to publish the statement to the recipients and the recipients must have a corresponding interest in receiving the statement ('the duty–interest test'). In applying this test, the court must have regard to all the relevant circumstances, such as:

(1) the seriousness of the allegation;
(2) the nature of the information and the extent to which the subject-matter was a matter of public concern;
(3) the source of the information;
(4) the steps taken to verify the information;
(5) the status of the information;
(6) the urgency of the matter;
(7) whether comment was sought from the claimant;
(8) whether the article contained the gist of the claimant's side of the story;
(9) the tone of the article; and
(10) the circumstances of the publication, including its timing.

The test for qualified privilege in the case of a publication to the world at large, for example in a newspaper, was whether the public were entitled to know the information and not whether a responsible journalist would publish it. It is important to note that a defendant cannot rely on facts of which it had been unaware at the date of publication, to support its defence of qualified privilege.

The courts have applied the Reynolds criteria in a number of cases since the House of Lords' decision in 1999. In interpreting the criteria, the courts have made it clear that they will expect the defendant to demonstrate responsible journalism before the privilege can be established. In particular, the courts will expect:

- checks to be made by journalists to verify their stories;
- the journalist to approach the subject of any allegations and put the allegations which are to be published to the person and ask for comment, giving the subject adequate time to respond on all of the allegations. The graver the allegation, the greater the need to give an opportunity to the subject of the allegations to comment;
- the journalist/publisher to delay publication if more checks must be made to verify the story, unless the story is objectively of an urgent nature (which is rare);
- the journalist not to rely heavily on draft or interim reports but to point to a concluded investigation before identifying the subject of any allegation. If the journalist waits until the outcome of an investigation, the defence is more likely to succeed.

As far as the courts are concerned, the desire to be the first to deliver a scoop and/or editorial pressure are not relevant to the consideration of urgency. The courts will also consider if the urgency alleged is borne out of the way the journalist/publisher has conducted his affairs.

Even if a newspaper, for example, can rely on the defence of qualified privilege in relation to the original publication of a defamatory article, it may not be able to do so in relation to fresh publications of the article stored in its online archive (as mentioned above, there will be a new publication every time someone views the article online). Publishers therefore face the burden of continually checking their archived materials.

Book publishers may have particular difficulties in relying on qualified privilege. This is because the lead-in time for a book is so much longer than for newspapers that the author and publisher will probably be expected by the court to have thoroughly satisfied the ten Reynolds factors. So for example, the author will usually have to have carried out rigorous checks of the facts as well as put the allegations to the claimant and printed his or her side of the story. Furthermore, if the publisher is put on notice about false information but continues to publish the book, then this could amount to malice which defeats a qualified privilege defence. The general rule therefore is that book authors and publishers should work on the basis that they will have to justify all defamatory allegations contained in the book.

Statements to and from those with a common interest may also be protected by qualified privilege – for example, between doctor and patient, or solicitor and client, company shareholders, employers (sharing references), or even members of a club. They must, however, be on an actual topic of shared interest, and be made without any hint of malice.

Statutory qualified privilege

The 1996 Defamation Act specifically grants qualified privilege, in the absence of malice, for fair and accurate reports of proceedings in public of any legislature, court, official public inquiry or international organisation or conference in the world as well as copies or extracts from documents required by law to be open to public inspection or published by any court, government, legislature or international organisation or conference in the world. It also provides a further category of qualified privilege including the following fair and accurate reports, but 'subject to explanation and contradiction':

(1) A copy or extracts of matter:

    a.   issued from an EU legislature, government or authority performing governmental functions (including police functions), the European Parliament or Commission, or an international organisation or international conference (attended by at least two governments);

    b.   made available by any EU Court or the European Court of Justice;

(2) Reports of any finding or decision of any EU associations promoting:

    a.   art, science, religion or learning;

    b.   any trade, business, industry or profession;

    c.   any game, sport or pastime;

    d.   charitable objects or other objects beneficial to the community;

(3) Reports of proceedings of any public meeting in the EU of a local authority, justice of the peace, official inquiry or held under a statutory provision;

(4) Reports of proceedings at any bona fide and lawful meeting in the EU concerning a matter of public concern;

(5) General Meetings of UK public companies.

However, this further category of qualified privilege will not be available if the claimant has requested a reply to be published and the defendant refuses or neglects to do so.

INNOCENT DISSEMINATION

A person who is not the author, editor or publisher of a statement complained of has a defence if he took reasonable care in relation to its publication and did not know, and had no reason to believe, that what he did caused the publication of a defamatory statement. Here 'publisher' means a commercial publisher, that is, a person whose business is issuing material to the public. A person is not considered to be an author, editor or publisher if he is only involved in the following:

(a) in printing, producing, distributing or selling printed material containing the statement;

(b) in processing, making copies of, distributing, exhibiting or selling a film or sound recording containing the statement;

(c) in processing, making copies of, distributing or selling any electronic medium in or on which the statement is recorded, or in operating or providing any equipment, system or service by means of which the statement is retrieved, copied, distributed or made available in electronic form;

(d) as the broadcaster of a live programme containing the statement in circumstances in which he has no effective control over the maker of the statement;

(e) as the operator of or provider of access to a communication system by means of which the statement is transmitted, or made available, by a person over whom he has no effective control.

This defence was tested in 1999 when a Dr Godfrey sued the Internet service provider (ISP), Demon Internet. In that case a defamatory article was posted on one of Demon's newsgroups. However, the posting was falsely stated to have been written by Dr Godfrey. He wrote to Demon requesting that the statement be removed. Demon did not take any steps to remove it and it remained in the newsgroup until the posting expired 10 days later. Dr Godfrey sued for libel and the ISP sought to rely on the defence of innocent dissemination. The court held that although the ISP was not the author, editor or publisher (as it fell within (e) above), it failed to take reasonable care in relation to the statement and knew about the publication of the defamatory statement. Once Dr Godfrey had given the ISP notice of the defamatory statement, the ISP could no longer rely on the defence of innocent dissemination. Therefore, ISPs who have been given notice of defamatory statements on websites hosted by them should ensure that they take reasonable care in relation to these statements.

The innocent dissemination defence has also been tested in relation to bookshops. In 2002, the court decided that a bookshop could not rely on the defence following the sale of an anti-racist pamphlet which included a defamatory statement. The man who the statement related to had written a letter of complaint to the bookshop and the bookshop continued to sell the pamphlet. The bookshop therefore could not establish that they had no reason to believe that what it did caused or contributed to the publication of the defamatory statement.

ISP LIABILITY

In addition to the innocent dissemination defence, Internet service providers were given further comfort with the enactment of the Electronic Commerce (EC Directive) Regulations 2002. Regulation 17 provides that where a service consists of the transmission in a communication network of information provided by a recipient of the service, or the provision of access to a communication network, the service provider is not liable for the information transmitted, on condition that the provider:

• does not initiate the transmission;
• does not select the receiver of the transmission; and
• does not select or modify the information contained in the transmission.

Transmission and provision of access includes the automatic, intermediate and transient storage of the information transmitted, insofar as the sole purpose is the transmission and provided that the information is not stored longer than is reasonably necessary. Thus ISPs and intermediaries which are merely conduits will not be liable. (As mentioned below, the position is different where an ISP hosts a website.)

Furthermore, the Regulations also limit liability for ISPs which cache information, that is, store information more locally to make more efficient the transmission of the information. The service provider is not liable for caching, on condition that the provider does not modify the information and complies with certain industry rules. A further requirement is that the provider acts expeditiously to remove information upon obtaining actual knowledge that the information at the initial source of transmission has been removed or ordered by a court to be removed.

The Regulations also state that where a provider of a service, which consists of the storage of information provided by a recipient of the service, i.e. where an ISP hosts a website for someone, the service provider will not be liable for the information stored at the request of the recipient of the service. The conditions are that:

- the provider does not have actual knowledge of illegal activity or information; or
- the provider, upon obtaining such knowledge acts expeditiously to remove or disable access to the information.

In the United States, ISP immunity from defamation actions has generally been granted by section 230(c)(1) of the federal Communications Decency Act 1996. This is achieved by stating that ISPs, and indeed any provider or user of interactive computer services such as libraries and schools, are precluded from being treated as publishers of any information provided by another content provider. The US Court of Appeals, Fourth Circuit confirmed in 1997 that the section covered tort-based lawsuits, including defamation, and that it extended to 'distributors' of such material, as well as 'publication', protecting ISPs further.

OFFER OF AMENDS

Defamation proceedings can be long and expensive. Where a defendant has published a defamatory statement, there is a method of speedily resolving the matter which aims to reduce expense. In order to achieve this, a defendant may offer to make amends by publishing, in a reasonable manner, a suitable correction of the statement complained of and a suitable apology to the aggrieved party, and to pay compensation and costs as may be agreed or determined. Thus, if the compensation under an offer of amends cannot be agreed between the parties, the matter will be determined by a judge.

The offer to make amends must be made before the defence is served and so the defendant must act quickly. If the offer is accepted, the party accepting the offer may not bring or continue defamation proceedings in respect of the publication concerned. If the offer is not accepted, the fact that the offer was made shall be a defence, unless the person making the offer knew or had reason to believe that the statement complained of referred to the aggrieved party and was both false and defamatory of that party. In any event, an offer to make amends may be relied on when arguing the amount of damages which should be awarded.

OTHER DEFENCES

Consent

Evidence of consent to publication is a full defence – although often difficult to prove, without signed statements. If you participate in the publication, for example by joining in a radio or TV discussion to put your side of the story, or by publishing your own statement alongside the offending version, then you may be held to have consented to publication taking place. However, the mere consent to be interviewed does not imply consent to specific libels. Consent can only be deduced from some positive act: silence does not imply consent, nor does the time-honoured phrase 'no comment'.

Death of the claimant

Libel is a purely personal action under UK law, and since the dead cannot sue personally, it is normally a complete defence to a libel action to establish that the person defamed is now dead. Even if the claimant was alive when the libel was published, but dies before the case is tried (or even in mid-trial), the action instantly dies too, and cannot be continued by the claimant's relatives or heirs. It may still be possible, however, to commit a *criminal* libel against a dead person (see below, p. 183).

Limitation

It is a defence to an action for defamation to prove that it is out of time, or in other words has been started too late. Claimants must bring their actions within one year from the date of publication. However, if the court considers that it would be equitable to allow the claimant to sue even if he or she is outside this time limit, it has a discretion to allow the claim to proceed if it would not prejudice the parties. Publishers with online archives should note that the time period of one year does not start from the date on which an article is uploaded onto the archive. Each time an article is downloaded and read by a web user it counts as a fresh publication with a fresh limitation period. It is therefore important to monitor archived articles and to remove any which, although perhaps not defamatory at the time the original story was published, are later rendered so by the occurrence of new events.

COSTS

The legal costs of bringing or defending an action for defamation often run into hundreds of thousands of pounds (and sometimes even exceed the £1 million mark).

The general rule in the English courts is that the losing party has to pay a proportion (e.g. 60–90 per cent) of the winner's costs. As mentioned above, the maximum general damages awarded have been about £200,000. It therefore comes as no surprise that it is frequently the costs of an action that become the driving force of the dispute. This is especially so if the person bringing the claim is funding the action by way of a conditional fee agreement (CFA) with his or her lawyer.

Under a CFA, a claimant's solicitors will usually only recover their fees in the event that either the claim succeeds or the defendant admits liability (e.g. in a settlement). The solicitors' fees are recovered from the losing defendant. A CFA is a kind of no-win-no-fee system. If the claimant wins, his lawyer will be able to charge a 'success fee', which can be an additional 100 per cent of the actual costs that have been incurred. So, if the defendant is unsuccessful in defending the claim, he may be liable to pay not only his own costs but also the claimant's costs plus the success fee. For example, if both sides' costs are £300,000 and the claimant's lawyer is working on a 90 per cent success fee, a losing publisher could have to pay £756,000. This is made up of £300,000 paid to the publisher's own lawyer and £456,000 to the claimant's lawyer at a recovery rate on the base costs of 80 per cent. The calculation is 80% × £300,000 = £240,000 for the claimant's base costs, plus 90% × £240,000 = £216,000 for the success fee. Furthermore, even if the defendant is successful, he will sometimes be unable to recover his own costs from a claimant who is funded by a CFA because the claimant may have no money.

After-the-event insurance policies (ATEs) are sometimes available to provide cover for a claimant's liability for the defendant's costs if the claim is unsuccessful, but these are very unlikely to be available for claims where the chances of success are not favourable. Also, some policies will be invalid if the publisher successfully justifies the claim (since the insurance would have been premised on the fact of the claimant telling the truth to his or her insurer). In a 2005 case, it was therefore decided that, in order to balance this unfairness to the defendant where a claimant is funded on a CFA with no ATE (and insufficient money of her own), the defendant can apply to the court for an order imposing a cap on the level of the claimant's recoverable costs (known as a costs-capping order). This goes a little way to redress the chilling effect on a publisher's right of freedom of expression by dissuading claimants' solicitors from taking on cases on CFAs.

SUMMARY CHECKLIST: DEFAMATION

IS IT DEFAMATION AT ALL?

• Is it a statement of fact, or an honest opinion?
• Has it been published yet? If not, is it too late to take it out, or tone it down?
• Is there any dangerous innuendo, or inference?
• Does it refer to an identifiable individual?

- Does it lower their reputation?
- Have we checked any 'fictitious' character names (for example in relevant directories)?
- Might this be repeating an old libel?
- Do we have an effective warranty against libel or libel insurance?

ARE THERE ANY DEFENCES?

- Is the statement (and any innuendo) substantially true? Can we prove it?
- Is this all 'fair comment', or are there (untrue) allegations of fact?
- Is this an honest opinion, or is there any malice?
- Is it comment on a matter of public interest?
- Is the statement privileged in any way?
- Was the defendant an ISP which was merely an information conduit, or was merely caching or hosting information?
- Has there been an offer of amends?
- Is the person concerned still alive?
- Did they consent to publication?
- Is it too late to bring a libel action?

CRIMINAL LIBEL

Some libels are regarded as being so serious that they may not only be actionable in the civil courts, but may also be prosecuted in the criminal courts as a crime. It has been an offence at common law since the thirteenth century to publish written libels (particularly, in those days, about the king or the great officers of state) and it may still be possible to bring a prosecution today if prosecution is in the public interest, for example to prevent some public disturbance such as a breach of the peace. Punishment on conviction may consist of up to one year's imprisonment or two years if the libel was known to be false, or a fine (or both), and either party may be bound over to keep the peace.

The crime consists in publishing a 'defamatory libel' (as opposed to a blasphemous or obscene libel) in written form – slander is not generally a crime (although public speakers may now commit other crimes, such as an incitement to racial hatred). A prosecution may be brought either where there is an actual likelihood of a breach of the peace, or at least where the libel is 'serious', rather than trivial or purely personal. Among the very few recent prosecutions were Sir James Goldsmith's prosecution against *Private Eye* in 1977, where there was some evidence of a sustained press campaign, and even bomb threats. Justification is not a complete defence in cases of criminal libel – public interest must be established as well.

Because of the public interest and public order element, it is possible to commit a criminal libel against a whole class of people (unlike a civil libel). Nowadays, however, prosecutions for class libels against, for example, Jews, blacks, or gays, are more often brought under public order or race relations laws. It is also possible to bring a criminal prosecution for words published about the dead – but, again, only if the intention or likelihood was to provoke the dead person's heirs or relatives to commit a breach of the peace.

MALICIOUS FALSEHOOD

Some untruths may not, strictly speaking, be defamatory and (for example) lower you in the estimation of right-thinking members of society, but they may still cause you harm. To say of a publisher or a literary agent, for example, that they had retired from business and were therefore no longer looking for authors, would not be defamatory – people do retire occasionally. If it was untrue, however, it might cause them considerable financial harm, in the shape of lost business, and if it was said maliciously they may have an action for malicious falsehood.

In order to succeed in an action for malicious or injurious falsehood, a claimant must prove:

- that the statement is false;
- that it was published maliciously ('malice', here means that the defendant knew the statement was untrue, and made it intending to injure the claimant or made it with a reckless indifference as to whether harm may be caused to the interests of the claimant); and
- actual financial loss or that it is likely to cause financial loss in his or her office, profession, calling, trade or business at the time of publication (or if the statement is published in writing or other permanent form).

The action was used by the actor Gordon Kaye to prevent the *Sunday Sport* tabloid from publishing an interview he made whilst in hospital just after undergoing extensive surgery for head injuries. Journalists had gained unauthorised access to Mr Kaye's hospital room to interview him. The court prevented publication of the interview on the grounds of malicious falsehood. The article falsely stated that Mr Kaye had consented to the interview (when he was in no fit state to do so). It was published maliciously as it was apparent to the journalists that he was not able to consent. Furthermore, the article was likely to cause damage as Mr Kaye had a valuable right to sell his story. It should also be noted that at the time there was no actionable right of privacy in English law. Such an action can now be brought as a breach of confidence in the light of the Human Rights Act 1998 (see chapter 8).

Since likely financial loss is an important element of actions for malicious falsehood, interim injunctions may often be more readily granted than they are in libel actions, and legal aid may also be available (when it is not for libel). However, the court must be convinced there is a serious risk of financial loss, and there must be a strong suggestion of malice.

NEGLIGENT MIS-STATEMENT

If a statement is not defamatory, or a malicious falsehood, or otherwise illegal, but nevertheless causes harm to people who rely on it, it might still expose the publisher to an action for damages if it was made negligently. Suppose that a leading medical textbook seriously mis-states a recommended drug dosage, or that a specialist financial journal gives a subscriber the wrong investment advice in its regular Advice column. Would either of these mis-statements be negligent?

Negligence is a particular kind of civil wrong (known in English law as a tort). It consists, briefly, in the breach of a duty to take care in a way which causes damage to others. To prove negligent mis-statement, therefore, it is necessary to prove five things:

(1) the person making the statement owed the claimant a duty of care;
(2) the statement was incorrect;
(3) the maker did not take reasonable care, i.e. he or she breached that duty;
(4) the recipient relied on the statement and it was reasonable for him or her to rely on it; and
(5) loss or damage was suffered which was reasonably foreseeable and caused by that breach.

DUTY OF CARE

There is no general legal duty to the whole world not to be careless. For a mis-statement to be negligent, it must be more than merely careless: the maker of the statement – the author or the publisher – must at the time the statement was made have owed the reader a specific legal duty of care. Such legal duties of care are not always easy to prove. They may arise in the context of a clear professional relationship (such as that between doctor and patient), or they may sometimes be assumed or implied in strongly similar circumstances, where any reasonable publisher (for example) would have foreseen the risk of injury to that particular reader, and taken suitable precautions to avoid it.

In the leading case of *Hedley Byrne v. Heller* (1964), the House of Lords confirmed as a general rule that:

> if A assumes a responsibility to B to tender him deliberate advice, there could be a liability if the advice is negligently given.

The crucial word in that proposition is 'assumes'. In that particular case, an advertising agency was retained by a new client for a major advertising campaign, and took out space ads in national newspapers and booked TV advertising slots, all at the agency's own financial risk. Understandably, the agency sought financial references from the new client's bank, which the bank duly gave, but 'without responsibility'. The references turned out not to be reliable and the agency lost a large amount of money. The House of Lords held that a duty of care could exist where a 'special relationship' was created, which might happen in the following circumstances:

- where the party seeking information or advice was 'trusting the other to exercise such a degree of care as the circumstances required';
- where that trust was reasonable; and
- where the other gave the information or advice 'when he knew or ought to know that the enquirer was relying on him'.

However, in that particular case, the bank had clearly given the advice 'without responsibility', and in the view of the House of Lords that disclaimer was sufficient to avoid liability – they had not 'assumed' responsibility.

In the case of a publisher who publishes statements for the whole world to read, it would be difficult to establish a specific legal duty of care unless it could be shown that there was a 'special relationship' with a particular reader, or group of readers. This is unlikely to exist in the circumstances of trade publishing, but it may possibly exist in the case of some specialist, professional or STM publishers, who give information or advice to a limited, specific market knowing that those people might reasonably be expected to rely on it. This might particularly be so in the context of a specific Advice service (or column) – the second of our two original examples – where answers to subscribers' queries are held out as being authoritative; a reader or subscriber relying (and known to be relying) on the skill and judgment apparently being offered might well – in the absence of any disclaimer – be able to prove that a sufficient duty of care existed, and claim damages for negligence if he or she suffered loss when the advice turned out to be wrong.

In the first of our two examples above, however – where a mis-statement is published in a textbook circulating generally to a wide readership – it is unlikely that any individual reader would be able to establish a similar duty of care, and negligence would be much harder to prove.

The same considerations would apply to mis-statements published on the Internet. Although statements made on a website will, by definition, be addressed to a very large audience (potentially, the whole world), there will also be instances where, for example, specialist advice is given to a particular individual or a group of Internet users, such that a duty of care could be established.

DISCLAIMERS

Some publishers seek to discourage negligence claims by printing general disclaimers of liability at the front of their books. Such disclaimers are usually unpopular with authors since they imply a lack of confidence in the text, and they are probably of limited legal effect. Even if it can be established that they formed part of the contract of sale (and disclaimers in small print tend not to be noticed at the time) they are still subject to the test of 'reasonableness' under the Unfair Contract

Terms Act 1977 (see p. 280) or the Unfair Terms in Consumer Contracts Regulations 1999. A court might well find in all the circumstances that the disclaimer was unreasonable – particularly if the publisher could easily have insured against the risk.

A specific disclaimer given in circumstances similar to the *Hedley Byrne* case above, however, might be effective if it made it clear that no responsibility for the statement(s) was being assumed.

OBSCENITY

INTRODUCTION

It is not a crime for an author to write obscene material, but it *is* a crime for a publisher (or anyone else) to publish it. It is also an offence for anyone to have it in their possession, with a view to publication for profit. Although authors are often asked in their publishing contracts to warrant that the material they produce is in no way obscene or indecent, this only gives a limited contractual remedy to the publisher against the author: the criminal offence will still be committed by the publisher and, in some cases, by the distributor, and it is they who will be prosecuted and possibly fined or sent to prison. Publishers should therefore take every possible precaution themselves against publishing obscene or indecent material, however innocently. This applies as much to text as to photographs or other illustrations, and increasingly to computer images (for example, on the Internet) as much as to printed matter.

OBSCENE PUBLICATIONS

Although the criminal offence of publishing an obscene libel is of some antiquity (obscenity having originally been dealt with under ecclesiastical law) what is or is not 'obscene' has never been defined very clearly. The law is now largely contained in the Obscene Publications Act 1959, and the test of obscenity is now contained in section 1 of that Act. Section 1 provides that an article, or any distinct item contained in an article, is obscene:

> if its effect ... is, if taken as a whole, such as to tend to deprave and corrupt persons who are likely, in all the circumstances, to read, see or hear the matter contained or embodied in it.

'Deprave' and 'corrupt' are strong words. They mean something considerably worse than simply shocking or disgusting, and one conviction (of the *Oz* 'School Kids' issue) was overturned in 1971 because the trial judge had wrongly directed the jury that obscenity could mean merely 'repulsive, filthy, loathsome, indecent or lewd'. An article is not obscene simply because it is repulsive or filthy. The prosecution must prove that its tendency is strong enough actually to deprave and corrupt a significant proportion of its likely audience; in other words, to pervert or corrupt their morals sufficiently for it to constitute a public menace. It is necessary for more than a negligible number of persons to see the material (see *R* v. *Perrin* below). Furthermore, the entire article 'taken as a whole' must have that tendency, not just one small bit of it.

It is important to note that obscenity is not just about sex. Anything tending to deprave or corrupt may be obscene, including material encouraging the taking of dangerous drugs or glorifying violence, particularly if it is expressly targeted at children or adolescents. But sex usually creeps in somewhere.

OBSCENITY OFFENCES

Publication

It is an offence under section 2 of the Obscene Publications Act 1959 to publish an obscene article. 'Publish' includes distribution, circulation, sale, hire or even free gift or loan. It also includes, where the matter is data stored electronically, transmitting that data. Publication therefore includes storing images on a computer and transferring them via the Internet. In *R* v. *Waddon* (2000), the Court of Appeal held that, even though the website in question was situated in the United States, publication took place in England because the defendant had transmitted the material to the website from England, which was then transmitted back to England when users there gained access to the website. However, the Court left open the question of whether publication would take place in England if the website was not intended to be accessible there, and suggested that this would depend on issues of intention and causation in relation to where publication should take place. TV and broadcasting are also covered under the 1990 Broadcasting Act. In 2002, in a similar case involving a website depicting 'people covered in faeces, coprophilia or coprophagia, and men involved in fellatio', the Court of Appeal further held that the jury only had to be satisfied that there was a likelihood of vulnerable persons seeing the material, not that such persons had actually seen the material, and also that the Crown in such a case did not have to prove where the major steps to publication had taken place (*R* v. *Perrin*). In that case, there was sufficient evidence of publication in the UK for jurisdiction to be satisfied.

Possession

The 1964 Obscene Publications Act added a further offence of having an obscene article for publication for gain, which now extends the threat of criminal penalties to printers, distributors, wholesalers, shopkeepers and booksellers. There may, however, be a defence of innocent dissemination where the person did not inspect the articles and had no reason to suspect they might be obscene (see below, p. 190).

Under section 85 of the Criminal Justice and Public Order Act 1994, publication of obscene matter was made a serious arrestable offence, which means that a police superintendent may authorise the holding of suspects for up to 36 hours without access to legal advice or even notifying relatives. On conviction for either offence (publication or possession), a sentence of up to three years imprisonment, with an unlimited fine, may be imposed.

DEFENCES TO OBSCENITY

Public good

No defence of literary or artistic merit had existed prior to the 1959 Act. It is now a defence under section 4 of the Act to prove:

> that publication of the article in question is justified as being for the public good on the ground that it is in the interests of science, literature, art or learning, or of other objects of general concern.

'Other objects' includes sociological, ethical, and educational merits, but must fall within the same general area as those listed. Mere therapeutic relief of sexual tension (seriously argued in one case) is *not* an object of sufficiently general concern.

The burden of proof is on the publishers, but they may call expert witnesses in their support. Penguin Books used the defence of public good successfully shortly after the Act was passed, in the 1961 trial of D.H. Lawrence's *Lady Chatterley's Lover*, and a succession of expert witnesses – including the Bishop of Woolwich – testified to the literary and sociological merit of the work 'taken as a whole'. Expert evidence may even be admitted to establish that a work, far from promoting or glorifying obscenity, deliberately shocks and disgusts so much that the likely audience will only be repelled: this defence was used (ultimately successfully) by Calder & Boyars Ltd in 1969 to defend the book *Last Exit to Brooklyn*, which contained graphic depictions of drug abuse, senseless violence, and sexual perversion. It seems likely now that any serious work of literature will have a strong defence, however graphic its contents, and more recent works, such as Brett Easton Ellis's *American Psycho* (and its recent, slightly toned down, Hollywood film adaptation), have not even been prosecuted.

Indeed, the Crown Prosecution Service appears to be recognising the increasing difficulty of securing a jury conviction on the 1959 test. In 1997, the library of the University of Central England in Birmingham was raided by the West Midlands Police pornography squad who confiscated a book about Robert Mapplethorpe and his work, and threatened to imprison the University's Vice-Chancellor unless he agreed to the destruction of two photographs in the book that were said to be obscene. However, the University stood their ground and, after a year of uncertainty, the Crown Prosecution Service decided not to prosecute and the book was returned to the University's shelves.

Arguably, the Act is also at odds with the new, more liberal British Board of Film Classification guidelines, as recently applied to such films as the sexually explicit film *Baise Moi*. It must also now be interpreted in line with the Human Rights Act 1998, which, as we saw in chapter 1, has been in force since October 2000 and incorporates various important rights and freedoms set out in the European Convention on Human Rights; freedom of expression (Article 10) in particular. This freedom is, however, subject to such restrictions as are 'necessary in a democratic society', such as the protection of health or morals.

Innocent dissemination

Under section 2 of the 1959 Act and section 1 of the 1964 Act it is a defence for someone found in possession of an obscene article to prove that:

(1) they had not examined the article; and
(2) they had no reasonable cause to suspect it was obscene.

Both conditions must be satisfied – once a wholesaler or bookseller has actually examined (in other words, personally inspected) an article it will be no defence to claim that they did not realise that it was obscene. This defence is therefore more likely to protect printers and distributors than booksellers, most of whom 'examine' their stock at some point, even if only to look at the cover or read the blurb.

INDECENT PHOTOGRAPHS

Although something which is 'indecent' is by definition less offensive than something which is 'obscene', special considerations apply to publications containing indecent pictures of children. Under the Protection of Children Act 1978 it is an offence to take, permit to be taken, make (e.g. by downloading from the Internet), distribute or show, possess with a view to distribution, or advertise, any indecent photograph of a child under the age of 18. The age limit was increased from 16 as of 1 May 2004 under the Sex Offences Act 2003, subject to the defence discussed below regarding photographs of children aged 16 or 17. The Criminal Justice and Public Order Act 1994 has extended the definition of 'photograph' for these purposes to include any 'pseudo-photograph', for example, a computer-generated image on the Internet (it has also made offences under the 1978 Act serious arrestable offences – see above, p. 188).

Whether or not a photograph is 'indecent' under the 1978 Act is to be decided by a jury according to 'the recognised standards of propriety'. These standards may of course change, which makes the task for publishers of illustrated or children's books of keeping within the law particularly difficult. Subject to the new defences below, the circumstances of the photography or the publication, or the motivation of the photographer, are all irrelevant: in one 1988 case, despite the fact that the 14-year-old girl concerned had clearly consented to the photographs being taken (in order to further her fashion career), and was photographed in the presence of her family and boyfriend, two or three of the photographs – showing her lightly clad, in underwear only, and 'in a provocative pose' – were held by a jury to be indecent.

More recently, the American photographer Tierney Gearon sparked an uncomfortable controversy when images of her own children playing naked in front of adults, and sometimes urinating or dressed in animal heads, were exhibited at the Saatchi Gallery in Hampstead. Scotland Yard's obscene publications unit threatened to seize the photographs unless they were removed from the Gallery, and also warned that thousands of copies of her book, *I Am a Camera*, should be withdrawn from bookshops by the publisher, or all concerned would face action under the 1978 Act. After a week-long furore, the Crown Prosecution Service lifted the threat of prosecution on the grounds that there was insufficient evidence to secure a conviction.

The Sex Offences Act 1993 offers a specific defence regarding photographs of children aged 16 or 17 where the following conditions are satisfied:

- at the time of the offence, the child and the defendant were married or civil partners of each other, or lived together as partners in an enduring family relationship;
- (in relation to the offences of taking or making indecent photographs, and possessing indecent photographs with a view to distribution only) the child consented to the photograph or the defendant reasonably believed that the child consented; and
- the photograph did not show a person other than the child and the defendant.

In order to reassure police officers and others (e.g. ISPs) involved in identifying and securing data for evidential and investigative purposes that they will not be prosecuted, the Act also creates a limited defence where a photograph is 'made' (i.e. usually, by computer download) for the purposes of the prevention, detection or investigation of crime, or for the purposes of criminal proceedings.

In spite of the outcome of cases like the Gearon photos, and the above defence relating to 16 and 17 year olds, at times of public concern about Internet pornography, paedophile rings and child abuse, it would be wise to take advice before publishing photographs of children that a jury might feel were indecent, particularly if they are in any sense provocative or suggestive.

POSTING INDECENT OR OBSCENE MATTER

Under section 85 of the Postal Services Act 2000, it is an offence to send any indecent or obscene article by post. It is also an offence under section 4 of the Unsolicited Goods and Services Act 1971 to send unsolicited material describing human sexual techniques, or unsolicited advertisements for such material.

BLASPHEMY

Despite calls for its abolition, there is still a common-law misdemeanour of publishing a blasphemous libel. As with defamatory, obscene and seditious libels, blasphemous libels were originally punishable because of the threat they posed to public order and the established institutions of the state, including the established Church. As late as 1917 it was still being said that blasphemous words were punishable 'for their tendency to endanger the peace then and there, to deprave public morality generally, to shake the fabric of society and to be a cause of civil strife'. It is unlikely that attacks on the Church of England would have that effect today, but the offence still exists.

Under English law blasphemy is limited to attacks on the *Christian* religion and it is arguable that the offence can only be committed against the tenets of the established Anglican Church (so that an attack on the beliefs of Baptists or Quakers, though probably anti-Christian, might not be blasphemous). It has never offered any protection to other religions such as Islam, and an attempt in 1991 to prosecute Salman Rushdie and the publishers of *The Satanic Verses* for blasphemy notably failed.

This antique law, left over from an age when scurrilous attacks on the Bible or Book of Common Prayer might provoke riots in the streets, was last used in 1979 in a private prosecution brought by Mrs Mary Whitehouse against the homosexual periodical *Gay News* and its editor, Denis Lemon, for publishing what she described as 'an obscene poem and illustration vilifying Christ in his life and in his crucifixion'. The poem, by Professor James Kirkup, and entitled 'The Love that Dares to Speak its Name', described a homosexual centurion's feelings at the scene of the Crucifixion, but did so in sexually explicit terms which would doubtless have been offensive to many Christians, although possibly not to the Christians who read *Gay News*. No evidence of literary merit was admitted (there is still no such defence for blasphemy) and the prosecution was not required to prove that there was any danger of breach of the peace (there clearly wasn't). It was not even necessary to prove that *Gay News* intended, in publishing that article, to shock or outrage Christians, but merely that they intended to publish it. In the view of the House of Lords, any publication might be blasphemous if it used indecent, intemperate or offensive terms likely to outrage and insult the religious feelings of the general body of Christian believers in society. This remains the test today. It is not necessarily blasphemous to attack or deny Christianity or the Church, if you do so in decent and temperate language, but it is blasphemous (whatever your intentions) if you do so scurrilously or offensively. *Gay News* was fined £1,000 (a suspended sentence against the editor was overturned on appeal).

Again, the law of blasphemy must now be considered in light of the Human Rights Act 1998, in particular Article 9 (freedom of thought, conscience and religion) and Article 10 (freedom of expression), subject to such restrictions as are 'necessary in a democratic society'. These restrictions include laws in the interests of public safety, public order, health or morals and the protection of the rights and freedoms of others. Indeed, the *Gay News* and *Satanic Verses* cases came under the scrutiny of the European Court of Human Rights in 1996 (before the coming into force of the 1998 Act), when the director of the experimental video *Visions of Ecstasy* challenged the British Board of Film Classification's refusal to give the work an 18 certificate. The video depicted the erotic fantasies of a character described as 'St Teresa of Avila' involving the crucified figure of Christ. It also contained lesbian fantasies involving the 'Psyche of St Teresa'. The European Court of Human Rights was satisfied that the work fell within the scope of the offence of blasphemy, as formulated by the House of Lords in the *Gay News* case, and that English law afforded adequate protection against arbitrary interference. It noted that the aim of the restriction was to protect against the treatment of a religious subject in a manner that was bound to outrage Christians, and that the high degree of profanation that had to be attained constituted a safeguard against arbitrariness.

Although there have been no further prosecutions since 1979, the crime of blasphemy still exists, and the Law Commission currently has no intention of revisiting the issue. (Interestingly, the gay campaigner Peter Tatchell of Outrage! was prosecuted under the Ecclesiastical Courts Jurisdiction Act 1860, not the law of blasphemy, for interrupting The Archbishop of Canterbury Dr George Carey's Easter Sunday sermon in 1998, and was pointedly fined only £18.60.) At the time of writing, a Christian group was threatening a private blasphemy prosecution against the musical *Jerry Springer – The Opera*, which features Jesus (proclaiming to be 'a bit gay'), Mary and God as guests on Jerry Springer's TV talk show, together with up to 300 swear words. A 2005 BBC screening of the musical, which has enjoyed an extended run since it premiered in 2002, reportedly sparked up to 55,000 complaints before it was even aired, and 8,000 after it had been broadcast. Until the crime of blasphemy is abolished, authors and publishers should be careful what they say about God and Christ, Christianity and the established Church, if they are planning to say it in indecent, offensive or intemperate terms.

SEDITIOUS LIBEL

Publishing a seditious libel is analogous to treason, although a milder form of offence. Like obscenity and blasphemy, the offence exists largely to control publications directed against the peace and good order of the state, and its institutions. It will not be seditious merely to criticise the Queen, or other institutions such as Parliament (few newspapers would survive if it were), but it may be if there was a seditious *intent*, for example to incite people to violence against the monarchy or to create anti-Parliamentary disturbances, and if there is also a *likelihood* that public disorder will result. Although it was argued in 1991 that Salman Rushdie's *The Satanic Verses* provoked hostility between Muslims and other citizens, it was held not to be seditious because there was no evidence that it constituted an attack on the state itself or its institutions.

INCITEMENT TO RACIAL HATRED

Most public order offences, including race relations offences, are now dealt with under the Public Order Act 1986. It is an offence to stir up racial hatred by, among other things, using threatening, abusive or insulting words or behaviour, publishing, displaying, distributing or possessing written material which is threatening, abusive or insulting, or distributing or showing or playing a recording of visual images which involves the use of threatening, abusive or insulting words or behaviour. Each offence may be punished on conviction by up to two years imprisonment or an unlimited fine, or both.

Note in each case the requirement that the medium used should be 'threatening, abusive or insulting'. There must also be either:

- a positive intention to stir up racial hatred; or
- a likelihood that it will be stirred up.

'Racial hatred' is defined in the 1986 Act as meaning 'hatred against a group of persons defined by reference to colour, race, nationality (including citizenship) or ethnic or national origins' (the requirement that such a group be in Great Britain was repealed by the Anti-terrorism, Crime and Security Act 2001). In early 2005, the former talk-show host Robert Kilroy-Silk caused an uproar by referring to Arabs as 'suicide bombers' and 'limb-amputators' in an article in the *Sunday Express*, but the CPS declined to prosecute, having determined that he had not intended to stir up racial hatred, and nor were his actions likely to do so. Note that religious or other social groups are currently not included as such – the purpose behind the legislation is to prevent *racial* discrimination, not discrimination generally. It was held in 1983, however, that an attack on the long-established Sikh community could be considered an attack on an 'ethnic' rather than merely religious group and much the same might be said of an attack on Jews. Further, at the time of writing, controversy surrounded the Racial and Religious Hatred Bill, which cleared the Commons in July 2005 but was reportedly set for a difficult time in the House of Lords. The Bill proposes extending the above offences to religious hatred, meaning 'hatred against a group of persons defined by reference to religious belief or lack of religious belief'. The Bill has already provoked significant debate, in particular in the aftermath of the July 2005 London terrorist tube and bus bombings. Its critics have voiced concerns that it will stifle free speech and be difficult to police.

CONTEMPT OF COURT

Publishing comments on matters which are currently being tried, or about to be tried, in the courts can carry a risk of a fine or even imprisonment for contempt of court. In the *Spycatcher* case (above) the *Sunday Times* was held to be in contempt of court for publishing extracts despite injunctions already granted against the *Guardian* and *Observer* (even though those injunctions were not in fact addressed to the *Sunday Times* directly). It is, of course, contempt of court to disobey any court order.

Under the Contempt of Court Act 1981, a person may also be guilty of contempt by publication where the publication creates a *substantial* risk that *active* court proceedings will be *seriously* impeded or prejudiced.

Proceedings are 'active' from the moment a case is scheduled for trial, or an arrest is made. Note that there must be a substantial risk of serious prejudice. Thus, the more distant the trial or the more peripheral the material published the less likely that a contempt will have been committed.

In *R v. Sherwood, ex parte Telegraph Group and others* (2001) – an appeal by media groups against an order postponing any reporting of the trial of the Sussex police officer, Christopher Sherwood, for the shooting of an unarmed man until the conclusion of the related trial of three other officers – the Court of Appeal formulated a three-stage test on restricting media coverage of court proceedings. The test attempted to balance the competing interests of Article 6 (right to a fair trial) and Article 10 (freedom of expression) of the European Convention on Human Rights (incorporated in the Human Rights Act 1998), stressing that the ban must be 'necessary', and was set out as follows:

- Would the reporting give rise to a 'not insubstantial' risk of prejudice? If not, that will be the end of the matter.
- If yes, would an order postponing the reporting eliminate the risk of prejudice? If not, that would, again, be the end of the matter. However, even if an order *would* achieve this objective, the judge must consider whether the risk could be overcome by less restrictive means.
- Even if there is no other way of eliminating the perceived risk of prejudice, the judge may still have to ask whether the degree of risk is tolerable in the sense of being 'the lesser of two evils'.

In the *Sherwood* case, it was held that, although the restriction was regrettable, it was unavoidable in order to ensure that the three officers in the second trial were given a fair hearing in accordance with Article 6. (In fact, reporting restrictions were eventually lifted after Sherwood was acquitted and the trial of the other defendants fell through.)

Under section 3 of the 1981 Act it is a defence for a publisher to prove that at the time of publication they did not know proceedings were active, provided they took all reasonable care, and had no reason to believe otherwise.

An additional 'public interest' defence is now available under section 5 of the Act, which provides that a publication made as, or as part of, a discussion in good faith of public affairs (or other matters of general public interest) is not to be treated as contempt of court if the risk of impediment or prejudice to particular legal proceedings is merely incidental to the discussion.

As the *Sunday Mirror* found out to its detriment in the 2002 *Leeds United* case, contempt of court can be a very serious matter. Eight weeks into the trial of the footballers Jonathan Woodgate and Lee Bowyer, who were accused of attacking a student outside a nightclub, the judge ruled that there was a 'clear and substantial risk' that the case had been prejudiced by the publication of an interview of the victim's father suggesting the attack had been racially motivated. The article led to the collapse of the trial, estimated to have cost around £8 million (and a subsequent retrial exonerating the two players). Although the Attorney-General decided that the paper's former editor, who had resigned over the affair, would not be prosecuted, the *Sunday Mirror* was fined £75,000 and ordered to pay the Attorney-General's costs of over £50,000. The paper was prosecuted for statutory contempt, not common law contempt – which would have required a deliberate or reckless attempt to prejudice the trial, and would usually carry a much higher fine. Two years later, *The Daily Star* was fined £60,000 for failing to heed the Attorney-General's guidelines issued after the alleged rape of a 17-year-old girl at the Grosvenor Hotel by a gang of footballers, requesting the media not to publish any material that could prejudice the identification of the suspects by the complainant. The paper's clear identification of the players Titus Bramble and Carlton Cole as potential defendants, at a time when the complainant had not clearly identified her alleged attackers, was held to create a substantial risk of serious prejudice. The players denied the allegations, and in the event no criminal charges were brought against them or anyone else.

James Steen, the former editor of *Punch*, was found guilty of common law contempt of court in 2002 when the House of Lords reversed a Court of Appeal ruling in his favour for publishing an article by David Shayler about the Bishopsgate bombing containing material subject to an injunction against the former spy and Associated Newspapers. Having re-examined the principles in the *Spycatcher* case, the House of Lords held that the material had been published in the knowledge that it would thwart the purpose of the injunction pending Shayler's trial, and had a significant and adverse effect on the administration of justice in the proceedings, by pre-empting the Court's decision on the confidentiality issues. This was held to be the case even if the injunction were drawn in seemingly over-wide terms. However, this was subject to the remedy of a third party whose conduct was affected by the order to apply to the Court for the order to be varied.

SUMMARY CHECKLIST: OTHER RISKS

- Is this a malicious falsehood?
- Is it negligent to make this statement? Do we owe any duty of care to particular readers?
- Might this be obscene? Taken as a whole, would it deprave or corrupt?
- Are we publishing it, or in possession of it?
- Can it be justified as being for the public good (for example on grounds of literary merit)?
- Are we disseminating it innocently?
- Would a jury think this photograph was indecent?
- Is this material blasphemous? Is it scurrilous or offensive about Christianity, or the Anglican Church?
- Is this a criminal or seditious libel, or an incitement to racial hatred?
- Might this breach the Official Secrets Act, or any duty of government confidentiality?
- By publishing this now, would we be in contempt of court? Would publication by us seriously prejudice active court proceedings?

Confidentiality and privacy

8

INTRODUCTION

These days, if a publication does not include exciting revelations or sexy photographs of a supermodel or an American actor it may be considered rather conservative. Happily, this chapter provides such revelations (albeit without the photographs). Those who wish to reveal sensitive commercial, governmental or private information should be aware that publication may be unlawful. The law of confidence protects information which is confidential to a person or a company. The UK courts have also applied the law of confidence to prevent the disclosure of private information. The law in this area is developing rapidly due to enactment of the Human Rights Act 1998 which brought in the right of privacy and the right of freedom of expression. This chapter first addresses confidential information before discussing the expanding area of privacy.

CONFIDENTIAL INFORMATION

There is a general rule of equity in English law that a person who receives information in confidence has a duty to keep that confidence and not disclose the information to others. Lord Denning put it well in a 1969 case when he said:

> No person is permitted to divulge to the world information which he has received in confidence, unless he has just cause or excuse for doing so. Even if he comes by it innocently ... once he gets to know that it was originally given in confidence, he can be restrained from breaking that confidence.

Are authors and publishers under a duty not to disclose or use information merely because it arrives on their desk in an envelope marked 'Confidential'? What if it is a completely unsolicited proposal – a fairly common publishing event – from someone they have never met? That will depend (in that particular case) on whether the information is indeed confidential and whether, in the circumstances, a duty of confidence arises. You do not make information confidential simply by stamping 'Confidential' on it (although this may often point towards the information being so). The law will prevent the disclosure of confidential information where:

(1) the information is confidential in nature;
(2) a duty of confidence arises; and
(3) there is no overriding public interest in disclosure.

INFORMATION OF A CONFIDENTIAL NATURE

Information may be of a confidential nature where it is the product of the human brain and not already in the public knowledge. In *Attorney General* v. *Guardian Newspapers* (1988) the court refused an injunction preventing publication in the UK of Peter Wright's book *Spycatcher* (the memoirs of a former MI5 officer), partly on the grounds that the book had already been published in Australia. The information should also be more than merely 'tittle-tattle'.

Plots and scenarios

In some cases, a plot or scenario may be protected if it was revealed in confidential circumstances. W.S. Gilbert obtained an injunction in 1894 to prevent unauthorised publication of the plot of his new play *His Excellency*, which was then in rehearsal but had not opened, on the grounds that the people seeking to publish it knew it had been obtained in breach of confidence. Publishers and authors would similarly be prevented from re-using the key elements of a scenario – plot, characters, dramatic ideas – which had been submitted to them, but rejected, if it could be established that they had been submitted in confidence and accepted as such at the time. There may also be an action for breach of copyright in the case of more developed material.

Developed concepts

If an idea is less than a completed plot or scenario, how far must it be developed before it is protectable by the law of confidence? Hughie Green, in a famous case, failed to protect the general ideas and format behind his game show *Opportunity Knocks* because so little of his own format had actually been put into fixed or developed form, or even written down: there were, for example, no scripts as such. However, in the case of *Fraser* v. *Thames TV* (1983) a much more developed concept – a television series about a three-girl band – was successfully protected by an action for breach of confidence. In this case, the concept was clearly identifiable, commercially attractive, original (and was not, for example, public knowledge) and capable of being realised in actuality. In contrast, in *De Maudsley* v. *Palumbo* (1996), the claimant had an idea for a new nightclub which would open all night, have separate dance areas, an acoustic design and top DJs from around the world. The defendant subsequently opened the Ministry of Sound nightclub which had a number of these features. The claimant's idea was held by the court to have been too vague and generally not novel enough to give the information the necessary quality of confidence to be protected. In order for an idea to be confidential, it must go beyond the identification of a desirable goal and needs a considerable degree of particularity. Simple ideas can be protected but they must not be vague.

The dilemma for an author who wishes to disclose information to a potential publisher is that if he only discloses an outline of the plot (while holding back essential detail), the information may not be detailed enough to be confidential. On the other hand, the more detail the author discloses, the more he has to take a risk that the publisher decides (whether deliberately or not) to commission another author to write a book with the same plot. Whether information is confidential is ultimately a question which can only be answered by taking all the circumstances into account. To minimise the uncertainties of the law, it is important that publishers and authors have clearly worded written agreements which specify what information is confidential and the circumstances in which it can be disclosed.

OTHER TYPES OF CONFIDENTIAL INFORMATION

Many other kinds of information may be confidential, including business proposals and reports, customer lists, interim reports from investigations, government and state secrets, ideas for new designs and technology and other trade secrets. In fact, a lot of financial and business information which has not been published is confidential.

Draft reports and opinions are obviously confidential. In *Sir Elton John v. Countess Joubeline* (2001) information from a confidential draft of a barrister's opinion, which had somehow been filched, was posted on a 'gossip' website. The opinion related to Elton John's court case against his accountants. The operator of the website created a link to the information from her home page. She was held liable for breach of confidence and the fact that the material was initially posted on the website without her knowledge was irrelevant once she became aware of it and allowed it to remain. She should have known that the information was confidential.

IS THERE A DUTY OF CONFIDENCE?

The circumstances in which a duty of confidence can arise are where:

*   *there is a relationship of confidence*, as for example between husband and wife, or doctor and patient;
*   *there is a contractual duty of confidentiality*, such as those included in many employment contracts or consultancy agreements; or
*   *the party receiving the information knows or ought to know that the information would be regarded as confidential* by the party to whom the information relates.

CONFIDENTIAL RELATIONSHIPS

Clearly, there are some close relationships, such as that between husband and wife, which the law will automatically regard as relationships of trust: the Duchess of Argyll found in a celebrated case in 1967 that information communicated confidentially to her by the Duke while they were married could not be published in later divorce proceedings. This duty of trust has been held to apply to secrets disclosed in other close or long-standing, personal, professional or business relationships of trust. Examples of such relationships include confessions made to a priest, information disclosed to doctors (although the courts have decided that there is no breach of confidentiality where doctors reveal prescription details without revealing the identity of the patients), solicitors or bankers and their clients, and secrets shared between partners of a firm or directors or shareholders of a company. It may well extend to ideas and other information disclosed by an author to his or her literary agent, but would not necessarily cover disclosures made to a publisher unless the author–publisher relationship was a fairly close or long-standing one. It would be unlikely to protect an unsolicited idea offered to a publisher by an author never previously dealt with: some other basis for protecting confidentiality would need to be found, such as a contractual agreement (see below).

CONTRACTUAL AGREEMENTS

Duties of confidence may be entered into contractually; for example, as part of a consultancy agreement, or disclosures of trade secrets made prior to a possible joint venture. Clearly, those seeking commercial backing for an exciting new idea will need to disclose at least some details of the idea in order to interest their potential partners, but they will only want to do so in circumstances of agreed confidentiality. A specific contract is therefore usually recommended – and is fairly common – in these circumstances.

The most common contractual obligations of confidentiality, however, arise out of contracts of employment. The relationship of employer and employee has always been regarded as a relationship of trust, particularly where the employee is relatively senior and has regular access to the employer's trade secrets. The general rule is that employees may not disclose confidential information acquired during the course of their employment, or use it for the benefit of others, either while they are employed or (usually more importantly) after they have left. The test most usually adopted is: would people of ordinary honesty and intelligence recognise the information as the property of their employers and not their own to do with as they like?

In the publishing context, the kind of information covered would include lists of customers, contacts or suppliers, advance price lists, pricing structures or mark-ups, contract terms, royalties or other financial information and future publishing plans. Documents as well as more general information would be caught, but they need not be taken away in physical form – an employee who memorised a list of customers for use in a future job might still be prevented from disclosing that information later. All kinds of publishing employees may be covered, including editorial, marketing, production and finance staff, particularly those at senior levels. To reinforce the general rule, confidentiality clauses are often specifically written into employment contracts. A confidentiality clause was successfully used by Tony Blair and his wife Cherie Booth QC in 2000 in obtaining an injunction preventing the publication by the *Mail on Sunday* of extracts written about the Blairs' family life by their former nanny, Rosalind Mark. It is, however, possible that in some circumstances where a contract of employment has been terminated as a result of a breach by the employer, the employee may be discharged from obligations of confidentiality under that contract. This was recognised as at least arguable in *Campbell* v. *Frisbee* (2002) where information from a former employee of Naomi Campbell, including information about alleged sexual encounters between Miss Campbell and the actor Joseph Fiennes, was published in the *News of the World*. However, even if an expressly assumed duty of confidence is found to be discharged on a serious breach of the employment contract, it is likely that a non-contractual duty of confidence may nevertheless exist.

For many employers, the greatest risk of disclosure of trade secrets comes when senior employees – such as marketing or other directors – leave to go to other jobs, or to set up on their own. For this reason, employment contracts for such staff often include restrictive covenants preventing the use of the firm's confidential information in the future, or for a limited number of months. Such covenants restricting future behaviour need to be very carefully drafted: the wider and more restrictive their terms, the more likely it is that a court might find them to be void as being in restraint of trade (see chapter 13). In the first place, the terms of such clauses will be strictly and narrowly construed against the person seeking to enforce them, so that, for example, an agreement not to 'disclose' company information will be just that, and may not prevent the employee from 'using' the information. Secondly, the information protected must truly amount to a trade secret of the firm. No employee can be prevented from using his or her general 'know-how' (often called 'life skills') in future jobs, even though that expertise will inevitably have been picked up in earlier employments. This is only reasonable – otherwise, as one judge put it, 'no servant could ever advance himself'.

REASONABLE EXPECTATION OF CONFIDENTIALITY

In the absence of a contract, a duty of confidentiality may be implied from particular circumstances, even if there is no relationship between the person whose confidential information it is and the recipient of the information. The question often asked is: would a reasonable person, standing in the shoes of the recipient of the information, realise on reasonable grounds that the information was being given to him or her in confidence? In the case of *Prince Albert* v. *Strange* in 1849, the Prince Consort was granted an injunction preventing the publication by an employee of their chosen printer of drawings and etchings which had been produced by him and Queen Victoria. The employee had been entrusted with the plates and other materials for a limited printing only, and clearly knew this – any further disclosure would have been a breach of trust. This would apply to any similar information improperly obtained, such as private letters (see the section on privacy below). In the Australian case of *Foster and Others* v. *Mountford and Rigby Ltd* (1976), adopting English law principles, the same implied duty of trust and confidentiality was held to apply to aboriginal tribal secrets disclosed to an anthropologist in the course of his research. The tribal elders showed him sacred sites, paintings and other objects, and shared secrets known only to male members of the tribe, and obtained an injunction limiting his right to publish them later in a book. The outcome might have been different if it had been clear to them from the outset that he was researching the information for publication in a book, but then he might not have been given the information.

A duty of confidence may arise where a person:

- is given confidential information from a person in circumstances where he knows or ought to know that a duty of confidence arises; or
- even if he is not given the information, he obtains or chances upon clearly confidential information in circumstances where he knows or ought to know that the information belongs to someone who can reasonably expect his or her confidential information to be protected. In this latter case, the person may have used surreptitious methods (such as a telephoto lens or listening device) to obtain the information or may have found a document in the street or been sent it anonymously.

Where information is conveyed in a social setting it is unlikely, in the absence of other factors, to give rise to an obligation of confidence on the part of the confidant. In *De Maudsley* v. *Palumbo* (1996) (see above), the claimant's idea for a new nightclub was disclosed to a friend around the table at a dinner party. Nothing was said to change what was a social setting into an occasion where confidence could be expected to be maintained. Where it is expressly made clear that the information conveyed or to be conveyed is to be treated as confidential, an obligation of confidence is more likely to be created – even in a social setting.

The information itself and the circumstances in which the party comes by that information will be of relevance in determining whether the other party has a duty of confidence. Clearly labelling documents with words to the effect of 'private and confidential' is also likely to point towards the information being so. In most circumstances in which someone finds or is the recipient of unsolicited information, it is obvious if the information is confidential. In *Imutran Ltd* v. *Uncaged Campaigns Ltd* (2001) the confidentiality of information regarding the claimant company's research into xenotransplantation (the replacement of human organs with those of animals), sent on CD-ROM to the director of an animal rights campaign company, was never in dispute. The documents comprised laboratory reports, minutes of meetings and correspondence. Interim injunctions preventing further disclosures of the information were granted pending trial.

THE PUBLIC INTEREST DEFENCE

It is important to be aware of the risks of publishing information which is potentially confidential. It is possible that an injunction may be granted to prevent publication and/or that an action for breach of confidence could be brought. Both have significant potential costs and damages implications – not to mention the possible embarrassment and inconvenience of having to recall a publication at the eleventh hour. However, it is a defence to an action for breach of confidence if the information is being published in the public interest.

Traditionally, the legal principle applied has been that there is 'no confidence in an iniquity'. This means that there is a public interest in the disclosure of crimes, misdeeds and fraud. However, the public interest defence only applies where the disclosure is to someone with a proper interest to receive the information.

In *Lion Laboratories* v. *Evans* (1984), former employees of the claimant gave information to the *Daily Express* newspaper that certain intoximeter devices were liable to error which was biased against motorists. The court refused to grant an injunction as it was in the public interest to know about this matter which was a serious question affecting the life and liberty of citizens. In contrast, where the *Daily Mirror* had obtained information by phone tapping that there were possible breaches of the jockey club rules by the jockey Johnny Francome, the court granted an interim injunction to prevent disclosure in the newspaper. It was held in *Francome* v. *Daily Mirror* (1984) that there was an arguable breach of confidence and although there might have been a public interest in disclosing the information to the jockey club or the police, there was no such interest in publishing the information in the media. What appealed to the public was not necessarily in the public interest.

Since the Human Rights Act 1998 has been in force, the right of freedom of expression is usually the starting point in considering the public interest.

ARTICLE 10 – FREEDOM OF EXPRESSION

Article 10 of the European Convention on Human Rights gives everyone the right of freedom of expression, including the right to impart information and ideas without interference from the state or public authorities (such as the courts). The right does, however, carry with it duties and responsibilities which make it subject to restrictions which are prescribed by law and necessary in a democratic society. One of these restrictions is for preventing the disclosure of information obtained in confidence, while another is to protect the interests of national security. It will therefore be up to the court to balance the right of those seeking to publish confidential information on the grounds that the disclosure is in the public interest against the right to stop such a publication under the law of confidence. The question is whether it is necessary in a democratic society to keep the information confidential or whether the public interest defence takes precedence.

PRIVATE INFORMATION

The UK courts have upheld people's rights of privacy by developing the tort of breach of confidence. Under the Human Rights Act 1998, the UK courts must not act incompatibly with the right of privacy enshrined in Article 8 of the European Convention on Human Rights. Article 8 gives everyone the right to respect for their private and family life, their home and correspondence.

There is an obvious potential for conflict between Articles 8 and 10 (the right to freedom of expression) and publishers and authors should be alert to the risks of an action for an unauthorised disclosure of private information.

The first question is whether the information is private. If it is, then the court must balance the right of freedom of expression against the right of privacy.

TYPES OF PRIVATE INFORMATION

To determine if information is 'private', the court will ask if the person in question can reasonably expect his or her privacy to be respected. The courts have noted that in many cases information is obviously 'private' in nature. This would include information relating to health, personal relationships and finances. Where the information is not 'clearly' private, the court may consider whether a person of ordinary sensibilities, in the shoes of the person in question, would find the publication of such information to be highly offensive. According to the European Court of Human Rights, private life includes a person's 'physical and psychological integrity'.

Relationships

Details of sexual relationships have been found to be a clear example of private information. However, there is a distinction to be drawn between long-term relationships, such as those in a marriage, and more transitory or objectionable relationships. This distinction was clearly made in A v. B *and another* (2002), in which a Premiership footballer failed to prevent publication of details of his extra-marital affairs. The more stable and established the relationship, the more likely it is that the court will prevent the disclosure of the information or say that the publisher of the information has violated the individual's privacy, since there is a higher standard of protection attaching to such relationships.

Medical information

Medical information is private. This not only includes notes of and treatment by clinical practitioners but also non-clinical forms of therapy. In *Campbell* v. *MGN Ltd* (2004), Naomi Campbell's therapy at Narcotics Anonymous sessions was held to be private and no less worthy of protection than treatment carried out by medical practitioners.

Daily life, home life and correspondence

Princess Caroline of Monaco was photographed during many day-to-day activities, a number of which were in public places. For example, she was captured shopping on her own, on horseback, on a bicycle, at a market, playing tennis, in a restaurant, skiing and tripping over an obstacle and falling down at the Monte Carlo Beach Club dressed in a swimsuit. The European Court of Human Rights in *von Hannover* v. *Germany* (2004) held the publication of those photographs represented an invasion of her privacy. Princess Caroline seemed to have been pursued relentlessly for many years by the paparazzi wherever she was and whatever she was doing. Thus there was a climate of continual harassment.

Home (and family) life and correspondence have been recognised as being areas subject to privacy, as identified in the wording of Article 8. 'Home' would include certain aspects of a person's business and professional premises and correspondence could include telephone calls made from business (and residential) premises. Emails are also likely to be covered by the concept of 'correspondence'.

CAN PRIVATE INFORMATION BE PUBLISHED?

Once it is established that the proposed publication contains private information, the next question is whether or not publication should be allowed. This is answered by the courts in weighing up the often-conflicting right of the individual to privacy under Article 8 against the right of freedom of expression under Article 10. The right of freedom of expression is not only the right of the publisher and author but also of the person who wishes to tell their story and the right of the public to receive the information. In a kiss-and-tell situation, the court must balance the right of the kisser (who is usually selling their story) with the privacy of the other party (who is usually a celebrity).

Neither human right takes precedence over the other and publication will be allowed only where the Article 10 right outweighs the Article 8 right. In striking the balance, the interference with either right must not be impaired more than is necessary and proportionate in a democratic society.

In analysing the competing rights, regard will be had to the 'public interest' in publishing (or not, as the case may be). This is distinct from information which may merely be interesting to the public. There are a number of factors which will be of relevance when considering what is in the public interest. We have already seen that the more stable a relationship which one party wishes to reveal and the other wishes to keep secret, the more likely it is that the court will protect the privacy of the relationship.

The claimant

The type of person the claimant is (in terms of their status) is of relevance because there is more likely to be a public interest in revealing private information about certain types of individuals. Information about political figures is more likely to be in the public interest than that about general celebrities, whilst information about celebrities is more likely to be of public interest than that about ordinary members of the public.

A distinction should also be made between those who actively seek publicity and those who do not. Those who seek publicity are less likely to be able to argue against publication of information of which they do not approve. In *von Hannover* v. *Germany* (2004), Princess Caroline, while undoubtedly a public figure, was not a person who had truly courted publicity and she did not fulfil a public function. Contrast this with celebrities such as the Beckhams, who can be said to have courted publicity. They failed to obtain an interim injunction to prevent the publication of the story of their former nanny, partly on the grounds that much information about them was already in the public domain and there was a public interest in publishing the information. The actress Jessie Wallace failed to prevent publication of the story of her former boyfriend about her private life. She was said to have previously sought publicity.

Where the individual seeking to resist publication is a role model, publication will more likely be deemed to be in the public interest. In *A* v. *B and another* (2002), the fact that the claimant was a professional footballer indicated that he was a role model for children. It was said (perhaps paradoxically) that undesirable behaviour by role models can set an unfortunate example.

Generally, publication of private information relating to children will not be in the public interest.

Setting the record straight

Where the public have been either directly or indirectly misled as to the truth regarding an individual, the public is usually entitled to know the real truth. In *Campbell* v. *MGN Ltd* (2004), Naomi Campbell had previously indicated that, unlike other models, she did not take illegal drugs. This was in fact not the case and it later transpired that she was an addict. She could not complain about publication necessary to correct the false image she had portrayed. However, in the court's view the newspaper in this case went beyond what was proportionate and necessary to set the record straight when it published additional details of the treatment she was receiving and photographs of her leaving a therapy session.

Subject matter

The subject matter of the publication is an important factor in determining whether private information can be lawfully disclosed or not. Different types of information are generally accorded different weight. Political expression (as distinct from merely personal information about a political figure) is regarded as the most important form of expression to protect in a democratic society. Educational expression is next on the scale of importance and then perhaps artistic expression. 'Gossip' and private information published merely for commercial profit fall below artistic expression in terms of the extent to which protection of it is important.

Matters of public debate will more likely be in the public interest. So, for example, if there is a contentious new law proposed, it is more likely that it is in the public interest to publish private information which is of relevance to that new law about a political figure involved in the debate over the new law. Such information might include the individual's policy in private where they have publicly stated something in apparent contradiction to support their party's policy. For example, if a politician is espousing the benefits of banning abortion and yet chooses to have an abortion herself, then it is more likely (but by no means certain) that the court will permit publication. However, if it is an actress who has had the abortion, it is less clear why it is in the public interest for the fact of her abortion (private information) to have been revealed.

Photographs

Photographs represent a special category of information which the courts regard as particularly intrusive when published. As such, publication of photographs of a person in a private situation is likely to impair a person's right to privacy more than is necessary and proportionate. The reason behind this approach seems to be that photographs have a more immediate, intrusive and long-lasting impact than a verbal description. In the Princess Caroline case, the fact that the photographs showed her going about her ordinary daily life and the climate of continued harassment persuaded the European Court of Human Rights to hold that there had been an invasion of privacy.

In *Theakston* v. *MGN Ltd* (2002), the court held that there was no breach of confidence in the newspaper printing details of the claimant's activities in a brothel but an injunction would be granted to prevent publication of photographs of the activities since the photographs were particularly intrusive. In *Campbell* v. *MGN Ltd* (2004), the newspaper's publication of information, including photographs of the model leaving a therapy session for a drug addiction, was not necessary (words having adequately corrected her false public image). In *Douglas* v. *Hello!* (2005), which concerned unauthorised and surreptitiously taken photographs of the wedding of Michael Douglas and Catherine Zeta-Jones, it was recognised that a person viewing the photographs in *Hello!* magazine would be in a position of a spectator of the wedding or, as one member of the Court of Appeal remarked, 'in some cases voyeur would be the more appropriate noun'.

REMEDIES FOR BREACH OF CONFIDENCE AND PRIVACY

In actions for breach of confidence, including privacy cases, the claimant may be entitled to several forms of remedy.

INJUNCTIONS

An injunction will often be the most important remedy to the claimant as it could prevent publication (or re-publication) of information giving rise to the action. The injunction could even be broad enough to cover the whole world, as was the case in *Venables and another* v. *News Group Newspapers* (2001), where an injunction was imposed preventing the disclosure of information leading to the identity or future whereabouts of the killers of James Bulger. Injunctions are always discretionary. Before publication, a claimant may apply for an interim injunction pending trial. At trial, the claimant can apply for a permanent or final injunction.

In a number of cases, the courts have indicated that there is a fairly high threshold to prevent publication pending trial. In *Cream Holdings Ltd* v. *Banerjee* (2004), a local newspaper wished to publish confidential information obtained by a former employee of the claimant company to support her allegations of financial irregularity. The court refused to grant an interim injunction as publication of the information was likely to be in the public interest. In the context of privacy, publication of an account by David and Victoria Beckham's former nanny about the couple was allowed in 2005. In the same year, publication of the story of the former boyfriend of actress Jessie Wallace regarding her private life was not prevented by the court. The Wallace decision even made reference to the fact that Article 10 could prevail over a written confidentiality agreement. However, since these interim injunction decisions, the Court of Appeal in the long-running case of *Douglas* v. *Hello!* indicated in 2005 that, in future, pre-publication injunctions to prevent the disclosure of private information pending trial are more likely to be granted, following the decisions in *Campbell* v. *MGN Ltd*, and *von Hannover* v. *Germany*. The *Douglas* v. *Hello!* (2005) decision, coming as it does after the decisions in the Beckhams' and in Jessie Wallace's respective injunction applications, would suggest that were the applications heard today, they may have been decided differently.

It is important to be aware of the risk of an injunction preventing a planned publication at the eleventh hour. This may have significant consequences financially and in terms of a publisher's reputation. Whilst newspapers and magazines may have a reserve article to use, the financial consequences for a book publisher are likely to be more severe as the book may have to be pulped.

DAMAGES

Damages for a tort, including breach of confidence, are to put the claimant in the position he or she would have been had the tort not been committed. In 'classic' confidentiality cases, such as where a trade secret is revealed by a former employee, damages would reflect the loss to the employer caused by the disclosure of the secret, provided that damage was reasonably foreseeable.

In privacy cases, the calculation of the loss suffered by the claimant is often hard to quantify in monetary terms. Damages have, however, been awarded for distress caused by the invasion of the claimant's privacy, although this is generally a relatively small sum. In *Cornelius* v. *de Taranto* (2001), the disclosure of medical information about the claimant by a consultant psychiatrist to another psychiatrist and the claimant's GP and solicitor, resulted in damages of £3,750. The nature and detail of the information disclosed, the character of the recipients and the extent of the disclosure were said to be material factors in assessing the true degree of injury to the claimant's feelings.

In *Adeniji* v. *London Borough of Newham* (2001), photographs of a child (taken without parental consent) which were used in a brochure advertising services offered by the defendant gave rise to damages of £5,000. The photographs were used in relation to titles including 'The strategy for children and young people who are infected by HIV or AIDS' but the child was not herself infected with HIV or suffering from AIDS.

In cases of commercial publication of private information, one might expect damages to be much higher but this has not usually been the case. In *Campbell* v. *MGN Ltd* (2004), Naomi Campbell was awarded £2,500 general damages for distress and injury to feelings occasioned by the invasion of her privacy by the newspaper for publishing details of her treatment for drug addiction. In *Douglas* v. *Hello!* (2005), the award for distress caused by the invasion of privacy by unauthorised photographs of their wedding was £3,750 for each of the couple. They also received £7,000 jointly for the expenses and disruption caused by having to select the authorised photographs to be published in *OK!* (with whom they had an exclusive contract) ahead of the planned publication date. It seems that individuals who court publicity (and in the case of Michael Douglas and Catherine Zeta-Jones who have commercially exploited their private information), damages will be less than for individuals who do not.

ACCOUNT OF PROFITS

Where the defendant has benefited from a breach of a duty of confidence or privacy, the court may order an account of the profits of that breach. The claimant must choose to seek this remedy as an alternative to damages, and it is at the discretion of the court whether to award such an equitable remedy. An account of profits is more likely to be awarded where the defendant has not acted innocently (e.g. by deceptively obtaining the confidential information). In *Douglas* v. *Hello!* (2005), the Court of Appeal indicated that had *Hello!* made a profit as a result of the breach of confidentiality, they would not have hesitated in awarding the couple an account of profits.

DELIVERY UP

At the court's discretion, material containing information in breach of confidence may be ordered to be delivered up or destroyed. Those involved in publishing should be aware of the costs and impracticalities involved.

COSTS

Although not strictly speaking a remedy for a breach of confidence or invasion of privacy, it is important to note that the loser is normally ordered to pay a contribution (usually about 60–80 per cent) of the winner's costs. In most recent cases, costs have significantly outweighed the damages awarded, with costs often running well into hundreds of thousands of pounds and sometimes into the millions. Thus in financial terms, the risk to a publisher of fighting a privacy action often comes down to costs. Further risk to the defendant can arise where the claimant's solicitors work under a conditional fee agreement, whereby they may not charge any fees if the case is lost, but agree a percentage uplift in their rate of fees for a 'successful' outcome. In rough terms, this is a no-win-no-fee agreement. Naomi Campbell's solicitors acted under a conditional fee agreement in her House of Lords appeal against the *Daily Mirror*. For more on conditional fee agreements see chapter 7.

OFFICIAL SECRETS

The Freedom of Information Act 2000 came fully into force in January 2005, potentially allowing individuals and businesses to access information held by public authorities which would not previously have been available. This could represent a significant commercial opportunity for businesses to find out more about their competitors' tenders and contracts with public bodies. The Freedom of Information Act is discussed in more detail in chapter 12.

However, in many respects we still live in a secret society. Civil servants are required under the Civil Service Management Code not to publish or broadcast personal memoirs reflecting their experience in Government, or enter into commitments to do so, whilst in Crown employment. Upon leaving the service, permission from the Head of the former civil servant's Department and of the Home Civil Service must be sought before entering into commitments to publish such memoirs.

Under the Official Secrets Acts of 1911 and 1989 it is an offence to publish several categories of official government or state information if publication may be prejudicial or damaging to the safety or interests of the state. In practice, this tends to affect investigative newspaper and TV journalists more than book publishers, but memoirs of former civil servants, especially those involved with the security services, can often run a serious risk of legal action. This may not only be prosecution under the Official Secrets Acts, but also civil action for breach of government confidentiality. These matters came to the fore in the *Spycatcher* saga in the 1980s, and in the David Shayler affair (both discussed below).

The 1911 Act

Although intended to apply to the spying activities of foreign enemy agents, section 1 of the 1911 Official Secrets Act still makes it an offence if any person for any purpose prejudicial to the safety or interests of the State:

- approaches, inspects, passes over or is in the neighbourhood of, or enters any prohibited place within the meaning of the 1911 Act;
- makes any sketch, plan, model or note which is calculated to be or might be or is intended to be directly or indirectly useful to an enemy; or
- obtains, collects, records or publishes, or communicates to any other person any secret official code word, or password or any sketch, plan, model, article or note or other document or information which is calculated to be or might be or is intended to be directly or indirectly useful to an enemy.

A 'prohibited place' might include an aircraft, a vessel or a power station, as well as more obvious military establishments, and an 'enemy' may include potential as well as actual enemies of the UK. 'Any person' might in theory include internal saboteurs or even journalists and authors, but the section has not successfully been used against non-spies, and an attempt by the Attorney-General in 1978 in the 'ABC' case to prosecute Time Out journalists Duncan Campbell and Crispin Aubrey under section 1, for a story including security revelations by a former soldier, was thrown out by the trial judge as being 'oppressive' (they were given lighter sentences under section 2 – now replaced by the 1989 Act).

The 1989 Act

Section 2 of the 1911 Act, so widely drafted as to include almost anything, was replaced on the recommendation of the Franks Committee. Offences are largely broken down to those most likely to be committed by 'insiders' and those most likely to be committed by 'outsiders'. The latter category is of most relevance to publishers and authors. There are specific classes of restricted information in the 1989 Official Secrets Act. They include, among others:

- security and intelligence
- defence
- international relations
- information which might facilitate a criminal offence.

In relation to 'outsiders', such as publishers, it is an offence to publish information which they know is protected by the 1989 Act and which originated from a Crown servant or government contractor. In most cases the prosecution will need to prove that the disclosure would be damaging to the security services or to the interests of the UK. Exactly what constitutes 'damaging' in this case will depend upon the type of information. The prosecution also need to prove that the author or journalist knew or had reason to believe that publication would be 'damaging'.

A further risk in relation to the 1989 Act is that the publisher could be charged with offences of conspiracy, incitement or aiding an insider committing an offence under the Act. Such an offence will apply to complicity with both current and former Crown servants, whereas the position for the 'outsider' offences as regards former Crown servants is unclear.

There are a number of other offences under the 1989 act, including:

- Disclosure of any information, document or article that the defendant knows, or has reasonable cause to believe, has come into his or her possession as a result of a breach of section 1 of the 1911 Act;
- Failure to return or failure to prevent unauthorised disclosure of any document or article which it would be an offence to disclose; and
- Disclosure of any information, document or other article which can be used for the purposes of obtaining access to any information, document or other article protected against disclosure by the 1989 Act.

In March 2002, the House of Lords, in upholding the decisions of Mr Justice Moses and the Court of Appeal, held in the David Shayler case that the provisions of the 1989 Act did not breach Article 10 (freedom of expression) of the European Convention on Human Rights, as enshrined in the Human Rights Act 1998. Shayler, a former MI5 officer, was charged with passing documents and information to the *Mail on Sunday* in 1997, which disclosed, among other things, that the agency kept files on a number of Labour ministers (at the time of writing, he had not been charged over his subsequent allegations, including that MI6 was involved in a plot to assassinate the Libyan leader, Colonel Gadafy). The judge held that the 1989 Act did not permit a defence that a disclosure was 'necessary in the public interest to avert damage to life or limb or serious damage to property'. The ban on disclosures by members or former members of the security and intelligence services was 'necessary in a democratic society, in the interests of national security', and was therefore compatible with Article 10.

In contrast, in July 2000, the *Guardian* and *Observer* successfully fought broad court disclosure orders obliging them to hand over e-mails sent to them by Shayler. In the absence of 'compelling evidence' that they were in the public interest, the High Court quashed the orders made by an Old Bailey judge, with Lord Justice Judge holding that they 'would have a devastating and stifling effect on the proper investigation of the Shayler story'. Interestingly, Shayler's 'gritty thriller about spies, sex and football', *The Organisation*, written while in exile in France, was also approved that month for publication by the Home Office, without a word being cut.

Breach of government confidentiality

Juries are not always as willing as governments would like to convict under the Official Secrets Acts, and where diaries or memoirs are concerned civil actions for breach of confidence are increasingly used to try and stifle publication on the grounds that every minister or government employee has a duty not to reveal government secrets. The confidentiality principles covering government secrets are the same as those set out above. An injunction might be granted if there is still a risk to national security. However, Jonathan Cape Ltd was allowed to proceed with publication of the *Crossman Diaries* in 1975 on the grounds that by then the revelations were too old to be dangerous.

The Attorney-General was more determined in 1985 and 1986, however, when attempting to suppress publication of former MI5 officer Peter Wright's memoirs, *Spycatcher*. While proceedings for breach of confidentiality were under way in the Australian courts, several UK newspapers began to publish extracts. In a succession of actions, the government obtained interim injunctions against the *Guardian*, *Observer*, and *Sunday Times* but meanwhile the book was published in Australia and became freely available throughout the rest of the world. The House of Lords finally lifted the injunctions in 1988 on the grounds that there could no longer be any public interest in suppressing 'secrets' that had become so widely public. As a final humiliation, the European Court of Human Rights later ruled that maintenance of the injunctions after general publication had taken place was an infringement of the right to freedom of expression contained in Article 10 of the European Convention (now encoded in the Human Rights Act 1998).

Where there has been a breach of an undertaking of confidentiality, the claimant (in these cases, the Crown) may be entitled to an account of profits in exceptional circumstances – rather than the more usual remedies of compensatory damages, specific performance and injunctions. In *Attorney-General* v. *Blake* (2000), the House of Lords held that the Attorney General was entitled to the money that remained payable (around £90,000) by Jonathan Cape Ltd to former secret agent George Blake under their publishing agreement. The 'exceptional circumstances' in that case included the fact that Blake – who was described by Lord Nicholls as 'a notorious, self-confessed traitor' – had 'deliberately committed repeated breaches of his undertaking not to divulge official information gained as a result of his employment' and had 'caused untold and immeasurable damage to the public interests he had committed himself to serve'.

DA-notices

The Defence Press and Broadcasting Committee was set up after the 1911 Official Secrets Act to issue Defence Advisory notices, or DA-notices (previously called D-notices) to the media, to advise on both general policy matters (there are currently five) and on the security implications of particular pieces of information. The notices are for guidance only, and have no legal status or authority and proceedings are rarely initiated following publication in apparent breach of a Notice. Publishers and authors should not rely too much on indications by the Committee that a publication will not threaten national security: prosecution under the Official Secrets Act could nevertheless follow.

SUMMARY CHECKLIST: CONFIDENTIALITY AND PRIVACY

Confidential information:

- Is it proposed that information of a confidential nature be published?
- If so, does a duty of confidence exist in relation to that information:
  - by way of a relationship of confidence;
  - by way of contract; or
  - through the recipient's knowledge that the information would be regarded as confidential by the person to whom the information belongs (or where the recipient ought to know)?
- If so, is there an overriding public interest reason why the confidential information should be published?

Private information:

- Is the information private? Consider:
  - Does the claimant have a reasonable expectation of privacy?
  - Obviously private information in fields of health, personal finances and relationships;
  - Information which, if published about the person of ordinary sensibilities, would be offensive to that person.
- If so, is the benefit of publication proportionate to the harm done by the violation of individual's right to privacy? Consider:
  - The type of individual to whom the information relates;
  - Whether publication would set the record straight;
  - The subject matter of the publication (including whether it is a matter of public debate);
  - Whether photographs need to be published to convey the information.
- Finally, give thought to the practicality of having to withdraw and/or replace the publication if an injunction is granted, and to the potential costs involved in legal proceedings, should they arise.

Additional considerations:

- Could publication be an offence under the Official Secrets Acts?
- Are any DA-notices relevant in relation to a proposed publication?

Copyright infringement

9

We saw in chapter 2 that copyright in the UK is not merely a personal licence to copy; its value lies primarily in the right to control (and if necessary, prevent) copying by others. In this chapter we will set out in detail exactly which activities a copyright owner may control in this way, and what remedies UK – and international – law provides against infringers. We will need to look in turn at the following:

- the primary 'restricted acts' under UK law, such as copying itself;
- secondary infringements such as possession or dealing with infringing copies;
- defences such as fair dealing, and the permitted acts which will not infringe;
- where infringement does occur, the civil and criminal remedies available in the UK against infringers;
- the legal protection available for UK works overseas, and for foreign works here.

PRIMARY INFRINGEMENT

Section 16 of the 1988 Act provides that copyright owners have the exclusive right to do the following 'restricted acts' in relation to most copyright works in the UK (but not always artistic works):

(1) to copy the work;
(2) to issue copies of the work to the public;
(3) to rent or lend the work to the public;
(4) to perform, show or play the work in public;
(5) to communicate the work to the public;
(6) to make an adaptation of the work, or do any of the above things in relation to an adaptation.

Anyone who does any of the above restricted acts to a relevant work without the licence of the copyright owner will infringe copyright in the work, unless one of the exceptions applies (see below, p. 224).

The key restricted acts for publishing purposes are 1, 2, 5 and 6, but before we go on to consider these in more detail, two further general points need to be made.

TAKING A 'SUBSTANTIAL PART' MAY INFRINGE

Any of the acts listed above may infringe copyright if they are done either in relation to the work as a whole, or to any 'substantial part' of it. It is therefore not necessary for an infringer to copy (for example) the entire work, as long as a substantial part is copied. This of course rather begs the question: what is a substantial part?

The 1988 Act itself gives no guidance, but in a long line of decided cases the courts have held that what is substantial is a question of fact and degree in all the circumstances, and depends more on the *quality* of what is taken than the quantity. The courts have also held that each case is one of feel and impression. The test is, first, to identify the features found to have been copied from the original work and, second, to ask whether those features form a substantial part of that work. One or two lines of text taken from a 500-page textbook might not be significant enough to amount to a substantial part of the whole thing, but centrally important dramatic lines from a novel or play might well be. Thus, as little as four lines from Rudyard Kipling's poem 'If' constituted a sufficiently substantial part in the 1920s when used without consent in a Sanatogen advertisement, and one verse out of four copied in the Robbie Williams/Guy Fletcher song 'Jesus In A Camper Van' was a substantial part of the claimant's song. A few bars from the 'Colonel Bogey' march infringed even though the full march lasted over four minutes, as did five minutes in a feature-length film based on four pages in a 126-page novel.

A key issue is often whether the part taken is commonplace or insignificant, or whether it includes some identifiable, distinctive flavour of the work.

In a recent case, IPC claimed that Highbury had infringed the artistic copyright in certain covers and articles in its *Ideal Home* publication. The Court dismissed the case referring to IPC's over-reliance on similarities common in the trade and on design elements which are not subject to copyright protection. The judge held copyright does not protect general themes, styles or ideas.

In the much-quoted words of one judge in 1916: 'What is worth copying is *prima facie* worth protecting'. If it is valuable enough to an infringer to be worth taking at all, it may well be important enough to be a substantial part.

INFRINGEMENT MAY BE INDIRECT

Any of the above infringing acts may be done indirectly as well as directly. Thus, copying a copy (or a copy of a copy) may infringe copyright just as much as copying directly from the original. In most cases of copying (for example from a book or journal) what is copied is not the author's original, but the authorised published edition, which is itself of course a copy.

Equally, copyright may be infringed by authorising (even impliedly) the infringement of others. There must, however, be a direct causal link between the 'authorisation' and the infringing act(s) which resulted. So the sale and supply of recording equipment with a copying feature expressly advertised as suitable for home copying might in some circumstances infringe, even though the infringements would actually be done by others, but the mere sale of blank DVDs by itself would probably not. Manufacturers of photocopying machines do not 'authorise' copyright infringement merely by selling and supplying their machines, but a university library or a business which installs a machine or a bank of machines and permits multiple copying knowing that most if not all of the copying will infringe copyright and does nothing to prevent it, may well be held to have 'authorised' those infringements.

COPYING

Although anti-piracy slogans such as 'Copying is Theft' are not always strictly accurate, copying the work, or a substantial part of it, without permission and in the absence of one of the exemptions, is probably the most common primary infringement. It often accompanies other infringements such as issuing copies to the public; indeed it would usually be difficult to do some of the other restricted acts without someone having copied first. A copy may still infringe even if its making is transient or incidental to some other use of the work.

Copying is widely defined in the 1988 Act (section 17) to mean reproducing the work 'in any material form' and this is expressly stated to include storing the work in any medium by electronic means. Any reproduction of any work in physical or retrievable form can therefore be caught under the definition. One case held that the use of small-scale copies of a third party's photographs as icons and banners on a website designed for the purpose of selling antiques online infringed the third party's copyright. In the Scottish *Shetland Times* case, it was held at least arguable on an interim application for an injunction that the copying verbatim of headlines by one website operator from another web site operator infringed copyright under section 17 of the 1988 Act, copying being storing the works by electronic means.

Whatever the medium, however, there must be some objective evidence that copying actually took place, and that the alleged infringing copy was derived directly or indirectly from the work in question. It will not often be possible to produce firsthand witness evidence of copying, of course (unauthorised copying is not usually done in public) – a court will therefore in many cases be prepared to make a presumption that copying must have taken place where:

- there is sufficient objective similarity between the work and the alleged copy;
- the alleged infringer had access to or knew of the original;
- no (credible) counter-evidence is produced to suggest that the alleged copy might have resulted from independent skill and effort (or been taken from some other source).

Under these circumstances there will be a strong inference that copying must have occurred, and in the absence of any defence (see below) this is likely to amount to copyright infringement.

Intention

It does not matter that the infringer did not consciously intend to copy; all the primary acts of copyright infringement are offences of strict liability, requiring no evidence of guilty knowledge or intent. An apparently innocent state of mind is no defence – neither is ignorance (for example, that the work in question was still in copyright, or even that it existed) and neither is honest mistake, such as a genuine belief that the copying in question was licensed by the copyright owner.

Evidence of this kind will of course be taken into account, and may provide a defence to any award of damages if there was no reason to believe the work was in copyright at all (see p. 224) but it will not otherwise prevent the acts concerned amounting to infringing acts. However blameless you think you are, if you in fact copy without permission you are very likely to infringe copyright.

In some cases, copyright infringement will occur even if the infringer does not consciously realise he or she is copying the work.

Plagiarism

There is a common misconception in some circles that copying someone else's work can somehow be legalised by the strategic alteration of a few words and phrases. This is entirely wrong, and highly dangerous. The mere fact that few passages are reproduced exactly, word for word, will not necessarily be sufficient to prevent what is copied from being a substantial part of the whole, particularly if the copying is extensive and blatant. It will also not give any protection against infringement of the separate copyright in the author's compilation of material, including the selection and arrangement of topics and headings. The question to be asked is very simple indeed: did copying actually take place? If it did – whether of the text, or the compilation – then no amount of subsequent tinkering with the wording or the arrangement will save the activity from being copyright infringement – provided that at least some substantial parts have been taken. The fact that all the material *could* have been obtained from elsewhere will also not alter the position if the infringer chose instead to save the time and effort and skill involved and copy from an existing compilation. In the 1985 case of *Geographia Ltd* v. *Penguin Books*, the selection and arrangement of map details including colours was accepted as protectable, although on the facts the copying was insufficiently substantial.

This is not to say of course that existing material and common sources cannot be relied upon in creating a new work – provided that they are not copied. It may also be permissible to reproduce limited extracts in the context of fair dealing for the purposes of criticism and review, but these must be accompanied by a sufficient acknowledgement (see below). There have often been borderline cases where there is a marked similarity between two works, and it is clear that much of the material in the new work has been derived from the thoughts and ideas in the existing one. Even without any acknowledgement this may be perfectly legal (if a little unprofessional). There is no copyright in ideas. However, over-reliance on any single existing work is generally inadvisable, and even though there may be no direct evidence of intentional copying, provided that sufficiently substantial parts have been taken a court may still be willing to infer that copying – however inadvertent – must have taken place.

Artistic works

The 1988 Act provides that the definition of copying in relation to an artistic work includes:

- making a three-dimensional copy of a two-dimensional work; and
- making a two-dimensional copy of a three-dimensional work.

A carving or sculpture which is copied from an original photograph may thus infringe copyright in the photograph even though the new work has added an extra dimension, and three-dimensional toys based on two-dimensional cartoon characters may similarly infringe copyright in the original graphic works. Conversely, a two-dimensional photograph or painting may infringe copyright in a three-dimensional work.

ISSUING COPIES TO THE PUBLIC

Under section 18 of the 1988 Act the issue to the public of copies of any work is a restricted act, and copyright in the work will be infringed if it is done without the copyright owner's consent.

'Issue to the public' is defined as the putting into circulation of copies in the EEA which were not previously put into circulation in the EEA by the copyright owner or with his consent or the putting into circulation of copies outside the EEA which were not previously put into circulation in the EEA or elsewhere. Under the Act issue to the public specifically does *not* include:

- any subsequent distribution, sale, hiring or loan of copies already circulating; or
- any subsequent importation of those copies into the UK or another EEA state but it does include putting into circulation in the EEA copies previously put into circulation outside the EEA.

Note that 'copies' are referred to in the plural, though there seems no particular reason why the issue to the public of a single copy should not infringe copyright also, in appropriate circumstances. However, it is likely that at least one physical copy of the work itself must actually be put into circulation, so that merely advertising or collecting orders will probably not of themselves amount to issue to the public, and there must be some evidence that the circulation which takes place is (at least potentially) to the public at large rather than to a small circle of friends or acquaintances.

RENTAL AND LENDING

Under section 18A of the 1988 Act the rental or lending of copies of certain works (including literary works) is a restricted act.

'Rental' is defined as making a copy of a work available for use, on terms that it will or may be returned, for direct or indirect economic or commercial advantage.

'Lending' is defined as making a copy of the work available for use on the terms that it will or may be returned, otherwise than for direct or indirect economic or commercial advantage, through an establishment which is accessible to the public.

'Rental' and 'lending' do not involve making a work available for on-the-spot reference use.

'Lending' excludes making available between establishments which are accessible to the public.

If the lending of a work results in a payment which covers the lender establishment's operating costs, there is no direct or indirect economic or commercial advantage.

In certain circumstances (principally the rental of sound recordings or films) authors who have transferred their rental rights are nevertheless entitled to claim equitable remuneration from the rental of their works.

PERFORMING, SHOWING OR PLAYING IN PUBLIC

Performing, showing or playing most works (but not artistic works) in public is a restricted act, which will infringe copyright if done without permission. 'Performance' includes delivery of lectures, addresses, speeches and sermons and can include presentation via any method of sounds or images, including sound recording, films, or broadcast as well as live recital. The audience does not need to be large, but in order to be 'public' must consist of more than a purely domestic or private gathering (even if some guests are present).

The Act (section 19(4)) provides a limited exemption for those (such as TV companies) whose electronic media for transmitting sounds or images are used by others (such as publicans, or club secretaries) for infringing performances: in such cases the person by whom the visual images or sounds are sent, and in the case of a performance the performers, shall not be regarded as responsible for the infringement. They may, however, be caught by other sections (see below).

COMMUNICATION TO THE PUBLIC

Communication to the public of most works is a restricted work. Communication means by electronic transmission and includes broadcasting and making available to the public in such a way that members of the public may access a work from a place and at a time they individually choose.

MAKING AN ADAPTATION

Making an adaptation of a literary, dramatic or musical work (not, incidentally, of an artistic work) is an act restricted by copyright. Doing it without the copyright owner's consent will amount to copyright infringement unless one of the exceptions (such as fair dealing – see below) applies.

However, adaptations for the purposes of copyright law are narrowly defined. What amounts to an 'adaptation' under UK law is defined in section 21 of the 1988 Act in relation to different kinds of works:

Literary and dramatic works

In relation to a literary or dramatic work, an adaptation means one of the following:

- a translation (normally from one human language to another);
- a dramatisation of a non-dramatic work (turning a novel into a screenplay, for example) or the converse: a conversion of a dramatic work into a non-dramatic work;
- a picturisation (conveying the story or action by means of pictures, in a form suitable for reproduction in a book, newspaper, magazine or similar periodical).

Musical works

An adaptation in relation to a musical work means an arrangement or transcription of the work.

Computer programs

An adaptation means an arrangement or altered version of the program or a translation of it. A translation involves a version of the program in which it is converted into or out of a computer language or code or into a different computer language or code.

Computer databases

An adaptation means an arrangement or altered version of the database or a translation of it.

SECONDARY INFRINGEMENT

As well as the key primary infringements of copyright set out above, sections 22 to 27 of the 1988 Act provide for further, secondary infringements. They include:

- importing an infringing copy;
- possessing or dealing with it;
- providing means for making it.

There are also secondary infringements of transmitting a work via a telecommunications system, permitting the use of premises for an infringing performance, and providing apparatus for one.

IMPORTING AN INFRINGING COPY

Section 22 provides that:

> the copyright in a work is infringed by a person who, without the licence of the copyright owner, imports into the UK otherwise than for his private and domestic use an article which is, and which he knows or has reason to believe is, an infringing copy of the work.

Guilty knowledge

Note that the person must *know* (or have reason to believe) that the article is an infringing copy – unlike primary infringements, which are all offences of strict liability (see above), it is an essential element of all secondary infringements that the alleged infringer should have known – or can be presumed to have known – the full significance of what he or she was doing. Proving – or inferring – such 'guilty knowledge' is a question of fact in each case: some defendants (such as rival publishers or experienced book importers) may be presumed to be more familiar with copyright transactions than others. Where there is some doubt whether importers have the necessary knowledge or not, it is usually advisable to remove any doubt by putting them on formal written notice that what they are doing is an infringing act. This is normally done by a letter before action – after receipt of such a letter it is not then open to them to claim that they had no idea that the copies concerned were infringing copies.

'Infringing copy'

An infringing copy is quite widely defined in section 27 of the Act to include as well as actual imports, copies that have not yet been, but are 'proposed to be', imported into the UK. Those copies may also include not only those which – if made in the UK – would have infringed the copyright itself, but also (under section 27(3)) those which would be in breach of an *exclusive licence* agreement relating to that work.

There is, however, a significant limitation on an exclusive UK licensee's rights to prevent parallel importation in section 27(5) of the Act, which makes it clear that any such rights will not be enforceable against imports from other member states of the EU.

> Nothing in sub-section (3) shall be construed as applying to an article which may lawfully be imported into the UK by virtue of any enforceable Community right within the meaning of section 2(1) of the European Communities Act 1972.

For more on parallel imports and Europe, see chapter 13, p. 324.

POSSESSING OR DEALING WITH AN INFRINGING COPY

Copyright may also be infringed by doing any of the following acts in relation to infringing copies without the consent of the copyright owner and (again) 'knowing or having reason to believe' that the copies are infringing:

- possessing them in the course of a business;
- selling or letting them for hire, or offering or exposing them for sale or hire;
- distributing them or publicly exhibiting them, both in the course of a business;
- distributing them other than in the course of a business, but still to such an extent as to affect prejudicially the copyright owner.

Possession may be by an agent or employee, but must be 'in the course of a business' (which the Act defines to include a trade or profession). On the meaning of this phrase generally, see chapter 11.

Note that sale or letting for hire need not be in the course of a business in order to infringe copyright, and neither need distribution if it is significant enough to affect the copyright owner prejudicially (so that handing out to a class of students course work books known to contain infringing copies of copyright text could well amount to infringement in itself, even though it is not in the course of business and the copying was done by someone else, if such distribution was likely – as it probably would be – to affect sales of the authorised editions prejudicially).

PROVIDING THE MEANS FOR MAKING INFRINGING COPIES

It is also an infringement of copyright in a work for a person, without the copyright owner's consent to:

- make
- import into the UK
- possess in the course of business or
- sell or let for hire (or offer or expose for sale or hire)

an article specifically designed or adapted for making copies of that work, knowing (or having reason to believe) that it is to be used for making infringing copies. Specialised photocopying or recording equipment might be covered, but only if specifically designed or adapted for making copies of the particular work concerned: the section is more likely to cover unauthorised dealings with negatives or plates.

OTHER SECONDARY INFRINGEMENTS

It is also an infringement of copyright in a work to do the following acts without the copyright owner's consent:

- transmit it via a telecommunications system (other than by communication to the public) knowing or having reason to believe that infringing copies will be made as a result;
- permit the use of premises for an infringing performance (unless whoever gave the permission believed on reasonable grounds that the performance would not infringe copyright);
- supplying infringing apparatus (such as film or recording equipment) knowing or having reason to believe that the apparatus was likely to be used to infringe copyright.

PERMITTED ACTS AND OTHER DEFENCES

If one or more of the infringing acts listed above is alleged, a number of legal arguments may be produced by way of defence. Here is a checklist of the likeliest possible defences.

SUMMARY CHECKLIST: LIKELIEST POSSIBLE DEFENCES

- the work concerned is not a copyright work at all (for example it is not a literary or other work, or it lacks the necessary originality – see p. 18);
- it is not a qualifying work by reason of first (or simultaneous) publication in the UK, or the author is not a qualifying person in the UK – see p. 33);
- it will not be protected under UK law for some other reason (for example, that it offends public sensibilities, or is fraudulent or otherwise unlawful – see below, p. 225);
- although it was a copyright work, the period of copyright protection has now expired and at the relevant time the work was in the public domain (note that copyright in some public domain works revived following the EU's Duration Directive; on this, and the term of copyright generally – see p. 35);
- the person alleging copyright infringement is not in fact the copyright owner (or the owner's licensee – see p. 237);
- no copying took place, and the work which allegedly infringes copyright was in fact the result of independent skill and effort – see p. 217);
- if copying did take place, the material copied is not significant or extensive enough to amount to a 'substantial part' of the copyright work concerned – see p. 216);
- the copying or other acts done were permitted acts, such as fair dealing (see below, p. 226);
- whatever took place, the copyright owner consented.

Most of the above defences are dealt with elsewhere in this book, as indicated, but we will look below at public policy (briefly) and permitted acts (in some detail).

PUBLIC POLICY

Although the boundaries of copyright are primarily defined by statute in the UK, the 1988 Act contains a number of general saving provisions (at section 171) for other existing rights – for example that the rights and privileges of the Crown and Parliament will not be affected by any copyright, and that a similar exemption applies to:

- any rule of equity relating to breaches of trust or confidence; and
- any rule of law preventing or restricting the enforcement of copyright, on grounds of public interest or otherwise.

This last proviso leaves scope for the courts to refuse to enforce any copyright on grounds of public interest or public policy, if it conflicts with 'any rule of law'. Although the old cases denying copyright protection to blasphemous or 'irreligious' works are unlikely to be followed nowadays, the proviso probably still gives judges sufficient grounds for denying copyright protection to a work which has already been held to be defamatory or obscene or where there is some other strong public interest argument against giving protection – but probably only if publication would actually be unlawful. It might also enable them to prevent a criminal from profiting from a crime, or from relying on copyright to protect a work which amounts to a fraud on the public (in one nineteenth-century case, an action against a book pirate failed because the religious work copied claimed to be a translation from an eminent German authority when in fact it was nothing of the kind).

The courts have held that this defence cannot be defined or categorised. It includes freedom of expression under the European Convention on Human Rights. It also includes:

- if the work is immoral, scandalous or contrary to family life;
- if the work is injurious to public life, public health and safety or the administration of justice; or
- if the work incites others to act in a way which would be so injurious.

PERMITTED ACTS

There are certain kinds of copying – generally non-commercial in nature – which may be done without infringing copyright if they come under the definition of one of the permitted acts set out in the 1988 Act. It would be a complete defence to any claim of copyright infringement to establish that the activity complained of was in fact a permitted act, although as we shall see motivation may be relevant too (for example in questions relating to fair dealing). The Act provides a long list of permitted acts, many of which are quite narrowly defined: we will consider below those of most relevance to publishing.

3-step test

Article 5.5 of the Directive provides, in wording taken from the Berne Convention, that any copyright exception must only be applied 'in certain special cases which do not conflict with a normal exploitation of the work or other subject matter and do not unreasonably prejudice the legitimate interests of the rightsholder'. This is likely to be a significant factor in future interpretation by UK courts of 'fair dealing' and other exceptions.

Temporary copying

Section 28A provides that copyright in most works is not infringed by the making of a temporary copy which is transient or incidental, an integral and essential part of a technological process and the sole purpose of which is to enable a transmission of the work in a network between third parties by an intermediary or a lawful use of the work. In addition, the temporary copy has to have no independent economic significance.

Fair dealing

Copyright in a literary, dramatic, musical or artistic work, or a typographical arrangement, will not be infringed by any 'fair dealing' with those works for the following purposes:

- research or private study;
- criticism or review;
- reporting current events.

'Fair dealing' is not defined in the Act, but it is an essential pre-requisite of all three of the above defences. It is not enough therefore merely to prove that copying (for example) was done for the purposes of research: it must have been *fair dealing* for the purposes of research. It will not succeed as a defence to a claim of copyright infringement otherwise. We will look at what is or is not 'fair' in the context of each individual activity. The test is an objective test. However, the intentions of the user are relevant to the question of whether the use is fair dealing. Other factors may include whether the original work has been published yet, and how extensive – and how important – are the extracts taken as a proportion of the whole (and in some circumstances how frequent).

Research or private study

Fair dealing for the purposes of research (for a non-commercial purpose) or private study is a permitted act and will be a defence to any claim of copyright infringement. In respect of research fair dealing has to be accompanied by a sufficient acknowledgement unless this is impossible for reasons of practicality or otherwise. The research or private study must genuinely constitute fair dealing, however, first and foremost: in this context this probably limits the defence to personal activities (such as personal copying) rather than acts undertaken collectively. In the case of copying, as a general rule the person doing the copying must be the same person as the person doing the research or private study. He or she may possibly ask a friend or some other agent, such as a librarian, to do it for them, and there seems no reason why more than one copy cannot be made, as long as all the copying is for the personal research or private study of the individual concerned. It will *not* be fair dealing if a librarian or teacher makes multiple copies on behalf of an entire class of students – even if individually they are all engaged in private study: this was confirmed as long ago as 1916 in the leading case of *University of London Press Limited* v. *University Tutorial Press Limited*, where the clear motive was not individual or personal, but a collective motive to save the users (examination candidates) from having to buy the original works themselves.

The 1988 Act also makes it clear (in section 29(3)(b)) that copying by someone other than the individual researcher or student will not be fair dealing if:

> the person doing the copying knows or has reason to believe that it will result in copies of substantially the same material being provided to more than one person at substantially the same time and for substantially the same purpose.

Research does not include commercial research. If the copying is by a commercial organisation for the purpose of commercial research, the use is not fair dealing.

Fair dealing for the purpose of research and private study specifically does not now include decompilation of a computer program – this is a separate permitted act (see below, p. 234).

Criticism or review

Section 30 of the Act provides that fair dealing with a work for the purpose of criticism or review (of that work, or another work, or of a performance of a work) does not infringe any copyright in the work, provided that it is accompanied by a sufficient acknowledgement and provided it has been made available to the public.

As with fair dealing for the purpose of research or private study, there are a number of points to note:

- In order not to infringe, the acts done must not merely be for the purpose of criticism or review, but must constitute *fair dealing* for that purpose. Any improper motive – such as an obviously commercial motivation – will weaken any defence of fair dealing at the outset. It will be a question of fact and impression in every case: in the *University of London Press* case referred to above, very extensive extracts were reproduced, with little or no attempt at 'critical' commentary, and the primary motivation behind the copying was clearly not critical at all but commercial.
- Fair dealing may be regarded as for the purpose of criticism or review, even though the criticism or review concerned may be of the theories or philosophy behind the work rather than its actual literary content or style, or of a class of works,

such as a style of journalism and, of course, the criticism or review need not be favourable. It must, however, have some significant element of genuine comment, or assessment.

- The term 'criticism or review' is interpreted liberally.
- The criticism or review must be accompanied by 'a sufficient acknowledgement'. This phrase is defined in section 178 of the Act to mean 'an acknowledgement identifying the work in question by its title or other description, and identifying the author' (unless the work is published anonymously, or is unpublished and the author cannot be identified). Crediting the title and the author will constitute sufficient acknowledgement, therefore; there is no requirement under the Act to credit the publisher or copyright owner (if different from the author). It is probably advisable to include as complete a credit as possible on each page where an extract appears, and a full copyright acknowledgement on at least one page, perhaps under the relevant acknowledgements section, or list of sources.

In the case of *Fraser-Woodward* v. *BBC*, the claimant owned the copyright in a number of photographs of the Beckham family which were first published in various tabloid newspapers. An episode of a TV programme featured images of the newspaper pages on which the claimant's photographs appeared. The defendant claimed this was criticism and/or review of tabloid journalism and the methods by which the tabloid press and the Beckhams built and exploited stories to their advantage. The Court stated that all that is needed is for there to be sufficient content to amount to criticism or review and gave the following guidelines:

- What is the real objective of the person using the copyright mark?
- Excessive use can render use unfair.
- What is the actual purpose of the defendant's mark?
- The amount of the work used can be relevant.
- What type of work is reproduced and in which medium is it used?
- Reproduction should not unreasonably prejudice the legitimate interests of the author or conflict with the normal exploitation of the work.

The use of the front cover of the claimant's magazine in an advertisement by the defendant which included the defendant's own magazine was not criticism or review. The Court found that the defendant's uses of the claimant's work was to advance the sales of the defendant's products.

Reporting current events

Fair dealing with a work (other than a photograph) for the purpose of reporting current events does not infringe any copyright in it, provided that it is accompanied by a sufficient acknowledgement (see above). The requirement of a sufficient acknowledgement does not apply to non-print reporting via sound recording, film, or broadcast where this would be impossible for reasons of practicality or otherwise.

The events being reported must be current, but the work copied or otherwise used need not be: it may count as fair dealing to reproduce part of an existing literary work (such as a political study, or a scientific report) for example, if it becomes relevant in reporting future current events. The purpose must be the immediate one of 'reporting' those events, not some wider or more long-term editorial purpose. Moreover the term 'reporting current events' is also interpreted liberally. Even if an event may only be of limited interest, it is still a current event. It appears that the threshold for showing something is a current event is not high or difficult to surmount. The distinction between current events and events which are currently of interest can become blurred.

In *Pro Sieben Media AG v. Carlton UK Television Limited* (1999) the pregnancy of Mandy Allwood, who became pregnant whilst undergoing a course of fertility treatment and was found to be carrying eight live embryos, was considered to be a 'current event' and the defendant's current affairs TV program relating to cheque book journalism, which featured an extract from the claimant's TV interview of Mandy Allwood, was deemed to be for the purpose of 'criticism or review'. The 1990 World Cup was also held to be a current event.

The Court of Appeal decision in *Hyde Park Residence Limited v. David Yelland and others* (2000) illustrates the subjective (and therefore unpredictable) operation of this fair dealing provision. The case involved an application for summary judgment by a security company owned by Mohammed Al Fayed on the basis of copyright infringement in respect of the publication of still photographs of Diana Princess of Wales and Dodi Al Fayed taken from security camera footage on a visit to the Villa Windsor in Paris. Al Fayed had alleged that this indicated that they planned to marry. At first instance, the Court held that the use of the video stills was for the purpose of reporting current events and fair dealing in all the circumstances. The Court of Appeal disagreed and upheld the claimant's appeal. On a liberal interpretation, the media coverage of Al Fayed's allegations was a reporting of a current event. However, the dealing with the photographs had not been fair. Their use was excessive in all the circumstances and the point could have been conveyed by text. Also, no fair-minded and honest person would have paid for the dishonestly taken stills in all the circumstances. The Court of Appeal stated that the Court must judge the fairness by the objective standard of whether a fair minded and honest person would have dealt with the copyright work for the purpose of reporting the relevant current events in the manner that the defendant did.

Note that these provisions apply to all works, *except* photographs.

Incidental inclusion of copyright material

Copyright in any work is not infringed by its incidental inclusion in an artistic work (such as a photograph), or in a sound recording, film, or broadcast. This is sometimes referred to as 'passing shot use'. The inclusion must, however, be truly 'incidental', which would probably exclude most deliberate acts designed specifically to add value, for example by dubbing in background music (deliberate inclusion of musical and allied works is now expressly ruled out by section 31(3) of the Act). Some other deliberate uses (such as the quotation of a few lines of a literary work by a character in a film) might nevertheless still count as 'incidental inclusion' in some circumstances, provided they amount to no more than passing shots.

The inclusion of badges and logos in photographs of football players in the defendant's football album was found by a Court not to be incidental inclusion.

Educational use

Sections 32 to 36 of the 1988 Act provide several somewhat limited exceptions to copyright infringement, designed to cover activities which are regarded as permissible under the general heading of 'education'. In the UK, these categories of permitted educational use are narrowly defined, so that much of the copying which goes on in schools and colleges (particularly if it is multiple copying) will not be permitted use under the 1988 Act and will still require the consent of the copyright owner. This can now be licensed under collective licensing schemes run by the Copyright Licensing Agency (see below, p. 231). This is in marked contrast to the copyright laws of some developing countries (at least, developing in the copyright sense) where 'educational use' has been notoriously widely defined to enable faculties – and the local photocopy shops – to reproduce entire text books more or less with impunity. This kind of educational piracy or wholesale copying (for example, of carol books for school choirs) is not possible in Britain under UK law, and what the law permits is strictly defined. The following acts are permitted.

Things done for the purposes of instruction or examination (section 32)

This is a very limited exception. In respect of literary works, the copying must be done in the actual course of instruction or preparation for it. It must be done by the teacher or student concerned, must not be via any reprographic process (such as photocopying or electronic copying), has to be accompanied by a sufficient acknowledgement and the instruction has to be for a non-commercial purpose. For literary works made available to the public, the instruction does not have to be for a non-commercial purpose but the copying has to be fair dealing with the work.

Actual examination use is also permitted, such as for the purpose of setting the questions, communicating them to the students or answering them if the questions are accompanied by a sufficient acknowledgement – this extends to reprographic copying but not of musical works. Any subsequent use of a permitted copy under this section (including selling or hiring it) will lose the protection – and will be treated as infringing use.

Anthologies for educational use

Again, this exception (in section 33) is extremely limited. The passage taken must be 'short', and must be in an anthology designed for educational use, which otherwise consists mainly of public domain material, and must be accompanied by a sufficient acknowledgement (see above). No more than two excerpts from the same author may be used in collections published by the same publisher within any five-year period.

Performing and recording by educational establishments

Section 34 provides that a performance of a literary, dramatic or musical work at an educational establishment (and in the course of its activities) by teachers or pupils will not count as a public performance for copyright infringement purposes, provided that the audience consists entirely of other teachers or pupils 'and other persons directly connected with the activities of the establishment' – this may include some parents, for example if they are also school governors, but not others: an 'open' audience of parents and other guests will almost certainly be a (potentially infringing) public performance.

The playing or showing of a sound recording, film, or broadcast under the conditions set out above would also not count as playing or showing the work concerned in public.

Section 35 provides that educational establishments may also record broadcasts, or copy such recordings under certain circumstances, without infringing copyright provided it is accompanied by a sufficient acknowledgement and the educational purposes are non-commercial; however, this exemption does not apply where there is a licensing scheme available, as there currently is, so licences would now be required from the Education Recording Agency (ERA).

Reprographic copying

Section 36 of the Act provides that reprographic copies (which include copies made by electronic means as well as photocopies) may be made of passages from published literary, dramatic or musical works by an educational establishment for the purposes of instruction, but *only* if:

- not more than one per cent of any work is copied in any quarter;
- no licences are available for such copying (about which the person copying knew or ought to have been aware); and
- they are accompanied by a sufficient acknowledgement and the instruction is for a non-commercial purpose.

Any subsequent commercial dealings with a permitted copy under this section (including sale or hire) will be treated as infringing acts. Educational licences for hard-copy and electronic reprographic copying are currently available in the UK from the Copyright Licensing Agency, who regularly grants such licences on behalf of publishers and copyright owners: it would be difficult nowadays for any teacher or librarian to claim that they did not know, or have any reason to believe, that such licences were available.

Details of the Copyright Licensing Agency are set out in Appendix B. The collective licences which it offers will cover multiple copying within defined limits depending on the terms of the particular licence. The licence will bring with it an indemnity from the Copyright Licensing Agency against any legal action by the relevant individual copyright owners, provided the terms of the licence are complied with.

Library and archive copying

'Fair dealing', for example for the purposes of research or private study, may well not cover all the legitimate copying a librarian needs to do. Sections 37 to 44 of the 1988 Act therefore provide certain additional exemptions, for librarians of 'prescribed libraries'. For some purposes, this covers all libraries in the UK, but for others excludes any library 'conducted for profit'. Under the Copyright (Librarians and Archivists) (Copying of Copyright Material) Regulations 1989 made under the Act, this would exclude any library or archive which forms part of, or is administered by, a body established or conducted for profit. For those purposes, this would almost certainly rule out research libraries in major oil companies (or law libraries run by law firms).

Articles in periodicals

Librarians of prescribed libraries (see below) may copy an article in a periodical without infringing copyright in the text, or any illustrations, or the typographical copyright, provided the following conditions are met:

(1) the librarian must be satisfied that the copies are required for the purposes of research for a non-commercial purpose or private study, and will not be used for any other purpose;
(2) no person may be supplied with more than one copy of the same article (or with copies of more than one article from any single issue of a periodical);
(3) the user must be charged a sum not less than the cost of making the copies (including a contribution to the general expenses of the library).

Libraries 'conducted for profit' are not prescribed libraries for these purposes.

Parts of published works

A similar copyright exemption exists for copying of parts of published works other than articles by librarians at prescribed libraries – again, libraries conducted for profit are excluded. The conditions are virtually identical to those set out above, applying to copying from periodicals, save that no person is to be supplied with a copy of 'more than a reasonable proportion' of any work (what is a reasonable proportion is not defined, but would clearly not include copying the whole work).

Public lending rights

Copyright is not infringed by the lending of a book by a public library if the loan is within the public lending right scheme, nor is it infringed by the lending of copies of a work by a prescribed library or archive (other than a public library) which is not conducted for profit.

Supply of copies to other libraries

All UK librarians, whether their library is conducted for profit or not, may copy and supply to librarians of prescribed libraries an article from a periodical or the whole or part of any literary, dramatic or musical work, unless at the time of the request they knew ('or could by reasonable enquiry ascertain') the name and address of the copyright owner. Again, only single copies may be made.

Replacement copies

Librarians of prescribed libraries may copy items from their holdings in order to preserve or replace them, or to replace copies in the permanent collection of other libraries which have been lost, damaged or destroyed. This exemption does not, however, apply where it is reasonably practicable to purchase a copy of the item in question to fulfil that purpose.

Copying unpublished works

All UK librarians may copy unpublished works made on or after 1 August 1989 and deposited with them, such as letters or manuscripts, without infringing any copyright. The conditions are similar to those listed above. The exemption does not apply if the librarian is aware (or ought to be) that the work had been published before being deposited, or that the copyright owner has prohibited copying of the work.

It will be seen that these statutory library exemptions are all fairly limited in scope, even where the library concerned is a prescribed library. Permitted copying is almost always restricted to single copies (which would exclude multiple copying of newsletters or journals to students or other users). In addition, in many cases the librarian must be 'satisfied' about the purpose for which the copies are to be supplied. This probably means that the librarian is at least expected to make reasonable enquiries of users and be reasonably satisfied with the response. This may be achieved by verbal questioning, but where a librarian (or the librarian's employer) is concerned about the risks of legal liability for copying which turns out to infringe (since copyright is infringed by the person making the copies, not the person making the request), it may be advisable for the librarian to obtain a signed declaration from the user before the copying is done. There is provision in section 37(2) of the 1988 Act for a declaration, which may be relied on in situations where a librarian is required to be satisfied as to any matter, and which will have the effect of transferring legal liability to the user, unless the librarian is aware at the time the declaration is made that it is 'false in a material particular'. The 1989 Regulations contain a prescribed form of statutory declaration for these purposes.

It is therefore possible for a librarian to avoid legal liability for single copying which turns out to infringe copyright. It is not, however, generally possible to avoid the risk of legal action by copyright owners for multiple copying in breach of copyright unless permission for that copying has been obtained from the copyright owner or under a collective licensing scheme operated on the owner's behalf, such as those offered by the Copyright Licensing Agency (see above, p. 231).

Parliamentary and judicial proceedings

Section 45 of the Act provides that copyright is not infringed by anything done for the purposes of Parliamentary or judicial proceedings. The Act defines 'Parliamentary' to include not only the UK Parliament, the Northern Ireland Assembly and the Scottish Parliament but also the European Parliament. Judicial proceedings are also widely defined to include, for example, tribunals. However, the copying must be done for the *purposes* of those proceedings, so that a solicitor copying evidence as part of pleadings prior to a trial will be protected, but a teacher or librarian copying Parliamentary or case reports for information or teaching purposes might well not be.

Sections 46 to 50 provide further exceptions regarding the proceedings of Royal Commissions and statutory inquiries, public records and other material open to public inspection or on an official register, and certain copying done by the Crown or under statutory authority.

Lawful use of computer programs

The Copyright (Computer Programs) Regulations 1992 provided new permitted acts in relation to computer programs, under which any 'lawful user' – who already had a right to use the program – may:

- make any necessary back-up copy of it;
- 'decompile' it, where necessary to create an independent program to run with it, or with some other program (not substantially similar to the program being decompiled);
- observe, study or test the functioning of a program in order to determine the ideas and principles which underline any element of the program, if he does so while performing any of the acts he is entitled to do; and
- copy or adapt it (for example, in order to correct errors) (sections 50A–50C of the 1988 Act respectively).

Databases

It is not an infringement of copyright in a database for a person with a right to use the database or a part of it to do, in the exercise of that right, anything which is necessary for the purposes of access to, and use of, the contents of the database or that part.

Designs and typefaces

Under sections 51 and 52, it does not infringe copyright in a design document or model (for anything other than an artistic work or typeface) to make any (presumably three-dimensional) article to that design, or copy such an article, or (inter alia) issue it to the public. Artistic works which have been exploited by or licensed by the copyright owner to be copied 'by an industrial process' and marketed (such as character illustrations licensed for merchandised goods), may be copied by making and exploiting similar goods without infringing copyright after a period of 25 years from the end of the year the original articles were first marketed. This section does not, however, permit copying or exploiting the artistic works concerned in any other way.

Under section 54, it is not an infringement of copyright in the design of a typeface (which is an artistic work) to do the following things:

- to use it in the ordinary course of typing, composing text, typesetting or printing;
- to possess an article for the purpose of such use; or
- to do anything in relation to material produced by that use.

This is despite the fact that such use may be based on an infringing copy. There may, however, still be a liability for secondary infringement, such as importing or possessing an infringing copy of the typeface design itself.

Transferring copies in electronic form

Where a copy of a work in electronic form – a software program, or a text on CD-ROM – is purchased with an express or implied licence to copy or adapt it (for example, permitting a back-up copy), then where the purchaser is freely permitted to sell or transfer it to someone else, that someone else may also copy or adapt it in the same way, without infringing copyright. A right to make a back-up copy, or any other licensed copy, can thus be passed on from seller to purchaser without the need for further licensing. However, any additional copy retained by the seller after the transfer of the licensed copy has taken place will be treated as an infringing copy.

Copying anonymous or pseudonymous works

For works made after 1 August 1989, copyright will not be infringed by any acts done at a time when:

- it is not possible 'by reasonable enquiry' to identify the author; *and*
- it is reasonable to assume copyright has expired or that the author died at least 70 calendar years earlier.

Complex transitional provisions apply to pre-1989 works. In addition, the above does not apply to Crown copyright works, or copyright works of certain international organisations.

Copying abstracts (section 60)

Section 60 of the Act permits the copying (or issuing to the public) of abstracts which accompany published periodical articles on scientific or technical subjects. Such abstracts are a common feature of medical and other scientific journals, and are frequently copied. The abstract must be primarily an abstract rather than anything more (such as an extended editorial): it must have the function of describing or summarising ('indicating') the contents of the article. The article must also have a 'scientific or technical' subject – although this sounds as if it might have rather a narrow scope, it may well be wide enough to cover abstracts of any similar specialist or professional articles, even in the social sciences or arts generally, provided they were pure abstracts accompanying the articles concerned.

The exception does not apply if there is a licensing scheme available for such use: there is not, at the time of writing, and the Copyright Licensing Agency seems to accept for the time being that the copying of abstracts under section 60 is generally permissible.

Copying for visually impaired people

Blind and other visually impaired persons (VIPs) benefit from two statutory copyright exceptions introduced under the Copyright (Visually Impaired Persons) Act 2002:

- an individual/personal right for every VIP to make 'accessible copies' for his/her personal use; and
- a multiple copyright right for 'approved bodies' to make copies on behalf of their members.

The second, collective copying exception does not have effect if, and to the extent that, a suitable licensing scheme exists.

There are a number of key provisos to these copyright exceptions:

(1) Both exceptions are subject to a requirement for copies to include a statement that they are made under the Copyright Act, and sufficient acknowledgement to the source.
(2) Copies must be made from lawful originals.
(3) There must be no accessible edition already commercially available.
(4) The accessible copy may not be transferred, sold, lent or hired, etc. without consent.
(5) In the case of multiple copies, copying may only be made by an approved body, which must notify rightsholders, keep records and allow reasonable audits.

Other permitted acts

Other permitted acts under the 1988 Act include the following:

- things done in reliance on a registered design (section 53);
- use of notes or recordings to report current events (section 58);
- public reading or recital of reasonable extracts (with a sufficient acknowledgement) (section 59);
- representation of certain artistic works on public display (section 62);
- copying an artistic work in order to advertise its sale (section 63);
- subsequent works made by the same artist (section 64);
- lending of works and playing of sound recordings (sections 66 and 67);
- incidental recording for the purposes of a broadcast (section 68);
- private photographing of a broadcast or recording it for the purposes of time shifting (sections 70 to 71);
- reception and re-transmission of a wireless broadcast by cable (section 73).

CIVIL AND CRIMINAL REMEDIES IN THE UK

What do you do if someone infringes your copyright? Perhaps equally importantly: what might they (and a court) do to you if you infringe theirs? In this section we will look at who can sue, and who can *be* sued, in UK courts, what civil remedies (such as damages) might be available to them, and in what circumstances, and finally – but increasingly importantly – what criminal penalties might apply.

WHO CAN SUE?

The copyright owner

Perhaps self-evidently, all copyright infringements are actionable by the copyright owner. It must be the correct copyright owner, however – as we saw in chapter 2, a typical publication such as a book or CD-ROM might contain several different copyright works, and there may be several different copyright owners: in order to bring an action for infringement, the copyright owner must be the owner of the particular copyright which has been infringed. So, if an illustration has been copied without permission, the owner of artistic copyright in that illustration may sue for infringement, but not, for example, the owner of literary copyright in the accompanying text – they are different copyrights, and may be owned by different people. The position would be the same with any separate, but associated, copyright – such as a compilation of the book as a whole, or an underlying computer program. If the text (or compilation, or computer program) was copied too, of course, then the owners of copyright in these works may have actions, but not otherwise.

The owner must also own the copyright at the correct *time* (in fact, two separate times):

- at the actual time when the infringement occurred. A subsequent copyright owner (such as a beneficiary under a will, or an assignee) cannot sue for infringements which took place before he or she became the owner (unless the rights of action have been assigned); *and*
- when the claim form is issued: you will have no cause of action if you do not own legal (or at least equitable) title to the copyright.

Joint copyright owners

Although a joint copyright owner cannot exploit the copyright without the consent of the others, any joint copyright owner can take legal action for infringement of the relevant copyright without needing to join the others in the proceedings (although the others, of course, may wish to join in).

Exclusive licensees

Section 101 of the 1988 Act provides that an exclusive licensee has the same concurrent rights and remedies as the copyright owner and can therefore sue for copyright infringement in the same way. Any infringer can be sued, except the copyright owner themselves.

The infringement must have occurred after the licence was granted, and while it was in force. The infringement must also fall within the terms of the particular exclusive licence concerned, of course, so that an exclusive licensee of English-language volume rights may bring an action against an infringing English-language paperback, but not against an infringing Russian translation on a website.

Although an exclusive licensee may seek an injunction, once the action is under way the copyright owner must be joined as a claimant (or added as a defendant) unless the leave of the court is obtained. The same point applies if the copyright owner commences proceedings. The court will usually only grant leave in exceptional circumstances – as in 1972, for example, when Bodley Head were granted leave to pursue an action on their own since the copyright owner – Solzhenitsyn – could not do so in Russia where the book concerned was banned.

Non-exclusive licensees may bring an action for copyright infringement if the infringing act is directly connected to a prior licensed act of the licensee. In addition, the licence has to be in writing, signed by the copyright owner and expressly grant the non-exclusive licensee the right to bring an action.

Other parties, such as agents, have no right to take proceedings for copyright infringement in their own name.

Presumptions on title

With old publishing records hard evidence of copyright ownership may be difficult to come by. The court will assist claimants in such cases by making a number of presumptions, spelt out in sections 104 to 106 of the Act. In each case, unless the contrary is proved:

- anyone whose name appears as the author on published copies of a work will be presumed to be the author;
- any such author will be presumed not to have written the work in the course of employment, or subject to Crown or other copyrights;
- where no author is named, but a publisher is identified, that publisher will be deemed to be the copyright owner, provided that the work otherwise qualifies for UK copyright protection on the basis of its country of first publication (see p. 34);
- where the author is dead or unknown (and cannot be ascertained by reasonable enquiry) it will be presumed that the work is original, and that the claimant's claims as to first publication are correct;
- where the work is a computer program, and is published bearing statements crediting a particular copyright owner, or relating to first publication in a particular country or issue to the public in a specified year, those statements will be presumed to be correct.

WHO CAN BE SUED?

Section 16(2) of the 1988 Act provides that copyright in a work is infringed by a person who, without the licence of the copyright owner, does, or authorises another to do, any of the acts restricted by copyright. As we saw above, these restricted acts may be primary infringements such as copying, or issuing copies to the public (above pp. 217 and 219), or secondary infringements such as importation or possession. Any 'person' who does, or authorises, any such acts, as defined, without permission, may thus be sued. This therefore includes the following.

Natural persons

This means human beings who do, or authorise, any of the restricted acts (on the meaning of 'authorise', see above, p. 216). In a publishing case, there may be several different infringements, such as copying, issuing copies to the public, importing, possessing, selling, hiring or distributing, and each person will be separately and personally liable for their own infringements. Several defendants may therefore be sued at once, including authors and publishers, printers, wholesalers and bookshop owners, even though the causes of action may be different.

Employees will often be personally liable even if they were acting in the course of their employment (in that case *both* employee and employer may be liable) and so may directors and agents.

Legal persons (such as companies)

In the case of many small companies the one or two directors in charge to all intents and purposes *are* the company. So although many of the infringements would have been done by the company and it will therefore be necessary to sue the company, it may be advisable to sue the directors personally as well (since small companies may conveniently cease trading, whereas directors tend to survive).

Joint infringers (or joint tortfeasors)

A common, concerted design by two or more persons to infringe may lead to both or all of them being sued jointly (even if one of them is outside the UK).

WARNING LETTERS

The first step in many actions for copyright infringement – indeed actions of any kind – is the sending of a warning letter. This is normal practice, and may give both sides the opportunity to sort the matter out (fairly) amicably without having to resort to costly and time consuming litigation. If a standard business letter does not produce the desired result, a more formal solicitor's letter, threatening specific legal action (and therefore called a letter before action) might concentrate minds sufficiently to stop the infringement and settle the matter on mutually acceptable terms. Whether or not a warning letter was sent may also have an impact on the question of costs later on: if there is time, such letters are therefore advisable. Courts may be less likely to award a successful claimant his or her costs if he or she did not send a letter before action, as litigation is now seen as a last resort and parties are encouraged to settle their dispute before commencing proceedings.

Where the infringement is a primary infringement – such as copying (see p. 217) there is no legal requirement to send a warning letter before commencing legal proceedings: indeed, there may be very strong reasons for *not* warning the infringer what is about to happen (see below, p. 244). With secondary infringements such as possession or dealing, however, it is necessary to establish that the infringer *knew* (or ought reasonably to have known) that the acts concerned were infringing acts (see p. 223), and for this reason it may be necessary to send a formal warning letter at the outset, putting the infringer on legal notice, which can then be produced at the trial as hard evidence of guilty knowledge.

Drafting warning letters requires some care: defamatory statements and malicious falsehoods must be avoided (see chapter 7), and in the case of letters sent to third parties such as distributors, any unlawful interference with contractual relations (see p. 67) must be avoided also.

A committee of some leading intellectual property practitioners have published a Code of Practice for pre-action conduct in intellectual property disputes. The Code's aim is to set out the steps which parties should follow where litigation is being considered. Although not binding, the Code represents the committee's assessment of what is reasonable pre-action behaviour in intellectual property law disputes. The Code lists various matters to be included in a letter before action and the defendant's letter of response.

INJUNCTIONS

An injunction is a discretionary court order, either commanding someone to do something or (more commonly) ordering someone to *stop* doing something and forbidding them from doing it in the future, or at least until the injunction is lifted. The latter, negative, version is often the most important and most urgent legal remedy a claimant will seek against a copyright infringer: once the infringement is discovered what the copyright owner usually wants most of all is for the defendant to be ordered to stop (or in some cases not to start: for example not to publish). Questions of financial compensation, though important, are usually less urgent and can be left to be dealt with by a suitable award of damages at the trial (see below, p. 242): an injunction, however, may be an urgent priority.

Five criteria which a court should apply in deciding whether to grant an interim, or pre-trial, injunction, were set out in a 1975 case known as *American Cyanamid*. This still appears to be good law. The five factors are:

(1) Is there a serious issue to be tried? An injunction will not be granted where the claimant does not have at least an arguable claim which would carry a real and substantial prospect of success at any trial.
(2) Would damages be an adequate remedy? If they would, then an injunction will normally not be granted (unless there is a serious likelihood that the defendant will never pay). A good example of this would be a permissions dispute, where the copyright owner concerned regularly grants permissions to others in similar circumstances, for fixed scales of fees.
(3) Where does the balance of convenience lie? If the disruption which granting an injunction will cause to the defendant is greater than the disruption which the claimant claims will be caused by continuing (alleged) infringement, then an injunction may well not be granted.
(4) Preserving the status quo. All other things being equal, a court may well simply seek to preserve the status quo: this may best be served by granting an injunction, or in some cases by *not* granting one.
(5) Relative strength of each party's case. This may help the court to decide, but only where one party clearly has a very much stronger *prima facie* case than the other.

Having weighed the above, the court may still refuse an injunction if it appears inequitable to grant one – for example if the claimant has delayed unreasonably. It is entirely at the court's discretion, depending on the facts in each case. If an injunction is granted, a court will usually require as a condition of granting it that the claimant gives the defendant what is called a cross-undertaking as to damages. This will protect the defendant against any loss or damage incurred as a result of complying with the injunction – for example by taking a book off sale on the day before publication – should the claimant's claim turn out to have been unfounded when it is finally adjudicated on, at the trial. Where the claimant is unable to give a sufficient cross-undertaking, the court may refuse to grant the injunction.

DAMAGES

It is not necessary in order to win an action for copyright infringement to prove financial (or any other) loss. If copyright infringement is proved, some damage will be assumed. There is a general burden of proof on any claimant to prove any *specific* loss or damage, but apart from that a court will usually be willing to make a general award of damages to compensate the claimant for what has happened. The basic aim is to restore the claimant to the position he or she would have been in had the infringement not occurred.

Not surprisingly, it is not always easy to arrive at a scientific method of quantifying the claimant's loss, particularly in publishing actions. Any one or more of the following criteria may be adopted:

- *Loss of profits* A court will take into account any reasonable expectation of profits, either based on evidence of previous publications or on reasonable commercial forecasts. Loss of likely subsidiary rights revenue (such as a US deal) will be as relevant as lost home sales, although a court will not compensate a claimant for possible future profits which are purely speculative. There is also a general duty on all claimants to take any reasonable steps to mitigate their loss where possible.
- *Damage to business* Compensation will often be given for general injury done to a claimant's business or trade, over and above lost sales.
- A *fair licence fee* Where the claimant normally grants licences for the use of the copyright material concerned, a more reasonable starting point for assessing damages might be to calculate a fair licence fee which might have been levied had the defendant sought a licence in the usual way. Evidence of current levels of licence fees in the market concerned will be borne in mind: the court may still award a higher figure if this calculation does not seem to go far enough to compensate the claimant properly.
- *Additional damages* Under section 97(2) of the 1988 Act, a court may award additional damages, as the justice of the case may require – bearing in mind all the circumstances, but in particular, *the flagrancy* of the infringement, and any *benefits* gained by the defendant.

It is important to note that damages are not available in copyright actions where at the time of the infringement the defendant did not know, and had no reason to believe, that copyright subsisted (at all) in the work concerned (section 97(1)) – however, other remedies, such as injunctions or an account of profits, may still be available in the court's discretion.

OTHER REMEDIES

Account of profits

This is an equitable remedy, available only as an *alternative* to damages (you cannot have both) where it seems more appropriate – once the financial information is known – to assess the profit the defendant earned from the infringement. It is unlikely that a claimant would opt for an account of profits unless the known profits were considerably more substantial than the sum a court would be likely to award in damages.

Delivery up

Section 99 of the 1988 Act entitles a copyright owner to apply to the court for delivery up of infringing copies which someone has in their possession, custody or control in the course of their business (innocently or otherwise). Proof of guilty knowledge is only required in the case of articles – such as machinery – specifically designed or adapted for making (infringing) copies. Under section 114 of the Act, the copies may be forfeited to the copyright owner, or destroyed, or otherwise dealt with as the court thinks fit.

Seizure

Copies which are found 'exposed or otherwise immediately available for sale or hire' (section 100) may be seized by the copyright owner without the need for any court order – however, there are serious practical restrictions: the local police station must be notified before any such raid takes place, no force may be used, and nothing may be seized from the infringer's permanent or regular place of business (since the section is primarily aimed at market stalls selling bootleg copies).

Confiscation by customs

Under section 111 of the Act, owners of copyright in a published literary, dramatic or musical work may give written notice to the Commissioners of Customs & Excise to treat infringing printed copies as prohibited goods for up to five years. This gives some scope for customs seizures where a tip off is received well enough in advance, but only applies to such works in *printed* form (and not therefore to computer software). There are however parallel provisions covering sound recordings and films.

Imports from elsewhere in the European Economic Area may be immune from prohibition under the free movement of goods provisions of the Treaty of Rome (see chapter 13).

Search orders

These are pre-trial court orders requiring a defendant to give immediate access to premises without notice and to allow property – such as incriminating documents – to be inspected and in some cases taken away by the claimant (generally the claimant's solicitor). Needless to say such an order (which is not just confined to copyright actions) is a drastic measure and its execution is closely regulated by the court. Generally speaking, such orders may be used only where such access is urgent and essential and where the claimant's case is very strong. There must also be a substantial risk that the defendant might destroy such evidence if given advance warning.

Freezing injunctions

Freezing injunctions may be granted in urgent circumstances by a court to prevent a defendant from removing assets (such as stock or money) out of the country – or otherwise putting them beyond the court's jurisdiction – in order to avoid judgment. The claimant must have a strong arguable case and there must be a significant risk that the assets concerned may be dispersed.

CRIMINAL PENALTIES FOR COPYRIGHT INFRINGEMENT

As well as the more familiar civil remedies which copyright owners may seek to obtain against infringers, such as injunctions and damages, the 1988 Act also provides *criminal* penalties of fines or imprisonment for a number of specific criminal offences. These are largely contained in section 107(1) of the Act. Under that section, a person commits an offence who, without the licence of the copyright owner, does any of the following acts in relation to an article which he or she knows (or has reason to believe) is an infringing copy of a copyright work:

(1) makes it for sale or hire;
(2) imports it into the UK, otherwise than for private or domestic use;
(3) possesses it in the course of a business with a view to committing any act infringing the copyright; or

in the course of a business:

(1) sells it or lets it for hire;
(2) offers or exposes it for sale or hire;
(3) exhibits it in public;
(4) distributes it; or
(5) distributes it otherwise than in the course of a business to such an extent as to affect prejudicially the owner of the copyright.

There are also separate offences under section 107(2) of the Act, of:

(1) making or possessing an article specifically 'designed or adapted' for making copies of a work, knowing (or – again – having reason to believe) that article is to be used to make infringing copies for sale or hire in the course of a business;
(2) communicating the work to the public either in the course of a business or otherwise than in the course of a business to such an extent as to affect prejudicially the copyright owner *and* in either case the defendant knows or has reason to believe that by doing so it is infringing copyright in the work; or
(3) the public performance of a literary, dramatic or musical work, or the playing or showing of a sound recording or film, where the person responsible knew (or had reason to believe) that copyright would be infringed.

Persons convicted of these offences are liable to criminal penalties including fines and terms of imprisonment ranging from up to six months (in the Magistrates' Court) to ten years (in the Crown Court). Further, under section 110 of the Act, directors or other senior officers of a company may be prosecuted personally if a relevant offence by the company is proved to have been committed with their 'consent or connivance'. Note, in all these cases, that proof of actual guilty knowledge or intent is not always necessary: evidence that the accused had 'reason to believe' infringement was occurring or would take place may also secure a conviction. In many cases, this may be established simply by sending a warning letter (see above, p. 240).

There are provisions in sections 108 and 109 for delivery up of infringing copies, and for police search warrants.

Criminal provisions have not attracted a great deal of legal attention, being seen as more relevant to the activities of obvious pirates and market traders selling bootleg tapes and CDs than to reputable individuals or companies. However, given the relative speed and cheapness of proceedings in the Magistrates' Court, and the significant criminal penalties available – potentially giving individuals as well as companies a criminal record – the criminal provisions of the 1988 Act may have considerable relevance to copyright owners seeking remedies against infringers, even where the alleged infringer may be a substantial and reputable company. The general trend seems to be a considerable increase in sentences passed.

INTERNATIONAL COPYRIGHT PROTECTION

UK copyright works are not only protected in the UK, under domestic UK law, but to a large extent internationally too. Equally, a great many foreign copyright works are protected here. This happy state of affairs is not the result of any all-embracing international copyright law, but has been arrived at piecemeal, over the years, by a combination of bilateral treaties between the major copyright nations, and, increasingly, multilateral Conventions to which most of the significant trading nations of the world now belong. We will look at these treaties and Conventions in more detail below. It is, however, essential to bear in mind from the outset that these arrangements are no more than treaties – in the case of many nations (including the UK) they may well have no legal effect unless and until the country concerned implements them as part of its own domestic law. Some countries are better – and quicker – than others about implementing their international treaty obligations; for example, despite being a founder signatory of the Berne Convention in 1886 (see below) the UK did not comply fully with its Berne obligations to protect moral rights of authors until the 1988 Act. So, whatever the treaties say, if you want to know what actual copyright protection is available in a particular country at any given time, the only way of finding out reliably is to look at their own domestic copyright law.

THE BERNE CONVENTION

The most important international copyright Convention today is the Berne Convention. Signed in 1886 by a handful of mainly European states and still going strong over a century later, it has now been acceded to by over 150 countries, including every EU member state and Russia, the USA and China. It has of course been revised over the years: the latest (Paris) Act dates from 1971. Not all members have yet acceded to the Paris Act: in cases of doubt, it is advisable to check with the World Intellectual Property Organisation (WIPO), which administers Berne and other intellectual property conventions (their address is set out in appendix B).

The levels of copyright protection required by Berne were strongly endorsed by the final (Uruguay) Round of the General Agreement on Tariffs and Trade (GATT), in particular in the associated TRIPS agreement (dealing with the Trade Related aspects of Intellectual Property Rights) which has now been adopted as a minimum international copyright standard by GATT's successor body, the World Trade Organisation.

For those who belong, the Berne Convention has a number of fundamental principles:

- A wide range of original 'literary and artistic works' are protected, defined to include 'every production in the literary, artistic or scientific domain, whatever may be the mode or form of its expression' – dramatic and musical works, films and photographs are expressly included and most member states now also protect computer programs (usually under literary works). Translations, adaptations and compilations are also covered.
- It is open to member states to require (as the UK does) that protected works must have been fixed in some material form (see pp. 20–1).
- Protection shall extend equally to works of authors who are *nationals* of a Berne member state, and to works of non-nationals which are *first published* in a member state. First publication includes simultaneous publication within 30 days (for the UK position, see p. 34).
- Authors shall enjoy, in Berne countries other than the country of origin, copyright protection for their works amounting to 'national treatment': in other words, the same rights which those other countries grant to their own nationals (and governed by the same domestic laws).
- Protection must not be subject to any formalities (such as registration) and must extend from the moment a work is created – or at least fixed in material form – for the rest of the life of the author and at least a further full calendar 50 years (within the EU this period was harmonised up to life plus 70 years as from July 1995: see p. 35). In the case of simultaneous publication in several Berne countries granting different terms of protection, the 'country of origin' shall be the one granting the *shortest* term;
- Authors shall have independent moral rights of paternity and integrity in their works (see chapter 3, pp. 44 and 47).

Generally speaking, authors shall have the exclusive right of authorising reproduction (and translation) of their works, but certain copying, for example fair dealing in the UK (see p. 226) may be allowed provided it 'does not conflict with the normal exploitation of the work and does not unreasonably prejudice the legitimate interests of the author' (this wording appears verbatim in a number of member states' copyright laws, but is often widely interpreted to cover copying activities such as large-scale educational copying which would be regarded as flagrant infringement in the UK). There are further exemptions, set out in an Appendix to the Paris Act, allowing in certain circumstances 'developing countries' to apply compulsory translation licences for limited periods 'for the purpose of teaching, scholarship or research' for works not otherwise available in the local language: these have also been a source of much controversy. A developing country is one regarded as such 'in conformity with the established practice of the General Assembly of the United Nations', but this strict rule has often been somewhat stretched.

WIPO Copyright Treaties 1996

Although the Berne Convention is periodically revised, usually via diplomatic conferences, it was by 1996 in serious need of updating to take full account of the digital environment. The member states met at a major session in December 1996, together with interested parties such as authors and publishers, users and intermediaries, and produced two major treaties: the WIPO Copyright Treaty and the WIPO Performances and Phonograms Treaty.

The 1996 WIPO Copyright Treaty has gone a long way towards meeting the need for a flexible right of Reproduction, a workable right of Communication to the Public, including making available and access via digital networks, modern 'fair dealing' exceptions, and provision for liability (or not) of intermediaries such as telecommunications companies and service providers, together with some agreement on anti-circumvention measures and remedies generally.

The TRIPS Agreement

The TRIPS Treaty is particularly concerned with intellectual property remedies and sanctions, setting out minimum compliance standards for member states to achieve initially by January 2000 (although some developing or East European countries may be given more time). Key provisions include:

- Article 41, requiring 'effective action' to be enabled, with 'expeditious remedies'.
- Article 50, requiring 'prompt and effective' provisional measures (such as injunctions).

The WTO offers a dispute resolution system to resolve disputes between member states, which has already proved effective. TRIPS treaty requirements can therefore now be a serious agenda item in dealings with WTO members, and (particularly) those countries wishing to join.

THE UNIVERSAL COPYRIGHT CONVENTION (UCC)

At the end of the Second World War neither of the two new superpowers, the USA and Russia, belonged to the Berne Convention. The new United Nations, and its educational and cultural arm UNESCO, were keen to bring the US particularly within the international copyright community, but the relatively long copyright term of life plus 50 years, and the ban on any registration formalities, among other things, proved continuing obstacles to US accession to Berne. UNESCO therefore sponsored an alternative Convention, the UCC, which was signed in 1952 and which the US, the UK and a number of other major copyright nations joined (although the UK did not finally sign up until 1957).

There is one important formality, but on the whole the level of copyright protection required by the UCC is somewhat lower:

- Works protected are broadly similar, and a similar 'national treatment' principle applies. Protection is again on the basis of either the author's nationality or the country of first (or simultaneous) publication.
- The minimum period of copyright protection is, however, the life of the author and 25 years only. In some cases this may be 25 years from first publication.
- Formalities (such as copyright registration) are permitted, but will be regarded as complied with if all published copies carry what has become known as the 'UCC copyright notice' – the copyright ©, the name of the copyright owner, and date of first publication – in no particular order, but 'placed in such manner and location as to give reasonable notice of claim of copyright' (Article Ill).
- There are developing country provisions similar to those in the Appendix to Berne.

Between 1952 and 1989 (when US accession to the Berne Convention came into effect) most UK published works carried the UCC copyright notice on their title pages, expressly in order to comply with UCC requirements and thereby secure effective copyright protection in the USA, a key English language market. Since US accession to Berne, such formalities should no longer be strictly necessary for the purposes of US protection (but registration may still be desirable, though – see below), but there are still countries which subscribe to the UCC but not to the latest (Paris) Act of Berne and most publishers will therefore probably continue to print the UCC wording. It is normally set out thus:

© Hugh Jones and Christopher Benson 2006

The word 'copyright' is sometimes added before the ©, but is not strictly necessary.

COPYRIGHT PROTECTION IN THE USA

For most of the nineteenth century, the USA granted little or no copyright protection to the works of foreign authors (indeed, such foreign copyrights were not recognised at all until the Chace Act of 1891). As a result, the works of European authors and composers such as Dickens, and Gilbert and Sullivan, were freely and frequently pirated in America, despite personal lecture tours and simultaneous 'authorised' performances. The Chace Act did finally provide copyright protection for foreigners, but only to citizens of those countries which either granted national treatment to US works or granted reciprocal protection under an international (bilateral) treaty. Thereafter, UK works could be protected in the USA, but (until fairly recently) subject to registration and renewal formalities. US copyright protection is still a formidably complex area of law. It is impossible in a book of this scope to do more than provide a brief overview of the current position: it cannot be stressed too strongly that for reliable answers to specific queries it is highly advisable to seek the advice of a specialist attorney.

US domestic copyright law was significantly revised by the passage of their current copyright law, the Copyright Act of 1976. The Act came into force on 1 January 1978: as a consequence, one of the first and most important questions to ask is whether the work concerned was created before or after 1978.

Works created before 1978

Before the 1976 Act came into effect, US copyright protection did not depend on the life of the author, but lasted for a fixed term of 28 years, calculated from the date of first publication, with a possible renewal for one further 28-year term, making 56 years in all. Protection also depended on compliance with a number of formalities (not as a prerequisite for copyright itself, but as requirements to institute litigation for infringement and obtain statutory (liquidated) damage and attorney's fees):

- an approved copyright notice (as in UCC above) printed on all copies published in the US;
- registration of the copyright at the Copyright Office;
- deposit of copies (a single copy in the case of foreign works);
- formal renewal at the end of the first 28-year term;
- compliance with the notorious 'manufacturing clause' (section 16 of the Copyright Revision Act 1909) which required that all copies published in the US should be typeset, printed and bound wholly within the limits of the US.

The last formal requirement in particular – a fairly blatant piece of protectionism – prevented many UK works from being protected at all in the USA, until the UK became a signatory to the UCC in 1957: from that point on, the only formality required in order to protect newly created UK works in the USA was the UCC copyright notice. On the whole, however, with one or two exceptions, existing UK works continued to be unprotected unless the full range of domestic formalities had been complied with.

Works created after 1978

For works created on or after 1 January 1978 (and for works created but not published before then), the 1976 Act provided a new term of copyright protection, in line with the UK and other Berne countries, of life plus 50 years (this was subsequently increased to match the new European period of life plus 70 years). For works which, as of 31 December 1977 were in either their original or renewal terms of 28 years, the 1976 Act provided that the second term of 28 years be extended by an extra 19 years, to 47 years – making a total of 75 years from first publication. Those copyrights already in their second, renewal, term at the time were automatically extended; those copyrights still in their first term had to be renewed in their twenty-eighth year in the normal way (but would automatically get the new 47-year renewal term). Special provisions applied to works of unknown authorship and works 'made for hire' (works made in the course of employment, or under certain commission arrangements). Copyright was not revived in pre-1978 public domain works. The term of copyright in work made for hire is now 95 years.

Certain registration formalities continued to exist, including the UCC copyright notice for foreign works, but the 'manufacturing clause' was considerably reduced in scope and finally expired in July 1986. Subsequent legislation has removed the requirement for registration of the renewal term for pre-1978 works.

US implementation of the Berne Convention and GATT

Following the Berne Convention Implementation Act of 1988, the USA finally acceded to the Berne Convention, with effect from 1 March 1989. Thereafter, in the spirit of Berne membership all formalities, at least as a pre-requisite to copyright protection, were swept away, and even the basic UCC copyright notice was no longer required. It is likely however, that UK works will continue to bear the UCC notice for some time to come, since among other things it will continue to provide evidence against any defence of innocent infringement under US law (which might otherwise reduce any damages). Indeed, copyright registration itself is still advisable in some circumstances for evidential purposes, and is required to maximise available damages, and to secure attorneys' fees in actions for infringement. Registration currently costs $30.

Despite Berne membership, the USA did not immediately grant retrospective copyright protection to all existing works of other member states: this did not happen until 1 January 1996, following US adherence to the 1994 GATT/TRIPS agreements (see p. 246). As of 1 January 1996, foreign works of Berne or GATT member countries – which includes the UK – which were still then protected in their country of origin, but which had entered the public domain for failure to comply with formalities in the USA, were restored to copyright protection for whatever remained of their domestic copyright periods. In the case of UK and other EU works, this meant up to an additional 20 years. US protection for such 'Restored Copyrights' was secured until 31 December 1997 by filing a Notice of Intent to Enforce with the US Copyright Office and can now be obtained by serving a notice directly on those concerned: those US publishers previously exploiting the work in reliance on its (then) public domain status (called Reliance Parties) have a 12-month sell-off period in which to dispose of remaining stock.

Reproduction for the blind or other people with disabilities

In 1997, US copyright law was amended to permit non-profit organisations or governmental agencies that provide specialised services to the blind and other disabled people to reproduce and distribute copies of previously-published, non-dramatic literary works in specialised formats (e.g. such as Braille, audio and digital text) exclusively for use by such people, without permission from (or payment to) the copyright owner. A similar copyright exception was introduced in the UK in the process of implementation of the EU Copyright Directive under the terms of the Copyright (Visually Impaired Persons) Act 2002.

US term extension

With respect to copyright duration, the Sonny Bono Copyright Term Extension Act (October 27, 1998), named after the now deceased former singer-turned-legislator, extended the term of works that were currently protected by copyright to life of the author plus 70 years (or 95 years after publication for anonymous works or works made for hire). Term extension was controversial in the USA, especially when combined with prior legislation which had restored some works to proprietary status from the public domain.

Digital Millennium Copyright Act

The Digital Millennium Copyright Act (October 28, 1998) (the 'DMCA') was the USA's implementation of the WIPO Copyright Treaty of 1996. The DMCA clarifies that a copyright work is protected regardless of media, and amends existing US copyright law to eliminate 'media-bias' (e.g. references to print). Controversial issues include the prohibition of the circumvention of copyright protection systems (given that the copying of some works in some circumstances might be fair use), proposals for the uncompensated use of digital materials for so-called 'distance education', and limitations on liability of online service providers for infringing materials being posted on their services. With respect to the latter, the service providers were given a 'safe harbour' if they took certain remedial steps 'expeditiously' upon being notified by a rights holder of the infringement.

TEACH Act 2002

The Technology Education and Copyright Harmonisation (TEACH) Act 2002 amended US copyright law to allow the use of copyright works in online instruction and for distance learning purposes, but subject to a number of provisos, including the following:

- Any copying must be from a lawfully acquired copy.
- The use must be in the context of mediated instructional activities analogous to live classroom teaching.

- The copying must be by, at the direction of, or under the supervision of, an instructor.
- The work copied should not be one primarily published for educational purposes.
- Technical protection measures must ensure access is limited to enrolled students, and to the relevant class session only.

In addition, there are limited provisions for educational institutions to digitise relevant portions of works not yet in digital form, including a proviso that no digital version should already be, or become, available.

Trade marks and passing off

10

TRADE MARKS

INTRODUCTION

Although copyright can be a powerful form of legal protection for published (and unpublished) works, there may be some key words, names or phrases, or other distinguishing signs (such as a logo), which have an established goodwill or reputation of their own in the market place and which may be protected independently as trade marks under UK law. They may include titles of books or journals, names of authors (such as Wisden), or names of characters ranging from Peter Rabbit to Harry Potter. They have become increasingly important to the publishing trade in recent years as a means of protecting properties with merchandising potential, but it is important to recognise that they are not just a useful means of protecting characters in children's books, and licensing T-shirts and novelty soap, but may also be an extremely valuable form of protection for database, reference and general publishing and all kinds of distinctive publishing marks. Publishers, authors and agents should at all times consider the trade mark implications of the material they are handling, for two reasons:

- to protect as soon as possible names or other signs with valuable trade mark potential;
- to avoid infringing any existing trade marks.

WHAT IS A TRADE MARK?

Under section 1(1) of the Trade Marks Act 1994:

> A trade mark means any sign capable of being represented graphically which is capable of distinguishing goods or services of one undertaking from those of other undertakings.

- *'Any sign'* Although 'sign' is not defined, section 1(1) of the 1994 Act goes on to specify that a trade mark may consist of 'words (including personal names), designs, letters, numerals or the shape of goods or their packaging'.
- *'Capable of being represented graphically'* This includes not only two-dimensional marks, but three-dimensional *shapes* (such as the famous Coca-Cola bottle) and *sounds* capable of being reduced to musical notation, such as advertising jingles.
- *'Capable of distinguishing goods or services'* This is a central requirement of any trade mark, and we will return to this later. For the present, note that the mark, in order to be registered, does not need to distinguish goods or services at the time of filing as long as it is *capable* of doing so. In addition, the proprietor has to have a bona fide intention to use the mark at the time the application is made.

WHAT MAY BE REGISTERED?

Under present UK law, all the following familiar publishing signs may be registrable as trade marks, *provided* the UK Trade Marks Registry is satisfied that they are capable of distinguishing the relevant goods or services from others:

- single letters, or sets of initials
- single words
- proper names
- names of authors
- names of characters
- titles
- phrases or slogans
- logos and other designs
- the distinctive shape or size of a publication.

Logos or designs (known as 'devices') are often more distinctive than ordinary words or phrases, and therefore easier to register: the first trade mark registered in the UK was the Bass triangle, and the Guinness harp was close behind.

As a general rule, words or other marks may *not* be registered if they are *generic*, or *descriptive* of the goods in question, and which consist exclusively of signs which (in the words of the 1994 Act):

- 'designate the kind, quality, quantity, intended purpose, value, geographical origin (or) time of production' of goods or services or which;
- have become customary in the language or practices of the trade.

However, such objections may be overcome with sufficient evidence of distinctiveness through use.

WORDS AND PHRASES

Given the above guidelines, the words most likely to be capable of registration as trade marks are those with no obvious descriptive or generic link with the product, which can be accepted as distinctive with no risk of confusion. The best trade marks are often invented words: meaningless but punchy and with no generic connection to anything at all, such as Kodak, Persil, Typhoo or Lego.

Known or existing words can be used, if completely unassociated with the product – 'Mars' for chocolate, for example. Composite words may also be registered successfully if 'invented', such as Coca-Cola and Starbucks. A common surname or a geographical name may be registered, but only with very strong evidence of distinctiveness. Buxton (for natural mineral water) managed to overcome this objection, but only after strong evidence of distinctiveness in the market place, and several years' continuous use.

Phrases and slogans may be registered, but not if descriptive.

TITLES

Although many titles may lack the necessary substance and originality to attract copyright protection, book, journal, or other titles may be registered as trade marks. However, whilst it may be difficult in the case of a single edition of a book to establish a sufficiently strong association or reputation in the market, serial publications such as directories, newspapers or magazines are more easily registered. *Hello!*, *OK!* and *Radio Times* are all UK registered trade marks for publications or magazines.

If no registration has been obtained (either because the application has failed or because none has been made) a title may still be protected by an action for 'passing off' (the closest English law has so far come to an unfair competition action). There must, however, be a *real* likelihood of confusion, and also actual or probable damage or loss, before a passing off action will succeed against a rival title: for more on this see below, p. 260.

AUTHORS' NAMES

It would be difficult to secure trade mark registration of an author's name unless there was very strong evidence indeed that it had become accepted as distinctive in its own right. This normally only applies to serial publications or to established works which have run to several editions. Wisden or Roget would be good examples.

A nom-de-plume may also be difficult to register, but the established user may well have an action for passing off against others using the same name. Similarly a signature (of a cartoonist, for example) may be hard to register if the name is simple or common. It should not be forgotten that an author has a statutory moral right in some circumstances to prevent false attribution to him or her of work which the author did not write (see chapter 3, pp. 51–3). There may also in some circumstances be an action for defamation (see chapter 7).

NAMES OF CHARACTERS

As Sir Arthur Conan Doyle found with Sherlock Holmes, there is no general right to prevent a fictional character's name being used by other authors in their own works. Disputes more commonly arise over unlicensed character merchandising. The owners of Ninja Turtles (which were merchandised almost entirely by licensees) were able to establish that the public was being misled into thinking that unlicensed T-shirts had come from the UK proprietors of the Ninja Turtles brand. Though the reputation of Ninja Turtles was very recent (a matter of months), thanks to massive TV exposure it was well established enough for the unlicensed merchandising to constitute passing off (see below, p. 260). However, the owners of the Spice Girls name failed to secure injunctions for passing off against unlicensed merchandisers since there was no real risk of public confusion between unlicensed goods and the legitimate rights owners. More recently the Courts have been more reluctant to protect rights in names or likeness. The Court of Appeal refused to allow Elvis Presley Enterprises Inc., which carried on merchandising activities, to register the names Elvis, Elvis Presley and the Elvis Presley signature as trade marks, holding that members of the public bought Elvis Presley goods because they bore his name or image, not because they came from a particular source. The same points arose in respect of the UK trade mark applications for the words Diana, Princess of Wales.

The Trade Marks Registry have issued guidelines on registering famous names as trade marks: they will not automatically refuse applications for famous names but will consider whether the name is descriptive for the goods and services in question. The Registry will not in general allow famous names to be registered for what they call 'mere image carriers', such as posters and photographs. The name of the famous person is not likely to be seen as an indication of origin but a description of the subject matter. The US rock group, Linkin Park, applied to register their name for a wide variety of goods, including image carriers. However, the Registry rejected the application for printed matter, posters and poster books.

HOW TO REGISTER A TRADE MARK

Provided there is no significant opposition, it is possible to secure UK registration for a registered trade mark in under a year. It is normally advisable to seek advice from a specialist trade mark lawyer before commencing an application.

Applications should be made to the UK Trade Marks Registry, who will need the following information:

(1) details of the applicant (for example, whether an individual, partnership or company, and whether or not resident in the UK);
(2) the particular goods or services for which the applicant is seeking to register the trade mark (see below);
(3) if a particular typeface, or a logo/device is involved, a representation of the proposed mark;

(4) a statement that the applicant (or a third party with the applicant's consent) is already using the mark in relation to the specified goods or services, or intends to do so.

Classes of goods and services

The UK Trade Marks Registry is divided into *classes* of goods and services. There are 45 classes in all, ranging from chemicals and drugs to clothing, games and playthings, and (of course) beer. Books are included in Class 16. Publications which are downloadable fall within Class 9 and publications which are non-downloadable fall within Class 41. It is possible to register a trade mark for certain online services and retail services including Internet and online shopping. One of the most important things to grasp about trade marks is that protection is given for specified goods or services. However, one application can be filed covering several (or all) of the 45 possible classes.

Advertisement and opposition

Once an application has been examined by the Trade Marks Registry, it is advertised in the *Trade Marks Journal* in order to enable other interested parties to oppose it if they think it will conflict with an existing mark (or prior application) of theirs, or otherwise cause confusion. Oppositions must be filed within three months of advertisement. If the opposition cannot be settled the matter may be resolved at a hearing, at which both sides may be represented.

Assuming that there is no opposition, or that any opposition is defeated, registration will then be granted for the particular goods and services concerned. Trade mark registration lasts for 10 years initially, but may be renewed indefinitely upon payment of renewal fees. The most famous marks are renewed regularly. Unlike copyright, therefore, which expires 70 years after the end of the year of the author's death, trade mark protection may be perpetuated forever – as long as your mark is used in relation to the goods and services it covers and is not challenged (for example, for becoming generic) and you remember to pay the renewal fees.

There is no legal requirement, incidentally, to use the ®, although most proprietors find it a useful warning that their mark has been registered. There is certainly no requirement on authors, or editors of dictionaries, to use the ® sign whenever the word occurs: such advertising is the responsibility of the proprietor. One often also sees the letters ™ in a circle: this has no legal significance whatsoever and indicates that the person using the mark regards it as a 'trade mark' whether it is registered or not. It should be noted that it is a criminal offence to represent a mark as a registered trade mark in the UK if it is not.

PROTECTION OF TRADE MARKS

The proprietor of a trade mark is in a very strong commercial position. Once the mark is registered, the proprietor acquires what amount to virtual monopoly rights over exploitation for that particular mark applied to the particular goods or services concerned. There may, however, be provision for individual words, or other elements, of the registered mark to be disclaimed – so that while 'Peter Rabbit' may be registered as a single mark, the individual words 'Peter' and 'Rabbit' may need to be disclaimed since individually they are too common, and non-distinctive of the particular goods concerned, to be protected. The Registry cannot, however, now insist on disclaimers and they have to be offered voluntarily.

TRADE MARK INFRINGEMENT

Section 10(1) of the 1994 Trade Marks Act provides that:

> A person infringes a registered trade mark if he uses in the course of trade a sign that is identical with the trade mark in relation to goods or services which are identical with those for which it is registered.

Section 10(2) further provides that infringement may take place where the sign is identical with the trade mark and is used in relation to goods or services similar to those for which the mark is registered or the sign is similar to the trade mark and is used in relation to goods or services identical with or similar to those for which the mark is registered in relation to, but where in either case there nevertheless exists a likelihood of confusion on the part of the public, including the likelihood that the public will associate the infringing mark with the registered trade mark. If the sign merely brings the registered trade mark to mind, this is probably insufficient.

Under section 10(3), infringement can occur if the mark is used in a way that 'takes unfair advantage of' or is 'detrimental' to the mark where the trade mark has a reputation in the UK. Confusion is not necessary. For use of registered trade marks in comparative advertising, see chapter 12.

Certain proprietors of trade marks are vigilant about any unauthorised use of their marks, and often write standard threatening letters to publishers when they spot 'their' word or other mark in, say, a book title. Care should be taken in writing such letters as in certain circumstances a person aggrieved by such a letter could bring an action in relation to the threat of proceedings being brought for registered trade mark infringement. Infringement is unlikely to occur, however, if the use is purely descriptive

You may even succeed in having an existing registration revoked if you can establish that the word concerned has become a generic term in its own right (inclusion in *The Oxford English Dictionary* is useful evidence, despite the editorial disclaimers one sometimes sees in dictionaries). In the Scottish case of *Bravado Merchandising Services Limited* v. *Mainstream Publishing (Edinburgh) Limited*, the registered owners of the trade mark 'Wet Wet Wet' (the name of a pop group) failed to prevent a publisher – Mainstream – from marketing a book entitled *A Sweet Little Mystery – Wet Wet Wet The Inside Story* as this was not trade mark infringement.

In another case, the judge referred to the Wet Wet Wet decision, stating:

It would be fantastic if the … trade mark legislation had the effect of enabling quasi censorship of books about people or companies just because those people or companies had registered their names as trade marks for books.

Where trade mark infringement does take place, however, the normal legal remedies will apply, including:

- an injunction to restrain infringing acts;
- an award of damages, or an account of profits;
- provisions for delivery up of infringing goods, material or articles.

EU AND INTERNATIONAL TRADE MARK PROTECTION

Registration of a trade mark in the UK only gives protection within the United Kingdom, and if trade mark protection in other territories – such as the USA – was required it had been necessary until fairly recently to pursue separate registrations in each individual territory, under the local laws concerned. For an international publishing business seeking worldwide protection, this can prove expensive; however, it is often worthwhile for distinctive international publishing marks, such as Encyclopaedia Britannica, and Grove's Dictionaries of Music, particularly as an added deterrent to piracy.

Community trade marks

It is possible to file one trade mark application to cover all the countries of the European Union including the UK via the Community Trade Mark Office in Alicante, Spain. Advertisement and opposition procedures are similar to those under UK law, and the period of protection is 10 years.

The Community Trade Marks Office examines applications on absolute grounds only, that is, for example, if the application is distinctive. It does not refuse applications on the grounds of earlier conflicting rights. It is cheaper to register a trade mark as a community trade mark rather than filing national applications in each of the member countries. Infringement of a community trade mark may be pursued centrally in one national court rather than (as at present) separately in each member state where infringement has occurred. A judgment in one member state may be enforced throughout the EU.

International trade marks

It is possible for UK companies to file one single application at the World Intellectual Property Organization (WIPO) under an agreement called the Madrid Protocol (to which the UK is a party) covering some or all of the over 60 countries who are signatories to the Madrid Protocol. Countries who have signed the Madrid Protocol include various European countries, the USA and Japan. Unlike the community trade mark, which is one 'all or nothing' mark, the Madrid Protocol system provides for a number of separate national trade marks and is a useful means of international trade mark protection as more countries sign the Madrid Protocol.

PASSING OFF

THE TORT OF 'PASSING OFF'

Even without a registered trade mark, it is still possible over a period of time to acquire goodwill in a distinctive name or title, or in the distinctive style, design or general physical appearance of goods (known as their 'get-up'). Under common law, such trading goodwill will be protected against rival traders who may seek to use it unfairly in order to enhance sales of their own (usually more recent) product. The general principle of law was stated as long ago as 1896 in the leading *Camel Hair Belting* case, as follows:

> The principle of law may be very plainly stated, that nobody has any right to represent his goods as the goods of somebody else.

Prior to that case, it might have been thought that 'Camel Hair Belting' was just about as generic a product description as it was possible to have, and that any rival trader seeking to start selling belting made out of camel hair could not legally be prevented from using the same generic description. However, 'Camel Hair Belting' had by the time of the action acquired such established goodwill, and such a distinctive reputation, in the market place that the action for passing off succeeded. Many publications, or lists, acquire a similar goodwill in their name or physical get-up – famous labels such as Puffin or, arguably, distinctive get-ups such as the Dorling Kindersley laminated white cover designs, would be similarly protectable under the law of passing off. Such common-law protection is not ideal and many of our trading partners, in Europe and the USA, deal with the matter somewhat more logically under fully fledged unfair competition laws. If the evidence is strong enough, however, our action for passing off can be an effective way of preventing such unfair competition under both English and Scots law.

In the *Jif Lemon* case, the Court identified three characteristics which must be present in order to create a valid case of action for passing off:

(1) a goodwill and reputation in the goods and services of the claimant by association with the get up in question so that the get up is identified by the public as distinctive of the claimant's goods and services;
(2) a misrepresentation by the defendant that his goods or services are those of the claimant;
(3) the claimant must suffer or is likely to suffer damages.

The weakness of passing off actions under English law is that, as a general rule, they will not succeed unless there is hard evidence of actual (or likely) loss or damage. There must also be a *real* likelihood of confusion in the market place – this can usually be established by market surveys, but these take time and are not always conclusive.

Passing off cases include the following: the publishers of the *Daily Mail* secured an injunction against a new evening newspaper called *The London Evening Mail*. The publishers of a series of free newspapers including *Bedfordshire on Sunday*, *Milton Keynes on Sunday* and *Hertfordshire on Sunday* were granted an injunction to prevent the free newspaper *Northants on Sunday*.

The publishers of the well-established *What's New In...* series of magazines secured an injunction against *What's New In Training Personnel* since in that case the risks of confusion, to public and advertisers alike, were great.

On the other hand, an injunction was refused to the claimant in respect of the two magazines *BBC Gourmet Good Food* and *Gourmet* as the court found the public would not be confused. In another case, it was arguable that the public would think *Management Today* and *Security Management Today* were linked, although the injunction was refused.

Most publishers, of course, go to considerable lengths to create and establish their own distinctive name and get-up, but there are always those who will seek to cut corners by linking their product unfairly to the goodwill established by someone else. Any new publisher launching a weekly trade journal for booksellers and publishers in the UK under the title *The Bookseller*, particularly if it used a similar design and get-up to the established organ, would almost certainly face an action for passing off. There might equally be an action for passing off against a publisher who tried to launch a new publication called, for example, *The Electronic Bookseller* if the get-up was confusingly similar and there was an implication – as there probably would be – that the new product was being launched by the publishers of *The Bookseller*, or under license from them, and carried with it their considerable reputation and goodwill.

If there is a real likelihood of confusion, and some evidence of loss, a passing off action may well succeed. It is, however, a question of fact in every case.

Where there really is no credible risk of confusion in the market place, an action for passing off will fail: in the case of *Mothercare UK Limited* v. *Penguin Books Limited* a passing off action to restrain the use of the words 'mother care' in the title of a book *Mother Care/Other Care* published by Penguin Books Limited failed. In the view of the Court of Appeal, the requirement for a successful passing off action that there should have been a misrepresentation (see above, p. 260) had not been established and the court 'was wholly unable to see any basis for saying that there was a misrepresentation in the title of the book. The book, taken as a whole, did not begin to suggest that the book had been issued or sponsored by, or was in any way associated with Mothercare'.

REMEDIES

Where passing off is established, the most effective remedy a claimant will usually seek is an injunction, and the usual considerations will apply (see above, p. 241). Damages, or an account of profits, will also be available in appropriate cases.

DOMAIN NAME DISPUTES

The value and importance of domain names (.com, .co.uk etc.) continues to grow. At the same time so does the number of domain name disputes. This is particularly so as more domain name extensions (e.g. .biz, .info and .eu), and multi-lingual domain names are added to the Web.

There are two principal types of domain name disputes, both of which arise where the defendant registers a domain name that is identical or confusingly similar to the claimant's trade mark. The first occurs where the defendant registers the name fraudulently, and is known as 'cybersquatting' (or 'typosquatting', where likely misspellings of the mark are registered). The second kind of dispute is where the defendant registers the name innocently and uses it for a legitimate website, but in circumstances where Internet users are likely to be confused into believing that the website is the claimant's.

A third type of dispute is where a 'spoof' or 'gripe' website is set up. One case involved the website NatWestSucks.com.

Under English law, the registration and use of a domain name in the situations described above may amount to common law passing off and/or registered trade mark infringement. The following principles have emerged.

CYBERSQUATTING

The Courts, starting with the High Court and the Court of Appeal in *Marks & Spencer* v. *One in a Million*, have shown a determination to stop cybersquatters. This has been on the basis that a cybersquatter registers a domain name as an 'instrument of fraud' and that this will inherently mislead Internet users as to the origin of the domain name or dilute the claimant's mark. It has been held that:

- The mere registration of a domain name will be unlawful where the name is identical or confusingly similar to a household mark that is exclusively distinctive of the claimant, even in the absence of attempted extortion or blackmail. The claimant will only succeed on this ground if the mark is very well known and distinctive, like the Marks & Spencer mark in the *One in a Million* case, such that consumers are *inherently* likely to be misled.
- The mere registration of a lesser-known mark, or of a mark which, although famous, is not exclusively distinctive of the claimant because it consists of a common or descriptive name, will be unlawful if coupled with attempted extortion or blackmail – e.g. the J Sainsbury mark in the *One in a Million* case.
- A 'pattern' of registering well-known marks as domain names will usually amount to good evidence of cybersquatting.

LEGITIMATE USE

Where the defendant is not a cybersquatter, the registration and use of the domain name will only be unlawful where traditional passing off or registered trade mark infringement principles apply. In broad terms, this requires the claimant to show that Internet users are likely to be confused into believing that the products or services offered through the defendant's website originate from or are otherwise connected with the claimant.

DOMAIN NAME DISPUTE RESOLUTION PROCEEDINGS

An alternative to bringing court proceedings is to file a complaint under the relevant domain name dispute resolution policy. ICANN (Internet Corporation for Assigned Names and Numbers) has established a Uniform Domain Name Dispute Resolution Policy (UDRP) in respect of .com, .net, .org and a limited number of country code domain names. A domain name can be either cancelled or transferred to the complainant. These proceedings are significantly cheaper and usually quicker than court proceedings. However, they generally only apply to cybersquatting or cases where 'bad faith' on the respondent's part can be shown. Damages cannot be awarded nor can costs. They also do not cover .uk country-code domain names. Nominet UK, the Registry for .uk domain names, has its own dispute resolution service which is very similar to the UDRP.

The three elements of UDRP

Complaints are decided by single to three member panels composed of legal practitioners from around the world. In order to succeed in the proceedings a complainant has to satisfy the following three elements.

The domain name must be identical or confusingly similar to a trade mark in which the complainant has rights

Decisions have protected registered trade names. Panels have also recognised that writers (such as Julian Barnes, Louis de Bernières and Margaret Drabble – one individual had registered the names of all three as .com domain names – which followed the successful result already obtained by Jeanette Winterson), actors (such as Julia Roberts), singers (e.g. Madonna) and sports stars (e.g. Venus and Serena Williams) can own unregistered rights in their names. (In contrast, as already seen, English Courts have traditionally been somewhat reluctant to enforce personalities' rights in their names, on the basis that, in general, their reputations do not grant them rights that extend beyond their core activities.)

The respondent must have no rights or legitimate interests in respect of the domain name

This may be demonstrated where the respondent is making a legitimate non-commercial or fair use of the domain name, without intending misleadingly to divert Internet users or tarnish the complainant's trade mark. A respondent was able to rely on this ground in brucespringsteen.com where he was using the domain name in connection with an unofficial Bruce Springsteen website. This proviso is also relevant to 'gripe' websites for persons who have genuine grievances or wish to express criticisms. Such views on a website may, however, be subject to defamation and trade libel laws and can, in certain circumstances, be removed from the Internet if a complaint is made against the Internet services provider (ISP) hosting the site.

The domain name must have been registered and be used in bad faith

This may happen if, for example, the aim is to resell it to the complainant or to a competitor for a sum exceeding the respondent's out-of-pocket costs or registering the domain name to prevent the complainant from reflecting its mark in that domain name or to disrupt the complainant's business.

Part V
Sales and marketing

Sale of goods and consumer protection

11

SALE OF GOODS

INTRODUCTION

Publishing is all about selling – or so, at least, every marketing director would tell us. Many other topics with legal significance are involved in the publishing process, of course, as we have seen – copyright, for example – but in a very real sense the act of publishing is the act of selling. No one who has been to Frankfurt could ever be in any doubt about that. However, this chapter is not about selling rights (for this, see chapter 5), but about selling the thing itself – the book, or the journal, the CD-ROM, or the online service. What happens in legal terms when X sells something to Y? Are any legal duties and obligations imposed on the seller, and are there any exceptions? Are there any specific duties owed to the public? What is the position of wholesalers and retailers?

Lawyers have traditionally called this area of law sale of goods, although for much of the high street or mail order selling which publishers do, consumer law is now a more helpful label. Even when the publication concerned is not 'sold' as such, but distributed free of charge (for example, a controlled-circulation newspaper paid for by advertising revenue) many of the same legal principles apply. We shall take a look at these basic principles in this chapter, and in the next chapter we will examine the special rules applying to advertising.

SALE OF GOODS AND CONSUMER RIGHTS

Although 'sale of goods' has a wonderfully Victorian ring to it, the law in this area has progressed significantly since that time. The first piece of legislation in this field was the Sale of Goods Act 1893, which was passed in an age when a man's word was his bond and merchants did not expect (or want) the law to interfere with free trade or freedom of contract. The law assumed, however, that the parties were dealing on more or less equal terms, and that in the case of contracts of sale there was a reasonably fair balance between the buyer and the seller.

Before the 1893 Act, the balance had become heavily weighted in favour of the seller. The basic rule of mercantile law was *caveat emptor:* let the buyer beware. The law would not protect a buyer from a bad bargain unless there was some obvious impropriety, such as fraud or duress, and buyers were expected to satisfy themselves about the suitability or quality of goods they were buying before buying them. Once the deal was struck, that was that: they must abide by their contract, however bad. This was all very well in the days when buyers could go to market and inspect what were then relatively straightforward goods (like horses or produce) for themselves, but as the Industrial Revolution developed, two things happened:

(1) goods became more complex and their defects became less visible – so that buyers often found they had to rely on the seller's description of the goods; and
(2) goods were increasingly mass produced, so that buyers were no longer making individual contracts which they could negotiate with each seller, but forced to deal on industry-wide terms and conditions, drafted entirely from the seller's point of view.

The 1893 Act went a long way towards restoring a fair balance between buyers and sellers. In particular, it introduced into all contracts for the sale of goods certain implied terms – for example, implied conditions that the goods would be fit for their purpose and of 'merchantable quality'. Although the 1893 Act has now been entirely superseded and amended by more recent legislation, many of these implied terms still form an important part of modern UK law. We will look at all of them below, in their modern context.

In today's consumer society, therefore, the law no longer assumes that well-informed buyers go about striking arm's-length bargains with individual sellers. That may be the commercial reality in some cases (a sale of stock between two publishers, for example), but in others the buyer (of a computer, for example, or an online purchase from a US-based website) may be negotiating at a distinct disadvantage, and may need more protection. We will therefore need to consider two different kinds of sale:

• sales between businesses (where the contract will usually prevail, subject to some important provisos, which we will consider below); and
• sales to the public, or 'consumer sales' (where the 'contract' may be hard to identify, and different provisions may now apply).

Both are now highly regulated, but in different ways. The original Sale of Goods Act 1893 has itself been replaced by a more modern 1979 Act (which in turn has been amended by the Sale and Supply of Goods Act 1994 and others), and has been added to by (among others) the Misrepresentation Act 1967, the Unfair Contract Terms Act 1977, and the Consumer Protection Act 1987. Supporting it all is a highly consumer-orientated European Commission, which has been responsible in recent years for a steady flow of Directives and other measures from Brussels on topics such as product liability, data privacy, and misleading advertising, all designed to protect the interests of consumers throughout the European Union.

Remedies for unsatisfied buyers, or consumers, may now therefore be found in a number of different places:

- in the terms of individual contracts;
- in civil liability for torts such as negligence or misrepresentation;
- (increasingly) in specific statutory duties, many of which are now duties of strict liability.

Let us start at the beginning, however, and consider what duties – and remedies – may exist under the contract of sale itself.

CONTRACTS OF SALE

What does the law understand by a sale? Consider some publishing examples:

- A publisher's rep visited a bookseller a couple of weeks ago, and the bookseller ordered several titles. The rep described one as being particularly suitable for a degree course taught at the local university, and the bookseller ordered 30 copies. The publisher has now supplied the books, but the bookseller has not yet paid for them.
- An online bookseller sells an electronic book (an 'e-book') to a customer (who owns the appropriate hardware) over the Internet. Before the sale the customer e-mailed the bookseller to say that the book is required to study modern history. The bookseller replied by e-mail and said that the e-book was suitable for that purpose, but in fact, the e-book is about medieval history.
- A publisher sells copies of a textbook on wholesale terms to an educational supplier. The supplier has its own standard terms and conditions.
- A UK publisher agrees to sell 20,000 copies of a new title to US co-publishers, in their imprint. The US publishers need the copies by a particular date, and make it clear that time is of the essence.
- An online e-publisher sells a novel to a customer who has paid by credit card. The novel contains a virus and is inaccessible.

In all these examples, the essence of the transaction is a contract for the sale of goods. But when is each contract complete, what are the terms and conditions of each one, and does the law imply any terms of its own? Equally importantly, if the buyer has any rights under the contract, against whom can those rights be enforced? In the case of the novel for example, is it the bookseller's fault that the e-book is defective: and does this mean that the bookseller is obliged to give a refund? Who is liable to whom, and when?

Contracts for the sale of goods

Some of these questions can be answered by first finding out whether a contract exists at all, and if so what kind. Contracts, as we saw in chapter 4, are fundamental to the publishing business, but may also essentially be very simple things. They may be created whenever X makes a promise to Y, and Y promises something of value in return: on that basis, all the above examples would clearly be contracts. They are also contracts of *sale*, because in return for an agreed price, it is intended that the buyer will get not only physical possession of the goods, but also the legal ownership of the goods (what lawyers call the 'property' or 'title' to the goods).

They are therefore different from contracts of hire, or contracts for services only, for an important part of the bargain is that the buyer will become the new legal owner. In the words of section 2(1) of the 1979 Sale of Goods Act, they are contracts 'by which the seller transfers or agrees to transfer the property in goods to the buyer for a money consideration called the price'. They are therefore covered by the Sale of Goods Acts, and this has a number of important results.

It is important to note that the Sale of Goods Act will apply equally to Internet sales. It is therefore essential to ensure that, especially where the buyer has to click through several online pages before a sale is made (e.g. payment details), both the seller and buyer are aware of the exact stage that a legal contract is made and all the terms of the contract are incorporated into the contract.

Contract terms

What are the terms of each contract? Do they have equal weight, or are some more important than others? Terms of a contract may be *express*, that is specifically set out and agreed by the parties at the time, or they may be *implied*, for example by a previous course of dealing between the parties, or by representations made by one party to the other, and on which the other party relied. Some terms may also be implied by statute: we will come to several important examples of these below.

Some terms may also be more important than others. A *condition* is a term which is fundamental to the bargain, which goes to the root of the whole contract. The price is often the best example, but terms relating to quantity and schedule might equally be conditions. Breach of a condition by a seller normally entitles the buyer to treat the whole contract as being revoked, reject the goods completely, and ask for his or her money back. A *warranty*, by contrast, is much less important. Despite the frequent appearance of the word 'warranty' in publishing contracts, in law a warranty is merely collateral to the main purpose of the contract. Breach of a warranty will not entitle a buyer to rescind the contract entirely or reject the goods, but will merely provide an action for damages.

OWNERSHIP AND TITLE

In a contract for the sale of goods, perhaps the most fundamental condition is that the buyer will acquire good title to the goods – in other words, become the legal owner, unhindered by any rival claims from elsewhere. This assumes, of course, that the seller owns the goods in the first place (and has not, for example, stolen them or have them on hire purchase). The normal rule in such cases (known to lawyers as the *nemo dat* rule) is that you cannot give better title than you yourself possess (*nemo dat quod non habet:* one cannot give what one does not have). If you don't own goods, then a person buying them from you won't own them either. There are exceptions to this general rule: where, for example, the owner has consented to the sale or has impliedly authorised the sale by his conduct. Therefore, a sale by a commercial agent would normally pass good title.

A seller who remains in physical possession of goods with the buyer's consent after a sale is completed (for example to repair them, or warehouse them) might also be capable of passing good title by delivering them to a new, second buyer, as long as the new buyer received the goods in good faith and without knowledge of the first buyer's rights. So if a bookseller sells the last signed copy of a Booker prize-winning novel to buyer A, who pays the price but leaves it in the shop to be collected later and the bookseller meanwhile re-sells it and hands it over to buyer B, buyer B might well become the new owner. Buyer A would of course have an action for the return of his or her money and possibly a claim for other damages, but would not be entitled to claim ownership of the book itself.

Similarly, a publisher who in similar circumstances sold a particular consignment of stock twice over would effectively pass legal ownership to the innocent final customer to whom the stock was actually delivered. In both cases, the seller (however dishonest) was in possession with the owner's consent, and can therefore pass on good legal ownership to someone buying in good faith.

Although this has the effect of protecting innocent book-buyers, it may leave publishers at some risk if they deliver stock on sale or return to a retailer and the retailer either fails to pay, or – worse still – goes bankrupt. Many publishing distribution contracts therefore contain express terms, known as 'retention of title clauses', which clearly stipulate that, even after they are delivered to the retailer, legal ownership of the goods remains with the publisher until they are paid for (or, in some cases, all outstanding debts are paid). If a major chain of bookshops (for example) calls in the receivers, such clauses are designed to ensure that relevant unsold stock can be reclaimed from the bookshelves by the publishers concerned, and will not belong to the bookshop's creditors. Nevertheless there are often practical difficulties in claiming title to specific stocks when they have become mixed with other stocks on the buyer's premises (how do you identify those which are yours?) and it may prove difficult to rely on a retention of title clause unless it is very carefully drafted.

IMPLIED CONDITION OF GOOD TITLE

With one exception, which we deal with below, section 12(1) of the 1979 Sale of Goods Act provides that in every contract of sale there is:

> an implied term on the part of the seller that ... he has a right to sell the goods.

This is so, whether the contract refers to the matter or not. There is a corresponding implied condition in contracts for future sales. Note that the 1979 Act implies a condition of good title into every such contract, not merely a warranty. This means that a buyer who does not get the legal title he or she bargained for may rescind the whole contract – understandably enough.

In addition to the condition of good title, section 12(2) also provides additional warranties that:

- the goods are (and will remain) free of any legal charges or 'encumbrances' which may restrict their use; and
- the buyer will enjoy 'quiet possession' of the goods.

What happens if you wish to sell the goods, but are genuinely uncertain as to whether you have the full legal right to do so? Can you sell 'such title as I may have'? Where there are difficulties in proving title, buyers may be quite willing to bear that risk as a commercial risk, particularly if you and they have dealt with each other regularly before. Section 12(3) of the 1979 Act provides for this situation, and provides specifically that the implied conditions and warranties above will not apply to such limited sales: there will in such cases only be limited warranties, for example that any charges and encumbrances which *are* known to the seller are disclosed to the buyer before the contract is made.

SUMMARY CHECKLIST: LEGAL OWNERSHIP IN SALES

To recap so far: to find out who owns particular goods, the questions to ask might be as follows:

- Does a contract of sale exist?
- Does the seller own the goods in the first place?
- If not, has the owner impliedly (or actually) authorised the sale?
- If not, does the seller possess the goods with the owner's consent, and does the buyer buy in good faith?
- Is there a valid retention of title clause?
- Is there any other restriction on title (for example, a sale of only 'such title as I may have')?

If we apply these criteria to our first contract of sale example (at p. 269, above), where the publisher has supplied the books, but the bookseller has not yet paid for them, it is likely that the publisher will have owned the books, and that a contract of sale exists. However, if there was a valid retention of title clause, the bookseller might not yet own the books. Even so, if (as is likely) the bookseller had physical possession of the books with the owner's consent, the bookseller might still effectively pass on legal ownership to a customer who bought one of them in good faith.

SALES BY DESCRIPTION

The seller's description of the goods may be such an important factor in the buyer's decision to buy, that it should in fairness be treated as a term of the contract.

Accordingly, under section 13(1) of the Sale of Goods Act 1979:

> Where there is a contract for the sale of goods by description, there is an implied term that the goods will correspond with the description.

Under section 13(1)(A), this term is a condition in England, Wales and Northern Ireland (a breach will entitle the buyer to reject the goods and get a full refund). Note that the implied condition applies only where the sale is *by* description, in other words where the description forms a significant part of the bargain, and is not merely incidental. So where a bookseller describes a text to a customer as being suitable for a certain syllabus, that might well be a sale by description. What if the jacket blurb carries a similar claim, but the bookseller, when asked, expresses no opinion on the subject? The customer's contract of sale is with the bookseller, not the publisher, so the description in the blurb would not become a term of the contract if the bookseller carefully remained distanced from it, or refused to endorse it. What if the book in question is simply selected, taken to the check-out till, and sold, without the printed description being referred to? This is a common situation in busy retail shops, particularly supermarkets. Probably, now, section 13(3) of the 1979 Act would apply, which provides that:

> a sale of goods is not prevented from being a sale by description by reason only that, being exposed for sale or hire, they are selected by the buyer.

Under such circumstances any description on the goods themselves would give rise to the implied condition under section 13(1), and if the goods did not comply with that description the buyer would be entitled to rescind the contract and reject the goods. The publisher might also be guilty of a false trade description under the Trade Descriptions Act 1968 and potentially fall foul of the provisions of the 'Unfair Commercial Practices' Directive 2005/29 once that is implemented into our domestic legislation (see chapter 12).

Equally, a description would also bind a publisher who sold direct to a customer by mail order or through the Internet, if it formed a significant part of the bargain. Quite apart from the Trade Descriptions Act implications, it would also constitute an implied condition of the contract of sale itself.

In the second 'Contracts of Sale' example (see p. 269), there may have been a sale of goods not matching their description if the text attached to the online description of the e-book was inaccurate. It is more likely that the e-book was not fit for the purpose for which it was bought (i.e. the study of modern history), when that was clearly communicated to the bookseller (see Fitness for Purpose on p. 277).

Sales by description might also bind a publisher selling stock, for example to a bookseller or wholesaler. The buyer could reject the goods if they did not comply with the description, even if the buyer had suffered no loss. This would be so, even if the buyer had inspected a sample – under section 13(2) of the 1979 Act:

If the sale is by sample, as well as by description, it is not sufficient that the bulk of the goods corresponds with the sample if *the goods do not also correspond with the description* (our italics).

Finally, note that unlike the implied terms of satisfactory quality and fitness for purpose (see pp. 275 and 277), section 13 applies to private sales as well as those 'in the course of a business'. Therefore, although a publisher selling its company car (for example) to an individual probably would not be subject to the satisfactory quality and fitness for purpose provisions, it would still have to ensure the car corresponded with its description.

MISREPRESENTATION

If a description cannot be incorporated as an implied term into the contract of sale itself, a seller might still be liable under the general law of tort for any misrepresentations made to the buyer, if the buyer relied on them and suffered loss or damage as a result.

Misrepresentations may be fraudulent, negligent or innocent:

- *Fraudulent misrepresentation* It is well-established law that sellers will be guilty of fraud (strictly speaking, the tort of deceit) if they cause loss or damage to buyers by intentionally misleading them with statements of fact knowing them to be untrue or not caring whether they are true or false. Not surprisingly, most of the cases involve used cars. In most cases, where fraud can be proved, the buyer may rescind the contract (so as to be restored to his or her original position), or alternatively claim damages.
- *Negligent misrepresentation* Even in the absence of actual fraud, the Misrepresentation Act 1967, section 2(1), provides that a buyer will still be entitled to damages, or to rescind the contract, if a misrepresentation was made negligently. Negligence, however, implies a duty of care, and may be difficult to prove: on negligence generally, see p. 185.
- *Innocent misrepresentation* In the absence of either fraud or negligence, where the misrepresentation was entirely innocent, the buyer's only remedy would normally be to rescind the contract. However, if this was no longer possible – for example, because the goods had been destroyed – a court may award damages in lieu, under section 2(2) of the 1967 Act.

SUMMARY CHECKLIST: DESCRIPTIONS, AND MISREPRESENTATION

- Is there a sale by description?
- Do the goods correspond with that description?
- Has there been any misrepresentation?

In our first contract of sale example (p. 269) the sales rep described one book as particularly suitable for a local degree course, and the bookseller ordered on that basis: the sale would probably therefore be a sale by description, and if the books did not correspond with the description the bookseller could rescind the contract (for breach of an implied condition) and return the books.

MERCHANTABILITY AND SATISFACTORY QUALITY

Under section 14 of the 1979 Sale of Goods Act (as amended) all sellers of goods who sell in the course of their business are bound by an implied condition that those goods should be of 'satisfactory quality' (formerly 'merchantable quality'). Prior to 1994, when the wording changed, there was considerable argument in the courts over what was or was not 'merchantable' (because the implied term was a condition entitling the buyer to reject the goods). The factors which might be taken into account clearly included fundamental defects in quality, such as exploding 'Coalite' (in one case) and a plastic catapult which broke and blinded a boy in one eye (in another case), but minor and less obvious defects were less clear, particularly if they were aesthetic rather than purely functional. Although the definition of 'merchantable quality' provided an objective standard of sorts, following the introduction of the Sale and Supply of Goods Act 1994 the test now is one of 'satisfactory quality', with clearer guidance as to the factors which may be taken into account.

Implied terms of satisfactory quality

Section 14(2) of the 1979 Act, as amended by the 1994 Act, now provides as follows:

(2)   Where the seller sells goods in the course of a business, there is an implied term that the goods supplied under the contract are of satisfactory quality.

(2A) … goods are of satisfactory quality if they meet the standard that a reasonable person would regard as satisfactory, taking account of any description of the goods, the price (if relevant) and all the other relevant circumstances.

Note that, for the 1979 Act (as amended) to apply, the seller must be selling 'in the course of a business'. The implied term will not apply to purely private sales. For most publishers, booksellers and distributors most of their sales transactions will clearly be in the course of a business. This applies equally to sales of stock between publishers, consumer sales in bookshops, or mail order sales. However, it is not necessarily enough to establish that the seller *is* a business – the sale itself must be 'in the course of' *that* business. It may be necessary to examine the transaction more carefully in borderline cases, for example when a publisher sells off a company car or a bookseller disposes of a computer. Arguably, neither of those transactions would be in the course of the seller's particular business (although they would be still subject to section 13 – sale by description). In the case of the car, this might particularly be so if it were a private car only occasionally used on company business. It will be necessary to look at all the relevant factors – particularly, perhaps, whether the sale appears in the accounts (and tax return) of the business concerned.

'Satisfactory quality'

Under the 1994 Act, quality factors which may specifically be taken into account (among others) include the following:

- fitness for all the purposes for which goods of the kind in question are commonly supplied;
- appearance and finish;
- freedom from minor defects;
- safety; and
- durability.

Any one or more of these factors may be relevant in deciding whether a reasonable person would regard the goods as satisfactory. Clearly, the first category is potentially the broadest, covering *all* the purposes 'for which goods of the kind in question are commonly supplied' – note, however, that the relevant purpose must be one for which such goods are *commonly* supplied, not some special or esoteric purpose not normally associated with the goods in question (for fitness for a special purpose, see below, p. 277). A scientific or technical textbook or CD-ROM with vital instructions missing so that it could not be used in teaching, or a cookery book without key ingredients or with the wrong quantities and therefore useless for cooking, would probably not be fit for all the purposes for which such books or CD-ROMs are commonly supplied, and since this would breach the implied condition that the goods would be of satisfactory quality the buyer would be entitled to rescind the contract, return the goods and ask for his or her money back.

'Appearance and finish' and 'freedom from minor defects' now appear for the first time, confirming the result of a 1988 case where a string of minor defects in an expensive Range Rover were held to make it unmerchantable (although it was still basically roadworthy). The buyer of a Rolls-Royce or a Range Rover is entitled to have higher expectations than the buyer of, say, a second-hand car whose only concern might be to get (relatively) safely from A to B. This flexible definition of what is or is not satisfactory quality must apply equally to publications. A buyer of an expensive multi-volume encyclopaedia might well be entitled to claim that it was not of satisfactory quality under the Act if the gold blocking on the spines came off after two weeks, whereas the buyer of a cheap paperback classic might be glad if the jacket stayed on at all.

'Safety' and 'durability' may be of vital concern to consumers, and so were expressly included in the 1979 Act by the 1994 Act. 'Durability' probably only implies durability for a reasonable time and depends on what is a reasonable duration time for those particular goods (in a 1987 case involving merchantable quality, a second hand Jaguar which was purchased from a motor dealer that seized up three weeks after purchase was not fit for its purpose). 'Safety' here probably only implies safety for reasonable or normal use – in one case involving pork chops which contained a harmful parasite, the buyer failed to prove that the chops did not reach the (then) standard of merchantable quality since the chops were only partially cooked, and normal cooking would have killed the parasite and made them perfectly safe to eat. Safety is clearly relevant for cars or electrical goods such as computer equipment – a CD-ROM or e-book containing a virus might not now be considered sufficiently safe to be of 'satisfactory quality'. Sellers also have statutory duties relating to safety under the Consumer Protection Act 1987 (see below, p. 285).

Exceptions

The implied term of satisfactory quality will not apply in the following circumstances:

- where the defect is specifically drawn to the buyer's attention before the contract is made;
- where the buyer examines the goods before the contract is made (and that examination ought to have revealed the defect); and
- where the sale was by sample, and the defect would have been apparent on a reasonable examination of the sample.

Note that the vital revelation, or inspection, must have taken place *before* the contract was made. In the case of sales by sample, section 15 of the 1979 Act provides similar implied terms that the bulk will correspond in quality to the sample, and will be of satisfactory quality except for defects apparent on examination.

SUMMARY CHECKLIST: SATISFACTORY QUALITY

- Is the sale in the course of the seller's business?
- Would a reasonable person regard the goods as satisfactory?
- Are they fit for all the purposes for which goods of that kind are commonly supplied?
- Is their appearance and finish satisfactory?
- Are they free from minor defects?
- Are they reasonably safe and durable?
- Was the defect brought to the buyer's attention before the contract was made?
- Did the buyer examine the goods before the contract was made? Ought that to have revealed the defect?
- Was the sale by sample, and would the defect have been reasonably apparent?

FITNESS FOR PURPOSE

In addition to the implied term that goods will be of satisfactory quality, there is a further implied condition imposed on the seller that goods will be reasonably fit for any *particular* purpose made known by the buyer. This implied condition is contained in section 14(3) of the 1979 Act, which provides as follows:

Where the seller sells goods in the course of a business and the buyer, expressly or by implication, makes known ... to the seller ... any particular purpose for which the goods are being bought, there is an implied condition that the goods supplied under the contract are reasonably fit for that purpose.

This will apply to any purpose (even if unusual), provided that the buyer has made that particular purpose known to the seller. The House of Lords (Scotland) in *Slater* v. *Finning* (1996) has clarified this by stating that there will be no breach of the implied condition of fitness where the failure of the goods to meet the intended purpose arose from an abnormal feature or idiosyncrasy, not made known to the seller, in the buyer or in the circumstances of use by the buyer. It is not relevant whether or not the buyer is aware of that feature. For example, if a publisher contractually agrees to provide textbooks suitable for 15-year-olds, it is unlikely that there would be a breach of section 14 if a 15-year-old recipient had learning difficulties, and actually needed simpler material.

The purpose may be made known expressly, or by implication, but it must be clearly made known, so that the seller is in no doubt that that is the purpose for which the buyer requires the goods, and for which he or she is paying the price. Where the circumstances of the sale indicate otherwise, the implied condition of fitness for that purpose will not apply. For example, where the buyer would have made the purchase anyway, and was clearly not relying on the seller's professional advice – or where it would have been unreasonable to do so – any statement by the seller about fitness for purpose will probably be regarded as merely ancillary, and will not form part of the contract. So where a student goes into a campus bookstore with a reading list, and selects a textbook on the list and buys it at the till, the purchase is clearly being made in reliance on the reading list, not on any extra encouraging remarks which the bookseller may add. In those circumstances if the book turns out to be unsuitable, the student's remedy – if he or she has one at all – would be against the lecturer who drew up the reading list, not the bookseller who sold the book, or the publisher who published it.

Suppose, however, that the student is clearly in some doubt, expressly asks the bookseller's advice as to whether the text is suitable for a specific course, and is advised that it is? In those circumstances, where the student clearly relies on the bookseller's skill and judgment, the bookseller will almost certainly be bound by an implied condition that the book is fit for that purpose.

An interesting question is whether a supply of software might be considered to be a supply of goods for these purposes, so that the same implied condition of fitness for purpose would apply. The Court of Appeal (1996) has decided that it may do. In that case a bespoke software package ordered by St Albans City Council to calculate the basis of the community charge in its area, and which miscalculated the population in a way which led to revenue and funding losses of £1.3 million (not all of which were awarded as damages by the Court of Appeal), was held not to be reasonably fit for the purpose for which it had been ordered, and was thus in breach of contract. The Court drew a distinction between a computer disk (which is 'goods') and a computer program (the code), which is not 'goods'. The Court decided that if a disk is sold containing a defective computer program, so that the program will not instruct or enable the computer to carry out the intended purpose, the seller will be in breach of the terms as to quality and fitness implied by section 14.

On the facts of the case, an employee of the seller went directly to the offices of St Albans City Council and loaded the defective code straight on to their computers from his disk. Will the statutory implied terms still apply? The Court said that they do not (because the program is not 'goods') but decided in favour of the buyer by implying a common law duty in the contract (because of the particular factual scenario) that the program was reasonably capable of achieving its purpose. Whenever a software package is required that is not 'bought off the shelf' (e.g. a specially tailored program for calculating royalties) it is important to include express provisions in the agreement between the parties covering the standard of work required (in case the statutory terms are not implied).

Since the Council was forced to deal on the computer company's standard terms and conditions, there was also an Unfair Contract Terms Act issue – see below, p. 280.

Publishers supplying goods or software direct would equally be bound in such circumstances, for example where a purchaser ordered a textbook, or a set of multiple-choice exam questions on CD-ROM by mail order, making it clear to the publisher that it was required for a specified course. If the wrong book or CD-ROM is supplied, even though it may in all other respects be of 'satisfactory quality', there will be a breach of the implied condition of fitness for purpose and the buyer will be entitled to reject the goods. Equally, a publisher selling stock to a retailer or wholesaler, knowing that it is required for further distribution or re-sale, would probably be bound by a similar condition if the goods for some reason turn out to be impossible to re-sell.

The only way for the seller to avoid such liability would be to establish:

(1) that no particular purpose was specified or implied (and was not already obvious, such as the 'purpose' of an umbrella or a hot water bottle); or

(2) that no opinion was expressed as to the fitness for that purpose of the goods in question; or

(3) that any unfitness which did appear stemmed from some other special circumstances unique to the buyer and not disclosed to the seller (or otherwise obvious) at the time – for example (as in one case) a perfectly good Harris Tweed coat which caused dermatitis to a lady buyer who did not disclose that she had abnormally sensitive skin.

SUMMARY CHECKLIST: FITNESS FOR PURPOSE

- Is the sale in the course of the seller's business?
- Has the buyer clearly made known a particular purpose?
- Was the buyer relying on the seller's professional advice or opinion?
- Did the unfitness stem from any other special circumstances, not disclosed at the time?

EXCLUSION AND LIMITATION CLAUSES

Is it possible to avoid or limit liability under such implied terms (of satisfactory quality etc.), for example by putting a clause in the contract in small print somewhere which specifically excludes or limits it? In most cases now, the answer is no – particularly where the exclusion clause attempts to avoid liability to consumers. However, some may still be permitted if they pass a test of 'reasonableness'. For disclaimers of liability for negligent mis-statements, see chapter 7, p. 185.

Exclusion clauses (sometimes called exemption clauses) were once widely used (and abused) in standard form contracts, and some of the more notorious examples would attempt total, blanket avoidance of any liability to consumers for any loss, damage or injury, and even for death. In many cases judges have refused to enforce such clauses if they were not properly brought to the notice of the consumer at the time of the contract (as in the infamous phrase 'for conditions see timetable'), or were unduly onerous or exorbitant (such as a £3,783.50 time penalty charged by a photographic library for a two-week delay in returning transparencies). In addition, because exclusion clauses were so destructive of the consumer's rights, they have generally been interpreted narrowly by the courts against the party trying to enforce them – so that a clause excluding liability for a breach of *warranty*, for example, would not avoid liability for any breach of a *condition*. This is known in English law as the *'contra proferentem'* rule, but even with this ammunition, courts have not always been able to prevent sellers from using exclusion clauses to avoid their proper obligations.

The Unfair Contract Terms Act 1977 was therefore passed to regulate the scope of exclusion clauses and other unfair terms by statute. The Act only applies to 'business liability' (generally in relation to acts done in the course of a business). Purely private transactions are outside the scope of the Act (with the exception of section 6, in relation to clauses that seek to exclude or restrict the statutory implied terms under the Sale of Goods Act 1979, which applies to all contracts). Also, importantly, under section 26, the Act does not apply to international supply contracts. This means exclusion or limitation clauses in a contract for the sale of goods made between parties whose 'habitual residences' are in different states will not be subject to the Act. Therefore, exclusion clauses in a publisher's contract for sale of 50,000 educational books to a US supplier would not be subject to the Act, but theoretically may be caught by equivalent US law.

Some liabilities – for example, for death or personal injury – may now never be excluded and others may only be excluded in certain circumstances. These largely depend on whether the purchaser is buying as a consumer, or negotiating freely in the course of a business (such as a publisher buying stock from another publisher). The following rules may apply.

Liabilities which may never be excluded

Any clause attempting to exclude liability for the following will be void and unenforceable:

- death or personal injury resulting from negligence;
- breach of the implied condition of good title (see p. 271).

Where the purchaser buys as a consumer

Stricter liability applies in the most common consumer situations where the seller is dealing in the course of a business but the buyer is *not*. A consumer is someone who does not make the contract in the course of a business and does not hold himself out as doing so. Under section 3 of the 1977 Act, any clause in a contract attempting to permit performance 'substantially different from that which was reasonably expected', or no performance at all (such as a 'force majeure' clause) will only be allowed if it satisfies a requirement of 'reasonableness'. What is or is not 'reasonable' depends on all the circumstances, including customs of the trade, the intention and knowledge of the parties and the relative strengths (or weaknesses) of their bargaining positions.

Section 3 also applies where the buyer (even though a business buyer) is obliged to deal on the seller's standard terms of business. Those companies whose negotiating strength means that buyers in effect have no choice but to deal on their standard terms should therefore bear in mind that those terms and conditions will now be open to legal challenge unless they are reasonable. This might apply to publishers, printers, or any other commercial suppliers, including computer corporations: in the 1996 case discussed above (p. 278), where bespoke software for a local council was held not to be fit for its intended purpose, the Court of Appeal upheld the original decision that an exclusion clause limiting liability to £100,000 (losses were £1.3 million) was unreasonable under the circumstances. The local council was under severe time pressure, had a limited choice of suppliers (all of whom dealt on similar terms), and at the time the computer company concerned had product liability insurance of £50 million.

Under section 2, liability for any loss or damage (except death or personal injury) may be excluded, but again only if reasonable.

Equally importantly, under section 6, the main implied conditions under the Sale of Goods Acts – that the goods will correspond with any description, will be of satisfactory quality and fit for their purpose, and correspond with any sample – can *never* be excluded where the buyer deals as a consumer.

Where the purchaser buys in the course of business

This covers the case of businesses contracting at arm's-length, as in co-publishing deals, or contracts with printers, agents or distributors. Here, where the bargaining positions are deemed to be somewhat better balanced (and insurance cover is more likely on both sides), more liabilities may be excluded. Liability for loss or damage (other than death or personal injury) may be excluded, but only if reasonable, and all the Sale of Goods Act implied conditions listed above (except the implied condition of good title) may be excluded, but again only if the relevant clause satisfies the test of reasonableness.

Finally, the Unfair Contract Terms Act 1977 does not apply to contracts relating to the creation, transfer or termination of a right or interest in any intellectual property (including copyright). It would therefore not apply to most author–publisher agreements.

The Unfair Terms in Consumer Contracts Regulations 1994, which implemented the EC Directive on unfair terms in consumer contracts, have been repealed and replaced by the Unfair Terms in Consumer Contracts Regulations 1999 (as amended by the Unfair Terms in Consumer Contracts (Amendment) Regulations 2001). The 1999 Regulations are not confined to exclusion clauses, and may apply to the majority of terms in particular contracts. They will also apply to contracts for the supply of services as well as goods.

The 1999 Regulations apply to 'consumers' who deal with 'sellers or suppliers'. A 'consumer' is a natural person who is acting for purposes outside his trade, business or profession. Only transactions by sellers or suppliers acting in the course of their business come within the Regulations.

The Regulations regulate the *clarity of language* in contracts and the *fairness* of terms. By Regulation 7, written terms of contracts must be 'expressed in plain, intelligible language'. Where there is any doubt as to the meaning of a written term, the interpretation most favourable to the consumer will prevail.

The 'fairness' provisions are the most significant because any unfair terms in contracts between suppliers and consumers are not binding on consumers. Two types of terms are excluded from the fairness test under Regulation 6(2): 'the definition of the main subject matter of the contract' and 'the adequacy of the price or remuneration, as against the goods or services supplied in exchange'. For the other qualifying terms, a term will be unfair if it:

- is contrary to good faith;
- causes a significant imbalance in the parties' rights and obligations under the contract;
- is to the detriment of the consumer.

All three requirements must be satisfied before a term is unfair. In considering the test, all the circumstances must be taken into account (e.g. other terms, nature of the goods or services involved).

Although the Regulations can be used by consumers to make claims in relation to individual contracts, consumers can also make complaints to the Director General of Fair Trading, who can seek injunctions to prevent the use of a term in a contract.

Additionally, the Regulations give a number of public bodies certain powers (e.g. to investigate and bring proceedings under the Regulations). That number includes the Information Commissioner, the Rail Regulator and the Financial Services Authority. The Regulations also give power to named private consumer organisations to apply for injunctions. At present, the only private consumer organisation given this power is the Consumers Association. We deal below with the wider use of injunctions for the protection of consumers' interests.

CONSUMER PROTECTION

NEGLIGENCE AND DUTIES OF CARE

So far, we have considered the remedies which a buyer of goods might have against a seller under a contract of sale. Some will be provided by the terms of the contract itself, and others under implied terms included by the Sale of Goods Acts, such as the implied terms of fitness for purpose or satisfactory quality. However, all these remedies depend on the contract of sale between the buyer and the seller. They will not protect anyone who is not a party to that contract. What happens if the defective goods cause loss or damage not to the buyer but to someone else – to the buyer's family or friends, colleagues at work, or even next-door neighbours? If the seller is not liable under the contract itself, does the manufacturer owe any general duty of care to such people, or to the public at large?

We have seen that, as well as contractual remedies, there may also be remedies in tort, for example for negligent mis-statement (above, p. 185) or for fraudulent or negligent misrepresentation (above, p. 274), where a duty of care can be shown to exist. Duties of care already exist between skilled or professional people such as lawyers and their clients, or between doctor and patient, and breach of such duties could well amount to negligence, but they were not generally regarded as existing between manufacturers and the general public. Not, that is, until 1932 and what is possibly the most famous case in English (and Scots) law: *Donoghue v. Stevenson*.

A shop assistant, Miss Donoghue, went with a friend of hers to a cafe in Paisley. The friend (not Miss Donoghue, notice) ordered ice cream for both of them, and ginger beer in a brown bottle. They had the ice cream, and drank half of the ginger beer, but hidden at the bottom of the ginger beer bottle were the decomposing remains of a snail. These remains came floating out with the latter half of the ginger beer at an inappropriate moment and – quite understandably – caused Miss Donoghue severe shock and gastro-enteritis.

Miss Donoghue had no action for damages against the cafe proprietor under the contract of sale, because the contract of sale was with her friend, not with her. The House of Lords held that, even so, the manufacturer owed a general duty of care to her as the ultimate consumer of the goods. In the immortal words of Lord Atkin:

> The rule that you are to love your neighbour becomes in law – you must not injure your neighbour; and the lawyer's question, Who is my neighbour? receives a restricted reply. You must take reasonable care to avoid acts or omissions which you can reasonably foresee would be likely to injure your neighbour. Who, then, in law is my neighbour? The answer seems to be – persons who are so closely and directly affected by my act that I ought reasonably to have them in contemplation

as being so affected when I am directing my mind to the acts or omissions which are called in question.

This duty of care is particularly strong when the goods are sold direct to the public in pre-sealed form such as canned or bottled goods – or perhaps today shrinkwrapped books or CDs – which cannot realistically be checked once they have left the manufacturer's warehouse. As Lord Atkin put it:

> A manufacturer of products, which he sells in such a form as to show that he intends them to reach the ultimate consumer in the form in which they left him with no reasonable possibility of intermediate examination, and with the knowledge that the absence of reasonable care in the putting up of the products will result in an injury to the consumer's life or property, owes a duty to the consumer to take that reasonable care. It is a proposition which I venture to say no-one in Scotland or England who is not a lawyer would for one moment doubt.

In cases since 1932, this duty has been extended to friends, family, guests, borrowers, employees and even bystanders. However, it is up to the person injured to prove that such a duty of care exists, and that – where it does – the manufacturer is negligent in failing to comply with it. In cases involving self-evident defects such as snails in ginger beer bottles, this may be relatively easy particularly now, but in other circumstances negligence on the part of the manufacturer may be harder to prove. It may require evidence of a failure in the production process, a design flaw, or defective instructions for use (where instructions are appropriate) and in many cases such evidence will be hard to obtain.

There may also be some difficulty in establishing negligence where the loss or injury is caused not by manufactured goods but by a statement of advice or assurance, even where the recipient has acted in reliance on that advice and suffered loss as a result: the difficulty will lie in proving that a duty of care already existed, or was assumed. Where a responsibility already exists, for example between professionals and their own clients, this will be fairly clear, and responsibility has been *deemed* to be assumed in some recent cases, for example involving negligent house surveys. But a business reference (such as a banker's or employer's reference) given to a third party, particularly with a disclaimer, might well not create a sufficient duty of care: there might perhaps be a general duty in such circumstances not to be dishonest or not to make statements which are known to be untrue, but otherwise it may be difficult to establish negligence based on a duty of care if the advice or opinion given turns out to be wrong. (On negligent mis-statement generally, see chapter 7, p. 185.)

For these reasons, some duties of care are now imposed on manufacturers directly by statute. There is also scope for certain enforcement bodies to obtain injunctions against traders who fail to carry out a service with reasonable care and skill (for further comment on this, see p. 286).

LIABILITY FOR DEFECTIVE GOODS

In one particular respect – that of product safety – the liability of producers and manufacturers for their products has increased dramatically in the UK and throughout Europe since the mid-1980s. Following the EC Directive on Product Liability of 1985, the UK passed the Consumer Protection Act 1987, which now imposes on producers and others considerably stricter liability for damage or injury caused by defective goods, without any need for the consumer to establish liability under a contract of sale, or to prove negligence or any other fault. Such strict liability is, of course, chiefly designed to cover those consumer goods with the greatest inherent dangers, such as cars, electrical goods, and – because of the risks to children – toys, but could equally well apply to a CD-ROM containing a virus, or even defective ink or paper if they were proved to have some harmful chemical side-effect.

Those liable under the Act include:

- producers of products (or extractors or refiners of natural products such as natural gas or oil);
- those who import products into the European Union; or
- those who sell goods under their own brand name (such as supermarkets).

Suppliers may also be liable as well as producers where they have supplied the defective goods to the producer (perhaps in the form of defective components) or to the final consumer (such as a retailer, if the producer is not readily identifiable).

What is 'defective'? A product is defective under section 3(1) of the 1987 Act:

if the safety of the product is not such as persons generally are entitled to expect.

'Safety' includes not only the physical safety of the consumer, but also covers any damage to property, although not loss of or damage to the defective product itself – if a CD-ROM causes damage to your data (for example corrupts your hard drive), you may claim for the loss of your computer, but not for the cost of the CD-ROM itself.

Under section 5 of the 1987 Act, 'damage' means death or personal injury or loss of or damage to any property (including land). However, there is no liability imposed in the case of loss or damage to property that is not ordinarily intended for private use and occupation. Note also that no damages will be awarded if the value of loss or damage (to property) would not exceed £275. Section 4 provides a number of defences. The strict liability under the Act may be avoided if:

- the defect was caused by compliance with any statutory or EU requirement;
- the defendant was not the actual supplier;
- the defective product was supplied privately and not for profit (for example, at a private dinner);
- the defect was not present when the product was supplied; or
- the state of scientific and technical knowledge at the time would not have enabled the producer to discover the defect.

In addition to these defences a producer of a defective product may also plead 'contributory negligence' on the part of the consumer – in other words, that the consumer's own negligence in using the product was at least partly to blame for the damage caused or injury suffered, and the damages awarded may be reduced accordingly.

SUPPLYING UNSAFE CONSUMER GOODS

As well as imposing strict liability for defective products on producers, the Consumer Protection Act 1987 also (in Part II of the Act as amended by the General Product Safety Regulations 2005 which came into force on 1 October 2005) imposes criminal liability on suppliers of consumer goods which are not safe. It is an offence, punishable by fine or imprisonment, to supply, offer or agree to supply, or expose or possess for supply, any consumer goods which are not reasonably safe (having regard to all the circumstances). 'Reasonably safe' means that there must either be no risk of death or personal injury, or at most a risk 'reduced to a minimum'. The Secretary of State may make safety regulations and issue notices covering specific goods from time to time. It is extremely unlikely that these would affect publications such as books and periodicals, which in themselves are unlikely to be unsafe, although they might become unsafe if, for example, they were sold to children with accompanying toys, games or other free gifts. It is also quite conceivable that an educational CD-ROM or multimedia package might contain unsafe items, particularly if aimed at young children.

Innocent retailers have a defence where they were unaware that particular goods were unsafe, or can establish that they took reasonable precautions and acted with due diligence (for example, by conducting random safety checks).

THE USE OF INJUNCTIONS FOR THE PROTECTION OF CONSUMERS' INTERESTS

Over more recent years, developments in consumer law have added to the weaponry available to the Office of Fair Trading (OFT) and other enforcement agencies. For example, under the Enterprise Act 2002, the OFT, trading standards authorities, 'sectoral' regulators and other 'designated enforcement bodies' (which we will refer to collectively as 'Enforcers') can apply to the court for orders to stop traders that they consider to be infringing the consumer protection legislation and where such infringements harm the 'collective interests of consumers'. The orders are known as 'Stop Now Orders'.

In addition to being available in the case of an infringement of the consumer protection legislation, Enforcers can also obtain Stop Now Orders against traders who fail to run their businesses (in relation to consumers) with reasonable care and skill.

The 2002 Act provides for three types of Enforcers:

- General Enforcers: essentially, the OFT and trading standards officers;
- Designated Enforcers: public or private bodies which are empowered by the Secretary of State by way of Statutory Instrument. The following bodies have been designated:

  The Civil Aviation Authority
  The Director General of Electricity supply for Northern Ireland
  The Director General of Gas for Northern Ireland
  OFCOM
  The Director General of Water Services
  The Gas and Electricity Markets Authority
  The Information Commissioner
  The Office of Rail Regulation
  The Financial Services Authority
  Consumers' Association (Which?);

- Community Enforcers: entities from other European Economic Area (EEA) States that are published in *E.C. Official Journal*.

A breach of a Stop Now Order would be a contempt of court and punishable by fine and/or imprisonment.

SUMMARY CHECKLIST: CONSUMER PROTECTION

- Does a duty of care exist?
- If so, does breach of that duty amount to negligence?
- Might the goods be defective goods?
- Is their safety such as the public is entitled to expect?
- Have unsafe consumer goods been supplied?
- Do any of the available defences apply?

Advertising and promotion

12

ADVERTISING

INTRODUCTION

There is a school of thought that if you invent a better mousetrap, the world will beat a path to your door. This may be true of mousetraps, and (perhaps) some essential professional texts, but as a general rule most publishers find it pays to advertise. As a result, as anyone who picks up a copy of *The Bookseller* will know, advertising is as prominent a feature of the publishing world as it is of any other major industry – perhaps more so – and can range from the modestly factual to the glossiest forms of hype. It is not, however, without its legal risks. We considered some of the general risks, which accompany all published text, such as defamation and malicious falsehood, in chapter 7. In this chapter we will take a look at the laws which particularly apply to advertising and promotional techniques, and which govern what you say in advertisements, and how you say it.

All advertisers sooner or later face the same universal temptation: to overstate the value of the thing being sold. You know the sort of thing: brilliant author, uniquely authoritative (or hysterically funny/thrilling/raunchy) work, miraculously good value at this never-to-be-repeated pre-publication offer. In a world increasingly dominated by the media, consumers are probably immune to much of this, and most of it is harmless enough. If it is no more than generalised hype, the law treats it, rather crushingly, as a 'mere puff', and gives it no particular legal significance. But beware: look again at the above blurbs. Are you simply throwing in the adjective 'authoritative' (for example) as a mere puff or are you actually stating – or implying – that your author or publication has specific authority (such as that of an examining board or Royal College)? Similarly, are you merely describing your product as being 'good value', or are you making a specific pre-publication offer? The difference could be highly significant. Where statements are made which *mislead* the consumer into buying something which he or she would not otherwise have bought, publishers may find themselves breaking the law. And the criminal law is often involved in this area of publishing, with fines and even imprisonment for those who infringe. It is therefore very much in publishers' interests to take care how they describe their publications.

TRADE DESCRIPTIONS

Trade descriptions are covered by the Trade Descriptions Act 1968. The Act applies between businesses, as well as to consumer advertising, and it covers statements relating to services (see below, p. 290) as well as to goods.

Under section 1(1) of the 1968 Act any person commits an offence:

who, in the course of a trade or business:
1. applies a false trade description to any goods; or
2. supplies or offers to supply any goods to which a false trade description is applied.

A trade description can include almost any feature or quality of the goods – their size, quantity, composition, manufacture, strength, accuracy, pedigree, official approval, testing or endorsement, or history, including previous ownership. Note however that, for the Act to apply, the description must be applied in the course of a trade or business: private sales are not covered.

Applying a trade description

A description can be 'applied' to goods by printing it directly on them (for example, as part of a jacket blurb), or by attaching it (perhaps via a label or sticker) or by marking it on to the packaging, or on anything in which, on which, or next to which the goods are placed, such as a spinner or other display unit, or adjacent point of sale material. Descriptions can also be applied, of course, by means of physically quite separate advertising, such as space advertising, leaflets, Internet links, catalogues and price lists, provided that the description is used in a manner 'likely to be taken as referring to the goods'. In fact, a trade description does not even need to be applied in physical form at all – it can be an oral description by the person supplying the goods, or even implied from the mere fact of supply if goods of a particular description were specifically requested. Most publishing advertising would therefore be covered.

False trade descriptions

What is 'false'? Section 3 of the 1968 Act helpfully tells us that false means 'false to a material degree': this includes statements which, though not strictly speaking false, are, nevertheless, misleading. So to describe a car as having 'one lady owner' might be a false trade description, even if the statement was strictly true in the sense that, out of five previous owners, only one was a lady. In the publishing context, any of the following may potentially be false trade descriptions:

- new, comprehensively updated, 1996 edition
- 30,000 articles with 12,000 illustrations
- specifically written for the GCSE syllabus

- as approved by the Royal College of Surgeons
- Windows and Mac.

In the case of *Southwark LBC* v. *Time Computer Systems Ltd* (1997), the defendants advertised a computer system indicating that certain software packages were preloaded and that customers could buy hard copies of that software together with instruction manuals at extra cost. The customer assumed the pictures of the software accompanying the picture of the computer meant that they were included in the price. The Divisional Court concluded that a reasonable consumer would have appreciated that that assumption was incorrect based on the clarity of the promotional material. Accordingly, no offence was committed. This case shows the importance of clear and unambiguous advertisements, particularly where pictures of the goods are displayed (e.g. a set of encyclopaedias to be sold over the Internet).

It may, however, be a false trade description to promote and package a book as if it were written by one of your best-selling authors, when in fact it was largely written by someone else: HarperCollins were prosecuted for this reason in 1991 by Warwickshire Trading Standards Officers, for publishing an 'Alastair MacLean' novel, jacketed in a style very like all his other successful thrillers, which although based on his own sketches with the full consent of his estate was in fact substantially ghost-written after his death by another writer altogether (named Alastair MacNeill). It was clearly in the interests of Alastair MacLean's estate – and his reading public – that his final work-in-progress should be published, but the court took the view that to package and sell it as a full-length Alastair MacLean novel was a false trade description. Although doubtless good in its own right it was not in fact a book by him, but by someone else. It is worth bearing in mind, therefore, that however understandable the motives – and continued use of a famous author's name and a strong brand identity are powerful motives – books should not be described in a way which misleads the public.

The Act applies to trade descriptions relating to *services*, as well as goods, and there have been many criminal prosecutions – not surprisingly – resulting from statements made in holiday brochures about non-existent hotels, restaurants, beaches and other facilities. Such criminal liability, contained in section 14 of the Act, might however also extend to a publisher who advertised facilities relating to books, such as '14 days free approval' or 'postage and packing free' when in fact these facilities did not exist, or did not extend to the particular books in question. It might well also cover advertisements relating to a help-line service with a CD-ROM or online product which either turned out not to exist at all, or not to include the full cover advertised. Under section 14, however (unlike section 1 above), the person making the false statement must either *know* it to be false, or make it recklessly.

Prosecutions and defences

Local Trading Standards Officers are given wide powers under the 1968 Act to investigate complaints and bring prosecutions, make test purchases, enter premises and seize goods and documents. Penalties, if convicted, range from a fine of up to

£5,000 on summary conviction to an unlimited fine and/or up to two years' imprisonment on indictment.

It is, however, a defence to a charge of applying a false description to prove (on the balance of probabilities) that the commission of the offence was the result of:

- a mistake;
- an accident, or some other unavoidable cause;
- reliance on information supplied by someone else; or
- someone else's actions or omissions;

provided that it can also be proved that 'all reasonable precautions' were taken and 'all due diligence' was exercised to avoid the commission of the offence (section 24). A similar defence is available to suppliers, such as wholesalers or booksellers, who may (under section 24(3)) prove that they did not know, and could not with reasonable diligence have ascertained, that the goods did not conform to the description.

A special defence is also available under section 25 to those people such as magazine and journal editors who innocently publish advertisements placed in their publications by others, if they can prove that the advertisement was accepted and placed in the course of their business *and* that they were not aware (and had no reason to be) that publication would involve an offence under the Act. The defence would also cover an innocent advertising agency placing an advertisement on behalf of a client.

MISLEADING ADVERTISEMENTS

As well as the criminal powers available to Trading Standards Officers under the 1968 Act, regulatory powers to prevent misleading advertisements are also given to the Director General of Fair Trading, under the Control of Misleading Advertisements Regulations 1988 (as amended). The Regulations were passed in order to implement the EC's Misleading Advertisements Directive of 1984, and give the Director General the power to seek injunctions in the courts, in order to prevent or halt the publication of most kinds of misleading advertisements, including press and magazine advertising, direct mailings, posters and leaflets (see also chapter 11, p. 286 for further commentary on the use of injunctions for the protection of consumer interests). They do not, however, apply to TV cable, or radio advertisements, which are regulated by separate, but similar, provisions under the Broadcasting Act 1990. By an amendment made to the Regulations in April 2000 the Regulations also cover the area of comparative advertising. We deal with this important subject later in this chapter.

An advertisement is misleading under the Regulations if it:

- 'deceives or is likely to deceive' those to whom it is addressed, or those it reaches; and
- because of this, 'is likely to affect their economic behaviour' (for example, by persuading them to buy the product), or otherwise injure a competitor.

The question of what is 'likely to deceive' was considered in a 1989 case involving misleading advertisements for a 'wonder' slimming product called SpeedSlim. Mr Justice Hoffmann, ordering an injunction, said:

> An advertisement must be likely to deceive the persons to whom it is addressed if it makes false claims on behalf of the product. It is true that many people read advertisements with a certain degree of scepticism. For the purposes of applying the regulations, however, it must be assumed that there may be people who will believe what the advertisers tell them, and in those circumstances the making of a false claim is likely to deceive.

MISLEADING PRICE INDICATIONS

Price is, of course, one of the key factors in the decision whether to purchase, and sellers of products and providers of services (such as restaurants) have proved highly inventive over the years in thinking up new ways to mislead and deceive consumers about the true price of what they are buying. Spurious 'bargains', non-existent 'sales' or 'reductions' and 'inclusive' prices (which turn out after all to omit significant items such as VAT or service charges) have all achieved consumer notoriety in their time – although not perhaps so much in the publishing trade, where recommended retail prices were enforced under the Net Book Agreement until 1995 (for RPM and the former NBA generally, see chapter 13).

Misleading price indications are now covered by Part III of the Consumer Protection Act 1987, and a Code of Practice made under that Act. Price Marking Orders (the latest Order is from 2004) are also made periodically, to guide retailers. It is an offence under section 20 of the 1987 Act to give any consumer in the course of any business an indication which is misleading as to the price at which goods, services, accommodation or facilities are available. A price is 'misleading' (or may *become* misleading) if as a result the consumer might reasonably be expected to think any of the following were the case:

- the price is less than it actually is;
- the price applies generally, when in fact it only applies to a particular item (such as an individual title, or service);
- the price is inclusive, when in fact extra charges are made (such as VAT);
- the price is a special or temporary bargain, when in fact it is not (for example, a spurious 'sale' or pre-publication offer);
- the price compares favourably with other rival products (e.g. 'we will beat any local price by £20'), or recommended prices, when in fact the comparisons are false.

Under section 24 of the Act, it is a defence for a publisher or other manufacturer to show that a recommended price was generally in force which was not followed by the retailer concerned. There is also a defence of innocent publication for newspapers, magazines and others who regularly carry such advertising, and a defence of incidental publication, in a book, newspaper, magazine, or on film, TV or radio, in a form other than an advertisement. Finally (as with offences under the Trade Descriptions Act), it is a general defence (under section 39) to show that you took all reasonable steps and exercised all due diligence to avoid committing the offence.

The Code of Practice gives further detailed guidance on matters such as price comparisons, statements about value or work, introductory offers and sales such as the National Book Sale or other special events, mail order advertising, and VAT, postage, packing and delivery charges. The Code, which is available from Trading Standards Offices, is intended for guidance only and does not create any separate offences, but may be taken into account in any prosecution under the 1987 Act.

COMPARATIVE ADVERTISING

One particularly dangerous temptation for advertisers is to indulge in what is known as 'comparative advertising' – advertising which makes direct comparisons (usually disparaging ones) with competitors' products: for example, that one make of batteries lasts longer than an identifiable rival battery, or that one car or computer is better value for money than another (illustrated) model. Magazines are prone to this, when comparing alleged circulation figures, actual readership, or advertiser satisfaction levels. The Advertising Standards Authority's (ASA) Advertising Code generally permits such advertising, 'in the interests of vigorous competition and public information', but makes it clear that:

> comparisons should be clear and fair. The elements of any comparison should not be selected in a way that gives the advertisers an artificial advantage.

This broadly tolerant view should not, however, mislead publishers into believing that comparative advertising is relatively safe. Very real legal dangers exist here – in particular, the following.

Control of Misleading Advertisements Regulations

UK legislation deals specifically with comparative advertising, implementing the EC Directive on Comparative Advertising. The UK implementation has taken the form of an amendment to the Control of Misleading Advertisements Regulations 1988. Section 4A of those Regulations (which was inserted by way of an amendment) provides that a comparative advertisement (one that expressly or impliedly identifies a competitor or the goods or services of a competitor) will only be permitted where:

- it is not misleading;
- it compares goods or services with the same function or intended purpose ;
- it objectively compares one or more material, relevant, verifiable and representative features of those goods or services (which may include price);
- it does not create confusion in the marketplace between the advertiser and competitor or between their goods and services, trade marks and trade names;

- it does not take unfair advantage of the reputation of a trade mark, trade name or other distinguishing marks of a competitor;
- it does not discredit or denigrate the trade marks, trade names, other distinguishing marks, goods, services, activities, or circumstances of a competitor;
- (for products with designation of origin) it relates in each case to products with the same designation;
- it does not present goods or services as imitations or replicas of goods or services bearing a protected trade mark or trade name.

A comparative advertisement referring to a special offer is not permitted unless it indicates in a clear and unequivocal way the date on which the offer ends or, where appropriate, that the special offer is subject to the availability of the goods and services. In addition, where the special offer has not yet begun, it should state the date of the start of the period during which the special price or other specific conditions shall apply.

The Director General of Fair Trading has the power to seek an injunction for advertisements that breach the comparative advertising provisions, in the same way as for other 'misleading' advertisements (see p. 291).

Trade mark infringement

If your advertisement shows, or otherwise uses, a rival's registered trade mark, you may be infringing that trade mark (on trade marks generally, see chapter 10). Under section 10(6) of the Trade Marks Act 1994, any such use:

> otherwise than in accordance with honest practices in industrial or commercial matters shall be treated as infringing the registered trade mark if the use without due cause takes unfair advantage of, or is detrimental to, the distinctive character or repute of the trade mark.

The Courts have taken a pragmatic approach to the interpretation of this sub-section and have been reluctant to find infringement where the advertisement in question was substantially fair, even if not entirely accurate, unless it is significantly misleading. For example, in a 2000 High Court action, British Airways failed in their action under section 10(6) (and for malicious falsehood) against the low cost airline Ryanair in relation to two of Ryanair's advertisements. One advert was headlined 'Expensive BA.....RDS' and the other 'Expensive BA', and both contained comparisons of flight prices between the two companies for return flights to various European destinations. The Court commented that 'one can almost say that no advertisement is complete without hyperbole and bluff' and summarised BA's complaint as being that Ryanair had exaggerated in saying that BA were five times more expensive, because they were actually only three times more expensive. The Court decided that the Ryanair advert was honest comparative advertising and suspected that 'the real reason that BA do not like it is precisely because it is true'.

However, advertisers must still ensure that their advertisements do not contravene the ASA code (as the 'Expensive BA…..RDS' advert did) (see p. 294) or the Control of Misleading Advertisements Regulations (as amended) (see p. 293).

Copyright infringement

If you reproduce a substantial part of a rival's copyright work – for example, packaging design, a title or logo, or distinctive typeface – in an advertisement without their permission, you may infringe their copyright in that work, and (subject to defences such as incidental inclusion, for example in a film) they would have the usual remedies for infringement (see chapter 9).

Malicious falsehood

If you publish an untrue statement, motivated by malice (or some other improper motive), and thereby cause loss or damage to someone else, you may be guilty of publishing a malicious falsehood or a trade libel (on this generally, see chapter 7, p. 184). The injured party may sue for damages and apply for an injunction: in one (1992) case between two computer companies, Compaq and Dell, the plaintiffs, Compaq, succeeded in obtaining an interim injunction on these grounds which prevented Dell from making untrue and misleading comparisons (particularly on dealer price) between the computer products of both companies.

Passing off

Although most comparative advertising seeks to *distinguish* one product from another, it is possible to refer to a rival's product in advertising in such a way that the public is given the impression that they are somehow approving or endorsing your own product, or that the products are linked, with the result that their own goodwill would be diluted and confusion would be caused. A good example of this was the 1985 case between McDonald's Hamburgers and Burger King, where McDonald's took action to prevent tube advertisements by Burger King bearing the words 'It's Not Just Big, Mac.' Although McDonald's failed on the ground of malicious falsehood, they succeeded in obtaining an injunction to prevent passing off; on the grounds that potential customers would be misled into thinking that there was an association between McDonald's successful Big Mac hamburger and Burger King, and that they could get a Big Mac at Burger King establishments. (For further treatment of passing off; see chapter 10, p. 260.)

Publishers would therefore be well advised to do all they can to make absolutely certain that statements made in comparative advertisements are fair comparisons, comparing like with like, that the quoted facts are true at the time of the advertisement, that they do not infringe any copyright or registered trade mark owned by rivals, and do not indulge in any form of passing off or in any other way mislead or confuse the public.

UNFAIR COMMERCIAL PRACTICES

In June 2005 we saw the publication of an important EC Directive, the 'Unfair Commercial Practices' Directive 2005/29 (OJ No L149; 11 June 2005). It has far-reaching controls over 'unfair' business to consumer commercial practices. Member states have until 12 December 2007 to implement the Directive by domestic legislation.

The Directive amends a number of related directives, including those on misleading advertising and for the protection of consumers in respect of distance contracts.

The Directive stipulates that a commercial practice is unfair if it is contrary to the requirements of professional diligence and it materially distorts or is likely materially to distort the economic behaviour of the average consumer whom it reaches with regard to the product in question. Under the Directive, commercial practices are unfair if they are misleading (e.g. the use of false information or by the omission of information) or aggressive (e.g. harassment, coercion or undue influence).

BRITISH CODES OF ADVERTISING AND SALES PROMOTION

In addition to the various legal controls mentioned above, the advertising industry has developed a parallel system of self-regulation, monitored and enforced by the Advertising Standards Authority (ASA). The ASA attempts to ensure that advertisements do not mislead, and are in the public interest, and may investigate complaints, publish findings and make references to the Office of Fair Trading, requesting the Office of Fair Trading to seek injunctions preventing offending advertisements. The ASA may also request newspapers and other publishers not to accept particular advertisements. In addition, the ASA's Committee of Advertising has issued a Code of Practice (the last edition came into force in March 2003) called The British Code of Advertising Sales Promotion and Direct Marketing. There are separate Codes covering TV advertising and radio advertising although effective from 1 November 2004, the ASA has assumed powers over advertising in this media from the communications regulator OFCOM.

The first Principle of the Advertising Code has become famous ('All advertisements should be legal, decent, honest and truthful') but there are many other provisions covering, among other things, safety, personal privacy, prices, free offers, guarantees, and comparisons with rival products (see above, p. 295). The Sales Promotion Code, similarly, provides for protection of consumers (especially children), competitions and prizes, and other promotions or incentive schemes. There are also separate Codes for alcohol and cigarette advertising and, importantly, for distance selling advertisements.

The Codes have no independent legal force, and are written in fairly general terms, but evidence that an advertiser has not complied with one or other of the Codes is likely to be taken into account in any court proceedings. It is therefore very much in publishers' interests to do all they can to see that their advertising complies with the Codes, and that copies of the Codes – which are usually available free of charge from the ASA (including on their website) – are on every marketing and advertising department's shelves.

The Committee of Advertising Practice (CAP) has prepared a range of guidance notes – 'Help Notes' – including one on the marketing of publications. This can be accessed on-line from CAP at www.cap.org.uk.

We give below an example of the 'key' points in the Help Note:

- All factual claims must be substantiated.
- Unproven claims contained in the title of a publication must be put in inverted commas.
- The first reference to the title should be followed by the author's name.
- Marketers offering 'new' publications should ensure that those publications have been available for no longer than a year.
- Marketers should not misleadingly describe pamphlets and the like as 'books'.

JURISDICTION

The number of consumers and businesses using the Internet continues to increase at a fast rate, as does the number of those providing and utilising online advertising and buying/ selling capability ('e-commerce'). Such an increase poses an interesting question about how the law governs such transactions, given that a website of one country is accessible from any country in the world.

One case where the problems of the worldwide web were exposed involved the huge US online web portal company Yahoo!. Yahoo! sold Nazi memorabilia (via online auction) on its US-based website (yahoo.com) presumably for the benefit of US citizens only. The items were not available on the Yahoo sites of other jurisdictions for obvious reasons (for example, the sale or promotion of Nazi-related items is prohibited by French law). However, as the website was accessible in France (even though France has its own French version of Yahoo! which did not have access to the material), an anti-racism group took Yahoo! to court in France to prevent sales of the paraphernalia to French citizens. The French court ordered Yahoo! to block the sale of Nazi items to French citizens or face fines of £10,000 per day. This was somewhat of a shock outcome not least because experts appointed by the court acknowledged that it was not, in practice, possible for Yahoo! to block all French users. The ruling would have huge repercussions (if upheld) as it puts online advertisers at risk of breaching the national laws of countries that they have no intention of targeting. However, Yahoo! sought and obtained a declaration from the US federal courts that the French ruling is unenforceable against Yahoo! in the US. Whilst national courts have often taken a pragmatic approach and generally only ruled against foreign sites that are actually targeted at users in the country in question, the significance of the French ruling should not be underestimated, and online advertisers and retailers should be wary of similar claims in the future.

Another interesting question is how the law governs Internet transactions from the point of view of consumers. For example, if an individual, who resides in the UK, purchases a new bestselling novel (in the US) from Amazon.com or equivalent US-based online retailer using a laptop while on holiday in France, in which country does the buyer seek a remedy if the book is not delivered and the retailer denies responsibility? Would it be his home courts (UK), those of the country where the purchase was made (France) or the country where the website is based (USA)?

Assistance has been provided by a binding EU Regulation on Jurisdiction, Recognition and Enforcement (which replaces the current Brussels Convention) to ensure that rules of jurisdiction and enforcement of judgments are dealt with consistently in the EU. The Regulation, which came into force in March 2002, broadly confirms the 'country of origin' principle that persons (including companies) domiciled in member states must be sued in their own courts. However, this is subject to certain exceptions. For example, in contracts for the sale of goods or delivery of services (including website services), consumers may sue in the courts of the place of performance of the contract. This will usually be in their home courts in a sale of goods case (place of performance is deemed to be where the goods were or should have been delivered). The same will probably apply in a provision of services case (place of performance is deemed to be where the services were or should have been provided).

SUMMARY CHECKLIST: ADVERTISING

- Is this statement a mere puff; or is it a trade description?
- Is it a false trade description?
- Might we have a defence, if we took all reasonable precautions, and used all due diligence?
- Is this a misleading advertisement?
- Are we making a misleading price indication?
- Are we indulging in comparative advertising?
- Are we infringing any trade marks or copyrights (or using a well-known personality for implied endorsement without their consent)?
- Are we following the ASA Advertising Codes?
- Have we advertised online, and, if so, have we considered the impact this may have in countries where the site is accessible?

UNSOLICITED GOODS AND SERVICES

One of the more notorious promotional techniques of the 1960s was 'inertia selling', an aggressive system of sending products – and invoices – out to people who had not ordered them in the hope that some at least would be passive or compliant (or intimidated) enough to buy them. The public outcry that resulted led to the passing of the Unsolicited Goods and Services Act 1971 (which has been amended by the Unsolicited Goods and Services Act 1971 (Electronic Commerce) (Amendment)

Regulations 2005 and the Regulatory Reform (Unsolicited Goods and Services Act 1971) (Directories Entries and Demands for Payment) Order 2005 which now, together with other legislation, severely restricts such practices.

Under section 2 of the 1971 Act, it is a criminal offence, punishable by fine, for anyone in the course of a trade or business to make a demand for payment for goods when:

- they know that the goods are unsolicited; they sent goods to another for the purpose of them acquiring them for their trade or business; and
- they have no reasonable cause to believe they have any right to payment.

Similarly, under section 24 of the Consumer Protection (Distance Selling) Regulations 2000 (which repealed section 1 of the 1971 Act), it is a criminal offence for anyone, in the course of a trade or business, to make a demand for payment of goods or services when:

- they know that the goods or services are unsolicited;
- they are sent to another person with a view to his acquiring them for purposes other than those of his business.

It is also a criminal offence (which is confirmed by section 24(5) of the 2000 Distance Selling Regulations) under such circumstances to make threats of legal proceedings for non-payment, or threaten any other sanctions, such as unfavourable credit listings. However, in the (familiar) situation where a publisher is not properly told (or refuses to believe) that an existing subscription has been cancelled, and keeps sending out publications, invoices and demands for payment, it was held in a 1973 case involving *Readers' Digest* that this did not constitute an offence under the 1971 Act, since the goods were not unsolicited but had been originally requested, and it could not be said that the publisher 'did not have reasonable cause to believe that there was a right to payment'.

The recipient of unsolicited goods, who has no reasonable cause to believe that the goods were sent for the purposes of a business, is under no obligation to return the goods or look after them, and (under section 24 of the Regulations, which as indicated repealed section 1 of the 1971 Act) may:

use, deal with or dispose of them as if they were an unconditional gift ... and any right of the sender to the goods shall be extinguished.

This is provided the sender sent the goods intending that the recipient could acquire them, (and did not, for example, send them by mistake) and provided the recipient had not in any way requested the goods, or agreed to acquire them or return them (for example if the recipient had previously signed a form agreeing to buy a book club's 'book of the month'). Following the introduction of the (2000) Regulations, there is no longer a 30-day or 6-month wait before you can keep unsolicited goods – the title to them passes immediately.

As the title suggests, the Regulatory Reform (Unsolicited Goods and Services Act 1971) (Directory Entries and Demands for Payment) Order 2005 lays down specific requirements as to how agreements may be made for entries in directories including the addition of a further method by which a person may agree to an entry where the entry is a repeat or renewal entry in a directory. If a publisher of a directory fails to comply with the specific requirements, any charge (for the entry) will be unenforceable (or recoverable) and the publisher could also be guilty of an offence if he demands payment.

DISTANCE SELLING

Distance selling (like distance learning) is less exotic than the name implies: it simply means contracts negotiated at a distance (rather than face to face), and includes Internet and mail order sales based on direct mail campaigns or telephone 'cold calling'. In the European Commission's view the development of new technology such as teleshopping and the 'Internet' required increased consumer protection within the EU, particularly for personal privacy, and so an EU Distance Selling Directive (1997) was enacted.

THE UK DISTANCE SELLING REGULATIONS

As we have seen the Distance Selling Directive has been implemented into UK law by the Consumer Protection (Distance Selling) Regulations 2000 (as amended by the Consumer Protection (Distance Selling) (Amendment) Regulations 2005 (see also above). The scope of the Regulations is very broad, covering goods and services, where the contract is made without any face-to-face contact between supplier and consumer. It does not, however, apply to business to business transactions (only business to consumer).

Distance contract

A distance contract is defined as 'any contract concerning goods or services concluded between a supplier and a consumer under an organised distance sales or service-provision scheme run by the supplier who, for the purpose of the contract, makes exclusive use of one or more means of distance communication up to and including the moment at which the contract is concluded'.

As the Regulations only apply to 'organised' distance-sales or service provision schemes, it is probable that they do not apply if a business:

- does not normally sell to consumers in response to letters, phone calls, faxes or e-mails (i.e. if a business conducts a one-off sales request, then it would not need to comply but if a business regularly deals with one-off requests and has the facilities to do so, then it would need to comply); and
- the business does not operate an interactive shopping website.

Key features

The Regulations may apply to any business that sells goods or services to consumers:

- on the Internet or digital television;
- by mail order, including catalogue shopping;
- by phone or fax.

In summary, the key features of the Regulations are:

- the consumer must be given (in good time before the conclusion of the contract) clear information about the goods or services offered;
- the consumer must be sent a confirmation by the supplier after making a purchase;
- the consumer has a seven-day cooling off period during which they can cancel the contract (if notice is given to the supplier in writing or other 'durable' form which probably includes e-mail).

Consumer information

The information that the consumer must be given includes:

- the identity and address (if payment is made in advance) of the supplier and his commercial purpose;
- a clear description of the goods or services;
- the price of the goods or services (including taxes) and delivery costs (where appropriate);
- information on the arrangement for payment, delivery or performance;
- the existence of the right of cancellation;
- the period that the offer or price remains valid.

In the case of telephone communication, the identity of the supplier and the commercial purpose must be made clear at the start of the conversation with the consumer.

Consumer's right to cancel

If within seven days after the contract, the consumer gives a notice of cancellation to the supplier, the contract will be cancelled. The notice of cancellation must be in writing or other durable form (as mentioned above, this probably includes e-mail).

Unless the parties agree otherwise, the consumer does not have a right to cancel in respect of certain contracts, including:

- for the supply of newspapers, periodicals or magazines (but not for the supply of books (for example from a book club);
- for the supply of services (but note the 2005 amendment of the Regulations);

- for the supply of audio or video recordings or computer software if they are unsealed by the consumer (although it is not clear whether this covers downloading computer software);
- personalised or specially made goods.

Once the contract is cancelled, it is treated as if it has not been made and the supplier must (as soon as possible and in any event within 30 days) reimburse any sums paid by the consumer under that contract.

These Regulations need to be borne in mind, especially with the growth of e-commerce and the increase of availability of online publications. For businesses conducting 'distance selling', it is important that the information to be provided to the consumer is clearly displayed.

DATA PROTECTION

Most businesses maintain a certain amount of information about individuals. For example, as advertising and marketing models become more sophisticated, business reliance on information about customers increases, and the type of information collected and used becomes more detailed. Also, a business involved with publishing, like any other business, will hold and use personal information about its employees, and other people with whom it deals including authors. It may also, of course, publish information that identifies individuals.

Use of information which relates to individuals is regulated in the UK by the Data Protection Act 1998 ('the 1998 Act'). The 1998 Act was brought into force to implement a 1995 European Commission Directive and provides the framework for the UK's data protection regime, with the detail being filled in by way of separate secondary legislation or regulations. It is important to note that contravention of the 1998 Act can be a criminal offence and directors and officers involved can also be held personally (and criminally) liable.

THE DATA PROTECTION ACT 1998

What does the 1998 Act cover?

The 1998 Act, which is enforced by the UK Information Commissioner, governs the 'processing' of information about individuals ('personal data') in the UK. Any business, person or company that 'processes' 'personal data' is known as a 'data controller' (except where that processing only takes place purely in accordance with the instructions of someone else in which case they will be known as a 'data processor').

- 'Data' is defined as information that is processed automatically (i.e. held on a computer) and information held in certain organized paper records (a 'relevant filing system'). In order for information held in a relevant filing system to be covered, that filing system must be structured by reference to individuals or to criteria enabling the user to readily access specific information relating to that individual.

- 'Personal data' is data that relates to individuals which can be identified from the data, or from the data and other information which is in, or is likely to come into, the possession of the data controller. Personal data can include expressions of opinion about the data subject and indications of the intentions of the data controller or any other person in respect of the data subject.
- 'Processing' is defined extremely widely and essentially includes any use of data from the collection and recording of data, the holding of data and the carrying out of any operation on data, to the data's subsequent disclosure and eventual destruction. The UK Information Commissioner has made it clear that the term will be interpreted broadly to include any conceivable operation on data.

In the case of *Durant v. Financial Services Authority* (2003) the Court of Appeal considered the definitions of personal data and relevant filing system in the 1998 Act. In terms of 'personal data', it took the view that incidental reference to a person's name will not necessarily be personal data about the named person. For the data to be 'personal data' it must affect an individual's privacy in some way, for example, the information has personal connotations or has the individual at its focus, rather than being a mere reference not associated with any other personal information.

The Court of Appeal also took the view that paper records would only qualify as a 'relevant filing system' where they are of 'sufficient sophistication to provide the same or similar ready accessibility as a computerized filing system'. In other words the files would need to be structured in such a way that it would be clear from the outset of a search whether specific information amounting to personal data is held and the structure of the files is so sophisticated to mean that specific criteria or information about a particular individual can be easily located.

The effect of the judgment is to limit the current extent to which information about an individual will be personal data and exclude all but the most organised of paper records from the scope of the 1998 Act. It remains possible that this interpretation will be investigated by the European Commission as part of a wider consideration of whether the 1998 Act adequately implements the European Directive.

What must be done before personal data may be processed?

Notification

If someone is a data controller processing personal data, generally speaking (there are some exemptions), they must notify the Office of the Information Commissioner that they are doing so.

Under the 1998 Act, notification must take place annually and the fee for notifying is currently £35.00. A notification involves giving certain information to the Office of the Information Commissioner including the data controller's name and address, a description of the personal data being processed, the purposes for which those data are processed and any recipients of the personal data and a description of any intended destination countries. The details of the notification will then appear on a publicly accessible register. Failure to notify or to notify the details of any material changes to personal data processing within 28 days of the change is an offence under the Act.

Compliance

The Act is based on eight 'Data Protection Principles' which must be observed by all data controllers whenever any personal data is collected and subsequently processed. These are summarised below.

* *Principle 1* Personal data must be processed fairly and lawfully and, in particular, shall not be processed unless at least one of a specified list of pre-conditions is met (for example, the data subject has given his consent or the processing is necessary for the performance of a contract to which the data subject is a party).
* *Principle 2* Personal data shall be obtained only for one or more specified and lawful purposes, and shall not be used in any manner incompatible with that purpose or those purposes.
* *Principle 3* Personal data shall be adequate, relevant and not excessive in relation to the purpose or purposes for which it is processed.
* *Principle 4* Personal data shall be accurate and, where necessary, kept up to date.
* *Principle 5* Personal data shall not be kept for longer than is necessary considering the purpose for which they are used.
* *Principle 6* Personal data shall be processed in accordance with the rights of data subjects under the 1998 Act (see below).
* *Principle 7* Appropriate technical and organisational measures shall be taken against unauthorised or unlawful processing of personal data and against accidental loss or destruction of, or damage to, personal data.
* *Principle 8* Personal data shall not be transferred to a country or territory outside the EEA unless that country or territory ensures an adequate level of protection for the rights and freedoms of data subjects in relation to the processing of personal data (see below for further comment on this principle).

Compliance with the first principle often takes the highest profile as it usually involves taking steps to give individuals certain information at the point at which personal data is collected from them– often (not always) it is necessary to obtain consent from the data subjects to use their personal data in the way intended by the person collecting them. 'Consent' is not defined in the Act but it is accepted that it must be specific, informed and freely given.

Sensitive personal data

The Act treats processing of certain kinds of personal data ('sensitive personal data') more strictly. For example, in order to comply with principle 1 in the case of sensitive personal data, at least one of an additional set of pre-conditions must also be satisfied which include obtaining 'explicit consent' from the data subject rather than mere 'consent'.

'Sensitive personal data' are personal data containing information relating to racial or ethnic origin, political opinions, religious or other beliefs, trade union membership, physical or mental health or condition, sex life, offences committed or alleged to have been committed by the individual and proceedings in respect of offences.

Rights of data subjects

The 1998 Act confers a number of rights on individuals in respect of their personal data. For example, individuals:

- may make written requests to those who process personal data about them (known as 'subject information requests') for a copy of the data including information as to what that data are used for, the recipients to whom it is or may be disclosed and the source of the personal data;
- have rights to prevent processing likely to cause substantial damage or substantial distress to them or to another;
- have the right to object to the processing of personal data about them for direct marketing; and
- are entitled to take action through the courts for compensation from data controllers for breaches of the 1998 Act.

How does the 1998 Act affect the publishing trade?

The 1998 Act may apply in a number of situations:

- For example, as mentioned above, it may be necessary, as with any customer-focused business, to collect and use personal information about customers. This may take the form of a mailing list of individuals or (possibly more likely in the case of a publisher) a list of individuals within customer organisations such as retailers. Any use of this information must comply with the 1998 Act. The most simple example is marketing – if there is a wish to contact a database of customers to try to sell a book, then it will be necessary to comply with the relevant provisions of the 1998 Act. This is likely to involve obtaining the consent of each person whose details are held for direct marketing, and giving them the right to opt out of direct marketing.
- Also, like any other data controller, the personal data must be held securely from unauthorised access. This will involve investing in up-to-date technology as well

as training staff and taking obvious steps such as locking filing cabinets that contain personal information.

* It is important to comply with all provisions of the 1998 Act in relation to data held about employees and any other data held about individuals.
* The content of some publications may also be affected by the 1998 Act. For example, a publisher may publish a directory of experts in a certain field (both online and offline) along with comments about each expert. It will have been necessary to obtain clear consent from each person included in order to use their information in this way (although it is appreciated that good practice would probably dictate that this procedure was followed anyway).

Journalism, literature and art

The 1998 Act contains a number of exemptions (covered generally below) which include an exemption relating to use of personal data for the purposes of journalism, literature and art. Personal data that are processed *only* for journalism, artistic purposes or literary purposes, are exempt from many provisions of the 1998 Act including many of the rights of individuals and the data protection principles (but are not exempt from the seventh data protection principle that relates to security measures, which continues to apply). The exemption only applies if:

* the processing is undertaken with a view to the publication of any journalistic, literary or artistic material; and
* the data controller reasonably believes that, having regard to the special importance of the public interest in freedom of expression, publication would be in the public interest; and
* the data controller reasonably believes that, in all the circumstances, compliance with the provisions covered by the exemption is incompatible with the purposes of publication.

When considering whether to publish the personal data, it is important to be able to satisfy each of the conditions and, in particular, take into account any relevant codes of practice in deciding whether a belief that publication would be in the public interest is reasonable. Relevant codes of practice include, for example, the code of practice issued by the Press Complaints Commission.

Human Rights Act 1998

When considering the application of the above exemption relating to journalism literature and art, and also when processing personal data generally, the application of the Human Rights Act 1998 will need to be taken into account. The Act only directly applies to public authorities and to acts of a public nature. However this does also extend to cover the judicial functions of courts or tribunals and provides that other legislation (including the Data Protection Act 1998) should be interpreted in a way that is compatible with the rights provided by the European Convention on Human Rights. As mentioned in chapter 8, Article 8 of the Convention provides that:

> Everyone has the right to respect for his private and family life, his home and his correspondence.

Article 10(1) of the Convention provides that:

> Everyone has the right to freedom of expression.

Although the Data Protection Act 1998 merely regulates the processing of personal information about individuals rather than offering statutory protection for individuals privacy rights, the effect of the Human Rights Act is that the courts considering a case concerning the publication of any information about an individual, will also need to balance these rights. This is particularly relevant to journalism, an area where there has been some significant case-law, generally, each case turning on its facts. The process of balancing the conflicting rights set out above as well as interpreting other legislation in a way that is compatible with the Convention rights is, at present, a delicate and often unpredictable exercise. The overriding consideration is that the Human Rights Act must be considered when interpreting any legislation, including the Data Protection Act 1998.

More specific information about the approach of the courts to issues of privacy and confidence since the Human Right Act and the relevance of recent case law to publishers can be found in chapter 8.

International sharing of personal data

Generally speaking, transfers of personal data to countries outside the EEA will only be allowed if the third country in question ensures an 'adequate' level of protection. Very few countries outside the EEA are deemed by the European Commission to have adequate protection. In the context of the US, certain measures have been put in place under which transfers of personal data can be made to US businesses who have signed up to a set of privacy principles similar to the data protection principles under the 1998 Act (because the measures will lead to a presumption of adequacy).

If the destination country outside the EEA does not have adequate data protection laws in place then the transfer will only be permitted in one of certain specified circumstances, such as where the data subject has consented, the transfer is necessary for the performance of a contract with the data subject or the rights of the data subject are protected by a contract based on European approved terms between the sender and the recipient of the data. It has become possible for multinational organisations to adopt binding corporate codes of conduct to ensure adequacy of protection for transfers of personal data to other group companies based outside the EEA. European guidance in the form of a checklist for the content of a binding corporate code and a procedure for making applications for approval of a set of binding corporate codes was published on 14 April 2005. However, the process for approval is complex and lengthy. It remains to be seen whether, in practice, binding corporate rules will be applied by only the largest multinationals.

Why comply?

Aside from the fact that many breaches of the 1998 Act are criminal offences under which directors or other officers can be personally liable, there is also the inconvenience factor. The level of awareness of individuals in the UK with respect to their data protection rights has increased over the last few years, and business competitors have been known to complain to the Office of the Information Commissioner where a rival is known not to be complying with data protection legislation. The administrative costs of dealing with complaints and, ultimately, investigations by the Office of the Information Commissioner can be very high and the Office of the Information Commissioner will publicise complaints which are upheld or successful prosecutions.

To force compliance, the Information Commissioner may serve enforcement and information notices, the latter requiring a controller to provide information to assist the Commissioner in determining whether the data protection principles have been broken. Going even further, the Commissioner may in certain circumstances apply to the court for an entry and inspection warrant.

Other exemptions

The 1998 Act contains a number of exemptions from some or all of the data protection principles and the other provisions such as:

- where national security is involved;
- where processing concerns the detection of crime or the assessment of taxation;
- where information must be made public by law;
- where the disclosure is made in connection with legal proceedings, or pursuant to a court order;
- for the purposes of research, history and statistics; and
- for processing for purely domestic purposes.

Achieving and maintaining compliance

Being compliant means having an up-to-date notification in place and internal procedures sufficient to ensure that in practice the organisation processes personal data in accordance with its notification and with applicable data protection law.

Generally, it is important to assess (and revise where appropriate) all data processing activities on a regular basis. Data protection notification must reflect the data processing activities in practice from time to time and relevant staff need to be aware of the impact of the Act and be appropriately trained. There should be suitable internal procedures in place to ensure the continuing compliance of the above and the effective handling of enquiries and complaints by individuals. This may involve appointing a data protection officer.

Finally, anyone publishing materials from which individuals can be identified should be extra careful to comply with the 1998 Act as well as the plethora of other laws covered by this book.

OTHER LAWS

Recent years have seen a number of other very significant items of legislation in this area, much of which has emanated from Europe. These laws have implications beyond the field of data protection but also have implications for data protection.

First, there are the Privacy and Electronic Communications (EC Directive) Regulations 2003 (the '2003 Regulations') which came into force in December 2003. The 2003 Regulations apply, among other things, to those sending electronic direct marketing communications such as by telephone, fax, e-mail or mobile text messages (SMS). In the case of marketing by e-mail or SMS, the default requirement is that it is only possible to send unsolicited communications in this way if the recipient has positively consented. There is an exception to this rule where a business is sending e-mail offers of its own similar goods or services to its existing customers who were offered an opt-out at the time their details were collected and at each time their details were subsequently used.

Second, under the Electronic Commerce (EC Directive) Regulations 2002, people sending commercial communications (including about promotions and discounts) must ensure that those communications are labelled as such as soon as they are received by the recipient and that they clearly identify the sender.

The Regulation of Investigatory Powers Act 2000 regulates, among other matters, the interception and monitoring of communications on networks including private lines such as the internal telephone network of a business. Monitoring is allowed only if the controller of the network has obtained a warrant, if both parties to the call consent, or if the purpose of the monitoring falls within the Lawful Business Practice Regulations 2000. These separate Regulations permit the monitoring of communications, for example to ascertain compliance with regulatory or self-regulatory business practices, to ascertain or demonstrate the standards achieved by those using the system for work or to detect or investigate unauthorised use of the employer's system. It is also possible to monitor (but not record) communications in order to establish whether a communication is work related. However, for any of the exceptions to apply, the business must first have taken all reasonable efforts to inform staff that monitoring takes place.

Finally, the Freedom of Information Act 2000 is likely to be of interest to publishing and related trades, not because they are likely to be directly regulated by the provisions of the legislation (which generally speaking places obligations on public authorities such as government or other public bodies), but because the legislation provides for general rights of access to recorded information public authorities hold. The Act offers the opportunity for anyone to make a written request for information held by a public authority, providing authors and journalists among others with wider opportunities to access previously unavailable information. The access rights under the Act only came fully into force in January 2005 and at the time of writing it is too early to tell how useful in practice the access rights will prove to be.

SUMMARY CHECKLIST: PROMOTION AND DATA PROTECTION

- Are we promoting unsolicited goods or services?
- If so, do we have reasonable cause to believe we are entitled to payment?
- Are we engaged in distance selling?
- If so, have we provided all the relevant information to the consumer?
- Are we using personal data in any way?
- If so, do we have in place a valid and up-to-date notification with the UK Information Commissioner?
- To the extent we need it, do we have the consent of the individual?
- Are we using any 'sensitive personal data'?
- If so, do we have explicit consent from the relevant individuals?
- Do we have procedures in place to ensure compliance and to handle complaints or subject information requests?
- Are we sending unsolicited communications?
- Do we make any transfers of personal data outside the EEA?
- If so, can we meet the requirement for adequacy of protection of the transfers?
- Are all relevant staff trained to understand the impact of the 1998 Act on their particular area?
- Do we have in place procedures to ensure ongoing compliance with data protection laws?

Distribution and export

13

INTRODUCTION

We looked in chapters 11 and 12 at the contracts which normally govern the sale of finished books and other manufactured products in the UK, and at the general law affecting consumer protection and advertising. We have seen that the law still attaches great importance to individual contracts, but increasingly regulates trading behaviour in the UK by means of statutory liability, especially where consumers are concerned. We have also seen how many of the statutes and other regulations now originate, not from Westminster, but from Brussels. In this final chapter, we shall turn a lot more of our attention to Europe. Distribution and the free movement of goods and services are key concerns of the European Union. So, also, are the goals of free, unrestricted, competition, and the famous 'level playing field'. Any publisher selling or distributing in the UK and Europe needs to bear these economic priorities very much in mind: agreements or trading behaviour which are found to be contrary to EC or UK competition rules, for example because they are monopolistic or otherwise anti-competitive, may be heavily penalised. This may affect distribution agreements, purchasing agreements and sales agency agreements, and potentially all commercial licensing of intellectual property, both within the UK and throughout Europe.

TRADE AND COMPETITION

Competition is a natural, some would say an essential, feature of healthy markets, and publishing is often highly competitive. Small publishers have a way of turning into larger publishers, however – or of being acquired by them (a process which may in itself require merger clearance, outside the scope of this book) – and large publishers may be able in time to influence, or even dominate, their particular market either by themselves, or as one of a group. Such groups can wield considerable market power. This is not in itself a bad thing: market power can encourage healthy rationalisation, and can benefit the consumer in many ways (by improving distribution, for example). It can cause legal difficulties, however, if it is used in an anti-competitive way, or leads to what are known as 'anti-competitive practices'. Anti-competitive practices can start quite informally, for example, over lunches between marketing directors, and may at first be nothing more than a (fairly) innocent exchange of views and gossip. When competitors have lunch, however, economists (and lawyers) start to feel nervous.

From such humble beginnings, price-fixing agreements may result, or divisions of local territories or market sectors, agreements on discounts or other terms of trade or other measures designed to restrict competition. Agreements or practices which restrict competition are very likely to be prohibited under UK and EU competition law, and are very likely to be unenforceable. They may even lead to large fines.

In these circumstances, great care needs to be taken when entering into commercial agreements, especially 'horizontal' agreements between companies competing at the same level, but also where there are 'vertical' arrangements operating at different levels up and down the distribution chain, for example between suppliers and agents or exclusive licensees.

We will look first at UK common law rules on what is known as restraint of trade, and then consider the UK and EC competition rules.

RESTRAINT OF TRADE

Since the early fifteenth century, the courts have refused to enforce contracts which are in unreasonable restraint of trade. Any such contract is *prima facie* void under English law. Each contract, of course, 'restrains' trade in some way, since it limits what one or both of the parties may do in the future, but it is only unreasonable restraints which will not be enforced. These most often occur in the context of restrictive covenants; for example, seeking to control rival activity by former employees, or former proprietors, of a publishing business, and may also occur with exclusive distribution or purchasing agreements.

An attempt to restrain a former marketing director from working in the same capacity for any comparable publishing company for the next five years would almost certainly be in unreasonable restraint of trade, for example – not only because of the breadth of the restriction (which would rule out a large proportion of the likeliest job options) but also because of the unreasonably long time during which the ban would operate. A restraint on working for any direct competitor for 12 months, on the other hand, might be regarded as reasonable, and therefore enforceable, but any attempt to impose wide-ranging bans over long periods may well be difficult to enforce, particularly if they would significantly limit the capacity of the person concerned to earn a living at all.

Anyone wishing to enforce restraints of trade will need to prove three things:

- that he or she has a legitimate interest worthy of protection (protecting the goodwill of the business, for example);
- that the restraint is reasonable between the parties themselves (and does not, for example, last for an unreasonable length of time or restrict too wide an area of activity); and
- that it is reasonable in the public interest.

Even if an individual contract may be enforceable between the parties, however, any business activity resulting from it which affects competition may still be caught by UK and EC competition rules. In fact, these currently impose a rather shorter duration (two or three years) on such restraints in the context of the sale of a business.

The scope of the principle has been considerably reduced by the modernisation of EC competition law in 2004, discussed below. Essentially, the common law rules may no longer be relied upon to avoid contractual obligations, at least as between businesses, in situations where there is no infringement of the EC competition rules.

UK AND EC COMPETITION RULES

The last few years have seen a significant convergence of UK and EC competition law, as a result of two key developments. The first was the entry into force of the Competition Act 1998, which introduced prohibitions of anti-competitive agreements and abuses of a dominant position that are worded in almost identical terms to those in Articles 81 and 82 of the EC Treaty. Questions arising under the Competition Act are interpreted in accordance with principles laid down in EC case-law. This is intended to ensure consistency and, most importantly for businesses, certainty. The second was the so-called 'modernisation' or decentralisation of the enforcement of the EC competition rules, under which the UK authorities and courts, in common with other Member States, are required to apply national and EC law in parallel, although with the EC rules enjoying priority.

The UK and EC competition rules can therefore now be described together. In each case, the principles and powers of enforcement are broadly similar. The key difference between the UK and EC rules is simply that whereas the UK rules apply to activities affecting trade within the UK (whether or not they also have a wider impact), the EC rules apply only to activities affecting trade between EC member states. A few differences of approach and procedure are highlighted where relevant.

The substantive prohibitions on anti-competitive agreements and abuses of dominance are addressed in turn.

ANTI-COMPETITIVE AGREEMENTS, TRADE ASSOCIATION DECISIONS AND CONCERTED PRACTICES

Scope of the prohibition

Article 81 of the EC Treaty, and the Chapter I prohibition of the Competition Act, apply to:

- agreements, including non-binding 'gentlemen's agreements', between 'undertakings' (anyone carrying on a commercial activity, so potentially including an author, commercial arms of government bodies such as HMSO and the Ordnance Survey, as well as the more obvious examples such as publishing houses). Agreements between members of the same group of companies are generally not caught, because they are considered to be within the same undertaking;

- decisions of trade associations, including for these purposes their rules, resolutions of their members or management, and recommendations to their members, even if not intended to be binding, or not fully put into effect;
- concerted practices, where, without expressly entering into an agreement, undertakings knowingly co-operate rather than compete, typically by informing a competitor of the action they propose to take, with the object or effect of influencing the competitor's own activities.

These agreements, trade association decisions and concerted practices (which we will refer to simply as agreements, in the interests of brevity) are prohibited if they have the object or effect of restricting competition within the UK (in the case of the UK rules) or the EC (in the case of the EC rules) and affect trade within the UK, or between EC member states.

The effect on trade between member states is relatively easily demonstrated: all that is required is that the agreement may have an influence, direct or indirect, actual or potential on the pattern of trade between member states. This effect may be demonstrated even in the case of an agreement between two UK businesses, for example if the agreement is likely to make it more difficult for businesses from elsewhere to enter the UK market. However, the absence of an effect on trade between member states is the reason why the European Commission currently tolerates national fixed book price schemes in countries such as Germany, as discussed below.

The rules give an illustrative list of restrictions of competition, including those which:

- directly or indirectly fix purchase or selling prices or any other trading conditions. This covers both horizontal price-fixing agreements – cartels – and vertical resale price maintenance, discussed below. Exchanges of information on prices and terms of trade are also very likely to infringe the prohibition;
- limit or control production, markets, technical development or investment. This applies to agreements which, for example, seek to impose production quotas;
- share markets or sources of supply. This includes agreements only to sell in certain geographic markets or areas, or not to sell outside a designated territory (for example, in distribution agreements);
- apply dissimilar conditions to equivalent transactions with other parties, thereby placing them at a competitive disadvantage. Discrimination usually takes the form of the operation of differential pricing or discount policies, favouring one customer or category of customers over another, although the mere fact of unilaterally charging different prices to different customers is not of itself prohibited; or
- make the conclusion of contracts subject to acceptance by the other parties of supplementary obligations which, by their nature or according to commercial usage, have no connection with the subject matter of the such contracts. Tying or forcing customers to stock a complete range of products of a particular brand may therefore be prohibited.

Appreciability

In order to fall foul of the prohibition, the restriction of competition and the effect on trade must both be appreciable. The Office of Fair Trading and the European Commission take the view that:

- an agreement will generally have no appreciable effect on competition if the parties' combined market share does not exceed 15 per cent in the case of agreements between non-competitors, and 10 per cent in the case of agreements between competitors; but
- agreements containing 'hard-core' restrictions such as price-fixing and market sharing, are likely to have an appreciable effect on competition irrespective of market share, as are agreements forming part of a wider network of agreements (such as a distribution network), the overall effect of which is to restrict competition.

The key to assessing market share, and thence appreciability, is market definition. This is considered briefly in relation to the prohibition on abuses of dominance below.

Consequences of infringement

The consequences of infringing the prohibitions are as follows:

- the parties are exposed to enforcement action by the competition authorities, possibly resulting in orders to terminate the agreement and, in the case of very serious infringements such as price-fixing and attempts to prevent exports, the imposition of fines of up to 10 per cent of the annual world-wide group turnover of each of the parties;
- the anti-competitive provisions of the agreement are void and unenforceable, although it may be possible to separate them out from the remainder of the agreement; and
- those who suffer loss as a result of the infringement can bring civil action in the national courts for damages and/or an injunction.

It should also be noted that individuals who dishonestly enter into horizontal cartel agreements by which businesses fix prices, share markets, limit supply or rig bids may be guilty of the cartel offence, introduced by the Enterprise Act 2002. Penalties include individual fines and imprisonment.

Exemption

Where the benefits of the agreement outweigh its anti-competitive effects, it may be exempted from the prohibition contained in Article 81 of the EC Treaty or the Chapter I prohibition. Following the modernisation of competition enforcement outlined above, it is no longer possible to notify the agreement to the Office of Fair

Trading or Commission for individual exemption. Instead, the criteria for exemption are examined as part of any overall assessment by a court or competition authority after the event. An agreement may be exempted if it:

- contributes to improving production or distribution, or promoting technical or economic progress; and
- allows consumers a fair share of the resulting benefit and does not impose on the parties restrictions which are not indispensable (as opposed to merely desirable) for achieving those objectives; and
- does not make it possible for the parties to eliminate competition in respect of a substantial part of the product market.

Rather than attempt to conduct the complex balancing exercise required to determine whether an agreement is individually exempt, it is generally preferable, where possible, to draft an agreement so as to fall within the terms of one of a series of 'block exemptions' adopted by the European Commission. An agreement satisfying the conditions set out in a block exemption regulation is automatically exempted from the prohibitions.

While there is a block exemption for so-called 'technology transfer agreements' (patents and know-how licences) there is no block exemption for copyright licences or assignments. In practice, the most common approach, where there is a possibility that the agreement will have an appreciable effect on competition, is to draft it in accordance with the general principles set out in the other block exemptions, so as to secure some degree of comfort by analogy.

Vertical agreements

For our purposes, the most important block exemption is the EC block exemption for vertical agreements. The block exemption theoretically adopts an economics-based approach. However, a close examination of the block exemption, and of the accompanying 44-page guidelines published by the Commission, reveals a large number of traps for the unwary. Drafting a distribution or other supply agreement requires expert advice if the pitfalls are to be avoided. The key features of the new regime, as it applies to re-seller agreements, can be summed up as follows:

- The block exemption applies to agreements for the purchase, sale or resale of goods, together with related licences or assignments of intellectual property rights, provided that those rights are not the primary object of the agreement. This means that the block exemption will not apply to a simple copyright assignment or licence unrelated to the sale of goods.
- The supplier's market share must be less than 30 per cent.
- Where the agreement imposes an exclusive supply obligation, the buyer's market share must also be less than 30 per cent.
- Above these figures, the agreement is not automatically exempt, but will not necessarily be prohibited: it may still be exempt, but its assessment will depend on an economic analysis of the market and of the parties' position on it.

- The re-seller must not be restricted in the customers to whom, or the territories in which, it can supply, except that it may be prohibited from soliciting business outside its territory or customer group where it has been appointed as the exclusive distributor to that territory or group, and other exclusive distributors have been appointed to those other territories or groups or the supplier has reserved them to itself. However, the distributor must always be free to respond to unsolicited orders from other territories and customer groups (known as 'passive sales'). Re-sellers must also be free to supply over the Internet: the supplier cannot reserve this sales channel to itself or to a specialist reseller. This area of resale restrictions is probably the most important area of the block exemption, and one of the easiest to get wrong when drafting.
- If the re-seller is prohibited from dealing in competing products, or is obliged to buy more than 80 per cent of its requirements of the products from the supplier, the maximum duration of the agreement is five years. It is not sufficient to provide for the agreement to roll over after that period: any continuation after the five years requires the consent of both parties.

An agreement which is exempt under Article 81 is also automatically exempt from the Chapter I prohibition. There is provision for UK block exemptions under the Competition Act, but there are none relevant to the publishing sector.

Resale price maintenance

Neither the EC block exemption nor the UK vertical exclusion apply where the reseller is restricted in its ability to set its own resale prices. Following the collapse of the Net Book Agreement in 1995, and the ruling of the Restrictive Practices Court in March 1997 that resale price maintenance for books was no longer in the public interest, resale price maintenance is prohibited in the publishing sector as it is in other industries. The European Commission does not take action against national systems of fixed book prices as long as they have no appreciable effect on trade between member states. In July 2001, therefore, having previously been satisfied with a purely national German fixed price scheme, the Commission accepted remedial undertakings from German publishers who had extended the scheme to cross-border book sales to consumers via the Internet, by refusing to supply Internet booksellers based in Belgium and Austria who wanted to sell books to German consumers at reduced prices.

In contrast, the Office of Fair Trading takes particularly vigorous action against resale price maintenance, with some of its highest profile cases to date being directed at agreements to fix resale prices.

Agency

There is no block exemption as such for agency agreements. This is because an agreement which is regarded as an agency agreement for the purposes of EU competition law is generally not within the scope of the EU competition rules.

Labels can be deceptive. As in other aspects of EU competition law it is the economic effect of the agreement that is important, and not the label that is attached to it. A personal agency agreement – as, for example, between an author and a literary agent – will not be regarded in itself as anti-competitive or objectionable under Article 85 since it will have no effect on competition: in economic terms, one person is simply stepping into the shoes of another. In legal terms, true agents in any particular transactions act only for the people they are appointed to represent (their 'principals'). They may, for example, seek out and pass on orders for their principals' products, but the customers are at all times their principals' customers, not their own, and their role is purely that of an intermediary. They accept no commercial or financial risk in performing their transactions. However, more general agency agreements where agents do more than simply represent their principals and also operate on their own account as independent traders, might well have competition implications and might well be caught by Article 81 or the Chapter I prohibition, since the 'agent' may in such cases not be regarded as an agent for the purposes of the competition rules. The point is that it is possible to control the agent's activities to a far greater extent than those of a distributor – including by imposing sales prices, territories and customers. These restrictions would be likely to be viewed as serious 'hard-core' restrictions if they were included in a distribution agreement.

Although not part of competition law, it is worth noting that throughout the European Economic Area, there is now legislation regulating commercial agents. For this purpose a commercial agent is a person who has continuing authority to negotiate or accept orders for the sale or purchase of goods on behalf of, and in the name of, his or her principal. These rules are implemented in the UK in the shape of the Commercial Agents (Council Directive) Regulations 1993. The Regulations contain provisions governing remuneration, such as terms of commission and also minimum terms of appointment and (in particular) termination, including mandatory compensation payable on termination. It should be noted that a number of European countries have legislation which is more extensive than that in the UK, often extending to services provided by an agent. In most cases the law of the country in which the agent is based does not allow contracting out.

The key factor which will determine whether an agreement is a true agency agreement for the purposes of competition law, or is a more arm's-length commercial arrangement between two separate business entities liable to have competition law implications, is the degree of financial or commercial risk borne by the agent. Relevant considerations will include the following:

- Does property in the goods vest in the 'agent'?
- Is the 'agent' required to contribute to the cost of sales promotion?
- Is the 'agent' required to contribute to stocking and transport costs?
- Does the 'agent' provide an independent customer service?
- Is the 'agent' responsible for non-performance of the sales contract by customers?
- Is the 'agent' required to make market-specific investments (i.e. which cannot be recovered on leaving the market)?

If the answer to any of the above questions is 'yes', it is likely that the agreement is not a true agency agreement for the purposes of EC and UK competition law and might well have competition law implications. If the relationship relates to goods then the EC and UK rules on Commercial Agents may also apply.

Abuses of dominance

Article 82 of the EC Treaty, and the Chapter II prohibition of the Competition Act, prohibit abuses of a dominant position on a market. In the case of the EC rules, the abuse must affect trade between member states, a concept which we have considered above.

The key to these prohibitions is market definition. The relevant market is defined by reference to product and geography.

The relevant product market is traditionally defined as the market for 'all those products or services which are regarded as interchangeable or substitutable by the consumer, by reason of the products' characteristics, their prices and their intended use'. This demand substitutability is the most important factor in market definition. A secondary defining factor is supply substitutability: the ability of suppliers of products which customers do not regard as substitutable to start producing demand substitutable products (for example, the ability of a publisher of one type of book to publish another type within a short period).

The relevant geographic market is the area in which 'the undertakings concerned are involved in the supply and demand of products or services, in which the conditions of competition are sufficiently homogeneous and which can be distinguished from neighboring areas because the conditions of competition are appreciably different in those areas'.

Market definition in the publishing sector follows these same principles. A key question will be the extent to which customers view one type of book as substitutable for another. However, this is tempered by supply substitutability – focusing entirely on demand substitutability would lead to the absurd situation of a separate product market for each book or author. A few guidelines can be drawn from the rather limited case-law:

- there are likely to be distinct product markets for the acquisition of content and rights, and for the supply of books to re-sellers. There are likely to be distinct markets for different types of book, for example paperback fiction and illustrated reference works. There may also be separate markets according to the sales channel;
- geographic markets will generally be world-wide in the acquisition of content and rights, national in book publishing (except in the case of scientific and technical publishing, where they may be world-wide), national in magazine publishing and possibly even narrower (regional) in the case of daily newspaper publishing.

Once a relevant market has been defined, it is necessary to assess dominance on that market. Dominance is 'a position of economic strength enjoyed by an undertaking which enables it to hinder the maintenance of effective competition by allowing it to behave to an appreciable extent independently of its competitors and customers and ultimately of consumers'. No single factor indicates dominance, but market share is an important one, a rule of thumb for likely dominance being a market share of around 40 per cent. In the publishing sector, market share can be calculated on the basis of the value of sales, or of the number of titles produced. Other factors, such as the ease of entry onto the market, will also be relevant in deciding whether a high market share is sufficient to confer dominance.

The Article 82/Chapter II prohibition also applies to conduct of undertakings which are collectively or jointly dominant, by virtue of links between them such that they adopt uniform conduct on the market.

It is important to note that it is not dominance itself which is prohibited, but abuse of that dominance. The abuse need not make its effects felt on the market in which the company is dominant. Using dominance in a particular publishing market to strengthen one's position in a related media content market, for example, might be an abuse.

The two prohibitions set out an illustrative list of abuses:

- directly or indirectly imposing unfair purchase or selling prices or other unfair trading conditions. This includes both excessive pricing and predatory pricing below cost in order to drive competitors out of the market;
- limiting production, markets or technical development to the prejudice of consumers;
- applying dissimilar conditions to equivalent transactions with other trading parties, thereby placing them at competitive disadvantage. This includes charging different prices to customers in the same circumstances without justification, or charging uniform prices to customers whose circumstances are different. Discounts which are not related to cost savings to the supplier, or intended to secure customer loyalty, may infringe the prohibitions if applied by a dominant supplier; or
- making the conclusion of contracts subject to acceptance by the other parties of supplementary obligations which, by their nature or according to commercial usage, have no connection with the subject of the contracts. The practice of tying the purchase of one product or service to the purchase of another, where the tie is not objectively justified (for example, on technical grounds) is similarly likely to be abusive.

To this list can be added conduct such as refusals to supply without objective justification: in short, anything which exploits the dominance or excludes competition still further. Dominant undertakings have a special responsibility not to allow their conduct to impair competition. Therefore a dominant undertaking may be unable to indulge in business practices which would be perfectly acceptable if carried out by a company without market power. The UK and EC prohibitions on abuses of dominance contain no provision for exemption, because the concept of abuse provides sufficient scope for a similar weighing-up of benefits and anti-competitive effects.

Abuse of copyright ownership

There is invariably a tension between intellectual property rights and competition law: the purpose of an intellectual property right is to confer a monopoly, and one of the functions of competition law is to regulate the way in which monopolies are operated.

It is important to note that the mere existence of copyright (or any other intellectual property right) will not necessarily define the relevant market. The English High Court decided in one case, for example, that it was not sufficient to define the market solely by reference to an intellectual property right. It was necessary to identify a product market in which the company concerned was dominant.

Refusals to license are a particularly complex area. It is relatively common for copyright owners to face complaints that they have abused their dominant position by refusing to license their copyright to an applicant, or have agreed to license only on unreasonable terms.

In the *Magill* TV listings case, finally decided in 1995, a refusal by the Irish State TV and radio company RTE and others who held the copyright in TV listings to supply details of the basic information on programme scheduling, in which they held a dominant position, to a new market entrant which wished to publish a weekly TV guide was held to be an abuse of a dominant position. This was despite the fact that RTE owned a copyright in its programme listings, and argued strongly that it was under no obligation to license them. The Court of First Instance and the full European Court both decided, on the contrary, that RTE's behaviour 'clearly went beyond what was necessary to fulfil the essential function of copyright as permitted in Community law' – which the European Court defined somewhat narrowly as being 'to protect the moral rights in the work and ensure a reward for creative effort, while respecting the aims of, in particular, Article 86'. Important features of this case were that Magill was seeking to enter a market for which the court found that there was clearly a demand and in which RTE was already present through its subsidiary. RTE, which owned the copyright in the TV listings, was attempting to use that copyright to protect its position in the downstream market of weekly TV guides, by refusing access to the raw material which was indispensable for the compilation for a weekly TV guide. All this supports – and extends – an important principal of EU law which is that while the ownership of restrictive intellectual property rights does not of itself create a dominant position and is not in itself anti-competitive (it is usually protected, with other forms of 'industrial and commercial property', in Articles 30 and 222) the use of those rights may be.

Magill, trumpeted at the time as imposing a duty to license, alarmed many copyright owners. However, it was clear at the time that *Magill* turned on its facts and, since then, a series of further judgments of the European Court of Justice and the Court of First Instance have clarified the scope of the duty.

In the 1997 *Tiercé Ladbroke* case, concerning the refusal to license the copyright in recordings and broadcasts of horse races, the Court of First Instance held that a refusal to license did not fall within Article 82, unless it concerned a product or service which was:

- essential for the exercise of the activity in question, in that there was no real or potential substitute; or
- it was a new product whose introduction might be prevented, despite specific, constant and regular potential demand by consumers.

In the highest profile and most recent case, in March 2004, the European Commission fined Microsoft €497 million (approximately £342 million) for abuses that included refusal to license. The Commission held that Microsoft had abused its dominant position in the market for work group server operating system software by refusing to license to Sun Microsystems and others the interface information required in order to allow their third party server software to communicate effectively with client PCs running Windows. Microsoft then appealed to the Court of First Instance (CFI) and requested an interim suspension of the Commission's orders.

Shortly after the Commission issued its decision in Microsoft, the European Court of Justice gave judgment in a further refusal to license case. This involved the refusal by IMS Health, a supplier of pharmaceutical sales data, to license its '1860 brick structure' (a format for dividing the German territory into geographic areas) to its competitor NDC.

The European Court of Justice held that the refusal by a dominant undertaking to license an IPR (intellectual property right) that is indispensable to operation on a downstream market constitutes an abuse of a dominant position where:

- the undertaking which requested the licence does not intend merely to duplicate the goods or services already offered by the intellectual property owner, but intends to produce new goods or services;
- the refusal is not justified by objective considerations; and
- the refusal eliminates all competition on that downstream market

It was at this point that Microsoft's application for interim suspension of the compulsory licence of the interface information came before the President of the CFI. A key argument of Microsoft was that its refusal was not an abuse according to the test set out in IMS, because Sun did not intend to provide a new product, but merely server operating systems competing squarely with Microsoft's own products. The President of the CFI took the view that a refusal could be abusive even where it did not exclude the development of a new product. In this interim application, the President of the CFI did not rule on the merits of the parties' substantive arguments, but merely concluded that Microsoft's arguments were not prima facie unfounded. He also noted that Microsoft's secret interface information, involving significant innovation, was fundamentally different in nature from the published TV listings data in Magill and the 1860 brick structure, which had been developed in consultation with the industry, in IMS. There might therefore be a higher threshold for ordering a compulsory licence of IPRs which reflect greater original creative effort than in cases involving 'commercial' information (the TV listings, the 1860 brick structure and the racing broadcasts). The EC courts seem to view such commercial copyright as inherently less valuable than creative copyright and this may have influenced their decisions. The common theme in these cases is that the copyright material acted as the gateway to a particular product or service market.

Investigation and enforcement

The competition authorities have extensive powers of investigation, including the power to request information and, less rarely exercised but rather more draconian, the power to conduct on-site investigations or 'dawn raids'. These investigations require careful handling and a rapid response. Failure to comply with the investigators' requirements may be a criminal offence, and may result in a prison sentence for directors and managers.

A key development in recent years is the increasing reliance of the authorities on evidence from whistle-blowers. The first member of a horizontal cartel or a price fixing agreement to come forward with evidence of the infringement will, if certain conditions are met, be entitled to 100 per cent immunity from penalty. A business discovering an infringement to which it has been a party therefore need to act very quickly if it wishes to ensure that it does not miss this opportunity.

ARTICLE 28: FREE MOVEMENT OF GOODS

Just as copyright ownership or licensing – though protected as such – must not be exercised in an anti-competitive way, or in abuse of a dominant position, so it must also not be allowed to interfere with the free movement of goods. The free movement of goods provisions of the EC Treaty are contained in Articles 28 to 30 (formerly known as Articles 30 and 36 respectively), and prohibit any 'quantitative restrictions' on imports or exports between member states. Put another way, there must be no internal barriers in the single common market: there must be free movement of goods within the EC (and, equally, free movement of services and information). Goods lawfully on sale in one member state may not be prevented from entering any other member state. This clearly outlaws quantitative restrictions imposed by states themselves, but it equally restricts geographical market divisions within Europe imposed by individual rights owners. This is of considerable significance to UK publishers, particularly in relation to English-language co-editions which will be on sale not only in the UK but elsewhere in Europe. The ownership of intellectual property rights is clearly incompatible with the principles of free movement, and in a number of recent decisions of the European Court of Justice national copyright protection, and the exercise of intellectual property rights generally, have increasingly given way to the overriding free movement of goods provisions of Article 28. Despite the fact that Article 30 specifically exempts 'the protection of industrial and commercial property' from the full effect of Article 28, this is subject to a proviso in Article 30 itself that restrictions on the free movement of goods shall not be allowed to constitute 'a means of arbitrary discrimination or a disguised restriction on trade between member states'.

Territories in Europe

Under co-publishing deals between, say, a UK and US publisher (see chapter 5), a schedule of world territories would normally be agreed: some would be exclusive to either side, and the rest would be 'open' markets, where either edition may sell. The US publisher would usually want exclusive rights to publish in North America, and the UK publisher might have asked for exclusivity in the UK and other territories of the former Commonwealth.

Traditionally, most of the rest of the world would have been regarded as an 'open market' – including (until now) European countries such as Holland or Belgium. In view of the free movement of goods provisions of Article 28, such an arrangement is now highly unsafe, and the UK exclusivity is almost certainly unenforceable against parallel importation of US (or any other) editions lawfully on sale in Holland or Belgium – or in any other member state.

Once the US edition is lawfully on sale in (for example) Holland, there is nothing the UK publisher can do under Article 28 (or Article 30) to prevent its importation into the UK. Our own Copyright, Designs and Patents Act 1988, in fact, expressly guarantees this under section 27(5) – nothing in that Act will prevent the importation of any article:

> which may lawfully be imported into the UK by virtue of any enforceable community right.

If UK co-publishers wish to achieve effective exclusivity for their own edition in the UK, therefore, they will now need to consider negotiating exclusive rights to the whole of the EU and EEA. Such agreements will still of course need to be permissible generally under EU competition law.

Exhaustion of rights

It seems appropriate that the last topic in a law book should be the doctrine of exhaustion. The free movement of goods provisions of Article 28 apply to goods lawfully on sale in any member state – in the case of copyright goods such as books, it might have been possible under Article 30 to argue that books licensed by the copyright owner for territory B only, but then re-imported via parallel importation back into territory A without the owner's consent, would be infringing copies in territory A and could still be excluded. However, in a leading 1971 case involving Deutsche Grammophon, the European Court of Justice decided that once copyright goods have been put on the market in any EC member state by the copyright owner or licensor, or with their consent, then their intellectual property rights restricting the distribution or circulation of those goods are 'exhausted'. Local, national, copyright cannot thereafter be used to prevent parallel importation from one member state to another. It is superseded by Article 30.

Exhaustion in relation to copyright only applies *within* the EU, however, and where the owner has *consented* – there is no exhaustion of rights if goods are marketed outside the EU (for example, in a third country such as the USA) and then imported into the EU. Similarly, if goods are released onto the market inside the EU without the owner's consent – for example via a compulsory licence in one member state – the rights will probably not be exhausted. In the case of *EMI* v. *Patricia* in 1989, the European Court of Justice held that records released lawfully marketed in Denmark, not with the consent of the copyright owner but purely because the term of local copyright protection expired, could be prevented from entering the German market, where copyright protection still remained in force. If the Danish recordings had been produced with the owner's consent, however, their rights would have been exhausted.

More recent case-law on international trade mark exhaustion is unlikely to alter fundamentally the basic position outlined above. In a case involving Silhouette spectacles, the European Court of Justice held that member states were not permitted to adopt rules providing for international trade mark exhaustion, i.e. to provide for exhaustion where goods were not placed on the market within the EEA by the trade mark owner or with his consent. The English High Court, in a case concerning Davidoff fragrances rather undermined this principle, when the judge held that the trade mark owner could be argued to have consented to the placing on the market within the EEA when he had not imposed constraints on their further sale, including possible sales *within* the EEA, following their first placing on the market *outside* the EEA. When the case was referred to Luxembourg, the European Court of Justice ruled in November 2001 that the trade mark owner's consent to the placing on the market within the EEA must be given 'unequivocally'. This consent could be expressed or could be implied from the circumstances surrounding the placing of the goods on the market outside the EEA. Consent cannot be inferred from the silence of the trade mark owner, nor from the fact that it did not reserve its rights or expressly prohibit the placing of the goods on the market within the EEA.

SUMMARY CHECKLIST: COMPETITION

- What is the relevant market?
- Are we dominant in it?
- Are we abusing our dominance?
- Do we have a sufficiently strong position in the market that any agreement into which we enter is likely to have an appreciable effect on competition?
- Is there an agreement between undertakings (or a concerted practice or trade association decision)?
- Does it affect trade within the UK, or trade between EC member states?
- Does it restrict competition?
- Is it automatically excluded or exempt?
- Is it likely to be eligible for individual exemption?
- Are we within the free movement provisions of Article 28?
- Should we be seeking exclusivity across the whole EC?
- Have we exhausted our rights?

Appendix A
A to Z glossary of legal terms

Action A legal action in a court of law, normally commenced by the issue of a Claim Form. A 'letter before action' (or "cease and desist letter") is often designed to avoid the need for this.

Applicable law The law which applies, for example to a contract, and which will govern any dispute arising under it.

Assignee Person to whom rights are assigned.

Assignment Formal transfer of ownership, for example in copyright. Assignments of copyright must be in writing and signed by or on behalf of the copyright owner.

Assignor Person assigning rights to another (called the assignee).

CIP (Cost Insurance and Freight) Delivery terms under which the price includes delivery to the buyer's own designated port of entry (but not normally all the way to the buyer's own warehouse) (compare FOB).

Claimant The complaining party who seeks a remedy via a court action. The party being complained about is called the Defendant. If the case goes to appeal, the party appealing is the Appellant and the party resisting is the Respondent.

Claim Form Issue of a Claim Form is the normal method of commencing an action (usually accompanied by Particulars of Claim).

Common Law A body of English law based on decided cases and developed by the judges over many centuries. Actions for breach of contract or negligence are common-law actions. It is no longer the primary source of new law in the UK, which largely now arises from statutes.

Condition Fundamental term of a contract, which goes to the root of the whole contract. Breach of a condition by one party normally entitles the other party to terminate the contract.

Consideration Something of value, usually given in return for a promise or undertaking: to be legally binding, most contracts must be supported by some valuable consideration.

Covenant A binding undertaking, often limiting future activity (such as a restrictive covenant).

Defamatory Statement A statement the meaning of which tends to make people think the worse of someone.

Defamation The law covering libel and slander.

Damages Remedy normally available to a successful Claimant. Awards of damages may be liquidated, to compensate for specific losses, or general, or sometimes punitive if the Defendant's behaviour has been particularly blameworthy.

Defendant The party being complained about in a legal action; they must defend themselves against one or more Claimants (see above).

Directive An EU law adopted by the EU Council of Ministers following circulation of a draft or proposed Directive by the EU Commission. Directives do not as a rule have direct effect as law in member states, but member states are required to implement them within a specified time limit.

EEA The European Union countries together with Norway, Iceland and Liechtenstein.

Estate Means of holding and administering property (for example, an author's, including any copyrights) after death: any property is normally vested initially in executors, for the benefit of any beneficiaries: if there are no desig-nated beneficiaries, there are complex statutory rules on entitlement to any assets.

Equity A traditional body of law developed over the centuries by English judges, parallel to the common law concentrating less on formal procedure and more on fairness and justice to the parties. Injunctions are mainly equitable remedies. An equitable interest or other entitlement may arise where legal ownership has not formally been transferred (via an assignment, for example) but where it is clear that it was intended to create an interest or it is fair to do so (perhaps where the price or part of it has already been paid).

Exclusive Licence Licence where the person granting the licence undertakes not only that there will be no other licensees, but also that there will be no rival exploitation by the licensor itself. Exclusive licences must be in writing and signed by or on behalf of the copyright owner.

FOB (Free On Board) Delivery terms under which the price paid does not normally include freight or insurance costs of transport to the buyer's warehouse or port of entry (compare CIF) but is normally based on delivery to the buyer's agent or shipper at the seller's port of shipment: traditionally legal title to the goods, and risk in them, was not transferred from the seller to the buyer until the goods 'passed the ship's rail'.

Grantor One who grants, for example, a publishing licence or sub-licence.

Indemnity A term in a contract under which the party giving it agrees to bear all the risks arising out of any breach of specified warranties and compensate the other party fully for any losses, damage, costs or expenses which may be incurred.

Indictment Formal criminal charge before a Crown Court.

Injunction A Court Order, either ordering someone to do something or ordering them to stop (or not to start).

Insolvency The condition of being unable to pay current or outstanding debts as they fall due. Insolvency of individuals (as opposed to companies) is commonly referred to as bankruptcy.

Libel A defamatory statement published in written or permanent form.

Licence A grant of rights, normally limited to a specific period of time (or limited in other ways, for example, territorially or to particular languages or formats or subject to other conditions). Licences may be sole, exclusive or non-exclusive. Licences may normally be revoked, for example for breach of their terms.

Minor Person under the age of 18. Contracts entered into by minors may be voidable under some circumstances.

Novation Fresh execution of contracts (for example, where a new owner of a publishing business wishes to re-confirm existing author contracts).

Prima Facie At first sight, or on the face of it.

Reversion Rights granted (for example, under a licence) may revert to the person granting them if a specified term comes to an end, or if the terms are breached.

Slander A defamatory statement made verbally, and not in permanent (for example, printed) form.

Sole licence A licence in which the person granting the licence (the licensor) agrees that there will be no other licensees, but that the licensor itself may reserve the right to exploit the rights concerned (compare exclusive licence).

Specific performance A court may in some circumstances make an order of specific performance ordering one party to perform one or more of their obligations under a contract, for example ordering a publisher to publish a book. The courts are reluctant to oversee the performance of contracts in such a direct way, where damages are an alternative.

Statutes Acts of Parliament: now the primary source of UK law (compare Common Law above). Statutory measures may include Statutory Instruments (SIs) and other orders made under Acts of Parliament.

Summary Conviction Conviction for a criminal offence by a magistrates' court. Penalties are normally lower than those following conviction on indictment before a Crown Court.

Tort A civil wrong (as opposed to a criminal wrong which is a crime). Examples of torts include negligence, defamation or passing off. Actions for tort may be commenced in the civil courts by the aggrieved parties (unlike crimes which are prosecuted by the authorities through the criminal courts). The most common remedy sought is an award of damages: in appropriate circumstances injunctions may also be granted.

Title Legal ownership, for example of specific goods or property.

Ultra Vires Beyond the given authority – an agent or an employee acting *ultra vires* is acting beyond his or her authority and the actions concerned may be challenged or declared void later (although authority may be implied in some circumstances).

Void Of no legal effect.

Voidable Liable to be declared void.

Warranty A term of a contract under which the party making the warranty gives certain guarantees, for example, that the subject of the contract (for example, a manuscript) is not defamatory or does not infringe any copyright or is not otherwise illegal. Breach of a warranty usually gives rise to an action for damages, and may sometimes entitle the other party to terminate the contract.

Work A literary, artistic or other creation, such as a novel or a photograph or a computer program. Most, but not all, original works of UK citizens, or first published in the UK, will qualify for copyright protection in the UK.

Appendix B
Useful adresses

Advertising Standards Authority
71 High Holborn
London WC1V 6QT

Agency for the Legal Deposit Libraries
100 Euston Street
London NW1 2HQ
publisher.enquiries@aldl.ac.uk

Association of Authors' Agents
AP Watts
20 John Street
London WC1N 2QR

Authors' Licensing & Collecting
Society Ltd (ALCS)
Marlborough Court
14–18 Holborn
London EC1N 2LE

British Copyright Council
Copyright House
29–33 Berners Street
London W1P 4AA

Copyright Directorate
The Patent Office
Harmsworth House
13–15 Bouverie Street
London EC4Y 8DP

Also The Patent Office
Concept House
Cardiff Road
Newport
South Wales NP10 8QQ

Copyright Licensing Agency
Saffron House
6–10 Kirby Street
London EC1N 8TS

Copyright Tribunal
Harmsworth House
13–15 Bouverie Street
London EC4Y 8DP

Design and Artists Copyright Society
Ltd (DACS)
33 Great Sutton Street
London EC1V 0DX

The Directory and Database Publishers
Association
P.O. Box 23034
London W6 0RJ

Educational Recording Agency Ltd
(ERA)
New Premier House
150 Southampton Row
London WC1B 5AL

The Independent Publishers Guild
(IPG)
P.O. Box 93
Royston
Herts SG8 5GH

Information Commissioner
Wycliffe House
Water Lane
Wilmslow
Cheshire SK9 5AF

Office of Fair Trading
Fleetbank House
2–6 Salisbury Square
London EC4Y 8JX

Patent Office (Including Trade Marks
Registry)
(Department of Trade)
25 Southampton Buildings
London WC2A 1AY

Performing Right Society
29–33 Berners Street
London W1P 4AA

The Publishers Association
29B Montague Street
London WC1B 5BW

Publishers Licensing Society Ltd (PLS)
37–41 Gower Street
London WC1E 6HH

Registrar of Public Lending Right
Richard House
Sorbonne Close
Stockton-on-Tees TS17 6DA

The Legal Deposit Office
The British Library
Boston Spa
Wetherby
W Yorkshire LS23 7BY
legal-deposit-books@bl.uk

Society of Authors
84 Drayton Gardens
London SW10 9SB

UNESCO
7 Place de Fontenoy
75700 Paris
France
(UCC Convention)

US Copyright Office
Register of Copyrights
Library of Congress
Washington DC 20559

World Intellectual Property
Organisation (WIPO)
34 Chemin des Colombettes
1211 Geneva 20
Switzerland
(Berne Convention)

Writers Guild of Great Britain
15 Britannia Street
London WC1X 9JN

Appendix C
Further reading and sources

FURTHER READING

Sheila Bone (ed.), *Osborn's Concise Law Dictionary*, 9th edition (Sweet & Maxwell, 2001).

J.M. Cavendish and Kate Pool, *A Handbook of Copyright in British Publishing Practice*, 3rd edition (Cassell, 1993).

Michael Flint, *A User's Guide to Copyright*, 4th edition (Butterworths, 1997).

Denis de Freitas, *The Law of Copyright and Rights in Performances*, 2nd edition (British Copyright Council, 1998).

Lynette Owen, *Selling Rights*, 4th edition (Routledge, 2001).

Lynette Owen (ed.), *Clark's Publishing Agreements*, 6th edition (Butterworths, 2002).

SOURCES

British Copyright Council www.britishcopyright.org

British Library (Legal Deposit) www.bl.uk

Department of Trade and Industry (publishing and intellectual property) www.dti.gov.uk

EU Commission (Directives and other information) www.europe.eu.int/comm/index_en/htm

EU intellectual property information europa.eu.int/scadplus/leg/en/S06020.htm

European Union (general site) www.europa.eu.int

Home Office (libel and other legislation) www.homeoffice.gov.uk

Law Society (solicitors) info.service@lawsociety.org.uk

Patent Office (copyright information, trade marks and patents) www.patent.gov.uk

Public Lending Right www.plr.uk.com

Society of Authors www.societyofauthors.org

The Publishers Association www.publishers.org.uk

UK Parliament (legislation) www.publications.parliament.uk

World Intellectual Property Organisation (WIPO) (Berne Convention) www.wipo.int

Index

Related titles from Routledge

Inside Book Publishing

Third Edition

Giles Clark

Book publishing today is a highly competitive and exciting international industry. *Inside Book Publishing* provides a wealth of essential information for anyone interested in a career in publishing, or in understanding how publishing works.

This fully revised, updated and extended edition covers:

- the history and current structure of the UK book trade

- the role of the author, authors' agents, packagers and booksellers

- copyright and contracts

- key elements of the publishing process: commissioning, editorial, design, production, publicity and promotion, sales and rights

- the business of publishing

- the impact of electronic publishing and online bookselling

- getting a job in publishing and career pathways

- information on organizations offering training for publishers, suggestions for networking opportunities, and an annotated guide to further reading.

Hb: 0-415-23005-5
Pb: 0-415-23006-3

Available at all good bookshops
For ordering and further information please visit:
www.routledge.com

Related titles from Routledge

Book Commissioning and Acquisition
Second Edition

Gill Davies

This new edition of a successful and highly-praised book provides an comprehensive introduction to the job of a commissioning editor. Gill Davies offers close guidance and support on how editors should approach this job. She demonstrates the main principles and practices involved in commissioning and acquisition, and covers difficult issues connected with judgement and decision making which are at the heart of the editor's job. Individual chapters address:

- how to choose what to publish

- proposing projects for publication

- from contract to delivery

- managing the publication process

- strategic and financial aspects of list building

- developing and maintaining a list

- teamwork and professional ethics.

The new edition also includes guidance on issues that have become more pressing since publication of the first edition, such as controlling email, the effect of digitisation, and inheriting other editors' lists as a consequence of take-overs and mergers. Extensive coverage is given to the perennial problems that editors face, particularly the most demanding: slippage and handling difficult authors. New case studies from a wide variety of publishing contexts illustrate the commercial and practical problems that editors must address in today's complex and challenging marketplace.

Hb: 0 415 31788 6
Pb: 0-415-31789-4

Available at all good bookshops
For ordering and further information please visit:
www.routledge.com